Communication Strategies

APPLIED LINGUISTICS AND LANGUAGE STUDY

General Editor
Professor Christopher N. Candlin, Macquarie University, Sydney

For a complete list of books in this series see pages v–vi

Communication Strategies: Psycholinguistic and Sociolinguistic Perspectives

Edited by

Gabriele Kasper
and
Eric Kellerman

LONGMAN
LONDON AND NEW YORK

Addison Wesley Longman Limited
Edinburgh Gate
Harlow, Essex CM20 2JE, England
and Associated Companies throughout the world.

*Published in the United States of America
by Addison Wesley Longman, New York*

© Addison Wesley Longman Limited 1997

First Published 1997

ISBN 0 582 100178 Paper

British Library Cataloguing-in-Publication Data

A catalogue record for this book is
available from the British Library

Library of Congress Cataloging-in-Publication Data

Communication strategies : psycholinguistic and sociolinguistic
    perspectives / edited by Gabriele Kasper and Eric Kellerman.
        p.   cm. — (Applied linguistics and language study)
    Includes bibliographical references and index.
    ISBN 0–582–10017–8 (pbk. : alk. paper)
    1. Communication.   2. Psycholinguistics.   3. Sociolinguistics.
I. Kasper, Gabriele.   II. Kellerman, Eric.   III. Series.
P91.C5615   1997
302.2—dc21   97–6433
                                                                          CIP

Set by 8H in 10/12pt Baskerville
Produced through Longman Malaysia, PP

APPLIED LINGUISTICS AND LANGUAGE STUDY

GENERAL EDITOR

PROFESSOR CHRISTOPHER N. CANDLIN

Macquarie University, Sydney

Contents

Contributors

Ellen Bialystok Department of Psychology, York University, Ontario, Canada

Heike Behrens Max-Planck Institut fuer Psycholinguistik, Nijmegen, The Netherlands

Nanci Bruhn Technische Universitaet Braunschweig, Institut für Psychologie, Braunschweig, Germany

Werner Deutsch Technische Universitaet Braunschweig, Institut für Psychologie, Braunschweig, Germany

Patricia A. Duff The University of British Columbia, Department of Language Education, Vancouver, Canada

Alan Firth Department of Language and Intercultural Studies, Ålborg University, Ålborg, Denmark

Rebecca Inscoe University of Illinois at Chicago, Department of English, Chicago, USA

Yves Joanette Ecole d'orthophonie et d'audiologie, Faculté de médecine, University of Montréal, Canada

Peter Lloyd Department of Psychology, University of Manchester, England

Gowert Masche Technische Universität Braunschweig, Institut für Psychologie, Braunschweig, Germany

Nanda Poulisse Engels Seminarium, University of Amsterdam, The Netherlands

Ben Rampton Thames Valley University, School of ELT, London, England

Ana Maria Rodino Harvard Graduate School of Education, Cambridge MA, USA

Steven Ross   School of Policy Studies, Kwansei Gakuin University, Hyogo, Japan

George Russell   Kyushu Institute of Technology, Kitakyushu City, Japan

Catherine E. Snow   Harvard Graduate School of Education, Cambridge MA, USA

Brigitte Stemmer   Kliniken Schmieder, Allensbach, Germany

Elaine Tarone   Institute of Linguistics, University of Minnesota, Minneapolis MN, USA

Thomas Tasker   University of Illinois at Chicago, Department of English, Chicago IL, USA

Johannes Wagner   Center for Applied Linguistics, Campusvej, Odense, Denmark

Deanna Wilkes-Gibbs   California, USA

Jessica Williams   University of Illinois at Chicago, Department of English, Chicago IL, USA

George Yule   Honolulu HI, USA

Acknowledgements

The publishers are grateful to the following to reproduce copyright material:

Cambridge University Press for our Figure 5.1 'Marshall and Newcombe's (1973) "two-route" model of the reading process as presented by Shallice', taken from Tim Shallice: *From neuropsychologty to mental structure* 1988, p. 71; Heinle & Heinle Publishers for our Figure 4.1 'The eleven pictures from Kellerman, et al (1990)' taken from *Developing communicative competence in a second language* edited by Eric Kellerman, T. Ammerlaan, T. Bongaerts and N. Poulisse; Routledge Limited for our Table 5.2 'Reading errors produced by two dyslexic patients' from *Deep Dyslexia* (1980) edited by M. Coltheart, K. Patterson and J. Marshall; and Addison Wesley Longman Ltd for our Table 9.1 'Dictionary entries for lexical items from *Longman Modern English Dictionary* (1968) edited by O. Watson.

Introduction: approaches to communication strategies

GABRIELE KASPER and ERIC KELLERMAN

In 1983, the predecessor of this present volume was published. Called *Strategies in Interlanguage Communication*, it was a collection of 12 papers on the subject of how what have traditionally been called *communication strategies* (CS) are used to tackle and overcome linguistic problems encountered during interaction involving non-native speakers. Some of the papers in that book are classics of their kind, yet when the idea for a second edition of the book was first proposed some ten years later, we both felt that so much new research had taken place in the intervening years, not to mention work in neighbouring fields which was both interesting and relevant that an entirely new book was required. However, continuity between the previous and the present volumes is maintained not only in the general subject matter, but also in the fact that four of the contributors to the earlier work, Ellen Bialystok, Gabriele Kasper, Elaine Tarone, and Johannes Wagner, appear here once again.

Early studies of communication strategies concerned themselves mostly with questions of definition, identification and classification. Of these, definition is obviously primary – it is closely tied to the adopted theoretical perspective, and identification and classification crucially depend upon it. We will therefore begin by discussing different perspectives on the construct and its disciplinary context.

1

Definition

In early work, most notions of CS restricted the concept to problem-solving activity. Compare:

> ... used by an individual to overcome the crisis which occurs when language structures are inadequate to convey the individual's thought.   (Tarone, 1977, p. 195)

> ... potentially conscious plans for solving what to an individual presents itself as a problem in reaching a particular communicative goal.   (Færch & Kasper, 1983d, p. 36)

> ... strategies which a language user employs in order to achieve his intended meaning on becoming aware of problems arising during the planning phase of an utterance due to his own linguistic shortcomings.   (Poulisse et al., 1984, p. 72)

These definitions have more in common, however, than their insistence on *problematicity* as definitional to CS. They all conceive of CS as mental plans implemented by the second language learner in response to an internal signal of an imminent problem, a form of self-help that did not have to engage the interlocutor's support for resolution (e.g., Færch & Kasper, 1983c, p. 36). The intraindividual, psycholinguistic view locates CS in models of speech production (e.g., Dechert, 1983; Færch & Kasper, 1983c) or cognitive organization and processing (Bialystok, 1990; Kellerman & Bialystok, this volume).

In contrast, Tarone saw CS as

> ... a mutual attempt of two interlocutors to agree on a meaning in situations where requisite meaning structures do not seem to be shared. ... attempts to bridge the gap between the linguistic knowledge of the second-language learner, and the linguistic knowledge of the target language interlocutor in real communication situations.   (1983, p. 65)

The inter-individual, interactional view of CS has been adopted from the vantage point of different theoretical orientations – for instance, pattern theory (Wagner, 1983), collaborative theory (Wilkes-Gibbs, this volume), conversation analysis (Wagner & Firth, this volume), and critical sociolinguistics (Rampton, this volume). For comparative discussion of the 'psycholinguistic' and 'interactional' approach, see Færch and Kasper (1984), Yule and

Tarone (this volume), and Aston (1993) for 'intraorganism' vs 'interorganism' perspectives on communication.

It is true that even in the early days of CS research, some opposition was voiced against problematicity as definitional to CS (Bialystok, 1984; Dechert, 1983; Wagner, 1983). These scholars argued that language use is always strategic, in the sense that actors purposefully select from a wide array of resources those which optimally and cost-efficiently achieve the purpose at hand – a position taken from different information-processing perspectives, speech-act theory and other theories of pragmatics (Brown & Levinson, 1987; Leech, 1983) and widely shared in the field of communication (e.g., Kellermann, 1991; Wiemann & Daly, 1994). During the early days of CS research, however, the majority opinion converged on regarding CS as a specialized problem-solving activity.

Identification

Identification of CS depends to a great extent on what one considers a CS to be, and in this respect, it matters very much whether one conceives of CS as intraindividual or interindividual events. In their chapter in this book, Wagner and Firth take the view that the only data that constitute evidence of strategic activity are those stretches of speech marked by a speaker in some way ('flagged') as requiring specific attention on the part of the listener. For those interested in strategies as underlying processes in the individual mind, observable evidence for strategic activity may be harder to come by. Its existence may be a matter of inference rather than direct observation. In fact, highly proficient non-native speakers have been shown to be very good at anticipating and circumnavigating bottlenecks such that there is no obvious trace of difficulty in their speech protocols (Færch & Kasper, 1983c), and it is only through the learners' retrospective commentary that the researcher is made aware of the existence of such difficulties (Poulisse, 1990).

Unless the task is such that it unambiguously elicits (usually referential) problems and their solution, researchers thus have to rely on two sources of evidence to identify CS: markers in the discourse and retrospective protocols. The first comprise explicit strategy markers – metalinguistic comments of the 'I don't know how to say this' sort – and implicit indicators such as an increase in hesitation phenomena (Dechert, 1983; Færch & Kasper, 1983b; Raupach, 1983). The second method involves play-back of the original discourse and self-identification of strategic activity by the informant. This form of self-report is, of course, subject to all the reservations that have been made about this data type in the literature (cf. Ericsson & Simon, 1980, 1984, for review). CS researchers who rely on self-report for strategy identification have referred to Ericsson and Simon's (1980, 1984) model of cognitive processing, pointing out that the 'problematic' information is under attention during task completion and hence reportable (Færch & Kasper, 1987b; Poulisse et al., 1987). Nevertheless, relying on one method of strategy identification seems risky; triangulation of different data types is advisable and has been employed successfully in research on CS in oral production (Poulisse, 1990; Poulisse et al., 1987) as well as in studies on lexical inferencing (Haastrup, 1987, 1991; Ross, this volume) and other modalities of language use and tasks (cf. studies in Færch & Kasper, 1987a).

Classification

Among second language acquisition (SLA) researchers, there has always been broad agreement as to what the various kinds of CS observable in non-native performance are. Most researchers will acknowledge that learners use their knowledge of other languages as well as various sorts of paraphrase, lexical substitution and gestures; they may also ask others for assistance, or surrender their immediate communicative goals. However, researchers differ in the way they treat observable strategic behaviours. The earliest, taxonomic, approach catalogued output differences (e.g., Tarone, 1977); a subsequent proposal related such output differences to a model of speech production (Færch & Kasper, 1983d), and the most recent scheme insists that categories for strategy classification should reflect distinct differences in processing rather than diverse types of linguistic form (e.g., Bialystok & Kellerman, 1987). For a detailed discussion of product- and process-oriented approaches to strategy classification, their underlying theoretical orientations and implications for research methods and 'teachability' of CS, the reader is referred to Yule and Tarone's chapter in this volume.

Communication strategies and SLA

SLA researchers' interest in experienced communication problems and their solutions, rather than efficient L2 use generally, is linked to the designated object of SLA research, the L2 learner. Relative to native speakers' linguistic competence, learners' *interlanguage* is deficient by definition. Such deficient competence gives rise to problems when the learner wishes to express a particular communicative intention in L2 and lacks the necessary resources for it. Yet the learner's dilemma, in and of itself, is an issue of L2 production – or, in a wider perspective, communication – and not immediately connected to L2 acquisition, unless there is a theory that explains why problem-solving activity in the form of CS is relevant to L2 learning.

Early work on CS discussed (though never empirically examined) the potential learning effect of CS. Adopting a hypothesis-testing model of L2 acquisition, Færch and Kasper (1980) argued that some strategic solutions may be incorporated into the learners' interlanguage: among the 'psycholinguistic', learner-internal strategies, (over-)generalization, transfer, or 'word coinage' ('morphological creativity', Poulisse, 1987) were seen as possible candidates, especially if such strategies elicited positive feedback. 'Interactional' strategies such as appeals for the interlocutor's assistance were seen as beneficial because they might prompt the desired lexical item from the other participant and make it available for incorporation into the learner's interlanguage lexicon. Appeals can serve to clarify productive and receptive problems, and the latter category has been pivotal in a different approach to L2 learning, Krashen's input theory (e.g., Krashen, 1985).

One of the central empirical problems arising from input theory is how learners can access comprehensible input. The most effective source of input seems to be conversational exchanges in which learners engage – either together with other L2 learners or native speakers – and in which they negotiate (referential) meanings (Ellis, 1994; Larsen-Freeman & Long, 1991, for review). Interactional modification, or conversational adjustments, such as confirmation checks, comprehension checks, and clarification requests operate on input which is too far ahead of the learner's current interlanguage competence and size it down to what the learner can manage. Since 'negotiation of meaning' is a joint enterprise between the learner and her interlocutor(s), the learner exerts a fair amount of control over just how much modification of the original input is needed in order to comprehend the interlocutor's contribution. While interactional CS are thus seen as directly beneficial to L2 learning because they serve to make input comprehensible, Larsen-Freeman and Long (1991) point out that all CS are helpful for acquisition because they enable learners to keep the conversation going and thereby provide more opportunities for input. Since psycholinguistic CS may be taken up as appeals, especially when they are flagged by 'strategy markers' such as increased dysfluency (Færch & Kasper, 1984), they can trigger negotiating activity and elicit processible input.

According to a substantial modification of input theory, comprehensible input is a necessary but not sufficient condition for L2 acquisition. As Swain (1985) demonstrated, despite ample availability of comprehensible input, learners may not acquire the expected level of proficiency unless they are forced to produce complex comprehensible utterances. CS, and especially the 'psycholinguistic' type where the learner relies on her own linguistic and strategic resources, are an important vehicle in producing 'pushed output', and in eliciting feedback on the strategic problem solution.

There is yet another theoretical vantage point from which CS are relevant for L2 learning. According to Bialystok's two-dimensional model of language use and development (Bialystok, 1990; Bialystok & Ryan, 1985), language acquisition proceeds from unanalysed to analysed knowledge and with an increasing degree of processing control. The cognitive taxonomy of CS proposed by the Nijmegen Project (e.g., Kellerman et al., 1987) can be mapped onto this model so that CS can be categorized as operating principally on either the 'analysis' or the 'control' dimension (Bialystok, 1990; Kellerman & Bialystok, this volume). An analytic strategy by definition requires that the learner has an explicit understanding of the conceptual features of the intended referent, whereas the decision on the type of strategy to opt for and how to apply CS sequentially (e.g., Kellerman et al., 1990), and to do all this in a timely and effective manner, are issues of processing control. Learners who use CS efficiently, then, display a high degree of processing control, and this is precisely what helps them compensate for lexical gaps, or for a low level of analysis of pertinent lexical items.

Despite their primary function in L2 communication rather than learning, there is a close connection between CS and L2 acquisition in SLA theories which emphasize the roles of input, output, feedback, and cognitive processing. Whether conceptualized as a cooperative venture or a purely cognitive process, the increased need to solve problems in establishing reference is both characteristic of language learners and instrumental in propelling their interlanguage forward.

Focus on lexis

Whereas no definition of CS limits the concept to any particular type of linguistic problem, in actual research practice researchers of different theoretical persuasions have focused on lexical difficulties. The concentration on lexis is an immediate consequence of the definitional criterion of problematicity and the related issue of awareness. CS had been defined by Tarone (1977) as 'conscious' and by Færch and Kasper (1980, 1983d) as 'potentially conscious', allowing the possibility that a speaker or hearer may not always be aware of using a CS but can become conscious of it after the fact, or that repeatedly used CS may become routinized. An early study by Glahn (1980) on the use of retrospective protocols in interlanguage research demonstrated that the criterion of 'consciousness' imposed a filter on possible candidates for CS. Glahn's subjects carried out a picture description task in L2 French and were asked to comment retrospectively on their choices of adjective morphology and vocabulary. Whereas subjects provided extensive comments on their problems in lexical knowledge and retrieval and the CS they adopted to solve them, they were unable to report on their morphological choices, even after they had been asked to focus their attention on adjective morphology in a second session of the experiment. The instruction did not seem to affect subjects' allocation of attention, or not to a sufficient extent: in order to accomplish their task, subjects needed to focus on the linguistic material with the highest information load and apparently had little attentional capacity left to select morphological markings consciously. Glahn's findings do not suggest that attention in speech production to redundant grammatical features is not possible, but they do indicate that unless learners' lexical knowledge is fairly adequate to the task at hand and their control of processing well developed, attentional capacity cannot be freed and reallocated.

Whatever conscious problem-solving learners may engage in when their morphological or syntactic knowledge is defective or uncertain, it seems marginal in information-focused tasks and difficult to operationalize. Lexical CS, on the other hand, are more readily identifiable:

1. Some CS types (paraphrase, circumlocution, and all interactional strategies) are overtly strategic, while other interlanguage productions (transfer, generalization, word coinage) are good candidates for CS, especially when the resulting lexical item is not part of the L2 lexicon.

2. A problematic slot for lexical selection or the CS itself may be flagged by strategy markers such as increased hesitation or identified through retrospective verbal report.

While the focus on lexical CS is thus to some extent an artifact of definition and empirical identifiability, it has obvious merits in its own right. Understanding lexical CS is particularly valuable because they are ubiquitously used – not only by L2 learners, as pointed out by CS researchers early on (Blum-Kulka & Levenston, 1983; Færch & Kasper, 1983d; Kellerman et al., 1987; Poulisse, 1990; Wagner, 1983) and as witnessed by the chapters in this book. In order to appreciate the full range of lexical strategic competence, however, a shift is necessary from L2 *learning* to a particular condition of *communication*. This condition is one where a speaker wishes to label a concept for which she does not have the lexical resources, or where these resources are available but cannot be recalled, or where available and retrievable resources cannot be used successfully because of contextual constraints. Here are some examples of each category (cf. Kellerman et al., 1987, p. 101):

Lexical item unavailable:
    discourse domain unfamiliar to native speaker
    child language
    L2 interlanguage
    L1 attrition
    pidgins
    non-lexicalized concept, e.g., in translation (when a concept is lexicalized in the source language but not in the target language) or lexical innovation

Lexical item irretrievable:
   any unimpaired language user (e.g., tip-of-the-tongue phenomenon)
   aphasic language users
Context constraints:
   expert–novice interaction
   listener's/reader's limited comprehension (children, L2
   learners, recipients experiencing language loss, recipients lacking domain-specific concepts or lexis)
   word definitions in monolingual dictionaries, e.g., through
   paraphrase, exemplification, semantically related lexical items
   (synonyms, antonyms, etc.)
   games and quizzes where players have to guess words (or referents).

Since productive lexical CS are used by all speakers or writers for a
variety of purposes, they constitute an important component of
any language user's strategic competence. But while some lexical
CS are general in the sense that they are not particularly tied to
lexical problem-solving – for instance, paraphrasing or substituting
can operate at the semantic, syntactic, and pragmatic level –
others operate directly on lexical knowledge and nowhere else.
This is true for strategies which rely on contiguous, contrastive
and hierarchical relationships between word meanings, and strategies building on rules for word formation, such as compounding,
pre- and suffixation, shift of word class, or inflectional derivation.
Such strategies operate in a modular fashion, lending support to
the hypothesis that lexical knowledge itself is organized in a separate module.

   There is thus a close link between strategies compensating for
lexical deficiencies and strategies for acquiring lexis. Such strategies both exploit and develop semantic connections in the
learner's mental lexicon and her knowledge of and skill in L2
word formation. They thus require analysed lexical knowledge to
operate on, and at the same time expand, the lexical component
of learners' analysed interlanguage knowledge. While some
authors deny a constructive role for CS in lexical acquisition (e.g.,
Kellerman, 1991), others emphasize their usefulness for precisely
this purpose (Nation, 1990). Consequently, on the much debated
issue of whether CS should be 'taught' (e.g., Dörnyei, 1995;
Mosiori, 1991; Yule & Tarone, this volume), two strong arguments

can be made in favour of incorporating lexical CS into an L2
teaching programme: a subset of psycholinguistic strategies helps
develop learners' analysed lexical knowledge, and interactional
strategies can serve to supply new lexical material in unanalysed
or analysed form. In our view, the narrow focus on lexical CS has been advanta-
geous. It has allowed researchers to identify sets of CS, and to
develop different theoretical models to account for the behaviours
labelled as 'CS'. Comparison of two approaches, as offered by Yule
and Tarone (this volume), has proved to be a useful method for
clarifying underlying assumptions, theoretical perspectives, differences in research design and categorization of data, and assessment of instructional benefits. To some extent, questions of
universal availability and sequential application of CS have also
been examined (Deutsch et al. and Russell, both this volume).
These issues clearly deserve more attention in future research,
because too little is known about CS employed by L1 and L2
speakers with different cultural and linguistic backgrounds
(though see Dickson et al., 1977).

Consistent with the early work on CS in non-native speaker production, this section has focused on *lexical* problem-solving strategies. Yet the relevant psychological literature and the more recent
studies on non-native speakers' CS use inspired by that research,
examine *referential* strategies. These are not just two labels for the
same thing: 'lexical' suggests a semantic view, whereas 'referential'
suggests a pragmatic view of CS. And indeed, the focus on different analytical levels of language and language use reflects the
traditional epistemological orientations of second language
acquisition research and cognitive psychology, whether in their
intra- or interindividual varieties. Consistent with their concern
for the acquisition and use of second *language* knowledge by L2
learners, interlanguage researchers have a prime interest in
uncovering the *linguistic* resources activated by L2 learners when
their required *linguistic* (L2) knowledge, such as vocabulary, is
insufficient to the purpose at hand. Just what the linguistic
resources are that learners draw on to compensate for lexical deficiencies provides a window on the current state of their interlanguage knowledge and is therefore a worthy candidate for close
examination.

Early work on referential communication, on the other hand,
examined the referring strategies of fully competent adult native

speakers – indeed, the designation 'native speaker' is never used because 'native speakerness' is taken for granted unless the contrary is specifically stated. Emphasis is given to the *cognitive* strategies underlying speakers' utterances, their changing assessments of the task requirements and concomitant adjustments of goal-oriented strategic behaviour, whereas little analysis is performed of the actual linguistic resources by which the strategies are implemented (but see Bongaerts et al., 1987; Carroll, 1980).

More recently, the concerns with linguistic resources on the one hand and cognitive processing on the other have crossed disciplinary boundaries. As several contributions to this volume demonstrate, second language acquisition researchers have examined CS within models of cognitive processing, while psychologists interested in child bilingualism have conducted close analyses of bilingual children's linguistic resources and observed the development of their dual linguistic knowledge and its use in referential communication tasks (see Deutsch et al., this volume).

Research methodology

The theoretical and analytical perspective adopted by investigators inevitably leads to differences in research methodology. The 'psychostrategist' tinkers carefully with all sorts of quantifiable variables. Because strategies are considered to be underlying psychological processes with no logical necessity for their behavioural outcomes to be clearly observable in speech, these researchers have had resort to tightly constrained methods of eliciting copious strategy tokens. The first method consists of posing language problems which subjects (note the terminology) have trouble solving; 'communicating' the carefully selected household object depicted in a photograph or drawing so that it can be identified by an imaginary person will result in a flood of strategies of the periphrastic kind (Bialystok, 1983b; Poulisse, 1990). Attempts to diminish the artificiality of such tasks have embraced story telling (though the story is usually the experimenter's with its carefully seeded lexical traps; cf. Dechert, 1983; Poulisse, 1990), descriptions of procedures like 'how to prepare/assemble a …' (Wagner, 1983; Yule & Tarone, 1990) and referential communication tasks involving novel abstract figures (Bongaerts et al., 1987; Russell, this volume). These are easy and reliable ways to collect data, and since they face different sorts of subjects with a common set of problems they are ideal for studying the effects of single variables on performance (language proficiency or linguistic/cultural background, for instance). However, because of their artificiality they seem to have allowed the 'sociostrategists' to occupy the high moral ground (see for instance the critiques offered by Yule and Tarone, and Rampton, in this volume of the typical tasks used by psychostrategists; also Lloyd for a justification). Fortunately, to redress the balance a little, analysis of strategy use in authentic and quasi-natural conversations has also been undertaken (Haastrup & Phillipson, 1983; Poulisse, 1990), but since the experimenter now has considerably less control over what subjects will say, so the surface manifestations of strategy use become more difficult to track down. This is where retrospective commentary by subjects of their own (videotaped) performance has proved useful. Here again, the use of conversation as one source of data is evidence of a desire to put hypotheses to the test in a situation that is more 'ecologically valid'. But even though the use of strategies is studied in spontaneous conversations, the goal is now not so much to understand the mechanics of interaction as to search for the commonalities that underlie strategic behaviour across tasks, to study the adaptations a speaker makes in terms of each task type (e.g., +/− interlocutor), and come to grips with the methodological issues involved in studying underlying processes in tasks with varying degrees of externally imposed control.

This volume

Recent work on CS in second language studies has increasingly recognized work in related fields such as sociolinguistics and psycholinguistics. While the chapters by second language researchers in this volume reflect this wider interest, we also thought it important to include a leavening of chapters by researchers in those fields whose work we believe should inform our own, even if they do not make use of or need the concept of *communication strategy* themselves. These latter contributions touch on referential communication, child bilingualism, mother tongue education, normal native adult interaction and language pathology. By considering what they have to say, second language researchers interested in communication strategies may acquire a broader understanding of the second language phenomena that interest them. At the same time, we would naturally like to think that the intellectual traffic will not be entirely one way, and that scholars in other fields may also benefit from exposure to some of the second language work currently being undertaken, as represented in this volume.

PART ONE

Psycholinguistic perspectives

The chapters in Part I have two things in common: they take a psycholinguistic, intraorganism view on CS (or contrast such a view with alternative positions), and they discuss or adopt as a model for analysis the CS taxonomy developed by the Nijmegen group (Kellerman et al., 1987). The first two chapters clarify some fundamental conceptual and theoretical issues in CS research and can thus be seen as further introductions to the book.

Yule and Tarone contrast the Nijmegen approach with a perspective on CS that emphasizes interaction, output strategies and teachability. They consider that an appropriate methodology for studying CS involves inspecting the differences between non-native and native speakers of the second language in performing linguistic tasks. These differences, which will very largely involve linguistic form, can function as the basis of appropriate pedagogical intervention by identifying areas where learners are in need of help in performing such tasks.

Based on Bialystok's two-dimensional model of language skills, *Kellerman and Bialystok* argue that non-native speakers' CS are just special cases of a wider class of strategic behaviours that characterize all language activity, adult or child, native or non-native, normal or pathological. This view of CS exposes the commonalities underlying all linguistic processing and considers a narrow focus on second language learners/non-native speakers as potentially obfuscating.

In her chapter, *Poulisse* seeks to explain the task effects on CS use found in the Nijmegen studies. Parallel to Kellerman and Bialystok's claim that CS are special cases of language as a fundamentally strategic activity, Poulisse argues that CS use abides by such universal principles as Grice's Cooperative Principle, Leech's principles of textual rhetoric, and Simon's 'satisficing' principle. These principles are implemented differentially in strategy use depending on task demands. Poulisse further demonstrates that self-corrections of slips of the tongue and automatic codeswitches are also guided by these principles. Irrespective of speaker status (e.g., native or non-native), the choices made in speech production appear to reflect the same principles of communication.

Russell's chapter reports on a replication of an earlier experiment in foreign language referential communication. Japanese learners of English participated both as L1 and L2 speakers when performing descriptions of abstract shapes. Following Kellerman et al. (1990), Russell shows that there is evidence for a hierarchy of strategies irrespective of language used: speakers prefer to describe a shape holistically either by analogy or geometric shape ('a rhomboid/a diamond'), then, if linguistic means are lacking, to partition it ('two triangles/two roofs attached at the base'), and finally, if all else fails, to linearize the figure by describing it literally like a set of route directions. While there is thus some support for a cross-linguistically valid CS sequence, Russell's study also suggests possible language- and culture-specific variation which requires further exploration.

Stemmer and Joanette extend the scope of enquiry to CS use by aphasic patients. Examining CS use at the phonological, morpho-syntactic, syntactic, and lexico-semantic level, the authors find that both conceptual and code compensatory strategies are used to express a target item. While there is no systematic preference for either strategy type at any processing level, the type of aphasia appears to influence strategy choice to some extent. Consistent with previous chapters in this section, Stemmer and Joanette note that aphasic patients use the same types of CS as unimpaired speakers.

1

Investigating communication strategies in L2 reference: pros and cons

GEORGE YULE and ELAINE TARONE

Introduction

In the decade since the publication of the then state-of-the-art collection of papers on communication strategies in Færch and Kasper (1983a), there has been continued interest in the ways in which second language (L2) learners make use of their interlanguage resources in attempting to create L2 reference. The basic challenge has remained essentially the same as that raised by Váradi (1983) a decade earlier when faced with a range of L2 referential expressions for the same observed object (i.e., *balloon, ball, air ball, special toys for children*): how do these observed 'creations' help us better understand what is involved in second language learning and use? While there has always existed a variety of different, though relatively compatible, perspectives on how to go about answering this question, how to conduct investigations and how to characterize the various forms produced by L2 learners, there has emerged, in recent years, a fairly serious challenge to the validity of much of the previous work done in this area.

In essence, there has been a marked divergence of opinion between those who are prompted by their investigations to propose additional categories, maintaining and expanding existing taxonomies (e.g., Tarone & Yule, 1987), and those who are prompted to deny the value of existing taxonomies and to propose a substantial reduction in the number of categories of analysis (e.g., Bongaerts et al., 1987). For ease of reference, let us characterize the first group as being rather profligate ('the Pros') in their liberal expansion of categories, and the second group as being rather conservative ('the Cons'), given their emphasis on parsimony. There are, of course, other differences in the focus of each of these two groups, with the Pros often exhibiting a preference for investigating variability in linguistic performance while the Cons emphasize the generalizability and psychological plausibility of their categories.

The noted divergence in analytic preference is accompanied by an equally marked divergence of views on the pedagogical implications of the research findings, with the Pros typically in favour of teaching the use of some communication strategies (e.g., Tarone, 1984) and the Cons expressing a strong opposition to any such teaching (e.g., Kellerman, 1991).

For students and teachers in the many fields related to second or foreign language education and research, this marked divergence of opinion may present a rather puzzling problem. If they choose to follow one school of thought, their research or teaching may be subject to criticism from those holding opposite views. If that potential opposition is interpreted as a source of conflict, then the whole area may be avoided, both in research and teaching. This would not be a desirable outcome. In this chapter, we will attempt to clarify the source of this puzzling situation, which may help researchers and teachers to decide, on the basis of their identified *goals*, how to approach the empirical data involved in L2 reference.

Pros and Cons

The most obvious way in which the two approaches differ is in the number of strategies considered necessary. Although some variation can be found in the terms employed by both groups as they developed their analytic frameworks over time, it is possible to capture the essential distinctions. In the typical taxonomic approach favoured by the Pros, there are both reduction strategies and achievement strategies recognized. Reduction strategies are associated with avoiding, changing or abandoning a communicative goal when faced with a perceived communication difficulty. Achievement strategies, also called compensatory strategies, are characterized by the use of alternative communicative resources (e.g., approximation, circumlocution, language transfer, word coinage) when faced with a perceived communication difficulty. Description and exemplification of these and related strategies can be found in Bialystok (1990), Færch and Kasper (1983d),

Paribakht (1985) and Tarone (1977). In opposing this taxonomic approach, a more recent perspective, favoured by the Cons, has focused on only compensatory strategies, divided into two types described as conceptual and code. A conceptual strategy is either holistic (i.e., using a term for a related substitute concept) or analytic (i.e., describing properties of the referent), whereas a code strategy involves using purely linguistic devices (i.e., L1 words, neologisms). Description and exemplification of these strategies can be found in Bialystok (1990), Bongaerts and Poulisse (1989), Kellerman (1991) and Kellerman, Ammerlaan, Bongaerts and Poulisse (1990).

Underlying these two different sets of descriptive terms is a fundamental difference in analytic perspective. The taxonomic approach of the Pros focuses on descriptions of the language produced by L2 learners, essentially characterizing the means used to accomplish reference in terms of the observed forms. It is primarily a description of observed forms in L2 output, with implicit inferences being made about the differences in the psychological processing that produced them. The alternative approach of the Cons focuses on a description of the psychological processes used by L2 learners, essentially characterizing the cognitive decisions humans make in order to accomplish reference. It is primarily a description of cognitive processing, with implicit inferences being made about the inherent similarity of linguistically different forms observed in the L2 output. The focus of the Pros is on the external and interactive while the focus of the Cons is on the internal and cognitive. In more familiar terms, it might be said that the Pros attempt to work from performance data to consider underlying competence while the Cons seek to characterize underlying competence in order to account for performance data.

Given this version of the Pros and Cons, it should be possible to treat the dichotomous categorization of processing possibilities (conceptual vs code) as 'a higher order description' (Bialystok, 1990, p. 114) that could be combined with the taxonomy of more specific instantiations devised to describe the linguistic performance of L2 learners. This type of compromise might take a form such as that presented in Figure 1.1 (overleaf). Although the combination of categories presented in Figure 1.1 may help clarify the relationship between the approaches of the Pros and Cons, it actually disguises a number of serious methodological and pedagogical differences that require further consideration.

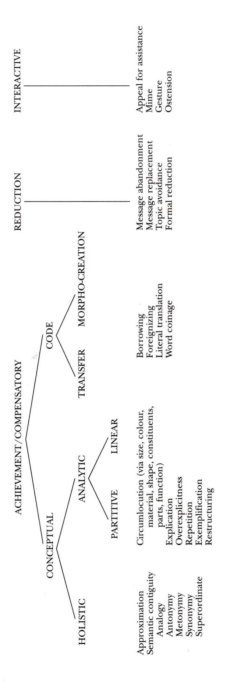

Figure 1.1   Types of communication strategy

Creating L2 reference

It is normally agreed that, as part of their general communicative competence, all adult language users make use of strategic competence or 'the mastery of communication strategies that may be called into action either to enhance the effectiveness of communication or to compensate for breakdowns in communication' (Swain, 1984, p. 189). Although the interest in most studies is in the types of communication strategies used by L2 learners, it has been emphasized (Kellerman, 1991; Yule & Tarone, 1990) that native speakers also employ communication strategies in their L1. This recognition of L1 communication strategy use has influenced research thinking in two quite distinct ways.

For the Cons, the relevant L1 has been the learner's L1. In their study of Dutch learners of English, Kellerman et al. (1990) reported that there was an overwhelming similarity between the strategies used in Dutch (the L1) and those used in English (the L2) immediately afterwards by the same speakers, when the same referential task was performed in that sequence. No results were reported for the reverse sequence. Moreover, there was a consistent hierarchical relationship among the strategies used, with the holistic being preferred over the analytic (only higher order descriptive categories were used). The advantage of this approach is in terms of the opportunity provided to ascertain the influence of a predisposition from a learner's L1 experience in the process of creating L2 reference. One example presented to illustrate the similarity of conceptual strategy used in describing an abstract shape is shown as (1), with the L1 version followed by the L2 version of the same speaker (from Kellerman et al., 1990, p. 175).

(1) (L1) De vorm van een hoefijzer ('The shape of a horseshoe')
    (L2) Erm, this is the figure that erm I do not know how they call it in English ... but it is the same figure. It has the same form as ... the things that horses wear under their feet, the iron things.

Using the Cons' analytic framework, we would say that this speaker uses the same ('holistic') approach to the task in both L1 and L2 versions. From this perspective, it is easy to see why the Cons might argue that strategic competence should not be taught. The L2 learner, producing the descriptions in (1), already knows how to use a holistic strategy to refer to the abstract shape in the L1 and can also use a similar holistic strategy in the L2 version. The use of a holistic strategy does not need to be taught. The observable linguistic differences in (1) between the actual forms used to encode the act of reference in the L1 versus the L2 are not considered significant in the Cons' approach.

However, such differences are what the Pros' approach tends to consider extremely interesting. The speaker in (1) has created a means of L2 reference via circumlocution using available higher-frequency L2 vocabulary when a specific, lower-frequency, vocabulary item was not known. If this learner used such a compensatory strategy in interaction with a native speaker of English, it would not only have a high chance of accomplishing successful reference, but also would be likely to elicit the specific vocabulary item ('Oh, you mean horseshoes') that the learner might wish to know. In fact, for the Pros, it is useful to compare the linguistic forms used by L2 learners and those used by native speakers of the target language for at least three reasons:

1. This comparison yields information about the structure of the learner's interlanguage grammar/lexis as compared to that of the native speaker of the target.
2. This information is helpful in understanding the relative success or effectiveness of learners' communication strategies as these are used in interactions.
3. This information can shed light on the way in which a learner's use of communication strategies in interaction can elicit the relevant 'negotiated input' from others (cf. Yule & Tarone, 1991).

As the reconsideration of the data in (1) suggests, the Pros' approach has focused on the relationship between similarities and differences in the expressions used by L2 learners and by native speakers of the *target* language. The relevant L1 for the Pros is not that of the learner, but that of the target language (TL) speakers. In their study of Chinese, Japanese, Korean and Spanish learners of English, Yule and Tarone (1990) reported on the wide range of differences, as well as similarities, between strategies used by learners and native speakers of English on the same tasks (only lower-order categories were used).

In that study, both the L2 learners and the native speakers of the TL were given a task which required that they make reference to

Table 1.1   Referring expressions used for one part of a coffee pot

---

Native speakers of English

(E2)   an object that it looks kinda like a thin metal long object with two disks both circular disk type objects on both ends one was smaller than the other one

(E4)   a device that caps the container but also has a plunger

(E6)   a sort of a I don't know what it is but on top had a round thing

(E8)   the strainer I'm not sure what it's called ... metal ... metal object with a long part that goes into the coffee pot

L2 learners of English

(S2)   another device which belong this object

(S6)   a look like two circles flat circles?

(S7)   a top and the top has a pole in the middle and in the top of this pole there are a little s like a little plate

(S9)   another piece which consist in two plates with a teeny piece of metal

(S11) the thing that you close has a round thing in the top

(S12) the little stick in the top of the cover

(Cl)   tick ... something like a ticket but head narr like a circle

(C2)   the cover the cover is a special kind of cover

(C3)   a cover

(J1)   cover

(J2)   the top the top is made ...

(J3)   a lid

(K3)   cap

---

real-world objects which were often unfamiliar to both groups of subjects. Table 1.1 presents the referring expressions used by the native speakers and the L2 learners of English as all attempted to refer to the metal inner workings of a Melior coffee pot.

It is clear from Table 1.1 that native speakers of English as well as L2 learners of English made use of communication strategies to refer to the object in question. Further, a similar general approach to the problem can be seen on the part of many subjects; for example, the use of an analytic strategy is shared by the two speakers in examples (2) and (3).

(2) (E2)   an object that it looks like kinda like a thin metal long object with two disks both circular disk type objects on both ends one was smaller than the other one

(3) (S7)   a top and the top has a pole in the middle and in the top of this pole there are a little s like a little plate

However, while an analysis within the Cons' framework might stop here, arguing that the underlying cognitive process was clearly the same and the differences in realization were merely surface differences, the Pros' analysis would pinpoint exactly where those surface linguistic differences lay, for these are precisely the differences which help to highlight the unique characteristics of the learner's interlanguage, as well as the way in which communication strategies can function in interaction between learners and native speakers to produce both successful transactions and negotiated input.

First, an analysis of the language used by learners and native speakers in Table 1.1 shows that the native speakers mostly seem to employ a somewhat larger subtechnical vocabulary than the L2 learners, using terms like *disk, plunger* and *strainer*. The learners' vocabulary, including *plate, circles, pole* and *stick*, tends to involve more implicit analogies. In this task, the native speakers can also be seen to use more analytic strategies, producing a greater volume of talk, than the learners who generally favour more holistic strategies. A general distinction can also be noted between the Spanish L1 learners who produce descriptive phrases and the Chinese, Japanese and Korean learners who prefer to use single lexical items to accomplish reference.

Another advantage of this approach is in terms of the opportunity provided to discover the ways in which learners use more versus less effective strategies in their attempts to create L2 reference, with the baseline of TL native speakers' attempts as a guide. Thus, for an object that all native speakers described successfully as a *tape dispenser*, there were clearly unsuccessful learner responses (*I don't know what this name*), some rather vague holistic (*an object designed to put another object*) and analytic strategies (*this is object, the measure is approximately three inch length and one half inch height ...*), as well as relatively successful L2 creations (*a device to put Scotch tape*). The concept of 'successful' or 'effective' strategy use is not addressed in the Cons' approach and will be reconsidered in the following section.

The point of eliciting L1 data from native speakers, as well as learners, within the Pros' approach, is to have some clear (and not idealized) illustrations of the target behaviour of L2 learners and to note the ways in which native speakers organize and manipulate certain types of general vocabulary when specific referring expressions are not available. Such data are clearly relevant in terms of the pedagogical orientation of the Pros' approach, as will be discussed in a later section.

Methodological issues

While both approaches described thus far have used research designs intended to elicit the creation of L2 reference under controlled conditions, there are notable differences in aspects of their methodologies. Taking Yule and Tarone (1990) and Kellerman et al. (1990) as representatives of the Pros and Cons respectively, we can point to some of those differences (summarized in Table 1.2, below).

1. As noted already, the Cons' approach uses learners as their own controls, with L1 performance being compared to L2 performance. The Pros' approach generally fails to elicit L1 performances and only compares the learners' L2 performance with that of TL native speakers. These differences in data base make sense given the fundamental differences in analytical perspective. The Cons' primary interest is in describing internal cognitive processes, whether in L1 or L2. The Pros are interested primarily in describing the forms used by L2 learners to accomplish reference in a given language, in comparison to the forms used by native speakers of that language for the same purpose.

2. To elicit L2 reference, the Cons in this study used abstract shapes whereas the Pros used real-world objects. Not all Cons' studies used abstract shapes in their elicitation tasks, as Poulisse (1990) demonstrates. However, the central focus of this study, comparing L1 and L2 strategies, is based solely on the abstract shape task. The effect of these different types of prompt can be seen in the data elicited. In describing abstract shapes, the L2 referring expressions often take the form of analogies (e.g., *horseshoes* in (1)). After analogies, speakers next used descriptions of parts of the shape (*two triangles ... their bases are ... put together*). In describing real-world objects, the L2 referring expressions more typically begin by naming (*it's a brush*). After naming, speakers tend to use descriptions of the object's possible function (*for comb the hair*) as well as its parts (*it has a handle*) and other features (*made of wood*). It is important to recognize that these differences in types of elicitation prompt will result in different patterns of L2

reference. The more abstract the prompt, the more likely that conceptually related analogies will be used. The more concrete and familiar the prompt, the more likely that simple names and everyday functions will be mentioned. This type of difference will contribute to the strong task-related effect on communication strategy use noted by Poulisse (1990) and Poulisse and Schils (1989). It may be that future investigations of L2 reference will have to include both abstract and concrete referents (cf. Paribakht, 1985) to explore fully learners' strategies and language in creating L2 reference. Greater recognition may also have to be given to the fact that claims about the nature of L2 referential communication are necessarily claims about L2 reference *on the specific task* faced by the learner.

3.   A related difference involves the presence of a listener or not while the learner is attempting to create L2 reference. For the Cons, there seems to have been no need for a listening partner in the shape-identification task. In some earlier reports where the Cons' studies *have* included a same L1 listening partner (e.g., Bongaerts et al., 1987; Poulisse & Schils, 1989), the results seem to lend support to the idea that there is an interlocutor-effect on choice of linguistic means used to accomplish reference (cf. examples where a local dialect of the Dutch L1 is used by participants in Bongaerts et al., 1987). However, the focus of the Cons on internal cognitive processes has resulted in no role for interlocutor-effects in more recent analytic frameworks.

For the Pros, a different L1 listening partner was present, performing an identification task, and able to give non-verbal feedback. In these circumstances, very few L1-related references were found. The presence of a listener, with a specific purpose dependent on the effectiveness of the learner's L2 reference, has a strong effect on the type of strategy and language used. As Tarone and Yule emphasize elsewhere (1989), within the Pros' approach, the nature and role of the addressee are seen as powerful influences on the speaker's performance, and by inference, may have a profound influence on the cognitive processes underlying that performance. It may be necessary in future studies to incorporate both a concern with the psychological processing of the individual speaker, performing in isolation, and an awareness of the sociocultural impact on that processing when the speaker has to make decisions concerning the knowledge, status and needs of the addressee involved in order to choose the best referential strategy.

We must also recognize that the presence of an addressee creates a quite different context for strategy use, allowing certain 'interactive strategies' (Tarone, 1977), such as appeal for assistance and mime to have referring function. While the Cons' approach categorizes mime as a conceptual strategy and ostension as a code strategy, distinguishing between the assumed psychological processes involved, the Pros would argue that those processes will necessarily be constrained by the speaker's assessment of the particular addressee's knowledge and status in the local interactive context.

4. On a more general level, there is a notable difference in the L2 learner population typically involved in the different approaches. The Cons have used only Dutch L1 subjects, which has the advantage of simplifying the elicitation of L1 performance on the task. The disadvantage may be that the performance of learners from a single L1 background, which is remarkably close, geographically, historically and socio-culturally, to English as the L2, will not generalize to the larger, extremely diverse, population of L2 learners around the world. For example, unlike Bongaerts et al. (1987), Chen (1990) found absolutely no code (or L1-based) strategies used by her Chinese subjects addressing English native speakers. The Pros have included learners from a variety of L1 backgrounds and essentially created cross-cultural communication dyads of non-shared L1s in their investigation. One result of this latter research design is, of course, a great reduction in the use of L1-based strategies. In addition, it can lead, for example, to the discovery of a strong tendency among Chinese L2 learners initially to attempt avoidance strategies (*sorry I don't know*) in the particular L2 reference task presented. It may be that more awareness of potentially diverse socio-cultural effects on L2 performance will have to be kept in mind in designing future studies of L2 referential communication, with more diverse L1 performances on tasks also elicited.

Pedagogical issues

Generally speaking, those adopting the Cons' approach see no point in teaching communication strategies, with some quite explicit statements against the notion: 'What one must teach students of a language is not strategy, but language' (Bialystok, 1990, p. 147) and 'Teach the learners more language and let the strategies

Table 1.2   Summary of differences between Pros and Cons

Pros	Cons
1. Profligate, liberal expansion of categories	Conservative, parsimonious reduction of categories
2. Taxonomic description of observed forms in output, external and interactive	Description of underlying psychological process, internal and cognitive
3. L2 learner performance compared to TL native speaker performance; many differences found	L2 learner performance compared to their own L1 performance: many similarities found
4. Elicitation prompts are real-world objects	Elicitation prompts are abstract shapes
5. Listening partner, with a purpose, present	No listening partner present
6. L2 learners with different L1s; L1s mostly dissimilar to TL	L2 learners with same L1; L1 very similar to TL
7. Communication strategies should be taught	Communication strategies should not be taught

look after themselves' (Kellerman, 1991, p. 158). It should be noted that such statements are not made on the basis of an educational research project by the Cons to find out whether teaching has a beneficial effect or not. To understand this opposition, it has to be understood that strategies employed in creating L2 reference are perceived within the Cons' approach to be essentially cognitive processes and that teaching them would amount to an attempt to teach cognitive processing. For adult learners, that cognitive processing is believed to have already matured through their L1 experience and hence need not be taught. Stated another way, L2 learners are already assumed to have sufficient *competence* from L1 learning to implement their chosen strategies and simply need to be taught the L2 linguistic forms which will enable them to *perform* that competence. There would appear to be no place in this perspective for the idea that developing L2 competence might come about as a result of L2 performance in successfully accomplishing L2 reference. via communication strategies in a classroom activity designed to promote strategy use.

It is possible to view the situation quite differently and to operate with the assumption that, in strategic terms, performance creates competence. Such an assumption seems to lie behind the Pros' approach. Generally speaking, those adopting the Pros' approach have been in favour of teaching communication strategies (e.g., Dörnyei et al., 1992; Dörnyei & Thurrell, 1991; Nattinger, 1988; Tarone, 1984; Tarone & Yule, 1989; Willems, 1987). It may simply be that this perspective is based on an assumed taxonomy of lower-order categories within which some strategies are perceived to be more effective than others in accomplishing L2 reference in specific circumstances. It may also be that the concept of 'teaching language' is viewed quite differently by the Pros. Rather than treating the L2 as something that is simply provided by teachers to learners, much recent thinking in L2 pedagogy has emphasized the provision of classroom activities and tasks in which learners develop a range of abilities in the L2. The language learned via such tasks may be unpredictable and may vary from one learner to the next. By employing tasks which introduce and foster different types of communication strategy, the Pros' approach not only promotes greater awareness, less inhibition and purposeful language practice, it provides relevant learner-produced L2 linguistic performances which can be reflected on later with a specific focus on form.

There have been a few studies designed, in one way or another, to assess the value of communication strategy teaching. In one early study by Brodersen and Gibson (1982), Danish learners of English were found to use more achievement and fewer reduction strategies after sessions discussing the effectiveness of strategies used by the learners themselves in tasks which had been videotaped. More recently, Mosiori (1991), focusing on only higher-order categories, reported no significant effects from an experimental study involving consciousness-raising about communication strategies among American undergraduates learning French. In contrast, Dörnyei et al. (1992) reported significant improvement in oral skills among Hungarian learners of English after training in lower-level communication strategy use. It may be that these different results are a reflection of different training situations and different categories of analysis. The definitive study on the value of communicative strategy teaching remains to be done.

Conclusion

We hope that we have provided fair representations of some divergent views on how L2 referential communication is to be conceived. We trust that we have also clarified how some compatibility between the analytic categories can be achieved and provided some guidance on what criteria should be borne in mind when future research on the nature of L2 referential communication is planned. In terms of teaching, it may be that two quite different perspectives will continue to exist. If the goal of teaching is seen in terms of developing cognitive processing via L2 referential communication tasks, then little benefit is foreseen. If that goal is conceived in more socio-cultural and interactional terms, with the nature of L2 referential communication treated as a function of addressee, communicative task and developing oral skills in the L2, then teaching communication strategies may be considered to have beneficial effects.

2

On psychological plausibility in the study of communication strategies

ERIC KELLERMAN and ELLEN BIALYSTOK

In Bialystok and Kellerman (1987), it was proposed that any attempt to produce a taxonomy of communication strategies as cognitive processes should meet three requirements: *parsimony*, *generalizability* and *psychological plausibility*. These three are considered desirable conditions for a proper account of strategic behaviour. The first requirement, *parsimony*, is that there should be as few discrete strategy types proposed to classify the data as possible. In the absence of other relevant criteria, Occam's Razor should be applied in favour of the most parsimonious taxonomy. The second requirement, *generalizability*, states that any proposed taxonomy should be equally applicable to all normally endowed speakers performing any task engendering strategic behaviour, irrespective of whether first or second languages are involved, and in the latter case irrespective of proficiency level or the particular coupling of the learners' native and non-native languages. The third and most important requirement, *psychological plausibility*, holds that any proposed taxonomy of strategies should be informed by what is currently known about language processing, cognition and problem-solving behaviour.

It is this last requirement we shall concentrate on here. To do this, we shall briefly summarize Bialystok's model of language proficiency and the Nijmegen taxonomy of communication strategies.[1] For more detailed discussion, we refer the reader to earlier work where these are discussed. For the former, see Bialystok (1990, 1991, 1992, 1994); for the latter, see Poulisse (1990). For modified views of the taxonomy, see Kellerman (1991), and especially Poulisse (1993), whose alternative will be discussed below

A model of language proficiency

Bialystok's model of language proficiency consists of two process-ing components, *analysis of knowledge* and *control of processing*. These components, each specialized for a different aspect of pro-cessing, are part of the mechanism responsible for language use and for advances in proficiency. They are domain-general cogni-tive processes which are applied to mental representations. This means that language learning and use take place by means of the same cognitive resources that are employed for the full range of intellectual accomplishments. The processing components are responsible for advances in proficiency because they lead to changes in the mental representations constituting knowledge of a domain. Development occurs in both on-line and off-line con-texts, so that the changes in mental representation occur both at the time these processes are being used (e.g., through correction, instruction, etc.) and when they are not currently in use (e.g., through reflection on the system, or by generalization from another system).[2]

Analysis of knowledge is the process by which mental representa-tions of information become increasingly structured. As an abstract representation itself, structure is also a form of know-ledge. Therefore, structure is both the principle by which know-ledge is organized and its instantiation.[3] Consider an example from children's understanding of geometric form. Young children at about two years old are unable to name or draw Euclidean shapes. They are perfectly capable, however, of drawing a sailboat with a triangular sail (Stiles et al., 1990). As their conception of 'sailboat' becomes analysed, the form of the sail can be isolated and represented as abstract new knowledge, 'triangle'.

The same procedure applies to knowledge of meanings or know-ledge of the world. Through the process of analysis, contextually embedded representations of words and meanings evolve into more abstract structures. As knowledge of meanings is analysed, words become organized by formal categories such as taxonomic structure (e.g., 'superordinate-basic level-subordinate'), and by for-mal linguistic categories, such as 'part of speech'. An early repre-sentation might be organized round the pair *dog* and *bone* because of their situational contiguity in the child's usual experiences. With ongoing analysis, this representation would undergo reorganiza-tion in two ways. A more formal representation of the meanings would come to relate such pairs as *dog* and *cat*, or *dog* and *collie*, because they are taxonomically linked. A more formal representation of language would relate such terms as *dog, cat*, and *bone*, because they are all nouns. Thus, both representations of meaning and representations of language are transformed through analysis. Analysed knowledge is structured and accessible across contexts; unanalysed knowledge exists only to the extent that it is part of familiar routines or procedures.

The second component is *control of processing*, or *selective attention*. In any cognitive activity, we are able to attend to only some selected portion of available information at any given time. Situations invariably present more information than it is possible to process, and cognition involves continual selection from that pool of information. In addition, every context brings perceptual or experiential biases that make some portion of that information salient. In conversational uses of language, we generally pay attention only to the meanings. Sometimes, however, other, more formal, aspects of the language are given attention, such as its syntax, its phonology, or the identity of the language itself. In reading, we must constantly redirect some attention to formal properties, in this case the printed or written text. Speaking to a non-native speaker may require that we redirect special attention to lexical choices. As a listener we may direct our attention to para- and extralinguistic aspects of a message – gestures, kinesics, intonation, the surroundings – as these may assist in the interpretation of the message. These changes in selective attention are central to language processing. However, the ability to orchestrate these changes in attention when the context assigns priority to other information develops gradually. The need for higher levels of control in processing can be determined both by the sheer quantity of information competing for attention and by the degree of correspondence between the perceptually salient aspects of the context and what the individual actually needs to attend to in order to process that information successfully.[4]

These two processing components describe operations that are applied to mental representations during language learning and use. The operations have the effect of increasingly structuring the organization of the representations (analysis) and increasingly directing attention to selected aspects of representations (control). They are ongoing processes whenever language is used. It follows that they are also used when communication strategies are employed. (For discussion of the application of the model to other areas, such as the study of reading deficits, reading comprehension, or metalinguistic awareness in mono- and bilinguals, see, for example, Bialystok, 1983b, 1993; and Bialystok and Mitterer, 1987, respectively.)

Taxonomies of compensatory strategies

In Kellerman (1991), a two-strategy taxonomy was presented which was based on the similar scheme used in the Nijmegen Project (e.g., Poulisse, 1987). The two strategy types are labelled *conceptual* and *code strategies*. *Conceptual strategies* manipulate the individual's knowledge of properties of the concept itself, including part–whole relationships, attributes and functions, and may also exploit episodic memory (Tulving, 1972). *Code strategies* manipulate the user's knowledge of word form by the construction of *ad hoc* labels for referents via languages other than the L2, or via derivational rules within the L2. One innovation associated with this division into *conceptual* and *code* is the subsuming of certain kinds of gestural behaviour under one or other strategy type (these have traditionally been lumped together in an independent category called *mime* in other taxonomies). In Kellerman's taxonomy, mimetic behaviour depicting semantic properties of the referent is to be seen as a manifestation of the *conceptual strategy*, while *ostensive definition* (pointing rather than naming, a 'pro-linguistic' device) is seen as a case of the *code strategy*. Similarly, what have been known traditionally as *word coinages* can be divided into those which are semantically based – the 'classic' example is Váradi's 'airball' for 'balloon', (Váradi, 1983) – and those rarely reported second-language innovations whose meanings are opaque to all but their users.[5]

The claim is that all utterances produced by a learner to compensate for the absence of a particular lexical item in the L2 can be classified according to one or other of these strategy types. The two-strategy taxonomy has been developed out of close scrutiny of learners' performance coupled to their retrospective comments. By positing the existence of no more than two strategies, each reflecting a distinct level of representation, that of concept and that of code, we distinguish between the strategic use of underlying sources of knowledge and the lower-level speech production processes ultimately responsible for determining the linguistic and phonetic form of utterances. The learners' ultimate choice between conceptual and code strategies will depend on a number of factors, among which we may assume at least the presence or absence of an interlocutor, assumptions of common ground, attentional resources, the type of task, the modes of communication possible (e.g., visual and auditory, or auditory alone), proficiency, the language selected, and the typological relationship between the learner's first language and the language of communication.

The two-way taxonomy is rooted in the distinction between the two types of knowledge representation (meaning and form) in long-term memory. Essentially, each of these types of knowledge is the basis for one of the strategies. But, as we have outlined in the previous section, the two cognitive processes of analysis and control are constantly being applied to mental representations, which are therefore shaped and influenced by them. These operations also give the two-way taxonomy its psychological plausibility.

Explanation of the strategies

How then does the analysis-control model account for the conceptual and code strategies of the modified Nijmegen taxonomy? The conceptual and code strategies refer to a distinction between two kinds of mental representation. The analysis and control processes refer to a distinction between two kinds of cognitive operation. In much information-processing theorizing, all cognitive performance can be explained in terms of operations (processes) acting on representations. Communication strategies, being the outcome of a normal cognitive activity, also require this type of explanation. The integration of the two schemes, then, is a means of anchoring a distinction between representations in a difference between processes. In this way, strategies are not only described, they are also explained.

Since the two processes are each capable of acting on two types of representation, there are four theoretically possible outcomes, as indicated in Figure 2.1. Our claim is that each of the strategy types may be viewed in terms of the demands made of analysis and control in the exploration of each type of knowledge. However, only three of the four possibilities describe plausible options for

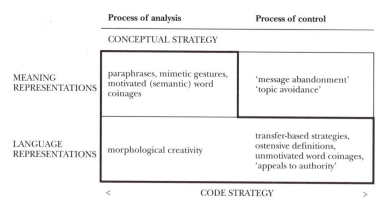

Figure 2.1   Operation of analysis and control processes on representations of meaning and language

compensatory strategies. The *conceptual strategy* is explained as the process of *analysis* operating on a representation of meaning; utterances (strategy tokens) fitting traditional descriptions such as *paraphrase, circumlocution* and some *word coinages* (those that are semantically motivated, like 'airball' for 'balloon') will be the outcome. To this group should be added *mimetic* or *iconic gesture*. When the process of analysis operates on language representations, we have a *code strategy*. There seems to be one obvious candidate to fill this cell. Here we posit the learner resorting to analysed linguistic knowledge to solve lexical problems. This could be accomplished by making use of productive grammatical processes in the L2, typically derivation (*steam iron* → **to ironize; to apply* → **appliance*, 'application' (examples from Poulisse, 1990)). In the Nijmegen scheme this sort of behaviour was called *morphological creativity*, though a better term might be *grammatical derivation*. This activity is linguistic rather than conceptual because it concerns first and foremost the exploitation of relationships between word *forms* (Miller & Fellbaum, 1991, p. 211), though of course there are semantic implications as a result.[6]

Moving across to the intersection of *code* and *control*, we see that the language representations cell contains semantically *un*motivated word coinages and ostensive definitions. Since we have claimed that the *code strategy* is based principally on linguistic representations, the exploitation of the control dimension would serve to focus attention on alternate means of labelling the target referent or concept. The first (or any other non-target) language would be a good source,[7] as would nonce labels created and accepted mutually for the sake of brevity and convenience. Also appearing in this cell is the traditional category known as 'appeals to authority', where the learner cedes the onus of solution by switching attention to another resource (an external authority, such as speech partner or dictionary). Since 'appeals to authority' are not autonomous solutions to lexical problems but merely defer them, these are not considered compensatory, and were not studied in the Nijmegen project. Yet it is perhaps possible to see how they could be accounted for in the present scheme.

Finally, we come to the last cell, the intersection of *meaning representation* and *control*. Here, we might insert 'appeals to authority' once more in the form of an expert source like an encyclopaedia, or traditional strategies like 'message abandonment' or 'topic avoidance', which imply the surrender of attempts to deal with conceptual complexities irrespective of the language of use. Like 'appeals to authority', message abandonment and topic avoidance are arguably not compensatory strategies at all (in the communication strategy literature, they are known as *reduction strategies*) and neither has been studied by the Nijmegen group.

Although the matrix in Figure 2.1 is a convenient way of depicting our model in that it makes the intersection of two types of representation with two types of process clear, it might leave the impression that the assignment of descriptive labels to the four cells, and especially to the two strategies, is categorical. The placement of *analysis* and *control* at the head of the columns might tempt one to conclude that they each have exclusive domains in which they function alone. This would be an unintended inference, however. The main point about language processing in terms of analysis and control is that these are two essential cognitive functions and that all language processing requires both simultaneously. Specific instances of language functioning, however, will tend to rely more heavily on one than the other – reading requires more control than speaking, and writing requires more analysis than listening (Bialystok, 1993). Communication strategies are called upon when the usual balance between analysis and control is disturbed (typically through inaccessibility of linguistic knowledge) so that one of the dimensions gains prominence. It is this disruption of the usual balance of processing, a disruption that may or may not be deliberately induced by the speaker, that makes this kind of communication strategic. (For discussion of the relationship between task and selection of analysis-based or control-based strategies, see Bialystok, 1990, Ch. 7.)[8]

Poulisse's approach to psychological plausibility

Though the issue of psychological plausibility has been strikingly absent in most discussions of communication strategies, it has recently also surfaced in Poulisse (1993), who specifically challenges the Nijmegen taxonomy on the grounds that in this very respect it fails to meet its own requirement. Poulisse's arguments are based on research on the bilingual lexicon, second language speech data (e.g., Poulisse & Bongaerts, 1994), the speech error literature, and a bilingual adaptation of a well-articulated model of monolingual speech production and comprehension, that of Levelt (1989). Her own view of psychological plausibility leads to a revised taxonomy that effectively adjusts the boundaries between the strategy types laid down in the Nijmegen classification.

The most striking difference between Poulisse's proposal and the Nijmegen taxonomy is the increase in the number of strategy types from two to three and the use of a different nomenclature (*reconceptualization, substitution, substitution plus*; see below) to label them. The new proposal is thus less parsimonious than Nijmegen's, but this in itself need be of no consequence if there are attendant gains elsewhere.

Poulisse criticizes the Nijmegen taxonomy for leaning crucially on the belief that strategies involving representations of meaning and form are themselves necessarily distinct, an assumption which she claims may artificially carve up what are in fact unitary operations. Since the present authors have levelled the same charge against the traditional taxonomies (e.g., Bialystok & Kellerman, 1987), this is an objection that requires some consideration.

Take the example of Nijmegen's *conceptual strategy*. As the name implies, this strategy is the outcome of an operation on meaning representations alone. In the original Nijmegen scheme, we distinguished two polar variants of this strategy – *analytic* and *holistic*. The first exploits features of the target concept itself, typically part–whole relationships, attributes and functions ('It has leaves, it's green and Popeye eats it to keep strong' for 'spinach'; example adapted from Poulisse, 1990), while the latter resorts to concepts in hierarchical relation, such as 'hypernym of' (e.g., 'bird' for 'sparrow'), 'hyponym of' (e.g., 'oranges and apples' for 'fruit'), and 'co-hyponym of' (e.g., 'peas' for 'beans').

As the Nijmegen term *holistic* implies, this sort of perspective involves abandoning the search for the target word in favour of a semantically linked concept whose form *can* be retrieved. However, Poulisse claims that there are no substantive *processing* differences involved in the strategic choice of, say, the equivalent *native* language label for the concept on the one hand, and the choice of a hypernym in the *second* language on the other (i.e., the uttering of L1 Dutch *mus* is equivalent to the uttering of L2 English 'bird' as compensation for the absence of the English target word 'sparrow'). This is because Poulisse, like many researchers (e.g., De Groot, 1992) assumes a spreading-activation model of lexical access, such that when a lexical item is accessed in one language, other same-language items to which it is similar in meaning are also activated, as are its functional translation equivalents in other languages familiar to the speaker. Therefore if a learner of French whose first language is English tries to access a lexical item meeting the feature specifications [+human], [+male], [+young] and [+French], he or she should activate *garçon*, but will also activate *boy* as well as *homme*. Thus 'specification of particular language' is seen as a component playing a role in lexical access akin to traditional semantic features. In this view, *boy* receives as much activation as *homme* does since they both differ by one feature from the target *garçon*, and so the system may on occasion accidentally yield either the word form with another language specification or a word form which differs by a single meaning feature – in both cases a slip involving just the single feature (see Poulisse & Bongaerts, 1994).

This view of the mental lexicon is founded in part on speech error data from second language learners (Poulisse & Bongaerts, 1994) and their similarity to certain kinds of L1 speech errors. Poulisse notes the occurrence of accidental substitutions of L1 for L2 words and blends of L1 and L2 words, supporting the notion that translation equivalents are also activated whatever the language in current use. Poulisse quotes examples of errors in the form of language blends such as /kweɪm/ (Du. *kwam + came*), and /eltʃʌθə/ (Du. *elkaar + each other*), where translation equivalents merge, as well as substitution errors where Dutch grammatical words like *maar* ('but'), *of* ('or rather'), or *ook* ('too', 'also') commonly appear in stretches of L2 English speech.

Since translation equivalents by definition share the *semantic* features of the concept they label (by virtue of being linked to a shared conceptual node), Poulisse compares these latter substitution errors to those (monolingual) errors which involve relations like antonymy ('low' for 'high', for instance) or co-hyponymy ('fingers' for 'toes').

Noting the similarity of the form of these speech errors to the strategic behaviour of learners solving their lexical problems, Poulisse calls the first of her three compensatory strategy types the *substitution strategy*, since second language learners may also *purposefully* utilize either the L1 translation equivalent or a semantically related L2 word to plug the gap created by the missing lexical item.

Building on this framework of activation during access as a model for describing the workings of CS, Poulisse proposes a second strategy type, termed the *substitution plus strategy*. This strategy is essentially a beefed-up *substitution strategy* where there is also adaptation to the target language via morphological and phonological accommodation. It can only occur when a substitution strategy has already been implemented. Its most obvious manifestations are 'foreignizings' of L1 words, but it is also taken to be at work in the morphological or phonological adaptation of pre-existing L2 lexical items so as to change their grammatical status (deriving a verb **ironize* from the noun *(steam) iron* and the productive verbal suffix *-ize*, for instance). In the Nijmegen taxonomy, the exploitation of the productive grammatical rules of the L2 was seen as an operation on the learner's linguistic knowledge, involving as it does relations between morphemes, and was therefore termed a *linguistic* (or *code*) strategy.

Poulisse's third strategy, *reconceptualization*, covers the rump of the Nijmegen taxonomy, the variety of conceptual strategy known as *analytic*. This strategy makes use of semantic or episodic properties of the target, expressed in linguistic units longer than a single 'chunk' (1993, p. 181). The fact that such a strategy does not rely on the substitution of existing single-word lexicalizations suggests to Poulisse that there is a different kind of process involved here, one requiring more planning and effort than either of the substitution strategies, since target concepts have to be 'unpackaged' and searched for appropriate and verbalizable properties. Utterances then have to be planned to integrate the selected properties. (Figure 2.2 below highlights the difference between the Poulisse and the Nijmegen taxonomies.)

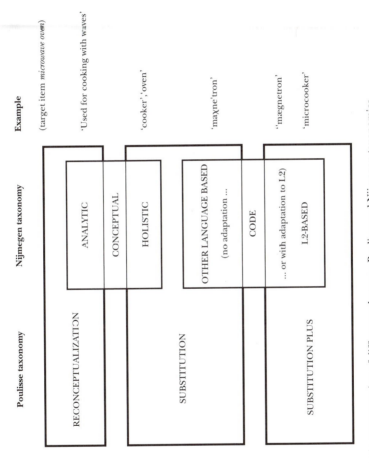

Poulisse taxonomy	Nijmegen taxonomy	Example
		(target item *microwave oven*)
RECONCEPTUALIZATION	ANALYTIC	'Used for cooking with waves'
	CONCEPTUAL	
	HOLISTIC	'cooker', 'oven'
SUBSTITUTION	OTHER LANGUAGE BASED	'maɣne'tron'
	(no adaptation ...	
	CODE	
	... or with adaptation to L2)	
SUBSTITUTION PLUS	L2-BASED	'mægnetron'
		'microcooker'

Figure 2.2   Schematic representation of differences between Poulisse and Nijmegen taxonomies

Discussion

Poulisse's proposal has the merit of being rooted in current views of linguistic processing and the bilingual mental lexicon. It is essentially an adaptation of a model of language production to account for the generation of solutions to failed lexical searches in L2. There is an assumption that by examining speech production on-line, one can also account for deliberative off-line behaviour when word-finding problems are encountered. In this respect, it seems to us that learners' behaviour is not so very different from that of 'native' speakers, who unproblematically measure their words in ordinary everyday conversation for purposes of affect or effect (e.g., Erickson, 1981, p. 245; Rampton, this volume).

From Poulisse's description of the above scheme, we see that the pressing into service by the learner of one lexical item for another is one strategy type (Substitution), while feature listing ('it's green, you eat it with potatoes and Popeye eats it' for 'spinach') and compounding ('cooking apparatus', both examples from Poulisse 1993, p. 181) are another (Reconceptualization). This distinction derives its psychological plausibility from a current model of bilingual access whose empirical base is largely founded on the study of cross-language priming effects (see De Groot, 1993, for a review).[9]

Poulisse's new classification also has its own problems of application. There seem to be two: the first is how to treat those fairly frequent CS tokens displaying a definition-like structure of [superordinate/'placeholder' noun or pronoun] + [specification]. Is a noun phrase (NP) like 'stuff to kill flies' (for 'fly spray') to be treated as one strategy (Reconceptualization), or two in tandem (Substitution *and* Reconceptualization), since 'stuff' is selected to label that part of the concept vacated by 'spray'? Or are only co-hyponyms to be considered adequate 'Substitutions'? If we are dealing with two strategies, then their obvious mutual affinity in these structures requires some explanation.

The second problem arises in connection with strategy tokens that exemplify superordinate categories by lists of category members (e.g., 'tables, beds, chairs and cupboards' for 'furniture').[10] Is the list of category members to be treated as Substitution or Reconceptualization? Presumably, attempted accessing of the lexical item *furniture* or its L1 equivalent will also activate all those prototypical category members. Perhaps one lexical item is a Substitution, but two or more a Reconceptualization on the grounds of requiring more processing effort. How, then, is an utterance like 'apples and things' (for 'fruit') or 'tables, etc.' (again for 'furniture') to be classified? Unfortunately, all the examples in Poulisse (1993) are at the co-hyponym level. Her distinction between Substitution and Reconceptualization seems in a number of cases to rest crucially on the idea of one lexical item standing in for another lexical item, with no modification. Since exemplification is a fairly common compensatory lexical device, its ambiguous status is a challenge to Poulisse's typology.

Moreover, the status of superordinates uttered without modification is also unclear. If a speaker, for lack of an English 'rose', says 'Percy tossed Keiko a flower' instead of 'Percy tossed Keiko a rose', this is Substitution in Poulisse's book. If the speaker says 'Percy tossed Keiko a red flower', this becomes Reconceptualization. However, 'flower' is a potential substitution for 'red flower, rose, red rose, red thing with thorns which the English grow in serried ranks', as well as for 'daffodil', 'bougainvillaea' and 'night-blooming cereus'. Who can know when a single lexical item is being substituted and not a complex of conceptual and episodic features? Introspection will probably not help here, since it is unlikely that a learner could examine these processes of lexical access; an account of their (partial) malfunctioning is probably the best one could hope for. And when such superordinates are uttered by native speakers, the choice may indicate no malfunctioning at all, but rather a context-driven adaptation (strategic) to a listener, or implicit acknowledgement of the dictates of style.

The modified Nijmegen classification scheme, with its two strategies, *conceptual* and *code*, seems immune to these problems. Exemplification, whether by one or more category members, whether qualified by *etc.* or *and things* or not, would all be classified as examples of *conceptual strategies*, as would superordinates, both modified and unmodified.

It is also appropriate to clarify the extent to which Poulisse's proposal is a true alternative to the model of strategic behaviour presented earlier, for Bialystok and Poulisse do not address the same questions. Poulisse's model queries the meaning-form distinction originally proposed by Nijmegen as the basis for distinguishing between types of strategy in the light of the spreading-activation model of bilingual lexical access. The Nijmegen group is fairly non-committal as to how the processes operate in real time (although see Poulisse 1990, Ch. 1), focusing instead on the types of representation that speakers/learners exploit. But Poulisse (1993) also offers a number of criticisms of the *analysis-control* framework as a viable model of CS use and it is to these that we now briefly turn our attention.

The first criticism is that Bialystok fudges the distinction between strategic and non-strategic aspects of language use, since her model does not account for the 'fast' or 'automatic' processes. As non-strategic language use is *automatic* language use, Poulisse continues, it is doubtful whether Bialystok can make claims about the imbalance in analysis and control invoked when the learner resorts to CS, since there is no way of knowing how these skills are exploited when strategies are *not* being applied.

This insistence on the distinction between strategic and non-strategic (automatic) language actually reveals a misapprehension about Bialystok's model, in that the description of language use in terms of cognitive operations (i.e., analysis and control) rather than linguistic principles makes *all* language use strategic. The term 'strategy' denotes the operation of the intelligent systems of information processing involved in all cognitive activity. Since the issue for Bialystok is to find a cognitive description to account for the development of language proficiency in terms of the two dimensions of analysis and control, the millisecond-by-millisecond workings of the speech production model are neither here nor there. Thus, and to return to a point made earlier, what makes CS salient is not the fact that they are strategic (since all language use is strategic), but that they make *unusual calls upon one or both of the two processing skills* in their execution. Furthermore, Bialystok has argued that it *is* possible to ascertain the relative amounts of analysis and control demanded by various kinds of task (see, e.g., Bialystok, 1991, for discussion; also Bialystok & Mitterer, 1987, and Ricciardelli, 1993, for empirical evidence of analysis and control in ordinary language use).

Poulisse also claims that Bialystok's notion of *control* fails to distinguish clearly among strategy types since it can be argued that one and the same strategy type can have elements of both control and analysis. In fact 'there is little reason to assume Analysis-based strategies ... require less control than Control-based Strategies' (Poulisse, 1993, p. 171). But as we suggested above, the more important point is that analysis and control are not two components in competition for a finite degree of processing space. Not only do strategies require some quantity of each component, but even if it were the case that analysis-based strategies required just as much control as 'classic' control-based strategies like ostensive definition, *they would still require more analysis.* And the same argument could be applied, *mutatis mutandis,* to control-based strategies.

Mimetic gestures are a case in point: the switch to a non-verbal medium requires control, but the implementation of the mime also requires analysis of the target concept, typically in terms of shape, position or movement. That is why we consider mimetic gesture as making greater demands on analysed knowledge than on control. Not so for ostensive definition, where it is clearly control that predominates. This last example conveniently brings us to another point raised by Poulisse (1993, p. 172), who maintains that if control strategies are typically used in contexts where there are high processing demands on learners (a job interview, for instance, where the discourse may be largely unplanned), switching to other reference systems to overcome linguistic deficits will demand even more attention in a situation where it is already in short supply. However, the very point of a control strategy is to reduce the processing burden – the switch to mime permits analysed knowledge to be exploited without overly taxing limited linguistic resources and so the communicative job gets done after all.

A last and somewhat surprising claim by Poulisse should not be left unanswered. It is that the *analysis-control* model cannot account for proficiency- and task-related effects in CS use, since '[w]hen we are dealing with adult L2 learners ... there is no reason to assume that the components of analysed ... knowledge and control ... are underdeveloped', presumably because adults have been through the language learning experience once before (1993, p. 172). While this may very largely be true for conceptual development, it does not necessarily apply at all to linguistic development, especially in the early stages of learning, and particularly in regard to formulaic speech. All the linguistic analysis and control available in the first language is of limited use in a second language in the initial stages and cognitive maturity and metalinguistic awareness can only help to the extent that the input can be segmented meaningfully. The explication of L2 linguistic knowledge and the development of control mechanisms also require development over time, even if they are assisted by cognitive maturity and metalinguistic insight. Progress in a language (or proficiency) may therefore be defined as the development of greater levels of analysis and control, resulting in the ability to perform more varied and difficult tasks in the L2. The development of proficiency has therefore been one of the principal objects of study in Bialystok's research programme. It is certainly not addressed in Poulisse's model.

Conclusion

Both Bialystok, the Nijmegen group and Poulisse have addressed the question of psychological plausibility in their work, though with different focuses of interest. While Poulisse is concerned with a model of speech production which will account for the generation of communication strategies, Bialystok is interested in showing that communication strategies are manifestations of the development of the cognitive processes of analysis and control. The Nijmegen group is more concerned with the types of mental representation available for exploitation by learners. Though it provides a good fit with Bialystok's model, the Conceptual–Code distinction (Kellerman, 1991) is not supported by Poulisse's analysis. However, Poulisse's modified taxonomy does not seem to be able to draw a clear distinction between Substitution and Reconceptualization strategies. Finally, it remains to be seen whether the model of bilingual lexical access she espouses stands up to further close scrutiny.

Since the two-way taxonomy of *conceptual* and *code* strategies is immune to the list/single exemplar problem that seems to trouble Poulisse's taxonomy, is still the more parsimonious option, and is furthermore quite compatible with Bialystok's model of processing (which has been shown to be applicable to other aspects of language use and proficiency such as reading comprehension and metalinguistic awareness), we believe that we have offered an account of strategic behaviour that directly addresses the question of psychological plausibility.

Notes

We would like to thank Theo Bongaerts, Clive Perdue, Nanda Poulisse and Nancy Wood for their comments on an earlier draft of this chapter. Needless to say, the present authors are entirely responsible for any warts on the version appearing here.

1. Actually, a subset of these is called *compensatory strategies,* used by non-native speakers so as not to compromise their target meanings despite lexical limitations.
2. For instance, the realization that the relationship of a puppy to a full-grown dog is analogous to that of a kitten to a cat.
3. Thus, it is one form of analysed knowledge to know that the category *furniture* consists of chairs, tables and other items, and that there are different sorts of chair (armchair, high chair, office chair); it is another to know that one form of structure is hierarchical organization.
4. For instance, the most salient aspect about one's interlocutor may be his or her foreign accent, necessitating extra control on the part of the listener to focus on the *content* of what is said.
5. Of course, these innovations abound in first language use. In British English we have a recent example in the verb *to gazump.* Scientists are particularly adept at coinages, and so, it seems, are their offspring: *Googol* (10^{100}) is an example of a word apparently invented by the nine-year-old nephew of Dr Edward Kasner. These two cases are examples of opaque coinages which have gained some acceptance.
6. Antonymy is a potential problem for the taxonomy since it is not immediately obvious whether learners' common exploitation of antonyms (*the water's not deep but* ... *{shallow}*; *the colour is not black but* ... *{white}*) is linguistic or conceptual. The same goes for pairs of words which are strong associates (*not pepper but* ... *{salt}*; *not dogs but* ... *{cats}*). In fact this is a controversial issue in psycholinguistics which we are not required to solve here. We assume that though there are obviously semantic links between *some* pairs of such terms, there are also associative links, a reflection of these terms' frequent co-occurrence. (See Levelt, 1989, Ch. 6, for discussion.)
7. As pointed out in Kellerman (1991, p. 151), some utterance tokens may well be the product of both conceptual and code strategies. Mimetic gestures are a case in point. And some utterances will be ambiguous: literal semantic transfers like **oldboy* (bachelor) from Finnish *vanhapoika* may be viewed either as conceptual or code strategy tokens (example from Ringbom, 1991, p. 177).
8. Bialystok (1990) differs somewhat from the present chapter in the way that the relationship between the analysis and control processes and the conceptual and code strategies is characterized.
9. Some recent work by Challis and Bartoszko (in preparation) casts at least *some* doubt on such models. In their experiments with proficient Polish learners of English, Challis and Bartoszko considered the effects of priming on a word fragment completion task after a period of study in which subjects had variously to translate subvocally, count vowels in, rate the pleasantness of meaning of, and form sentences with Polish and English words. Interestingly, no cognates were used

as stimuli (for the distinction between cognates and non-cognates in terms of bilingual storage, again see De Groot, 1993). Challis and Bartoszko report no cross-language priming effects from English to Polish, and Polish words only primed English equivalents if the Polish words had been translated earlier in the study condition. The results of this study certainly argue against the existence of a component [+specific language], equivalent to traditional semantic features like [+male], [+young], etc., arranged in some sort of bilingual semantic network.

10. Perhaps it is worth remembering that from a cross-linguistic point of view, some languages simply do not have superordinate terms for categories Anglophones take for granted. *Nut* is a case in point: in French, for instance, one cannot refer to a generic nut, but only to types of nut, whatever we were taught about *noisette* at school. A *bag of mixed nuts* will thus become much more specific once translated into French. See also Klima and Bellugi (1979) for discussion of the expression of superordinate categories in American Sign Language.

3

Compensatory strategies and the principles of clarity and economy

NANDA POULISSE

Introduction

One of the most striking findings of the Nijmegen studies of how Dutch learners compensate for lexical problems while speaking English (Bongaerts & Poulisse, 1989; Kellerman, 1991; Poulisse, 1990) was the powerful effect of task in the selection of particular strategy types. Moreover, the realization of the learners' compensatory strategies (CpS), that is, their syntactic form, the amount of information included in them, and the modality (speech, gesture) used to encode them, also turned out to be task-related. In more controlled tasks (reference to 'difficult' real-world objects and novel abstract shapes in the absence of an interlocutor), learners generally went to great lengths to solve their lexical problems, using extensive analytic (descriptive) strategies in the object reference task or a combination of such strategies and holistic strategies (which explore hierarchical relations between lexical items, for example, co-hyponymy or hypernymy) in the abstract shapes task. In more naturalistic tasks (retelling in English a brief story originally heard in Dutch and informal conversation with a native speaker of English), learners tended to use a variety of shorter strategies, including not only less detailed analytic strategies, but also a fair number of holistic and transfer-based strategies.

In this chapter, it will be argued that many of these task-related differences can be explained in terms of two general principles of communication: the Principle of Clarity and the Principle of Economy. These two principles, which have been discussed in the literature under these and other names, require the speaker to be informative and clear on the one hand, and brief and economical on the other (see, e.g., Grice, 1975; Leech, 1983; Levinson, 1987;

49

Sperber & Wilson, 1986). The important role these two principles play in communication has been amply documented in L1 studies of communication (see the studies mentioned above as well as, e.g., Brown, 1965; Clark & Wilkes-Gibbs, 1986; Krauss & Weinheimer, 1967; Olson, 1970; Sacks & Schegloff, 1979; Wilkes-Gibbs, this volume). Here, it will be shown that these same principles also play an important role in L2 communication. They not only influence the use of CpS, but also, it will be suggested, affect the production of code-switches and self-corrections by L2 learners.

The Principles of Clarity and Economy

To explain the differences in CpS use according to task, it is necessary to have a closer look at the notion of CpS when learners find themselves unable to communicate their intended messages in the preferred manner. Following Levelt's (1989) model of speaking, we may summarize what happens as follows: At step 1, speakers conceptualize a message, adhering to general principles of communication and taking into account the situation, the preceding discourse, the knowledge they share with their interlocutor(s), and so on. At step 2, they start the encoding of this message, but run into problems, most typically because their lexicon does not contain the words they had planned to use. They then have the choice between giving up (i.e., using an avoidance strategy) or encoding their message in an alternative way (i.e., using a CpS). The latter solution will presumably involve replanning the original message at the level of conceptualization: it will either require a complete reorganization of the original plan in the case of analytic conceptual strategies, or the substitution of some meaning or language elements to allow for the selection of an alternative lexical item in the case of holistic conceptual strategies and transfer strategies.[1] It seems likely, then, that while planning the use of a CpS, the speaker will again follow general principles of communication and will take the situation, the preceding discourse and shared knowledge into account. In other words, CpS use is probably subject to the same principles and constraints that affect the production of any other utterance.

There are two well-known principles of communication that seem particularly relevant to CpS use. They are the Principle of Clarity and the Principle of Economy. Although these principles have been discussed in the literature under several different names – only Leech (1983) actually uses the terms Clarity Principle and Economy Principle – there seems to be general consensus as to their definitions. The Principle of Clarity requires speakers to produce clear, intelligible messages and the Principle of Economy requires them to do this with the least possible expenditure of effort. To comply with both principles simultaneously, speakers must strike a balance between the intelligibility of their messages and the processing effort they and their listeners put into the production and reception of these messages. Or, as Kasher (1977) has put it: 'Given a basic desired purpose, the ideal speaker chooses that linguistic action which, he believes, most effectively *and* at least cost attains that purpose' (cited in Levinson, 1987, p. 75). This also means that speakers will try to solve their communication problem by using CpS in the most effective and economical way possible.

In an article on the inferential implications of minimization in linguistic expression, Levinson (1987) gives various examples to illustrate how the Principles of Clarity and Economy (in his terminology the Principles of Quantity and Relation, cf. p. 67) work in ordinary language use. The usage of names to refer to persons, for instance, allows speakers to comply with both principles simultaneously. Names enable the listener to recognize that a mutually known person is being referred to (i.e., they are clear), and because of their brevity, they require little processing effort (i.e., they are economical). Of course, there are situations where names cannot be used to refer to persons, for instance when the speaker is not sure that the name is known to all the participants in the conversation. In this case, the speaker may still use the name with a rising intonation and followed by a pause in which the listeners can indicate whether or not they recognize who is being referred to. If there is recognition, reference is established in the most economical way possible, while if there is not, the speaker may continue with increasingly more elaborate references until recognition is achieved. Levinson illustrates this with the following example from Sacks and Schegloff (1979, p. 19):

A: ... well I was the only one other than that the uhm tch Fords?,
     uh Mrs Holmes Ford? You know uh // the the cellist?
B: Oh yes. She's she's the cellist. [at the double slashes]
A: Yes
B: Ye//s
A: Well she and her husband were there ,,,,

In addition to the above studies, which specifically dealt with principles of communication, there have been a number of studies in the area of referential communication which attest to the operation of the Principles of Clarity and Economy. In these studies, subjects were typically asked to refer to a number of objects or pictures presented in an array of more or less similar objects or pictures. Most importantly, the studies showed that the length of the speakers' references depended on the setting, the linguistic context and the presence of a listener.

Brown (1965, p. 265) noted that when the elements of a set of referents were similar to each other, speakers used longer names to distinguish the elements from each other than when the elements were dissimilar. In other words, when the task required the subjects to produce longer references to make sure that they were clear, the subjects were prepared to invest the extra effort. This finding was replicated by Krauss and Weinheimer (1967) in a study of references to similar and dissimilar colours, and again by Olson (1970), who also observed that when referring to an object in an array of similar objects, say a black square in an array of black and white squares and circles, 'the speaker simply provides the necessary information to differentiate the alternatives he has seen – he does not try to imagine all the possible alternatives from which the intended referent could be differentiated in all contexts' (Olson, 1970, p. 266). Thus, speakers only make their references as informative as necessary (so as to be clear); at the same time they also make them no more informative than necessary (so as not to waste effort).

The linguistic context also affects the length of references. In several studies, subjects were asked to go through a series of trials in which they had to refer to the same set of objects or pictures in such a way that a listener, sitting behind a screen with the same set of pictures in a different order, could identify them. It turned out that these subjects would gradually shorten their references. Krauss and Weinheimer (1964), for instance, showed that speakers tended to start with fairly lengthy references, like *the upside down martini glass in a wire stand*, when first referring to a particular figure, but after one or more trials, speakers and listeners generally agreed upon a name, such as *martini*. This finding was replicated with the same figures for Dutch L2 learners of English at different proficiency levels (Bongaerts et al., 1987) and with different figures for native speakers of English (Clark & Wilkes-Gibbs, 1986). Clark and Wilkes-Gibbs interpreted their data as evidence for a collaborative theory of communication in which speaker and listener cooperate in an attempt to minimize their joint efforts (see also Wilkes-Gibbs, this volume). In trial 1, speaker and listener still needed to describe the figures because a common perspective still remained to be established. On subsequent trials, the speaker could rely on the listener's remembering previous descriptions. Once operating on common ground, speakers could safely assume that a name like the *ice-skater* would be interpreted as an abbreviation of the original *the next one looks like a person who's ice-skating, except they are sticking two arms out in front.* Therefore, by trial 6, speakers were generally able to be much less detailed, and hence to save a great deal of effort, in their references to the figures.

A third factor which proved to influence the length of referential phrases was feedback. Krauss and Weinheimer (1966) conducted an experiment in which half of the subjects received concurrent feedback from the experimenter-listener, who was in a different room, while the other half received no concurrent feedback. Moreover, half of the subjects in the concurrent feedback condition and half of those in the no concurrent feedback condition received confirmation that the listener had correctly responded to their message after all trials (100 per cent confirmation). The other subjects received such confirmation after 50 per cent of the trials only. The study revealed that subjects' references were longer when concurrent feedback was withheld and confirmation was given after only 50 per cent of the trials. Further evidence of the importance of feedback was provided by the study mentioned above, in which speakers had to refer to sets of similar and dissimilar colours (Krauss & Weinheimer, 1967). Some of these speakers were placed in a monologue condition, while others performed the same task in a dialogue condition. It turned out that speakers in the dialogue condition, who were obtaining feedback, produced shorter references than speakers in the monologue condition. This finding is probably due to the fact that when there is no interlocutor present, speakers cannot establish whether their utterances are sufficiently informative. Hence, they will need to provide all information considered necessary for reaching their communicative goals. Conversely, when the listener is present and 'collaborative' in the sense of Clark and Wilkes-Gibbs (1986), the listener may indicate when sufficient information is given and thus may save the speaker the effort of providing more.

The studies discussed in this section illustrate how the Principles of Clarity and Economy work in native-speaker communication. We may conclude that speakers generally try to adhere to them, but that in doing so they are constrained by the physical setting and the linguistic context in which they are operating, and by the presence of a collaborative listener. In the next sections, it will be shown that the Principles of Clarity and Economy work similarly in L2 communication.

The Principles of Clarity and Economy and the use of compensatory strategies

In the preceding section, we have seen that the most efficient way to establish reference to a person is by using this person's name (Levinson, 1987). The same is true for references to objects or other concepts. If there is a commonly accepted word in the language to refer to a particular concept, then this is generally the most preferred means of reference. To call a spade a spade is both clear and economical. The problem for CpS users, of course, is that they cannot use the most preferred means of expression for the simple reason that they (or the person(s) they address) do not know (or may not know) the required word. Thus, the most efficient way of communication, using the concept's conventional name, is not available to them.

If the Principles of Clarity and Economy apply to CpS use, in spite of the fact that the clearest and most economical means of reference are ruled out, we should find that CpS users will nevertheless try to produce references which are clear and effective, that is, which enable them to reach their communicative goals while attempting to keep their own (and their listeners') processing efforts to a minimum. If it is possible for CpS users to reach their goals with little effort, the expectation is that they will do so. If this is not possible, however, they will need to make a choice between being clear and reducing effort. Depending on the (perceived) importance of the communicative goals and the availability of resources, they may decide to lower their aspiration levels and use CpS that may be less clear but also less costly in terms of processing effort. This kind of behaviour is known as 'satisficing' in the problem-solving literature (Simon, 1957). It enables problem-solvers to maintain the balance 'between the time (and effort) required to meet needs and the total time (and effort) available' (Simon, 1957, p. 272).

The CpS collected in the Nijmegen Project show that the speakers were very often trying to adhere to both the Principle of Clarity and the Principle of Economy. This came out most clearly in the interview task, where the subjects would often start the solution to L2 lexical problems by using Dutch words, presumably hoping they would be understood by the interlocutor. If the interlocutor indicated she understood these CpS, reference would have been established in the most economical way possible (see example (1)). If the listener had not understood the CpS, subjects would usually proceed in the way described by Levinson (1987), and would gradually add more information while continually checking understanding until they reached their communicative goals (see example (2)) or were satisfied with the result (see example (3)).[2]

> (1) S: erm you understand **narcissen?**
> I: mm
> S: and uh roses
> I: oh nice yeah (daffodils; 206t4)

> (2) S: …. and erm, I've a great uh box uh with uh beams
> I: beams?
> S: erm 1 those uh 1 little <**touches the beads in her earrings**>
> I: oh the beads yeah (beads; 213t4)

> (3) I: <laughs> yeah, what is she studying in Antwerp?
> S: erm, yeah 1 I don't know how to say it in English, it's uh, **tolk, I don't know**
> I: it's what sorry?
> S: **tolk yeah, a man or woman**
> I: talk
> S: **uh which uh, who, translate, uh, when you're talking English and there's a Russian man**
> I: oh yeah
> S: **she understands you and, then she translate it in Russian for the man**
> I: hoh, translator, translator I should say
> S: yeah, yeah (interpreter; 204t4)

The interview task also enabled the subjects to reach their goals with a minimum of effort because they could rely on the interlocutor for help. Although offering help did of course increase the effort expended by the interlocutor, it seems that in some cases the joint effort could be minimized in this way. Example (4) also illustrates the role of the interlocutor in a joint attempt to solve the problem. After the interlocutor's initial guess of 'cauliflower' was rejected by the subject, who obviously did not know this word, the interlocutor proceeded to name some of its characteristic features like 'hard' and 'big'. Finally, this resulted in the subject's acceptance of the interlocutor's first suggestion.

(4) S: erm 1 'n bloemkool uh, **white it'll uh, uh it looks like a flower, white, it's ook uh, very erm, hard, uh very** 2 erm
 I: maybe cauliflower is it?
 S: a cauliflower erm, yeah I don't think it's white
 I: yeah, **and hard**
 S: yeah and
 I: yeah, **big**
 S: **it looks like, little flowers**
 I: yeah
 S: yeah?
 I: cauliflower yeah
 S: cauliflower mm, yeah, I also put it in yeah (cauliflower; 209t4)

Finally, the fact that the interview took place in a relevant setting and provided a linguistic context occasionally allowed subjects to be both clear and economical in their use of CpS. The setting, for instance, allowed them to refer to objects by pointing at them or touching them. The linguistic context sometimes allowed them to make do with a vague word like *thing* because the message would be clear from the context anyway. Consider example (5), in which the interviewer and the subject were discussing the work involved in freezing vegetables.

(5) I: oh, do you help freezing?
 S: well, freezing now, we have to erm 2 put the uh, peas out of the uh
 I: oh yeah
 S: **thing** <laughs> (pod; 108t4)

The same is true for the story retell task, in which the problems to be solved were presented within the context of the story. Again, this enabled the subjects to reach some of their goals with a minimum of effort. In one of the stories, for instance, the subjects' references to 'a wig', worn by a salesman, tended to be quite short. They usually consisted of two words only, for example, *fake hair, false hair, artificial hair, unreal hair,* or even just *hair* or *some other hair.* Even the last example proved to be perfectly acceptable in the context, because the subjects had just made clear that the salesman was bald.

The possibility of obtaining feedback in the interview task, and hence of checking the comprehensibility of their CpS and the presence of a linguistic context for the lexical problems encountered in both this and the story retell tasks constitutes a plausible explanation for the relatively large use of transfer strategies, holistic strategies, and short analytic strategies in these tasks. Although some of these strategies were intrinsically not very clear, they were clear enough when used in context, so that they allowed the subjects to reach their goals with a minimum of effort.

There were also cases where it was not possible for the subjects to reach their goals at little cost. For instance, in the object reference task, where there was no opportunity to get feedback and no linguistic context to aid the interpretation of the subjects' references, the only way for the subjects to reach their goals was to expend a lot of effort on elaborate descriptions of the objects presented. In virtually all cases they used fairly lengthy analytic conceptual strategies in which they mentioned two or three, and sometimes even as many as seven, of the characteristics of the intended object. The reason why the subjects were prepared to spend so much effort on their references in this task is certainly related to the task demands. The instructions required the subjects to refer to the targets in such a way that a native speaker of English would later be able to identify the objects while listening to the recorded transcripts. Since there were no time limitations which might have excused them from producing lengthy strategies, the subjects had no other option than to try their best. Even so, in this task too there were limits to the amount of effort expended. Subjects did not, for instance, mention 'irrelevant' properties such as the size of the *baby's bib*, the headlines of the *newspaper*, or the colour of the *clapper* on the bell (Eric Kellerman, personal communication). Clearly then, while prepared to expend effort in order to achieve the goals imposed on them, the subjects were still trying to maintain some sort of balance (see also Rodino and Snow's discussion of 'distanced communication' in this volume).

In general, if a choice had to be made between being clear and saving effort, the subjects appeared to be led by the importance of the goal. When they did not consider the intended referent to be very relevant, they were inclined to put less effort into their CpS.

In the story retell task, for instance, there was a story in which a bicycle-manufacturer tried to bribe a judge by giving him an electric drill. Now it did not really matter whether the present to the judge was an electric drill, an ordinary drill, or just any tool, and it turned out that only one of the subjects made an attempt to specify that the drill was of a special kind. Conversely, in another story, which featured a rabbit expressing the wish to buy a pleated skirt, 23 of the 45 subjects used CpS to convey the fact that the skirt was pleated. A further six of the subjects attempted to express the concept 'pleats' but gave up, while four more indicated that the skirt was of a special kind. The amount of detail provided in the story of the rabbit was almost certainly due to the punch line of this story hinging on the very fact of the skirt being pleated. Clearly then, the pleats were a relevant detail which could not simply be left out and for this reason the subjects were prepared to put a great deal of effort into the communication of this point.

In the interview task, too, the subjects would not go into details which they considered irrelevant. This is illustrated by examples (6) and (7), where holistic strategies were used which did not really convey the subjects' intended meanings:

(6) S: and so the 1 uh a man 1 I knows, a man uh who 1 s it's uh, **an uncle** of me ... (acquaintance; 310t4)

(7) S: we had to wait for the bus for uh th, uh **half an hour** (three quarters of an hour; 203t4)

In both cases, subjects' retrospective comments revealed what they had really wanted to say and hence that CpS had been used. The subjects who used these CpS obviously preferred maintaining the fluency of the conversations to communicating the two intended concepts accurately.

It was observed that in the interview task, the subjects would often use transfer strategies without any morphophonological adaptation to English to refer to concepts which they perceived to be typically Dutch, such as *Sinterklaas* ('Santa Claus'), *HTS* (a Dutch type of higher education) and *boerekool* (a Dutch dish). This *use of* unadapted transfer for language- or culture-specific concepts has also been noted by Færch and Kasper (1986) for Danish speakers. Some students participating in the Nijmegen project indicated that it was too complicated to communicate these concepts in English so that they had not even tried. In their opinion, the effect was not worth the effort. Again, this demonstrates that they tried to maintain a balance between the goal to be achieved and the effort to be expended.

The Principles of Clarity and Economy and other aspects of L2 communication

To demonstrate the importance of the Principles of Clarity and Economy, and their pervasiveness in language use, I would now like to discuss some of the findings of two studies dealing with other aspects of L2 use. The first of these studies concerns the occurrence of self-corrections, while the second examines the occurrence of code-switches in L2 learner data.

Self-corrections

Research on L1 and L2 speakers' self-corrections of slips of the tongue has also shown that in correcting errors, speakers seem to adhere to the Principles of Clarity and Economy. The more serious they consider their errors to be (from a social, communicative or linguistic point of view), the more willingly they appear to put in the extra effort required to repair them. Again, speakers adapt the effort they expend to the importance of their goals.

The role of social acceptability in a speaker's decision to correct an error was established by Motley, Camden and Baars (1982) in an experiment in which they induced socially less acceptable speech errors like *tits fall* for *fits tall* and *ball cunt* for *call bunt* as well as neutral speech errors like *wits fall* for *fits wall* and *ball hunt* for *hail bunt*. Subjects took great care in correcting errors which would result in taboo phrases. They produced only 12 such errors as opposed to 56 neutral ones. Measurements of the subjects' galvanic skin responses often showed that the subjects had started the taboo phrases, but were able to intercept them pre-articulatorily. Usually, this resulted in partial errors like *cool kits* for *tool kits*, in which the taboo word /*tits*/ was intercepted just in time. The fact that 'taboo errors' were corrected in time to avoid the taboo phrases more often than 'neutral errors' were corrected suggests that speakers were more intent on the correction of errors which they considered socially unacceptable.

In their decisions to correct errors, speakers also appear to take into account how disruptive an error is for communication.

Fathman (1980) noted that most of the self-corrections produced by children concerned semantic rather than structural errors. Cutler (1983) observed that lexical stress errors are frequently corrected when the stress shift results in a change of vowel quality (62 per cent), for example when a full vowel is replaced by a reduced vowel or vice versa, but much less frequently (23 per cent) when no such change is involved. In addition, Cutler reports that people sometimes use prosodic means to mark the correction of lexical errors, which may impair communicative success, but never mark phonetic errors. And finally, Levelt (1983) found that corrections of real errors (where a wrong word or sound is selected) tend to be produced immediately after error detection, whereas corrections of words that are merely inappropriate (i.e., technically correct words, but ambiguous or lacking in precision or coherence) are often postponed. As a result, really erroneous words are often interrupted, while inappropriate words are generally completed. Again, one of the reasons for this could be that erroneous words are more likely to hamper communication than inappropriate words, so that speakers find it more important to correct errors and to do so immediately.

Another possible reason for the difference in error-repairs and appropriateness-repairs is that errors generally result in linguistically unacceptable utterances, while inappropriate words do not. Because of this, speakers who are about to produce an error may feel more obliged to cut off the original utterance than speakers who realize that they have selected a word which is not really optimal. The last group of speakers may decide to finish the inappropriate word so as to gain time for the selection of a better word without appearing dysfluent. How much effort they will invest in finding a more felicitous word will not only depend on their goals but also on personality traits. The greater their ambition and desire to be precise, the more likely they will be to correct inappropriate words.

In the case of second language learners, the influence of linguistic acceptability on self-corrections seems to be particularly strong. A comparison of the self-corrections in the L1 and L2 descriptions of the abstract novel shapes which had been collected as part of the Nijmegen Project on CpS showed that the speakers repaired a larger percentage of the speech errors they had produced in English than of the speech errors they had produced in Dutch (L2 English: 59 per cent vs L1 Dutch: 37.4 per cent; see

Poulisse, in press). Presumably, the increased attention to error correction in the L2, which concerned lexical as well as phonological errors, is due to the fact that the learners, being placed in a test-like situation, felt it was important not to make too many mistakes. It is also worth noting, however, that the two least proficient groups of L2 learners, who obviously had least attention to spare for error correction, repaired a smaller percentage of their L2 speech errors than the most proficient group of learners (grade 9 students: 53.4 per cent, grade 11 students: 54.3 per cent; 2nd-year university students: 71 per cent).

Clearly, then, self-corrections also exhibit the joint operation of the Principles of Clarity and Economy. Speakers devote much attention to the correction of those errors which they think are important to repair and less to the correction of other errors or phrases which are merely inappropriate. They do not expend a disproportionate amount of effort on error correction, however. Particularly beginning L2 learners, whose ordinary speech production already takes up a great deal of their attentional resources, are somewhat restrained in their correction of errors.

Code-switching

Another aspect of language use which seems to be affected by the speakers' adherence to the Principles of Clarity and Economy concerns code-switches. In a study of L1 use in L2 production, for which the same corpus of Dutch L2 learner English was used as in the Nijmegen Project. Poulisse and Bongaerts (1994) observed that L2 learners often switched to the L1 unintentionally. Thus, subjects would frequently use Dutch words while speaking English. Interestingly, most of the words involved in these switches were either function words (N = 316), like *ook* ('too'), *dit* ('this') and *dan* ('then'), or editing terms (N = 302), like *of* ('or') and *nee* ('no'). Content words, like *vol* ('full'), were also involved, but much less frequently (N = 131). The occurrence of these language switches was proficiency related, the grade 9 students switching 463 times in this way (in a dataset of 2,795 words), the grade 11 students switching 235 times (in a dataset of 3,199 words) and the 2nd-year university students switching 51 times (in a dataset of 3,361 words).

Poulisse and Bongaerts (1994) have equated the occurrence of these unintentional switches with speech errors (or slips of the tongue) similar to lexical substitution errors involving semantically related words, like 'low' for 'high' and 'fingers' for 'toes', observed in native language speech (Fromkin, 1973). They argue that these switches tend to occur particularly often when the intended L1 words or expressions are much more frequent, and hence easier to access, than the corresponding L2 words or expressions. Since function words and editing terms tend to have a high frequency, this would explain why these words are so often involved in these switches. To explain why less proficient L2 learners make more of these switches than more advanced L2 learners, Poulisse and Bongaerts point to the fact that the difference in frequency between L1 and L2 words is largest for beginning learners. For low proficiency learners, L1 words are more easily available than L2 words; consequently, L1 words are more likely to be selected by accident.

A second explanation for the fact that function words and editing terms are so frequently involved in unintentional language switches is that these words tend to be less important from a communicative point of view than content words. For this reason, L2 learners, and particularly the less proficient ones, who have little attention to spare, probably pay less attention to their selection. This interpretation is supported by the fact that relatively few of the accidentally selected L1 function words were corrected by the learners, viz. 30.7 per cent, as opposed to 53.4 per cent of the L1 content words.[3] Again then, these data illustrate the operation of the Principles of Clarity and Economy in L2 communication. L2 learners pay more attention to the selection of content words, and hence make fewer mistakes in the selection of these words, because they carry more meaning and are therefore considered to be more worthy of investing effort into than function words.

Conclusion

In this chapter I have discussed certain task-related differences in the use of CpS by Dutch learners of English. These differences not only concerned the types of CpS which the learners chose to solve their communication problems, but also the ways in which instances of each type had been realized. The observed differences could be explained in terms of the combined operation of the Principles of Clarity and Economy. Learners generally tried to produce CpS which were clear and effective while keeping their own (and their listeners') processing efforts to a minimum. This approach proved very successful, particularly in the interview task, where subjects were able to obtain feedback and help from the interlocutor, and where the physical setting and the linguistic context contributed to the clarity of strategies. If clarity at the cost of little effort could not be achieved, as for instance in the object reference task and sometimes in the story retell and interview tasks, task demands and the assumed importance of reaching the communicative goal determined the amount of effort learners were prepared to expend on their CpS.

To illustrate further the importance of the Principles of Clarity and Economy for studies of L2 communication, I finished this chapter with a brief discussion of L2 learners' self-corrections and code-switches. It appeared that in these areas, too, speakers' behaviour is governed by their wish to maintain a balance between being clear and being economical.

Notes

The author would like to thank Theo Bongaerts and the late Paul Werth for their thoughtful comments on earlier versions of this chapter.
1. See Poulisse (1993), where these strategies have been renamed: analytic strategies have become 'reconceptualization strategies', and both holistic and transfer strategies are now called 'substitution strategies'. See also Kellerman and Bialystok (this volume) for a reaction to this reclassification.
2. All examples are taken from the Nijmegen Project. Numerals in the text indicate the length of pauses in seconds. Pauses shorter than one second are marked by a comma (','). Rising intonation is marked by a question mark. In the examples 'I' stands for interviewer, a native speaker of English, and 'S' stands for subject. CpS are in bold type when this is necessary to distinguish them from the context. Relevant information on the subject's and the interviewer's behaviour is given between angular brackets (e.g., <laughs>). The examples are followed by the target word and a code indicating which subject produced it in which task. Thus, '208t1' indicates that this extract was produced by subject 208 in task 1. The first digit indicates the subject's proficiency level, 101 being a subject of the highest and 301 a subject of the lowest

3. Yet a third explanation discussed by Poulisse and Bongaerts (1994) is that function words tend to be shorter than content words. As a result, there is less time for speakers to discover mis-selections and correct them. This explanation is also compatible with the error correction data. Poulisse and Bongaerts (1994) note that the three explanations need not exclude each other and suggest that all three factors (frequency, semantic importance, and word length) contributed to their results.

4

Preference and order in first and second language referential strategies

GEORGE RUSSELL

Introduction

In Kellerman, Ammerlaan, Bongaerts and Poulisse (1990), an attempt was made to compare L1 and L2 strategic language use and to consider strategies in terms of mental processes rather than linguistic products. In a shape-description task, Kellerman et al. (1990) observed the use of referential strategies by Dutch speakers of English as a second language, both in L1 and L2. They classified these strategies as holistic, partitive, or linear, and proposed a hierarchy of preference, based on subjects' usage, of holistic over partitive over linear. The hierarchy was, they claimed, operational both for pairs of L1 and L2 descriptions (cross-language) and for single descriptions (within-language).

In consideration of the relationship between strategy use in L1 and L2, the present study replicates Kellerman et al. (1990), but with Japanese non-native speakers of English as subjects, to examine whether the hierarchy operates among these speakers as well. Of particular interest to the present study is a possible influence

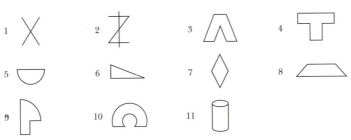

Figure 4.1 The 11 pictures from Kellerman et al. (1990)

65

of cultural differences. While it has been suggested that a specific first language should not affect strategies at the level of processing (see Bialystok & Kellerman, 1987), one may consider whether the linguistic similarities between English and Dutch, as well as the cultural similarities between English and Dutch people, may have influenced the results of Kellerman et al. (1990).

Referential strategies in L1 and L2

A hierarchy of preference

Kellerman et al. (1990) had 17 Dutch students of English describe 11 shapes (shown in Figure 4.1) in Dutch and English, so that a native speaker could draw the shapes after listening to a recording of the descriptions. Subjects received no feedback when describing the pictures, Dutch descriptions preceded the English descriptions by about a week; the Dutch ones were done first so that subjects would have to solve only the problem of how to describe the shapes, and not be burdened with the additional problem of making use of a non-native language. Subjects were unaware of the second part of the task until the time they had to perform it, presumably to control for planning variables.

Kellerman et al. classified the referential strategies used by their subjects into three types. The first type was holistic, where a speaker made an attempt to describe an entire shape (Picture 7, for example, might be described as 'a diamond'). The second was partitive, where the speaker described the shape part by part (Picture 7 might be described as 'two triangles put together'). The third was linear, where a shape was described line by line (Kellerman et al., 1990, pp. 168–9).

Kellerman et al. argued that there was a preference governing strategy selection, a preference for holistic over partitive, and of partitive over linear. Speakers first attempt to use a holistic strategy (H) when making a referencing decision (in this particular case, when describing a picture), because such a strategy requires the least amount of effort, a general problem-solving principle. When speakers are unable to use a holistic strategy – that is, when they lack the language to make a holistic description possible – they will attempt a partitive strategy (P). Similarly, when they are unable to use a partitive strategy, they will attempt a linear strategy (L).

According to the same principle, Kellerman et al. claimed, there is a preference in combinations of strategies within a single picture description. A description may start at a holistic level, proceed to a partitive level, and then proceed to a linear level, or proceed from a holistic level directly to a linear level. However, a description is not likely to violate the hierarchy; that is, it is not likely to start at the linear level and proceed to the partitive level, or proceed from the partitive to the holistic level. Thus, the following level changes in strategy combinations are the ones to be expected:

1. H
2. H, P
3. H, L
4. H, P, L
5. P
6. P, L
7. L

(Kellerman et al., 1990, p. 171)

Kellerman et al. claimed that the hierarchy also operated across languages. The study yielded 183 L1–L2 pairs of description; in 164 of the pairs, the referential strategies used were essentially the same in L1 and L2, and in 18 of the 19 remaining pairs, all of the L1 descriptions were holistic, while all of the L2 descriptions were partitive or linear. Thus, Kellerman et al. argued, an L2 description tends not to contain a strategy that is at a level in the hierarchy higher than that of the one contained in the corresponding L1 description. For example, if an L1 description is holistic, a corresponding L2 description may be holistic, partitive, or linear, but if an L1 description is partitive or linear, the corresponding L2 description will probably not be holistic. The contention seems reasonable, as it is unlikely that speakers would have a word or term in their second language to refer to a shape or concept but not have an equivalent word or term in their first language. Kellerman et al. offer the following model to predict cross-language strategy use:

	L1		L2
If strategy	H	then	H > P > L
	P		P > L
	L		L

(Kellerman et al., 1990, p. 172)

By postulating a hierarchy that controls both L1 and L2 referential strategies, Kellerman et al. contend that strategic behaviour in L1 and L2 is the same; that is, it involves the same general problem-solving behaviour. This argument appears in other studies originating from Nijmegen University; particularly relevant to a consideration of Kellerman et al. is Bongaerts and Poulisse (1989) (but see Bongaerts et al., 1987).

In a task similar to that of Kellerman et al. (1990), Bongaerts and Poulisse (1989) had subjects describe 12 pictures in their L1 (Dutch) and L2 (English). In classifying the picture descriptions, Bongaerts and Poulisse adopted two basic perspectives from Clark and Wilkes-Gibbs' (1986) study of L1 referential communication: holistic and segmental (cf. Wilkes-Gibbs, this volume). Bongaerts and Poulisse note that the two categories established in Kellerman et al. (1990), partitive and linear, can be considered subsets of segmental. They found that in both languages, subjects predominantly opted for holistic perspectives, on an average of 69.57 per cent in Dutch and 69.27 per cent in English. Looking at the English descriptions which corresponded to Dutch holistic descriptions, a total of 323 cases, Bongaerts and Poulisse found that in 193 cases the subjects had no lexical problems in using the same holistic image in English, in 64 cases subjects tried to use the same image even though there were lexical problems, in 30 cases the subjects used a different holistic image in English, and in only 36 cases did the subjects not use a holistic perspective in English. Bongaerts and Poulisse claimed that the preference for a holistic perspective was so great that subjects tended to look for ways to keep the perspective in L2 before considering a non-holistic alternative. Further, they argued, the strength of the preference in both L1 and L2 showed that when native and non-native speakers are faced with the same kind of problem in a task such as describing abstract shapes, the problem will be approached in the same manner whether the speakers are using their first or second language.

Culturally appropriate referents

While Bongaerts and Poulisse (1989) note lexical problems involved in the maintence of a holistic perspective, they do not specifically address the issue of cultural appropriateness. If, in a description task such as that in Bongaerts and Poulisse or Kellerman et al. (1990), subjects use a holistic image in L1 that is known within the culture of the L1 but is unlikely to be known within the L2 culture, will the subjects approach the problem of making a reference in L2 as a lexical problem and look for an alternative holistic image? Conversely, will they abandon the holistic perspective, or abandon the description altogether? Although this issue was not discussed specifically in Kellerman et al., they do report instances of subjects using the Dutch word 'wybertje', a Dutch diamond-shaped licorice candy, to describe Picture 7 (indeed, as will be noted later, 'wybertje' appears in an English description). This word, and perhaps the subject who used it in English would agree, would not be useful in helping an English speaker not familiar with Dutch culture to draw the picture. How then may a concern for cultural appropriateness specifically affect strategy use?

There are few L2 communication strategy studies that specifically look at differences of strategy use among subjects of different linguistic and cultural backgrounds. One of the few is Yule and Tarone (1990), which employed South American and Asian speakers of English as a second language, as well as native English speakers. Yule and Tarone sought to establish that there were three considerations for a speaker when making a referencing choice: the speaker's language ability, the speaker's general knowledge, and the speaker's assessment of the listener's general knowledge. It is in the assessment of another's knowledge that cultural variables become important; when one is speaking to someone of a different culture, one must consider whether differences in culture mean gaps in knowledge. Yule and Tarone offer a particular instance of a cultural assessment from their data: a native Spanish speaker describing, in English, an object to a native Korean speaker, uses the image of the key which opens a can of sardines but then abandons it, assuming that the Korean, a member of a different culture, might not be aware of this particular image. The contention of assessment of knowledge is plausible; however, Yule and Tarone also report some puzzling results which belie the contention. In a task requiring subjects to explain how to use a coffeemaker, almost all of the second language speakers used the word 'coffee', while only one of the native English speakers did. The others, even though talking to other native English speakers, used words like 'powdery substance' (Yule and Tarone, 1990, p. 188). Surely the speakers believed that their partners knew the word 'coffee'. Why, then, didn't they use it? Yule and Tarone only report this non-usage; they do not comment upon it. This lack of commentary limits the usefulness of Yule and Tarone for the study of communication strategies and cross-cultural variables.

A study of particular interest to the present study is Dickson, Miyake and Muto (1977), which was specifically concerned with referencing by Japanese subjects. The study required Japanese college students to write descriptions of abstract shapes. A group of other Japanese and a group of American college students were asked to identify the shapes after reading, respectively, the original descriptions or English translations of them. The students who wrote the descriptions were instructed either to describe what the shape looked like – which Dickson et al. term a 'metaphoric' description – or to describe the shape according to its geometrical components – which is termed an 'analytic' description.

Dickson et al. considered metaphoric descriptions as likely to be holistic, and thus their categories are comparable to those of Kellerman et al. (1990) and Bongaerts and Poulisse (1989), with analytic descriptions corresponding to segmental (partitive or linear) descriptions. Dickson et al. hypothesized that metaphoric descriptions were more easily influenced by a given culture than analytic descriptions were, because metaphoric descriptions were more likely to concern specific culturally defined experience. Among the data collected for their study, Dickson et al. found metaphoric descriptions, such as 'abacus' and 'wine [i.e., sake] cup', which they considered to be culturally biased.

Dickson et al. manipulated their subjects' production of analytic and metaphoric description. If their subjects had been allowed to select metaphoric or analytic descriptions according to their own preferences, there may have been a relationship between the type of description selected and the perceived potential readers (Japanese, American, or both) of the descriptions. Considering Dickson et al.'s contentions, the subjects may have produced more metaphoric descriptions if they had been told to describe for Japanese readers, and more analytic descriptions if they had been told to describe for Americans. Such language usage would be perfectly in line with Kellerman et al.'s hierarchy. On the other hand, considering Bongaert and Poulisse's assessment of the strength of the preference for holistic perspectives, the subjects may have produced different, less culturally biased metaphoric descriptions for American readers, which would not contradict Kellerman et al.'s hierarchy.

In any case, the findings of Dickson et al. seem to support the idea that the hierarchy of preference will be as operational within the referential strategy usage of Japanese speakers of English as a second language as it was with that of the original Dutch speakers in Kellerman et al. Accordingly, the present study offers the following hypotheses:

1. As with the Dutch native speakers, the Japanese native speakers will not, for a given picture, use a strategy in L2 at a higher level than the strategy used in L1 for the same picture.
2. As with the Dutch native speakers, the Japanese native speakers will proceed, within a single picture description in either L1 or L2, according to the hierarchy of referential strategies.

The investigation

Subjects

The subjects who participated in the present study were 21 native speakers of Japanese. Fifteen were female and six were male. Subjects ranged in age from 19 to 31, with a mean age of about 24. The length of time spent in the USA varied from one month to four years, with a median length of almost one year.

All subjects were students at the Hawaii English Language Program (HELP), an ESL programme attached to the University of Hawaii. Subjects' enrolment in HELP ranged from one month to a year and three months, with a median length of enrolment of six months. In addition to HELP, all subjects had had at least three years of English education at the high-school level. Eleven also reported at least one year of college-level English education, with one attending college in the USA and four reported having English education in Japan outside the established educational system.

To examine a possible effect of proficiency, the present study took note of HELP rankings of subjects' English abilities. All HELP students are pretested before entering the programme, and are ranked from term to term in several skill areas. Areas deemed relevant to this study were Communication Skills, which involves listening and speaking skills, and Structure, which is concerned with facility with English grammar. In Communication Skills, seven subjects were ranked as intermediate and 14 as advanced.

Intermediate Communication Skills students are considered to have enough English-speaking ability to meet the demands of everyday needs, and, in addition, to carry on conversations on familiar topics. Advanced students are considered to have the English-speaking ability required to express complex time relations in narrations, participate in conversations on unfamiliar topics, and manage potentially difficult social situations. As for Structure, nine subjects were ranked as intermediate and 12 as advanced. An intermediate Structure student is expected to have a working knowledge of English verb tenses. Intermediate students study conditionals, modals and perfect tenses, and advanced students study subordinate clauses.

Procedure

Subjects were asked to describe, in both Japanese and English, the 11 shapes used in Kellerman et al. (1990). In the original study, as was noted, subjects described the pictures in Dutch first and in English second. To account for a possible effect of description order, the present study employed counterbalancing. Eleven subjects first described the pictures in Japanese, and ten first described them in English. The pictures themselves were counterbalanced, except for Picture 1, which was always presented first as a practice picture. In the first session, a subject described the pictures from number 2 to number 11, and, in the second, from 11 to 2. The two picture description sessions were scheduled one week apart. At the conclusion of the first session, subjects were told that there would be a second, but were not informed of the nature of the task they would perform then.

Sessions for all subjects were conducted by a native speaker of Japanese, usually assisted by the experimenter. In both sessions, the subjects received instructions in Japanese. Subjects were told to describe the pictures in Japanese so that a 'nihonjin' (a Japanese) could draw them after listening to a recording of the descriptions, and to describe them in English so that an 'amerika-jin' (an American) could draw them after listening to a recording. As in the original study, no feedback was given during the descriptions.

Retrospective data were collected, according to principles stated in Færch and Kasper (1987b) and Poulisse, Bongaerts and Kellerman (1984, 1987). Retrospection sessions (not announced in advance) were conducted in Japanese. Subjects listened to a recording of their descriptions immediately after the task, and were asked to comment freely about their language use; they could request that the tape player be stopped when they wanted to say something. Some subjects were eager to comment in detail about both L1 and L2 performances, while others would wait to be questioned. When the experimenter wanted to question subjects, he would stop the tape and ask the native-speaker assistant to speak to them in Japanese. Most questions concerned why a subject had chosen a particular word or phrase or why a description had been abandoned; generally, subjects frankly assessed their confidence or lack of confidence in their language choices or elucidated the problems which led to abandonment. Yes/no questions were not asked, nor was there any mention of the terminology of key interest to this study: referential strategy, holistic, partitive, linear. Subjects were not told that they would be asked to comment upon their performances until they had completed the 11 descriptions. However, since the task was performed on two occasions, it can be surmised that subjects expected that they would comment on the second occasion as well. Retrospections were recorded and used in determining instances of strategy use.

After the sessions, the experimenter transcribed both English and Japanese descriptions, and both sets of transcriptions were checked by Japanese native speakers. Determinations of strategy use were made using these transcriptions. Strategies were classified as holistic, partitive, or linear, following Kellerman et al. (1990). The experimenter's strategy designations were checked against those of a Japanese native-speaker colleague. At first, only original strategy levels and changes in level had been noted. However, in the course of checking, it was determined that every instance of strategy use had to be recognized. For example, if a subject used two holistic descriptions, such as 'uh:: (.) kore wa batsu desu ne. ((laugh)) [H] ekkusu no katachi desu. [H]' ('Uh, this is a cross. It's the shape of an x.') (38–J1) (see Appendix 4A for transcription conventions), two tokens of strategy use had to be noted (see Appendix 4B for more information on counting strategy tokens). After the transcripts were reanalysed for strategy tokens, the experimenter and the Japanese native speaker independently re-evaluated the transcriptions. Inter-rater reliability

Results

Tokens of strategies used by subjects for all descriptions are shown in Appendix 4C, see page 92. Since 21 subjects each had to describe 11 pictures, there were potentially 231 pairs of Japanese/English descriptions. However, there were 17 instances in English and one instance in Japanese in which a description was abandoned. Concerning abandonments in English, ten occurred when the Japanese descriptions were done first, and only seven occurred when the English ones were first. This outcome should be considered in terms of Kellerman et al.'s (1990) contention that doing a description in L2 first added an extra cognitive burden to subjects. While a number of subjects in the present study found it stressful to do the English descriptions first, this particular order did not seem to affect the number of abandonments.

In any case, of the remaining 213 pairs of descriptions, 200, or 98.6 per cent, show strategy use in which all tokens are at the same level in English and Japanese, or in which the token at the highest level in English corresponds to that at the highest level in Japanese. This is an even greater percentage than was shown in Kellerman et al., which was 164 out of 183, or 89.1 per cent.

Of the 13 pairs in the present study that show a difference in level between L1 and L2 strategies, ten conform to the holistic–partitive–linear hierarchy proposed by Kellerman et al. and three violate the hierarchy. While these results are not as striking as the 18 conforming pairs and one violating pair found in Kellerman et al., the sample is too small for statistical analysis.

Kellerman et al. did not report the percentages of the different types of strategies used by their subjects. Whatever the percentages may have been, holistic strategies were used overwhelmingly in the present study. In 179 pairs, 84 per cent of all complete pairs, both the English and Japanese descriptions contain at least one token of holistic strategy use, an even greater percentage of holistic strategies than found in Bongaerts and Poulisse (1989).

Violations of the proposed holistic–partitive–linear order within a single description, also not reported by Kellerman et al., were more frequent in the present study than those across languages. Of 444 completed descriptions, 52 (11.9 per cent) violate the pro-

Table 4.1 Violations of the proposed strategy order within single picture descriptions

Tokens	Total	As proposed	Violations	% of violations
1	166	166	0	0
2	144	139	5	3.4
3	81	60	21	25.9
4	31	17	14	45.1
6	13	6	7	53.8
7+	4	1	3	75

posed order. Of these violations, 31 are in Japanese and 21 are in English, a difference which is not statistically significant according to chi-square analysis. Further, there is neither a significant chi-square value when one compares the number of violations in the first description session with the number in the second, nor when one compares the number of violations occurring when the English descriptions were done first with the number when the Japanese ones were first.

Examination of tokens shows that there may be a process involved in the violation of the proposed order. In Table 4.1, descriptions are ranked by number of strategy tokens within each description, from one token to seven or more. The table shows, for each rank, the total number of descriptions, the number of descriptions that follow the proposed order, and the number of descriptions that violate it. As descriptions display a greater number of tokens, the percentage of violations increases. It is impossible, of course, to violate the order if there is only one token. When there are two tokens, violations are rare, comprising only 3.4 per cent of all two-token descriptions. It seems, however, that as subjects elaborated upon descriptions – that is, as they supplied more information – the more likely they were to violate the order.

Chi-square analysis showed no relationship between English proficiency, as determined by either Communication Skills or Structure level, and violations of the order in English descriptions. However, it must be conceded that the HELP placement levels are not the firmest measures of proficiency. If other measures had been used, some effect for proficiency might have been suggested.

While the present study showed no effect of proficiency, there seemed to be a relationship between violations in Japanese and

Table 4.2   Violations of the proposed strategy order in English compared with violations in Japanese

English behaviour	Subjects with two or more violations in Japanese $N=9$	Subjects with one or no violations in Japanese $N=12$
Predicted order	77	116
Violations of order	15	6
Abandoned descriptions	7	10

$\chi^2(2, N = 21) = 7.71, p < .05$

Table 4.3   Abandonments in English compared with violations of the proposed strategy order in Japanese

English behaviour	Subjects with two or more violations in Japanese $N=9$	Subjects with one or no violations in Japanese $N=12$
Completed descriptions	92	122
Abandoned descriptions	7	10

$\chi^2(1, N = 21) = 0.16$, ns

violations in English. Twenty violations, 38.5 per cent of the total, were found in ten English–Japanese description pairs, and it appeared that those subjects who had a number of violations in their Japanese descriptions also tended to have violations in their English ones. To test for a possible relationship, Japanese subjects were divided into two groups: those subjects who violated the order two or more times in Japanese and those who violated the order once or not at all in Japanese. Chi-square analysis revealed that the former group had significantly more instances of violations in English (see Table 4.2). There may be a question as to whether the significant difference was due to the number of violations or the number of abandonments. However, when abandonments were compared with all completed descriptions, no significant difference was found between the two groups of subjects (see Table 4.3). Therefore it seems that those subjects who violated the order in L1 were more likely to do so in L2, and that strategy choice is somewhat subject to individual variation.

Discussion

Hypothesis #1

With only three cases of cross-language strategy order violations in the present study, Kellerman et al.'s (1990) idea of a cross-language strategy hierarchy seems to be supported. Nevertheless, it may be worthwhile to look at the three cases of hierarchy breakdown and attempt to account for subjects' behaviour. In one case, linguistic categories may have contributed to a strategy classification problem. Describing Picture 1, Subject 36 said, in Japanese, '((breath)) nihon no boo ga, kurosu shite imasu [L]' ('Two lines are crossing') (36–J1), and, in English, 'a character of:: x. [H]' (36–E1). The loan word 'kurosu', normally a noun, becomes a verb when attached to 'shite imasu'; this use of 'kurosu' as a verb leads to a linear classification. If the word had been used as a noun, the strategy classification would have been one linear token and one holistic token. It may be argued that this classification decision is product-oriented. However, since Subject 36 did not report any problems with either description, the classification choices must stand in order to conform to the categories of Kellerman et al. A description such as 36–J1 thus suggests that linguistic structure has some relationship to strategy classification.

In another case, Subject 38, for Picture 10, used a partitive approach in Japanese by mentioning two circles and started on the holistic level in English by mentioning one:

'(5) kore wa, ee:: (1) um:: (1) en wo, futatsu egaite, [P] ee nishurui no chiisai en to ookii en (.) o egaite, [P] (.) ee shita sanbun no ichi shihoo o katto shite ((laugh)) imasu. [P] node shita ga taira ni nattemasu. [P] ((sniff))' ('This, uh, um, draw two circles, uh, draw two types, a large circle and a small circle, and all around the bottom third [they are] cut. And so the bottom has become flat.') (38–J10); 'This is, uh, like a circle::, [H] but um (.) uh:: (.) third one cut off in a uh:: very end. [P]' (38–E10).

It is difficult to draw any conclusions from this pair of descriptions. Subject 38, one of the more proficient in English, stated in retrospect that the problem she had with Picture 10 was that she did not know how to describe the thickness of the circle in English. However, there was no mention of thickness in her Japanese description; rather, she described the picture as composed of two circles. Hence, her L1 strategies were classified as partitive, and, therefore, at a lower level than the holistic strategy she used in L2.

Perhaps the most interesting of the three cross-language violations is that committed by Subject 33. In her Japanese description, which was done first, she offered a pure linear approach, one of only seven in the data:

'(4) mazu heikoo ni, nagai sen to mijikai sen o, hikimasu- [L] shita::
a (1) nihon (1) hiite [L] a- hidari a-migigawa no hoo ga mijikaku.
(1) shite [L] sono mijikai hoo no sen ni, (1) onaji gura-i (1) nagasa onaji gura-i hida:: (.) chigau migi:: ni sen wo hiite kudasai. [L] soshite s::ono, owari no ten to, nagai hoo ga ue no hoo no ten wo, (1) en no yoo ni musun::de kuda(sai). [L]' ('First, in parallel, draw a long line and a short line. The bottom .... uh, draw two lines, uh, the left, uh the right side is short, and at that short line, about the same, with a length about the same, lef–, no at the right, please draw a line. And please connect with a circle that end point and the long top part's point.') (33–J9).

In English, she opted for a holistic/partitive strategy combination:

'(4) you write circle [H] and then (1) cut(t::) fou::r ah quarter? [P]
(2) a::nd (.) cut (3) uh:: (1) something. [P] ((laugh))' (33–E9).

When asked during retrospection what she meant by 'something', she pointed to the picture, and did not seem to be satisfied with her English description. Kellerman et al. acknowledged that linear descriptions were difficult to do, which might be one reason that the preference for linear strategies is low. However, the fact that linear descriptions are difficult may allow for the possibility that a speaker may use linear strategies in L1 but not attempt them in L2, rather opting for a strategic approach at the holistic or partitive level, however unsatisfying the results may be. Kellerman et al. conceded that, in a case in which a word is lacking in both L1 and L2, it is possible for a speaker to use a partitive or linear strategy in L1 and a holistic strategy employing a 'bad analogy' in L2, but then argued that the fact that such an option was not taken by their subjects provided evidence for the operation of the hierarchy (Kellerman et al., 1990, p. 172). However, Subject 33 seems to have opted for an unsatisfactory description in L2 at a higher level than her L1 description. Nevertheless, little can be concluded from a single pair of descriptions.

As has been noted, the lack of cross-language hierarchy violations may have been due to the preponderance of holistic strategies in both English and Japanese descriptions. It may be that such a pre-ponderance gives strong support to the idea of a preference for holistic strategies, asserted not only by Kellerman et al. but also by Bongaerts and Poulisse (1989) and even Clark and Wilkes-Gibbs (1986). However, it is worthwhile to consider what other factors may have influenced this considerable production of holistic strategies.

Bongaerts and Poulisse reported that once their subjects used a particular perspective with success, they tended to continue with that perspective in subsequent picture descriptions. Ammerlaan (1984) noted the same tendency, although the tendency was not mentioned in Kellerman et al. In the present study, it was observed during the description sessions that subjects tended to repeat, as they performed succeeding descriptions, certain linguistic struc-tures that seem to be appropriate to introduce or frame holistic strategies. Table 4.4 (overleaf) sets out examples of such linguistic frames used by subjects, a number of whom seemed to use similar structures in English and Japanese. Subject 40 tended, in both English and Japanese, to construct each description as a noun phrase, and all but one of these noun phrases contained a holistic description. Subjects 32, 33, 34 and 38 tended to use 'kore wa' ('this (is)') in Japanese and 'this is' in English. It seems that a holistic image is most likely to follow 'kore wa' and 'this is'. Other construc-tions that seemed to be built around holistic strategy use include '_____ ga arimasu'/'there is a _____' (Subject 21) and '_____ o kaite kudasai'/'draw (a) _____' (Subject 39; see also Subject 29).

It is reasonable to believe that the framing language reported herein is a consequence of a preference for holistic strategies, and it is beyond the scope of the present study to determine how much the language reflects the preference and how much the lan-guage itself influences holistic choices. However, one might con-sider, for example, Subject 33's attempt to describe Picture 2 in English, the last description done in her second session. She had described nine of ten previous pictures using 'this is'. For Picture 2, she said, 'this is e- you write zed, [P] (.) z:: an::d (.) middle:: of z::, (.) you add (.) i. (.) letter i. [P]' (33–E2). It appears that it was necessary for her to abandon the 'this is' frame in order to offer a partitive approach to Picture 2. Another example comes from the performance of Subject 38. Subject 38, the only one who knew the English words 'trapezoid' and 'cylinder', abandoned her description of Picture 7: 'this is i don't know ((laugh))' (38–E7). In retrospection, she stated that she did not know the English word,

Table 4.4 Linguistic structures repeated by subjects that may be conducive to the use of holistic strategies

Subject	Order	Japanese structures, descriptions containing them	English structures, descriptions containing them
21	J, E	kami no mannaka ni ___ arimasu [in the middle of the paper, there (is a) ___] 1 3 5 ___ kaite arimasu [___ is written] 2* 4 ___ ga arimasu [there (is a) ___] 7 8 10 11	there is a ___ 11 11 10 8 7 6 5 4 3 2*
22	E, J	___ katachi desu [a shape of a ___] 11 10 7 5 ___ o kaite kudasai [please draw (a) ___] 1 11 1	this is ___ 4 5 6 7 this (shape) is (like) ___ 1 3* 11 there is ___ 2* 8
23	E, J	kore wa ___ [this (is) ___] 8 7 6 5 4 3	this is ___ 1 5 7 8 please draw ___ 3* 4 9 10
24	J, E	___ o ka(ku) [draw (a) ___] 2* 3 4 5 7 9 10 11	looks like ___ 11 10 NP (+ elaboration) 1 10 9 7 6 5 4
25	E, J	kore wa ___ 11 10 7 5 4 3	(a) letter ___ 2* 3 4 5 the shape is like ___ 5 6 7 8 9 10*
26	J, E	kore wa ___ 4 5	this is ___ 1* 6 this/it looks like ___ 11 10 9 8 7 5 4 this/it seems to ___ 3 2*
27	E, J	___ katachi op kaite kudasai [please draw the shape of (a) ___] 1 11 10 9 8 7 6 5	it is ___ 3 4 this is ___ 5 6 7 8 9 10 11
28	J, E	NP 1 4 5 6 7 10 11	looks like ___ 1 11 10 5 4 3 this is ___ 9 6
29	E, J	kami no mannaka/chuuo ni, ___ o kaite kudasai [in the middle/center of the paper, please draw a ___] 1 11 10 9 ___ o kaite kudasai 8a 7 6 4 3 2*	in the middle, ___ 1, 2* you (should) write ___ 2* 3 4 5 7 8 you draw ___ 9 10* 11
30	E, J	NP 1 11 10 9 8 7 6 5 4	this is ___ 6 7 8

Table 4.4   (continued)

Subject	Order	Japanese structures, descriptions containing them	English structures, descriptions containing them
31	J, E	kami no mannaka/chuuo ni, ___ kakarete/egakarete imasu [in the middle/centre of the paper, ___ has been hung/drawn] 2* 3 4 5 7 8 10 11	there is (a) ___ in the centre of the paper 1 11 10 7 ; there is (a) ___ 8 6 5 4 3 2=
32	E, J	kore wa ___ 1 11 10 9 8 7 6 5 4 3 2*	this is ___ 1 4 5 6 7 8 9 11
33	J, E	kore wa ___ 2* 5 6 7 8 10 11	this is ___ 1 11 10 8 7 6 5 4 3
34	J, E	kore wa ___ 1 2* 3 4 5 6 7 8 9 10 11	this ___ 1 11 10a 9 8a 7 6a 5 4 3 2 ; this is (a) ___ 1 11 10a 9 8a 6a 5 4
35	E, J	___ katachi (desu) [(it's) the shape of ___] 1 11 10 9 4 3	NP 3 4 5 6 9 10*
36	J, E	___ jootai (desu) [(it's) a condition of ___] 3 6 9 ; katachi (desu) 5 10 ; ___ desu [(it) is (a) ___] 4 7 8 11	NP 1 6 5 4
37	J, E	___ kaite (aru) [___ is written] 4 5 ; NP 1 6 7 8 11	NP 1 5 ; looks like ___ 11 10 ; like a ___ 4 3 2*
38	J, E	kore wa ___ 1 3 4 7 8 10 11	this is ___ 1 11 10 9 8 7a 6 5 4 2*
39	E, J	___ o kaite kudasai 1 11 8 7 6 5 4	draw (a) ___ 1 2* 3 4 6a 8 9*a
40	J, E	NP 3 4 5 6 7 8 11	NP 1 11 10 8 7* 6 5 4
41	E, J	___ desu 1 11 8 6 5	it's/it is ___ 1 3 4 5 6 10 ; it's like ___ 3 4 10

Key:
21–41 subject numbers   J Japanese
1–11   description numbers   E English

*   descriptions without holistic strategy tokens
a   abandoned descriptions

but her inability to fit a description readily into her 'this is' formula may have led to her not considering a partitive and/or linear approach.

Among the factors which may have affected subjects' strategy choices, the possible influence of the pictures themselves must be considered. Kellerman et al. noted that some of the pictures lend themselves more readily to holistic descriptions than others, although they do not report which of the pictures their subjects were more or less likely to describe holistically. In the present study, of the 58 completed descriptions that included no holistic strategies, 40 (or 69 per cent) were of Picture 2. In fact, only Subject 26 offered a holistic strategy, a summary image, when describing Picture 2; in English, '((breath)) uh:: it it looks like a:: (1) mark of (1) uh:: american (.) doll. dollar. ((breath))' (26–E2). On the other hand, all descriptions for Pictures 4, 5, and 11 contained at least one holistic strategy. This suggests that the task itself was geared to the production of holistic strategies. Indeed, the 11 pictures chosen by Kellerman et al. were those to which a group of Dutch speakers could most easily assign a name. Perhaps a picture description task could be designed using pictures that were composites of common shapes; it would be interesting to observe whether such pictures lead to the production of more partitive descriptions.

Finally, the preponderance of holistic strategies in the present study should be considered in terms of Dickson et al.'s (1977) claim of the potential cultural bias of metaphoric (i.e., holistic) descriptions, countered with Bongaert and Poulisse's (1989) argument for the overwhelming preference for holistic perspectives. There is a need to consider whether any of the Japanese descriptions were specifically geared to cultural knowledge particularly possessed by the 'nihonjin', for whose benefit the subjects were instructed to describe the pictures, and, if so, what the subjects did in English to make their descriptions more understandable to the 'amerikajin' for whom they had been instructed to describe.

The Japanese descriptions, it should be noted, suggest a far-reaching Western influence upon the subjects. Of the Japanese descriptions, 79 (34.3 per cent of all completed ones) contain at least one reference to a letter of the Roman alphabet. Other images used in Japanese descriptions which could be considered 'Western' are the diamond (the loan words 'daiya' or 'daiyamondo', six descriptions, with four referring specifically to playing cards), the dollar sign, the Greek letter omega, and a Coca-Cola can (one

Table 4.5   Holistic images in Japanese descriptions that may be culturally specific; English descriptions for corresponding pictures

Subject picture	Order	Culturally specific holistic image in Japanese	Holistic image in English
24–4	J, E	totsu to yuu ji o kaite (write the character for convex')	looks like (.) t.
28–4	J, E	oototsu no oo. (the 'oo' (concave) of 'oototsu' (unevenness))	looks like t:: intersection. on the road.
30–4	E, J	oototsu no totsu. (the 'totsu' (convex) of 'oototsu' (unevenness))	a letter d [*sic*]
34–4	J, E	oototsu no totsu	the word t::.
40–4	J, E	oototsu?	alphabet (uh) t::.
26–4	J, E	yubinkyoku no maaku (the (Japanese) postmark)	english letter t.
29–4	E, J	nihon no posutomaaku (the Japanese postmark)	a you write (.) t::.
25–9	E, J	benjo (a (Japanese) toilet)	TOILET? not toilet ((breath)) slipper.
34–9	J, E	toire no benki (a (Japanese) toilet)	like helmet uh in a::
27–5	E, J	ka-kamaboko (boiled fishpaste)	this is a letter d::
25–11	E, J	yamamoto yama no nori no kan (a can of Yamamotoyama seaweed)	a:: chalk.
29–10	E, J	kamakura (an igloo shape)	[none]

description each). Nonetheless, at least 12 Japanese descriptions contained images that might be considered culturally specific to a Japanese experience. These images are set out in Table 4.5. Four of them concern the Chinese character 'totsu' and/or the character combination 'oototsu', two concern the mark used by the Japanese post office, two the Japanese floor-level toilet, one boiled fishpaste, one a brand of seaweed, and one a shape that resembles an igloo.

Table 4.5 shows that in all but one case there was a holistic image used in the corresponding English description. Subjects used 'T' in the English descriptions corresponding to those containing the Chinese character and the postmark (Subject 24 also used 'T' in his Japanese description). Subject 27 used the image of the letter D in her English description of Picture 5, as she used it along with the fishpaste image in Japanese. Subject 25 tried to use the image of a toilet in English, but abandoned it, and used that of a slipper. When doing his Japanese descriptions, he used both images to describe Picture 9. Subject 34 used the image of a helmet in English rather than the toilet image. In his retrospective interview, he admitted that he did not think that the image of a Japanese toilet was appropriate for the 'amerikajin'. Only for 'kamakura' was there no corresponding holistic image. However, in her descriptions for both pictures, Subject 29 used the approach of starting with a larger image and removing parts of it to arrive at the actual shape. In her Japanese description, 'kamakura' was offered at the end as a summary image. Since she did her Japanese descriptions second, it is unknown whether or not she had considered 'kamakura' at the time of her English descriptions.

Subjects seemed to have used alternative, assumedly less culturally specific holistic images in L2, supporting the contentions of Bongaerts and Poulisse, instead of moving to the partitive and/or linear level as potentially more culture-free, as implied by the contentions of Dickson et al. However, any imagery in the English descriptions possibly culturally inappropriate for the 'amerikajin' may support, or qualify, the claim that subjects assessed a listener's cultural knowledge. Nearly all English descriptions that might be considered culturally inappropriate involved a misuse of English loan words. Subjects 21, 22 and 29 used the word 'cup' (Japanese 'koppu', a glass) to describe Picture 11. For Picture 7, Subjects 26, 28 and 35 used 'daiya' (Japanese for 'diamond', particularly the rhomboid shape associated with it), and 26 and 32 used 'trump' (Japanese 'torampu', playing cards). Only Subject 26, in her use of 'daiya', was uncertain about her word choice; the others had felt they had used an English word properly. The only remaining culturally problematic description is Subject 28's of Picture 9: 'this:: is a:: like a chinese (2) chopping knife.' (28–E9). In retrospection, she admitted that the image might not be useful to the 'amerikajin'.

To conclude this discussion of cultural appropriateness, it can be said that the subjects of the present study took cultural concerns into account when choosing strategies for picture description, but such concerns resulted in the choice of an alternative holistic image rather than a move down the hierarchy. However, as with the considerations of other factors influencing strategy use, when considering the question of cultural appropriateness one has to accept the overwhelming number of holistic strategies as the key characteristic of the data of this particular study.

Hypothesis #2

While there was a lack of hierarchy violations in cross-language pairs of descriptions, there was a greater number of order violations within single descriptions in either language, and it is worthwhile to look at the situations in which the order breaks down.

One type of situation occurs when subjects move between descriptions of the one-dimensional lines and of the two-dimensional sections that make up geometric figures. The proposed order dictates that descriptions on the two-dimensional (i.e., partitive) level precede those on the one-dimensional (i.e., linear) level. However, in ten descriptions, the one-dimensional level precedes the two-dimensional level. An example is Subject 21's description of Picture 6:

> 'um:: shironuki no sankakukei ga arimasu. [H] (.) ee:: (.) chokkaku sankakukei desu. ((breath)) [H] (1) (e) (3) (m) MIJIKAI men ga, hidari::gawa ni kite ite, [L] nagai men ga, migigawa ni shita o shite arimasu. [L] (2) (u::) chokkaku no kakudo wa, suihei:: (e) suichoku hookoo o ((laugh)) muite imasu. ((breath)) [P]' ('Um, there's an outlined triangle. Well, it's a right triangle. The short side has come to the left and the long sides are put on the right and bottom. The right angle is set in a horizontal/vertical direction.') (21–J6)

She first offered two holistic strategies by describing the figure as a triangle ('sankakukei'). She moved to the linear level by describing two sides ('men'). When she described the right angle ('chokkaku no kakudo'), she moved back to the partitive level, and thus violated the hierarchy. It has been noted that as the number of strategy tokens for a given description increases, the more likely the order is to be violated. A possible reason for the increasing likelihood of an order violation is that as a speaker adds more information when describing a geometric shape, the more likely he or she is to move from a one-dimensional

level back to a two-dimensional one. Thus there are more possibilities of a breakdown occurring as descriptions become more
elaborate.

Similar problems occur in seven descriptions, five of them produced by Subject 29, that start with a figure larger than the target
shape and then call for parts of this figure to be removed. In these
descriptions, a line is described as dividing the shape, and then
the parts to be removed and/or the parts to be retained are
mentioned. This procedure was used in both of Subject 29's
descriptions of Picture 5. Here is the English description:

'(6) um:: at first you write circle [H] and then (.) um:: you (2)
draw? (1) ((cough)) li::ne (1) um:: (1) li::ne (1) from? middle? [L]
(1) and then, middle, from (2) left to right [L] (1) and then you::
(4) erase:: (.) half circle. [P] (2) ((laugh))' (29–E5).

She described a shape holistically ('circle'), then divided it linearly
('line') and then stated what was to be removed partitively ('erase
half circle'). It is possible that the partitive and linear classifications
made in this study are ultimately product-oriented, which suggests
that the partitive/linear distinction is not valid. Perhaps partitive
and linear strategies should be collapsed into segmental strategies,
the category used in Bongaerts and Poulisse (1994).

However, a narrower categorization of referential strategies into
holistic and segmental will not explain away the most common
type of order breakdown. Thirty-two descriptions, more than half
of those that violate the proposed order, conclude with a holistic
image that usually seems to summarize the description. Seven
descriptions, four of which were produced by Subject 26, begin
and end with the same image, as in 'it looks like a:: wood. [H] (1)
uh:: (2) when somebody cut the wood in the middle (1) um:: you
can see the circle on the wood o-on top of the wood. [P] (3) it
looks like a piece of wood. [H]' (26–E11). In 16 descriptions, the
summary image is different from an initial holistic image, as in
'ah:: (.) it:: looks like a profile of bird ((breath)) [H] (ano::) (2)
put the quarter of circle (1) on the square. [P] (2) uh:: some
people may think ((breath)) it's uh like a human's profile. [H]'
(26–E9). Of these 16, five involve an initial holistic image which is
to be cut down to produce the desired shape – for example,
's::quare (2) [H] kore wa nan daroo (2) square minus:: (2) two
squ::are from-ah from:: (.) left side (1) left side and uh:: right side
(1) [P] so:: (1) looks like (.) t. [H]' (24–E4). In the remaining

nine, a final holistic image concludes a description previously on the partitive and/or linear level, as in both of Subject 38's descriptions of Picture 4 – in English, '(4) this is u::m (1) mix of:: two:: rectangle, [P] and uh:: (3) mix (wa) (um) (can i say) ((inaudible)) connecting with:: uh:: shape like uh:: alphabet (.) t::. [H]' (38–E4).

Kellerman et al. did not comment upon any such use of summary images by their subjects. However, in a list of descriptions of Picture 7, a pattern similar to those reported in the present study appears. Subject 9 started with a holistic image, 'it's er a square with er', then moved to the partitive level, 'the corners are not of 90 degrees you have er ... this ... well this is like two triangles ... put together', then to the linear level, 'but the line where they are put together has vanished so you have', then back to the holistic level, 'it's like a 'wybertje' (laughs)' (Kellerman et al., 1990, p. 171). Ammerlaan (personal communication) noted that the summaries that occurred tended to be marked by pauses, intonation changes, or lexical markers that indicated that the subject had finished his or her initial description, and implied that the summaries should be considered as following, and not as part of, an instance of strategy use. Kellerman (personal communication) supports Ammerlaan's contention by referring to Clark and Wilkes-Gibbs' Principle of Distant Responsibility (Clarke Wilkes-Gibbs, 1986) which states that when communication is not in a face-to-face situation and a speaker (or writer) does not receive immediate feedback from a listener (or reader), the speaker will tend to add extra information to ensure that the communication will be understood. The summary images may be viewed as such extra information.

These arguments are difficult to refute. In the retrospective data collected for the present study, subjects were not asked, nor did they report, if they had 'finished' their descriptions at a certain point before they stopped talking. Only in the situation of abandonments is it clearly marked where one description ends and another begins. In any case, if the Kellerman et al. data were to be re-examined, one might find occurrences of summaries comparable to those in the present study. However, evidence is needed to support classification of a summary as lying outside an instance of strategy use. Collecting such evidence would require a new study with new retrospective data. Otherwise, the phenomenon of strategies within a single description following the hierarchy remains to be demonstrated.

Conclusion

The present study considers whether L1 and L2 referencing behaviour is identical by replicating Kellerman et al. (1990) but with Japanese speakers of English as a second language as subjects. Of particular interest is the proposal that there is a hierarchy of preference of holistic strategies over partitive strategies and of partitive strategies over linear strategies, both across and within languages. The present study found so few cases of cross-language hierarchy violations that it cannot dispute the first part of the proposal. A possible explanation for the lack of violations is the preponderance of holistic strategies, which may support the idea of a strong preference for holistic strategies, as argued in Bongaerts and Poulisse (1989), but which may have been built into the task itself. In any case, this preponderance influences all considerations of the data, including that of cultural appropriateness. Nonetheless, an examination of the few violations that occurred suggests that certain assumptions behind the hierarchy, such as avoidance of poor analogies, may not always hold, and that more violations may be found if more data are gathered.

As for within-language violations, many more cases occurred. Some cases seem to suggest that the partitive/linear distinction be reconsidered. Other cases involved the use by subjects in the present study of a summary holistic image that seemed to violate the proposed order. However, the data of the original study need to be re-examined to see if there were as many summary images as in the present study. Further, it has to be determined whether summary images should be classified as occurring inside or outside a given instance of strategy use. Without further investigation, the claim for the operation of a hierarchy of strategies within a single description cannot be supported.

Appendix 4A: Transcription conventions

hai	normal utterances.
HAI	utterances spoken with a noticeable increase in stress.
(eeto)	utterances guessed at.
::	extended speech sounds.

?	rising intonation, such as that suggesting a question.
´	slightly rising intonation, such as that suggesting the continuation of an utterance.
.	falling intonation, such as that suggesting the conclusion of an utterance.
(1)	pauses of one second or more.
(.)	pauses of less than one second.
-	breaks in utterances without a pause.
((inaudible))	utterances which are too unclear to be transcribed.
((laugh))	laughter by a speaker.
((breath))	the audible breath of a speaker.
(21–J1)	identification number of a description.
	21 – Subject 21 (subjects are numbered from 21 to 41; numbers 1 to 20 are reserved for the subjects of the original study).
	J – Japanese description.
	1 – Picture 1.
[H]	holistic strategy token.
[P]	partitive strategy token.
[L]	linear strategy token.

Appendix 4B: Counting strategy tokens

Here are some basic principles that the present study followed in enumerating tokens of strategies. Each principle is followed by an example or examples from the transcripts. English translations of Japanese comments are in italics.

1. Do not consider an immediate repetition to be an additional token.

'((breath)) cross::. [H] (5) cross and uh:: ((sniff)) when you wrong answer, (.) you got (1) this:: mark. ((sniff)) [H]' (24–E1)

2. Do not consider an immediate correction to be an additional token.

'ha::lf circle:: [H] (3) in the:: (3) ee:: to looks like ((laugh)) (1) horse:: (3) horse fee::t [H] AH. horse foot.' (24–E10)

3. Consider each new holistic image to be an additional holistic strategy token.

'the style is look-looks like rainbow. [H] (3) but um:: (4) or:: arch. [H]' (28–E10)

4. Consider each additional description of a complete shape to be an additional holistic strategy token. '(uh::) looks like (.) po::le [H] . but it's not so long. [H] (3) yeah. about about (2) uh thirty:: (.) centimeter? something like that. [H]' (28–E11)

5. Consider an order to move an entire picture to be a token of holistic strategy use.

'(umhm) (7) uhm:: (1) at first you write (.) vu::i? [P] (1) and:: (2) um (7) ((suck)) ((inaudible)) (6) (e wa) at first you wri::te vui::, and agai::n you write vui::, (1) outsi::de? [P] (3) um:: (2) and you turn (2) the paper. [H]' (29–E3)

6. Consider each description of a part of the shape to be a token of partitive strategy use.

'uh:: (1) this is:: like a mix of:: quarter of circle, [P] (.) an::d rec- rectangle. [P]' (38–E9)

'((laugh)) this is:: (2) uh:: (1) LOOKS LIKE p letter:: [H] (1) uhuh:: an::d (1) (and uh) also it's:: (.) it's style blo::ck? block or bro::ck-bri::ck, [H] (1) but it doesn't have a poi::nt ins- you know in inside the p:: (1) p-p has:: p has a:: (.) ho::le (inside) in it. but it doesn't have it. [P] (.) and uh:: (1) ((tongue click)) (2) sh::it (1) the:: (.) the right s::-the p:: has the right hand-right side of the (1) p letter::, [P] (2) it has a edge it's not rou::nd (.) shape. [P]' (32–E9)

7. Consider a mention of a line to be a linear token. Compare the following:

'wri::te z:: [P] (1) and (8) (chokusentte nante yuu *how do you say straight line?*) and uh (1) wri::te (7) uh write uh write z:: and:: wri::te (.) uh:: (1) la::ne [L] (1) uh li::ne (.) above (.)z.' (24–E2)

'uh draw:: z, [P] (1) and uh:: (.) like a:: (.)uh:: (1) i. [P] (1) in the middle.' (39–E2)

8. When a subject mentions a shape and then mentions a part or parts to be cut out of that shape, consider the mention of the complete shape to be a token of holistic strategy use, and the mention of each part to be cut out to be a token of partitive strategy use.

'((sniff)) nante yuun da kore wa *how do you say this?* (5) first (1) wri::te triangle, [H] and:: (3) minus:: (1) uh:: (2) little:: triangle from top. [P] ((breath))' (24–E8)

'eh (wakan- *i don't understand*) (6) um:: at first you write circle [H] and then (.) um:: you (2) draw? (1) ((cough)) (2) li::ne [L] (1) um:: (1) li::ne (1) from? (1) middle? [L] (1) and then, middle, from (2) left to right [L] (1) and then you:: (4) erase:: (.) half circle. (2) ((laugh)) [P]' (29–E5)

9. Note an abandonment when a strategy is interrupted by a statement of a problem. The subject may or may not start over after the abandonment.

'(ee) triangle [Ha] (4) (um) (5) sq squa::re [Ha] no triangle (nantakkana *how do you say it?*) (3) triangle squa:: (1) squa::re (8) eh i forgot the:: na::me. ((laugh)) (13) um:: (3) eh TRIangle and uh:: ((breath)) (3) um:: (5) etto (desu ne) *well*, squa:: squa::re (3) triangle:: ah i forgot.' (29–E6)

'tri::angle:: [Ha] (1) triangle and uh:: (3) left oh-left corner is:: [Pa] (.) (nante yuu *how to say?*) (3) left corner is:: (3) wakannai *i don't understand* (2) ((sniff)) (10) (nan to yuu *how to say?*) (10) ((breath)) difficult. ((breath)) (4) to (11) a triangle [H] and uh:: (1) right side is:: long. [P] ((breath))' (24–E6)

10. Do not consider statements of difficulty following completed descriptions to be abandonments.

'um:: (9) um:: (11) uhm:: (3) e::xample (2) bow::l [H] or:: (.) di::sh? [H] (1) put on the opposite side. [H] (3) i i don't know how to say. ((laugh))' (28–E8)

Appendix 4C (overleaf)

Appendix 4C: Subject performances

No.	Order		1	2	3	4	5	6	7	8	9	10	11
								Strategy choices					
21	J, E	J	133	222	11	1	133	11332	(1a)11	1133	11221	12	11
		E	13	222	1111	112	133	13	11	133	112	112	1
22	E, J	J	11	23	112	12	1	12	11	11	111	122	1
		E	1	23	11	1	13	12	13	333	122	123	121
23	E, J	J	1	233	121	(12a) 132	1122	1222	1	13333	122 2221	1123 2232 12223	11
		E	1	222	22	132	1	33	11	13333	(12a) (122a) 122222		1
24	J, E	J	1	23	1211	1111	1	133	1	133	(12a) (1a)11	1321	1
		E	11	23	112	121	12	(12a) 12	1	12	1	11	(12a)1
25	E, J	J	11	233	11 (3a)22	13	1	122	1	(11a) (12a)1	1112	(222a) (1a)1 22	11
		E	22	22	11	1222	11	(1a)1	1	(1a)12	(1a)1	333	1

Appendix 4C   (continued)

No.	Order		1	2	3	4	5	6	7	8	9	10	11
								Strategy choices						
26	J, E	J	11	231	1132 211	111	1131	1331 2	111	11	1212	1221	11232
		E	111	231	1111	1	111	1133	1111 1112	1221	121	1	121
27	E, J	J	1	233	132	12	111	122	11	133	112	11	1
		E	1	23	111	1112	113	123	11	13	122	11	1111
28	J, E	J	1	23	111	1	1	1	1	11	1	11	1
		E	1	23	11	1	11	12	1	111	1	11	111
29	E, J	J	1	222	1321 1	121	1132	132	1	(133a)	1322 2	22321	1
		E	1	22	221	1	1332	(11a)	111	(133a) 132	1322 2	2232	12
30	E, J	J	1	22	1	1	1	1	1	1	1	1	1
		E	1	(2a) 22	(11a) 1	132	1	133	131	(1a) 1 2	(2a) 1 21	1	1
31	J, E	J	1	23	1	1	1	1	1	1	(2a) (2a) 12	1	1
		E	1	233	11	(11a) 1	12	1	1	13	(2a) (1a)	1	1

Appendix 4C (continued)

No.	Order		Strategy choices										
			1	2	3	4	5	6	7	8	9	10	11
32	E,J	J	11	23	131	13	11	12(2a) 322	11	1	112	12	1
		E	133	23	131	11	1(1a) 2	12	1111	1133	1122 2	11	11
33	J,E	J	1	22	1331	13	(11a) 1322 1	1122 2 1	11	1233	(333a) 3333 122	113	(1a) (1a)12 1
		E	1	22	1	1	1	1	1	1	122	1	1
34	J,E	J	1	23	11	11	11	1	111	111	1122	1	11
		E	13	23	11	11	122	(a)	11	(a)	121	(111a)	1111
35	E,J	J	3	23	12	12	11	12	11	12	12	122	1
		E	3	22	1	1	1	2	1	23	23	22	1
36	J,E	J	3	23	122	1	11	1	1	1	12	12	1
		E	1	32	122	1	1	1	2	12	122	12	11
37	J,E	J	1	2	1	1	1	1	1	1	(1a)22 22	1	1
		E	1	2	1	1	1	(a)	(a)	(a)		1	1
38	J,E	J	11	23	11	21	(1a)1 2	121	1	1	21	2222	1
		E	1	23	(12a)	21	12	1311	(a)	1	2	12	1

Appendix 4C (continued)

No.	Order		1	2	3	4	5	6	7	8	9	10	11
									Strategy choices				
39	E,J	J	1	23	11	1	11	1	1	1	12	1	1
		E	1	22	1	1	1	(12a)	31	12	(12a)	11	1
40	J,E	J	1	23	1	1	1	1	1	1	22	122	1
		E	1	23	1	1	1	1	2	1	(a)	1	1
41	E,J	J	1	323	112	11	1	1	12	1	2211	11	(1a)11
		E	(1a)1	23	1132	11	133	(13a)	(a)	(3a)	(1a)	12	11

Key:
1–11 – pictures
21–41 – subjects

E – English
J – Japanese

1 – holistic strategy tokens
2 – partitive strategy tokens

3 – linear strategy tokens
(a) – abandonment

5

Strategies in verbal productions of brain-damaged individuals

BRIGITTE STEMMER and YVES JOANETTE

1. Introduction

The notion of 'strategy' has been applied broadly to such different research areas as problem-solving, reading comprehension and second language acquisition (Færch & Kasper, 1983a; Newell & Simon, 1972; Sternberg & Powell, 1983; Van Dijk & Kintsch, 1983). One of the motivations for investigating strategic behaviour has been to gain insights into the psychological processes underlying such verbal (or non-verbal) behaviour. However, conceptions and definitions of strategies and criteria for their classification have been criticized on various grounds (e.g., Kellerman, 1991; Oxford et al., 1992), one of which pertains to the lack of psychological plausibility of proposed strategies in terms of their compatibility with language production, cognitive and problem-solving processes (Kellerman, 1991, p. 145). One possible way of throwing light on the psychological processes underlying strategic behaviour is to investigate the verbal output of language-impaired individuals relative to normals. The goal of this chapter is thus to investigate the nature of the verbalizations produced by language-impaired patients in an attempt to infer the strategic behaviour underlying the verbalizations and to relate them to processing mechanisms. The investigation is based on a review of specific studies with illustrative references, and focuses on verbal productions. Although such an endeavour may provide useful insights, our approach is subject to various limitations due to the particularities of the population investigated. Hence, we shall first discuss the types of patient investigated and the difficulties one should anticipate when dealing with language-impaired individuals.

1.1 Classifying language-impaired individuals

Many factors have been described which may influence the strategic behaviour of second language learners. These include age, level of education, type and number of second languages acquired, and mode and length of acquisition, to name only a few. Although group homogeneity may pose a problem in second language acquisition research, one is confronted with a much more complex picture when investigating brain damaged individuals. We can only touch upon some of the problems pertinent to the current chapter which concern the types of patient we will report on, aphasic patients. The term aphasia will be used to refer to language impairments based on lesions in the central nervous system, most commonly located in the left hemisphere of right-handed individuals. Classificatory systems are not without problems and explanatory paradigms of aphasia are by no means homogeneous. They do not necessarily reflect the clinical characteristics of the patients, which, in turn, vary widely from one patient to another (for a classification of aphasia and aphasic syndromes see, for example, Benson, 1988; Caplan, 1987; Lecours et al., 1988). Linguistic, psychological or philosophical investigations of language are more concerned with theories of language organization or methodological questions and thus operate with idiosyncratic classifications which have little or no correlation with the classic clinical/anatomical syndromes. In the latter approach, labels are attached to clusters of observed symptoms which tend to occur together. However, almost half the aphasic patients do not clearly fit any single syndrome (Goodglass & Kaplan, 1972), and language patterns may change during the course of the disease, rendering the previously assigned syndrome invalid. The classification of aphasia is thus incomplete and many inadequacies exist. However, for lack of a 'better' classification scheme, and as a point of reference, we will employ the labels of Broca's, Wernicke's, conduction and anomic aphasia throughout the chapter. We will also refer to agrammatic aphasia as an aspect of Broca's aphasia and paragrammatic aphasia as an aspect of Wernicke's aphasia. Table 5.1 summarizes the characteristic symptoms of these syndromes (Benson, 1988), and Appendix 5A provides speech examples for each syndrome. Note that there is considerable individual variation and that the overall severity of symptoms varies with each patient.

Table 5.1   Syndromes of aphasia (adapted from Benson, 1988, p. 269)

	Conversational output	Oral comprehension	Repetition	Naming	Reading comprehension	Writing
Broca's	Non-fluent	Relatively preserved	Disturbed	Disturbed	Disturbed	Disturbed
Wernicke's	Fluent, paraphasic	Disturbed	Disturbed	Disturbed	Disturbed	Disturbed
Conduction	Fluent, paraphasic	Relatively preserved	Disturbed	Disturbed	Relatively preserved	Disturbed
Anomic	Fluent	Relatively preserved	Relatively preserved	Disturbed	Relatively preserved	Relatively preserved

1.2   Identifying strategic behaviour in brain-damaged individuals

The identification and analysis of any strategic behaviour relies largely on the inferences we make from subjects' verbal and non-verbal behaviour in relation to their communicative intentions or goals. Investigating the strategic behaviour of language-impaired patients entails a variety of problems not encountered in normal subjects. First, it is difficult, and at times impossible, to reconstruct the word or message the patient intended to convey. The utterances produced may sound distorted and incomprehensible to us (even if we assume that the articulatory organs function reasonably well). This situation is aggravated by the fact that the opportunities for communicating metalinguistically with the patient may be restricted, or not possible at all. Furthermore, production problems may be accompanied by comprehension problems, or by attention, memory, or other physical and psychological impairments. Researchers have tried to circumvent these problems by designing particular tasks in which the target items are known or imposed on the subject, such as picture naming, word and sentence repetition, or judgement tasks. Despite these efforts, however, the problems inherent in research with this population remain and it cannot be emphasized enough that one should keep the ensuing limitations in mind throughout this chapter.

Considering the problems we encounter with brain-lesioned patients, it is not surprising that there are hardly any studies which are *primarily* concerned with investigating the strategic behaviour of such patients in order to gain insights into underlying psychological processes. One of the few studies investigating adult aphasics' strategies from videotaped patient–therapist interactions is Penn (1984, cited in Lesser & Milroy, 1993). The author identified five categories of compensatory behaviour:

1. simplifying or condensing the message
2. elaborations
3. repetition
4. use of stereotypical chunks
5. strategies related to the sociolinguistic demands of the situation.

However, the author's focus was not on trying to relate strategic behaviour to psychological processes but rather on the role such strategies play in therapeutic intervention. Although many efforts have been made to describe the deviant or erroneous verbal productions of these patients, there is a lack of studies attempting a *systematic* classification or *taxonomy* of strategic behaviour of this population group and relating such behaviour to processing mechanisms. We have thus attempted to provide a general (and by no means exhaustive) review of the deviant or erroneous behaviour generally observed in certain aphasic syndromes and an explanation of this behaviour in terms of suggested processing mechanisms.[1] Considering the difficulties outlined above, inferring the strategic behaviour from the deviant and erroneous production and relating them to underlying processing mechanisms must necessarily remain general and suggestive.

Following the higher-order classification categories for communication strategies proposed by Færch and Kasper (1983d) and the Nijmegen taxonomy for compensatory strategies (e.g., Kellerman, 1991; cf. the preceding chapters in Part I of this volume), we will distinguish between *reduction* (*avoidance*) and *achievement strategies, retrieval* and *compensatory strategies*, and *conceptual* and *code strategies* in aphasic patients' linguistic performance. First, we will describe deviations at the phonological level, followed by a discussion of morphosyntactic alterations. Then we will consider syntactic deviations, and, finally, we will turn to disturbances at the lexico-semantic level.

2.   The phonological level

2.1   *Description of deviations*

As has been pointed out before, it is difficult to infer the intended word from an error. This is particularly true for errors made at the phonological level, as the experimenter has to decide whether a produced sound is indeed an error or a phonological variant. Therefore, specific target items are elicited and evaluated in terms of the patient's knowledge about their initial phonemes, syllable structure, stress pattern, or mapping of phonological and semantic features.

A word produced by an aphasic patient can deviate from the intended target item in various ways (Lecours et al., 1981) (see Appendix 5A, Examples 1 and 2). In *phonemic deviations*, sound elements in the produced item differ from the target. For instance, in *phonemic paraphasia*, the patient replaces one phoneme by another phoneme (e.g., *keams* for *teams*), deletes one or several target phonemes (e.g., *Fance* for *France*), adds one or several phonemes to the target item (e.g., *papra* for *papa*), or displaces a target phoneme (e.g., *ploriferation* for *proliferation*) (Ryalls et al., 1988). Another type of phonemic deviation is *phonemic télescopages*, where segmental components of at least two target words are combined to generate a single word-like entity such as *animal + mammal = mamimal* (Ryalls et al., 1988). *Formal verbal paraphasia* denotes a phonemic error which results in a legitimate word, such as *pat* instead of *bat*.

Compounded deviations (see Appendix 5A, Example 1) are a combination of phonemic and verbal paraphasias such as the production of *rnge* /rInj/, where the patient selected the item *orange* instead of the target *apple* and, at the same time, deleted the first vowel. Finally, a patient may produce *neologisms* (see Appendix 5A, Example 1) which designate 'a sequence of phonemes (a) which abide by the phonotactic rules of the speaker's tongue, (b) which is uttered as if it were a single word or locution although it does not occur in appropriate dictionaries, and (c) which cannot be positively identified as a phonemic paraphasia' (Ryalls et al., 1988, p. 372).

2.1.1   Constraints on phonemic errors

After describing various forms of phonemic deviations, one may wonder whether such deviations are constrained in any way. There is indeed evidence that phonemic errors obey normal phonological processes such as syllabification, stress assignment, or vowel reduction (Béland et al., 1990; Caplan, 1992). This suggests that basic phonological structures are preserved. Investigations of slips of the tongue in normal subjects have demonstrated similarities in the discourse production of normal and aphasic subjects, such as exchanges, substitutions and deletion of segments (for an overview, see Caplan, 1992). However, common phonemic errors produced by aphasics, such as exchanges and duplications of consonants in onsets and codas, or exchanges and duplications of entire syllables, are rarely, if at all, observable in normal slips of the tongue. Finally, phonemic paraphasias are subject to different constraints in different patients (Nespoulous et al., 1984). They can arise during the phonological planning of single words as well as during the integration of single word forms into utterances (Pate et al., 1987) and may be similar across different modalities (Caplan et al., 1986). Furthermore, the number of syllables in a word and, to a lesser degree, word frequency and word length have an impact on a patient's ability to plan the sound structure of a word (Caplan, 1992).

2.2 Processing mechanisms

Difficulties in producing the sound of a word may be due to disturbances at different stages in processing, such as accessing or retrieving lexical phonological representations, or, during utterance planning, after the form of a word has been accessed but before its actual articulation.[2] The question then arises whether we are able to point to the stage of processing at which the impairment occurs.

2.2.1 Problems at the access/retrieval stage

According to Caplan (1992), helpful indicators for locating problems at the access or retrieval stage are the inability of the patient to produce a word from a semantic stimulus such as a picture or a definition. At the same time, the patient does not encounter difficulties with a non-semantic stimulus such as word repetition, or a semantic stimulus such as answering questions about a picture. Furthermore, the patient benefits from phonological and semantic cueing or prompting

As will be discussed in section 5, semantic paraphasias may be attributed to disturbances affecting semantic or conceptual representations. However, there is also a possibility that semantic paraphasias reflect the patients' inability to access a particular morphophonological form. This hypothesis is supported by experimental findings, indicating that the lemma of a word (i.e., information about word meaning and the syntactic information associated with it) is separated from its phonological form (Levelt et al., 1991). The production of a semantically associated or related word, superordinate term, phrase, or synonym may thus reflect different achievement strategies, that is, retrieval strategies or compensatory strategies. The patient may employ semantic paraphasias in an attempt to activate phonological representations as described in procedure-based activation theories (for review, see Levelt, 1989; Newell & Simon, 1972) or in spreading activation theories (see, e.g., Dell, 1986; Morton, 1969; Rumelhart & McClelland, 1986). At the same time, however, the patient may also employ such semantic paraphasias in order to compensate for failure to access the phonological form.

2.2.2   Problems at the planning stage

Lesser and Milroy (1993) hypothesize that the retrieval of word fragments such as phonemic paraphasias may reflect a disorder of the phonological output lexicon. According to Caplan (1992), characteristic features which may indicate difficulties at the sound planning stage, that is after a word's form has been accessed and before that form is actually articulated, are (a) phonemic paraphasias which are closely related to their target items, (b) multiple attempts by the patients to produce the correct form of a target, and (c) similar phonological errors across modalities. Compensatory strategies, or, more precisely, code strategies, are the most probable candidates to operate at the sound planning stage.

Joanette et al. (1980) and Valdois et al. (1989) have investigated sequences of phonemic approximations relative to the target in conduction aphasics, Broca's aphasics, and Wernicke's aphasics. Whereas conduction aphasics and Broca's aphasics tended to improve their approximation to the target with repeated attempts, Wernicke's aphasics showed an irregular progression or no progression towards the target. It was suggested that the internal phonological representation and monitoring mechanisms were, to a certain extent, preserved in all aphasic syndromes investigated. However, whereas conduction aphasics made use of the correct production of phonemic sequences in their items by preserving these phonemes in the approximations which followed, Wernicke's aphasics did not. This was interpreted by Valdois et al. (1989) as indicating that Wernicke's aphasics, relative to conduction aphasics, are not able to monitor self-correction processes initiated by a comparator mechanism for error detection in order to arrive at the correct production. However, it is difficult to decide whether the impairment is at the planning or the monitoring stage since all aphasics produced phonemic deviations indicative of an impairment at the planning stage. Perhaps the *type* of impairment at the planning stage is different in various aphasic syndromes, as reflected in the irregular or absent progression towards the target item in Wernicke's aphasics compared to conduction aphasics. It could thus be this difference at the planning stage which influences the monitoring behaviour.

2.3 Summary

There is evidence that the basic phonological structures are preserved in Broca's, conduction, and Wernicke's aphasia. It has been suggested that the observed phonemic deviations are due to problems either at the retrieval or at the sound planning stage. Phonological and semantic cueing points to the employment of retrieval strategies in order to gain access to a particular morphophonological form. However, semantic paraphasias may also reflect the usage of compensatory strategies, more specifically, conceptual strategies. In the case of already accessed word forms, the production of phonemic paraphasias and phonemic approximations is indicative of the employment of code strategies. Evidence from the qualitative difference of phonemic approximations in conduction and Wernicke's aphasia suggests that different processing mechanisms may be impaired in the two aphasia syndromes. However, retrieval strategies and the two types of compensatory strategy appear to be used in both aphasia types. Although there appears to be a tendency for code strategies to be dominant in Wernicke's aphasia and conceptual strategies in conduction aphasia, at the present no clear picture emerges

3   The morpho-syntactic level

3.1 Description of deviations

It has been observed that bound grammatical morphemes (e.g., inflectional suffixes) and free grammatical morphemes (functors) are selectively vulnerable in both Broca's and Wernicke's aphasia. The extent and the nature of these deficits depend on the structure of the patient's native language (Bates et al., 1987; Menn & Obler, 1990). Omissions and substitutions of morphemes have been reported to occur in both aphasic syndromes. However, omission errors were more common in Broca's than in Wernicke's aphasics, and occur more frequently with free morphemes than with bound morphemes (Bates et al., 1991; Menn & Obler, 1990). Menn and Obler (1990, p. 1374) compared the omission rates of the most comparable free morphemes across 12 languages in agrammatic patients. Generally, their findings suggest that the morphemes omitted most frequently are auxiliaries and empty main verbs (have/be), followed (in descending order of frequency) by pre-/postpositions, personal pronouns, articles, lexical verbs, nouns and coordinate conjunctions. Discourse-controlled free grammatical morphemes, such as initial text connecting conjunctions ('and', 'and then', 'so') and Japanese sentence-final particles, were overused.

With regard to morpheme substitution, it has been shown that the substituting item usually remains within the same set or class as the intended target item. For example, a preposition is substituted for another (incorrect) preposition (Jarema & Kadzielawa, 1990; Miceli & Mazzucchi, 1990). Or, when bound morphemes were substituted, Miceli and Mazzucchi (1990) reported that verb inflection errors occurred within the set of verb inflections appropriate to the conjugation to which the verb belonged. Furthermore, morphologically illegal forms were never produced and incorrectly produced inflections were in close relationship to the target. Similar to the observations at the phonological level, successive approximations and self-correction also occurred at the morphological level (e.g., '*die ... der ... das ... die ... den ... den Hund*') (Bates et al., 1991).

3.2   Processing mechanisms

Bates and Wulfeck (1989, p. 131) point out that generally speaking there are very few quantitative or qualitative differences in the morphological symptoms displayed by the two aphasia groups in a richly inflected language. The production rate, the non-hesitant, seemingly effortless production of well-formed though incorrectly applied morphological options and complex syntactic structure seem to indicate that Wernicke's aphasics have fewer problems retrieving stored knowledge than applying and monitoring the information retrieved. If the impairment is at the level of inhibition of automatic processing, as some authors have suggested (Blumstein & Milberg, 1983; Goldstein, 1948; Milberg & Blumstein, 1981), then one should generally observe less strategic behaviour since automatic processing is 'less' observable than controlled processing. Furthermore, one would expect more compensatory strategies to occur rather than retrieval or reduction strategies. The speech of Broca's aphasics, on the other hand, with its frequent hesitations, long pauses, structural simplicity and the patients' avoidance of complex utterances and phrases would suggest problems at the level of retrieving information or at the level of transforming conceptual knowledge into linguistic form. Thus, observations such as false starts and grammatical approximation would be indicative of retrieval strategies. Controlled processing (Shiffrin & Dumais, 1981) involves some measure of consciousness or awareness of various components. The frequent hesitations, long pauses and avoidance behaviour would be indicative of such awareness. Furthermore, controlled processing can also function as a monitoring device. The repair of produced items may be interpreted as indicative of such monitoring.

The avoidance behaviour displayed by Broca's aphasics, characterized by their production of minimal syntactic structures, failure to employ more complex syntactic structures and dysfluency, suggests the employment of reduction strategies, as reflected in the high number of omission errors in free morphology. Wernicke's aphasics, on the other hand, do not display such avoidance behaviour. On the contrary, 'they barge ahead and attempt complex constructions, making a less systematic array of substitution errors' suggestive of the usage of compensatory strategies (Bates et al., 1991, p. 140). The usage of reduction strategies by Broca's aphasics is thus reflected in either omission of free morphemes or in substitution of simpler, more frequent and/or less marked morpho-syntactic structure. The usage of compensatory strategies in Wernicke's aphasics, on the other hand, reveals itself in more complex constructions and a less systematic array of substitution errors. The different strategic behaviours displayed in the two aphasic syndromes may, in this case, express different underlying processing mechanisms.

The substitution errors observed with bound morphemes in both Broca's and Wernicke's aphasics may reflect the employment of compensatory strategies, that is, code strategies. This interpretation would be supported by the observation that in the substitution of free as well as bound morphemes, the category of the intended target item is preserved. The appropriate form can either not be retrieved (in case of Broca's aphasia) or not be appropriately applied or monitored (in case of Wernicke's aphasia). Whereas Broca's aphasics compensate for failure to retrieve the target item, Wernicke's aphasics compensate for difficulties in monitoring the slot once it has been filled. All things considered, these findings suggest that different processing mechanisms underlie the same type of strategy.

3.3 Summary

Morpheme omission and substitution is found in Broca's and Wernicke's aphasia. However, the dissociation between frequent omission of free grammatical morphemes and substitution of bound grammatical morphemes is typically impoverishment or simplification of syntactic structure in spontaneous speech (see, e.g., Bates & Wulfeck, 1989; Caplan, 1985; Menn & Obler, 1990). With regard to strategic behaviour, this suggests that agrammatic patients typically employ reduction strategies.

4 The syntactic level

4.1 Description of deviations at the syntactic level

Several features have been described as characteristic of sentence production in agrammatic patients, the most common one being the preservation or even overuse of canonical word order (Bates & Wulfeck, 1989; Bates et al., 1991; Caplan, 1992; Menn & Obler, 1990). This tendency is accompanied by a lack of word order variation and frequent absence of relative clauses and other subordinate clauses, resulting in underrepresentation or absence of embedded sentences. However, it has also been reported that Dutch-speaking patients went counter to the tendency to produce canonical word order when using non-finite verb forms, which require a word order different from the canonical one (Kolk et al., 1990). By using a non-finite verb, these patients avoided the necessity of computing verb agreement. This interpretation would be supported by the more general observation that agrammatic patients tend to avoid complex grammatical constructions and attempt to self-monitor (Linebarger et al., 1983). At the clause level, simplification of all constituents, and particularly the structural simplification of noun phrases, is common. Within the clause, the near absence of optional elements of the verb phrase and the omission of content verbs (see previous section) has been reported.

It is difficult to establish whether syntactic simplification is the result of avoiding problems at the morphological level (cf. section 3), or of avoiding problems at the level of syntactic computation, which, in turn, may affect the production of morpho-syntactic markers. Evidence in favour of the latter assumption would be the observation that sentence planning strategies in aphasics are influenced by the structure of the patient's native language. For example, Italian aphasics avoided low-frequency phrase structures even when those structures required no extra morphological marking (Bates & Wulfeck, 1989). They also produced more relative clauses than their English counterparts, reflecting the generally more frequent employment of sentence embedding in Italian relative to the English language (Bates et al., 1988). The degree to which syntactic devices, such as declensional or inflectional morphology, are used in different languages (such as English, German, Italian and Serbo-Croatian) has been shown to influence the expression as well as comprehension of sentence meaning (Bates & Wulfeck, 1989; Caplan, 1992).

Although agrammatic and paragrammatic aphasics produce similar errors in sentence production, paragrammatic patients differ from agrammatic patients in their fluent production of 'long and complex sentences, with multiple interdependencies of constituents', interspersed with neologisms (Butterworth & Howard, 1987, p. 23). The output of paragrammatic patients may thus be the result of achievement rather than reduction strategies.

4.2 Processing mechanisms

Basing themselves on Garrett's (1980, 1984) model of language production and Kolk et al.'s (1990) adaptation theory, Menn and

Obler (1990, p. 1384) advance the hypothesis that agrammatic patients suffer from syntactic output processing difficulties. The authors view the difficulties at the morphological level as closely related to difficulties in syntactic computations. The dissociation between omission of free grammatical morphemes and substitution of bound grammatical morphemes (see section 3) in agrammatic patients points to differential treatment of the two classes in normal syntactic production. The retrieval of erroneous verb forms might have its origin in either of two different points in output processing: the level at which lexical items are found for concepts and aspects of meaning related to sentences. Garrett (1984) has called this the functional level. Or it could be the level at which information about the form of words and sentences is specified, which Garrett (1984) labels the positional level.

The close relationship between morphological and syntactic processing is further supported by the observation that some agrammatic patients present with morphological and syntactic problems only in relation to sentence planning and production, without showing any disturbances of processing function words or bound morphemes in isolation (Caramazza & Hillis, 1990; Nespoulous et al., 1988). Furthermore, patients have been reported to demonstrate problems at the morphological level, independently of whether the morphological items occur in isolation or in co-text. At the same time, these patients also exhibit problems at the sentence level. Caplan thus hypothesizes that

> agrammatic patients whose omission of function words and bound morphemes only occurs in sentence production and not in single word processing tasks will have disturbances affecting the construction of syntactic structures. ... It may be that certain forms of agrammatism are accompanied by significant disturbances in the production of syntactic phrases because the disturbance affecting the function word/bound morpheme vocabulary elements arises at a stage in sentence planning intimately connected to the elaboration of syntactic structures.   (Caplan, 1992, p. 347)

As for processing mechanisms in paragrammatic patients, it has been suggested that the syntactic and morphological errors in paragrammatism reflect an impairment of these patients' ability to monitor output (Butterworth 1982; Butterworth & Howard, 1987; Kolk et al., 1990). This would suggest that there may be different underlying processing mechanisms in which paragrammatism differs from agrammatism in terms of sentence production. Agrammatism would reflect a disturbance of one basic aspect of the sentence-building process – the construction of syntactic form – while paragrammatism would result from a disturbance of control mechanisms that monitor the speech planning process (Caplan, 1992, p. 350).

4.3 Summary

The avoidance of complex grammatical constructions as demonstrated by the preservation or overuse of canonical word order, the lack in word order variation, and the structural simplification of noun phrases is reflected in the employment of reduction strategies by agrammatic patients. The paragrammatic patients' fluent output and more complex sentence productions with embedding of constituents is suggestive of the usage of compensatory strategies. The impairment of different processing mechanisms appears to be responsible for the agrammatic or paragrammatic output, respectively. In accordance with observations at the morphological level, the observed differences in strategic behaviour thus seem to reflect these processing differences.

So far, we have discussed impairments at the phonological, morpho-syntactic and syntactic level. We have also mentioned at various points the possibility that the patient may have problems in finding the proper word for a concept. We will turn to this issue next.

5 The lexico-semantic level

A common disturbance following a brain lesion is the difficulty a patient can have in using the right word in order to express a concept. Indeed, the occurrence of so-called word-finding difficulties or anomia is part of the semiology of nearly all types of left-brain-damaged aphasic patients (Lecours & Lhermitte, 1979) and can also be found in right-brain-damaged individuals (Joanette et al., 1990) or in patients with non-focal lesions such as in dementia of the Alzheimer type (Habib et al., 1991).

5.1 Description of verbal behaviour at the lexico-semantic level

In the previous section, we have referred to the frequent omission of free morphemes, reflecting the employment of reduction strategies as a typical characteristic of Broca's aphasia. One major reason for these omissions is the difficulty the patients have finding the right word. Whereas the absence of production cannot be analysed in itself, one can explore those instances in which patients with word-finding difficulties resort to other means to express a target item.[3] Two main groups of search strategies in anomic patients, semantically bound strategies and lexically bound strategies, have been identified by LeDorze and Nespoulous (1989). This distinction corresponds to conceptual and code strategies, respectively. The prototypical and most commonly used conceptual strategy is exemplified by circumlocutions such as *the thing to put cigarettes in* for 'ashtray'. The use of code strategies is reflected in the patient's recourse to information about the target, such as the number of syllables, the first or the last letter of the item, and so on. The successive verbalizations of phonologically impaired approximations of the target item constitute further examples of code strategies (see section 2.2.2).

5.2   *Processing mechanisms*

There is a common consensus that language-specific knowledge is largely preserved in aphasic syndromes (Bates & Wulfeck, 1989; Bates et al., 1991; Goodglass, 1990; Menn & Obler, 1990). Accordingly, the problem associated with naming can lie either in an inability (a) to activate automatically the semantic representation, which is frequently conceived in terms of a disturbance of the permanent lexical semantic representation of a word, or (b) to activate consciously the semantic representation corresponding to the concept to be expressed, or (c) to access the lexical form of the word corresponding to the semantic representation. It has been suggested that circumlocutions, which provide the interlocutor with semantic cues about the target item, are evidence that the patient did indeed identify the semantic target and that the problem lies in gaining access to its lexical form (LeDorze & Nespoulous, 1989). However, one can question this interpretation since providing these semantic attributes does not necessarily ensure that the specific semantic concept was indeed identified by the patient. It could be the case that the patient only activated a number of features in the semantic network, without being able to activate the specific, isolated concept being sought. In other words, conceptual strategies should not be conceived of as proof of the integrity of the semantic representation. Accordingly, conceptual strategies may reflect an impairment at the level of the semantic representation of words, or at the level of access to the lexical form of words corresponding to the semantic representation.

Similarly, code strategies have been taken by some researchers to indicate that the semantic concept was in fact identified and that it was only the expression of the lexical item corresponding to this concept that was the source of the problem. In this case, the usage of code strategies could point to a lexical deficit. Again, the situation might not be as clear as it seems. Given the intimate and mutual relationships between the semantic representation on the one hand, and the lexicon on the other hand, it could be that the lexical item was not retrieved adequately due to a weakened semantic representation. In this case, a code strategy could thus reflect a semantic deficit.

5.3   Summary

In sum then, although reduction strategies expressed in omission errors are frequently observed in anomic patients, conceptual and code strategies are also commonly employed to arrive at the target item. Given the current stage of knowledge, it is not possible to view either of the two strategies as indicating an impairment at a particular processing stage. Both types of strategy can be indicative of an impairment at the level of the semantic representation of words or at the level of access to the lexical form of words.

5.4   Priming studies

In an attempt to gain more insight into the semantic processing of words, researchers have resorted to employing particular techniques, such as priming. In simple priming, two stimuli are presented: the target item and a prime which precedes the target item. The prime is usually a picture or a word and is in some way related to the target item. The subject is shown the prime and then asked to make a response to the target item, such as deciding whether it is a word or non-word. A facilitation effect such as a shorter reaction time to and/or better performance on the target item is usually observed. For example, presenting the word *zebra* as a prime followed by the word *dog* will result in a shorter reaction time in a lexical decision task than presenting *cloud* as the prime. In semantic network theory (Collins & Loftus, 1975), this suggests that the presence of a prime pre-activates semantically related nodes in the network. Thus, a string of letters which corresponds to one of these pre-activated nodes is easier to recognize as forming a word than a string of letters which does not correspond to any of the pre-activated nodes.

As shown by Milberg & Blumstein (1981), Wernicke's aphasics demonstrate semantic priming effects in a lexical decision task although they failed on matching pictures to spoken words. Broca's aphasics, on the other hand, who could match words and pictures, did not show any priming effects. The authors concluded that Wernicke's aphasics still retained some semantic knowledge of a word but were not able to use their residual semantic knowledge in conscious processes. Broca's aphasics, who were able to access the semantic knowledge consciously, had a disturbance of the unconscious processes making use of this knowledge. Using an expanded priming paradigm with automatic and controlled priming conditions, Gagnon et al. (1989) tried to induce distinct strategies in order to test different components of the lexical-semantic processes. Three aspects of the priming tasks were changed in order to induce either an automatic or a controlled condition: (a) the time between the first occurrence of the prime and the beginning of the target, referred to as stimulus onset asynchrony (SOA); (b) the proportion of related/unrelated primes; and (c) the instructions given to the patients. In order to favour automatic access to semantic representation, the SOA was short (300 msec), the proportion of related/unrelated primes was high (3/1), and the instructions to the subject did not emphasize the usefulness of the primes in relation to the targets. The reverse situation applied for the controlled condition: the SOA was longer (1000 msec), the proportion of related/unrelated primes was low (1/3), and instructions emphasized that the prime could provide cues as to the nature of the following target. It is assumed that automatic priming depends on the passive propagation of activation through the semantic network, whereas controlled priming is thought to reflect active, consciously driven activation of the semantic network. Hence, if the lexico-semantic deficit is due to some alteration of the semantic network itself, both automatic and controlled priming should be affected. Conversely, if the lexico-semantic deficit is to be attributed to the processes needed in order to explore the semantic network consciously, then it is controlled priming rather than automatic priming that would be affected.

Investigating aphasic left- and non-aphasic right-brain-damaged subjects, Gagnon et al. (1989) found that both automatic and controlled priming conditions were unaffected in the two groups, but all brain-damaged subjects showed lowered performance in the semantic judgement task. It was concluded that when the brain is afflicted with some lexico-semantic deficit, these deficits appear to express the limitations of look-up mechanisms needed for the conscious and most effortful activation of the semantic network.

In summary, distinct strategies are not only the expression of compensatory behaviour on the part of the patient, they can also be induced in patients in order to test different components of the lexico-semantic processes and the way they can be affected by a brain lesion.

After this discussion of achievement strategies in reaction to lexico-semantic deficits and the use of strategies as a means of exploring semantic representations and access processes, the next section will discuss particular patterns of errors displayed by patients in single word reading.

5.5   Single word reading

As described in previous sections, aphasic patients usually show a variety of symptoms including, in many cases, reading disorders. Sometimes, reading problems are the dominant or only symptoms. Such reading disorders are referred to as acquired dyslexia. Although there is a wide variety of acquired dyslexias, we will focus on two types which have been discussed extensively in the literature: *surface dyslexia* and *deep dyslexia* (for review, see Coltheart et al., 1980; Marshall & Newcombe, 1973; Patterson et al., 1985). We will briefly characterize these disorders and then give an account of the processing mechanisms which have been suggested as being impaired in these disorders.

5.5.1   Surface dyslexia

Errors made by patients with this disorder when reading words aloud typically resemble unsuccessful attempts to arrive at the correct pronunciation. For example, these patients may produce the following reading errors:

guest as 'just'
disease as 'decease'
island as 'izland'
unite as 'unit'
broad as 'broke' ... break ... braid ... brode'
route as 'rote' ... rut-th ... rout'
listen as 'liston' ('that's the boxer')
begin as 'beggin' ('collecting money')
omit as 'ommit' ('that's the name of the prophet of Islam')
(Marshall & Newcombe, 1973, p. 183ff.)

The observed irregularities are thus words or non-words, with the vast majority of errors resulting from faulty grapheme–phoneme translation. Often, patients apply the most regular letter–phoneme rules in a given language. The meaning these patients assign to the words is frequently based on the pronunciation of the word produced. For example, when questioned about the meaning of the items produced, the surface dyslexic patient described by Marshall & Newcombe (1973) explained 'the famous boxer' for the item *liston* (thus referring to the boxer Sonny Liston), or described *beggin* as 'collecting money'. A small number of errors are visual confusions, such as 'police' for *polite*.

The reading aloud of presented words is not affected by such factors as concreteness or abstractness, and the errors produced are not semantically related to the word to be read. However, high frequency words and regular words are read more successfully than low frequency and irregular words (Bub et al., 1985). These observations, together with the type of errors described above, indicate the employment of code strategies.

5.5.2 Deep dyslexia

Whereas in surface dyslexia the erroneous words produced do not bear any semantic relationship to the target item, in deep dyslexia such a semantic relationship is the cardinal symptom. Furthermore, these patients show more problems in reading a word if the word is a low-frequency word, an abstract word, or a function word, and they are unable to read non-words. Although, at times, the patient may notice the error, in many cases the errors go undetected. Coltheart et al. (1980) provide a list of reading errors in two deep dyslexic patients, a selection of which is presented in Table 5.2.

Table 5.2   Reading errors produced by two dyslexic patients (Coltheart et al., 1980, p. 416ff.)

Semantic paralexias	Derivational paralexias	Visual paralexias	Function-word paralexias
block>boulder	tackling>tackle	tying>typing	where>because
thermos>flask	assaulting>assaulted	goggles>gaggle	my>me
probing>digging	delight>delightful	signal>single	the>is
pair>two	reality>real	edge>wedge	both>perhaps
most>big	think>thinking	loose>noose	under>in
direct>straight	worth>worthy	grief>greed	just>it

Semantic paralexias and derivational paralexias are the most frequent errors. Visual and function-word paralexias, where the produced item is not necessarily related to the target item, are also observed. A combination of these categories, such as visual-semantic paralexias, is also noted. Whereas semantic paralexias point to the use of conceptual strategies, derivational paralexias reflect the employment of code strategies. Function-word paralexias seem to reflect a combination of both types of strategy.

5.5.3   Processing mechanisms

One way of understanding these disorders is to interpret them by reference to a simple functional architecture of normal word-reading, such as the 'two-route' model of the reading process proposed by Marshall & Newcombe (1973, p. 188ff.; see Figure 5.1). It is true that although much more sophisticated and explicit models have been proposed since (see, e.g., Behrmann & Bub, 1992; Patterson et al., 1985), but this simple representation serves well to illustrate the point to be made here. Essentially, this representation suggests that reading a word aloud can be executed at least in two ways, using one of two cognitive routes. The first route is the semantic route. In this case, the meaning of the word is extracted from its written form, fed into the semantic system and thereafter reproduced orally. An alternative way is the grapheme–phoneme conversion route. In this second case, it is not the meaning of the word that is extracted. Instead, the written form of the word is transcoded into its oral form by using the conversion rules of a given language.

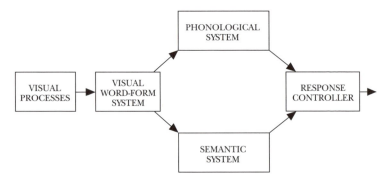

Figure 5.1   Marshall & Newcombe's (1973) 'two-route' model of the reading process as presented by Shallice (1988: 71)[4]

By reference to this representation, or functional architecture, it is thought that in deep dyslexia the grapheme–phoneme conversion route is no longer available. Hence, the patient has to rely upon the semantic route in order to read the word aloud. This causes the problems described above since all the information related to the form of the word cannot be processed. The situation is different for surface dyslexia. In this case, it is the semantic route that is no longer accessible. Thus, only the non-semantic rules of grapheme–phoneme conversion can be applied. This explains why these patients are sensitive to the complexity of word forms and unable to identify the word or to consider irregular word characteristics.

5.5.4 Summary

It has been suggested that there is a tendency for code strategies to appear in surface dyslexic patients, whereas conceptual strategies dominate in deep dyslexic patients, although in the latter case, code strategies are found as well. Two different processing mechanisms have been proposed to account for the two different types of dyslexia. These different processing mechanisms thus seem to be rejected in the two types of strategy employed by these patients. The fact that code strategies are also employed by deep dyslexic patients may be interpreted in two ways. Either the underlying semantically oriented processes are expressed through both types of strategy or the processing mechanisms attributed to deep dyslexia are not as clear-cut as proposed in the two-route model.

That the latter may indeed be the case is supported by more complex processing models underlying dyslexia.

So far, we have described typical deviations in the communicative behaviour of patients who have suffered some form of brain damage. An attempt has been made to derive strategic behaviour from such deviations. Processing mechanisms responsible for the various forms of observed impairment were suggested and the extent to which strategic behaviour reflects such mechanisms was also discussed. We have also demonstrated how a 'reverse' approach, starting from the concept of different types of strategy, can be employed in order to infer different processing mechanisms. In the final section, we will demonstrate how the notion of communication strategy can be applied to rehabilitation programmes for brain-damaged patients.

6   Strategic approaches to the rehabilitation of aphasic patients suffering from lexico-semantic deficits

One of the biggest challenges in clinical aphasiology is, of course, the development of adequate rehabilitation programmes that will support the patient's recovery process, or compensate for his or her impairments. Rehabilitation procedures have not only shown a positive effect on the acceleration of spontaneous recovery processes, but can also induce improvement in long-standing aphasias where the spontaneous recovery process has terminated. Although most recently, rehabilitation programmes have focused on a pragmatic approach to intervention, the efficiency of rehabilitation programmes has been most thoroughly studied in relation to lexico-semantic deficits. Not surprisingly, many of these rehabilitation programmes have been aimed at enhancing achievement strategies such as those illustrated in the preceding sections.

The first example illustrates a rehabilitative measure based upon the enhancement of retrieval strategies. Until the early 1970s, the approach to the rehabilitation of aphasia was little influenced by cognitive neuropsychology and followed a basically pedagogical approach. The somewhat implicit postulate was that the aphasic individual with anomia had lost words which he or she had to re-learn. The goal of many rehabilitation programmes was thus to restore the normal, adequate and standard access to the word that was missing through a re-learning programme for those words. However, there were two problems with this approach. First, we now know that the words are not lost *per se*. Secondly, as pointed out by Holland (1977), the rehabilitation programmes were exclusively based on the production of a particular item which was viewed as the norm. In fact, Holland (1977) was among the first to insist that such a normative approach could even induce in the subject a loss of spontaneously occurring compensatory strategies. For example, in patients with long-standing anomia, the typical normative approach of the 1970s would have been to support the patient's effort to produce the lexical item exactly as expected, even though in doing so the patient was deprived of using such compensatory strategies as circumlocutions. As a result, some patients could neither produce the expected lexical item, nor use compensatory strategies; a spontaneous strategy was replaced by muteness! Alternatively, pursuing an approach directed towards communicative effectiveness, a rehabilitative programme could focus on a refined use of such strategies, since lexical access remains difficult. Thus, rehabilitation serves to enhance spontaneous compensatory strategies instead of aiming to replace strategic behaviour with more normative but rather inefficient language use. However, as Penn (1984; cited in Lesser & Milroy, 1993) has pointed out, spontaneously acquired compensatory strategies can also be counter-productive, depending, for example, on the frequency and context of use. Nonetheless, instruction in production and comprehension strategies has become an integral part of current aphasia therapy (for a detailed account, see Milroy & Lesser, 1993).

The second example describes a rehabilitative measure which also aims to enhance the use of compensatory strategies. However, in this case, the approach is based on a cognitive model which targets the stage in processing at which the impairment occurs. In a seminal paper, De Partz (1986) demonstrated that the performance of a patient with deep dyslexia could be improved by enforcing the use of a particular processing route when reading aloud. As discussed above (see section 5.5), patients with deep dyslexia are not able to use the so-called grapheme–phoneme conversion route in order to read aloud a written word. However, they are still able to use the semantic route. The rationale of the rehabilitative measure was to use this still available route in order to compensate for the non-available grapheme–phoneme conversion route. Similar to the priming studies referred to previously (see section 5.4), this approach is centred on intentionally employing particular strategies in order to provoke a specific processing mechanism.

7   Conclusions

The purpose of this chapter was to infer from the erroneous or deviant verbal productions of brain-damaged subjects the strategies used in order to communicate, or arrive at a target item. At the phonological level, both conceptual and code strategies were identified. It was concluded that neither of the two strategies could clearly be assigned to a specific processing level. At the morpho-syntactic level, a tendency to employ reduction strategies was observed in Broca's aphasics, whereas Wernicke's aphasics appeared to rely more on compensatory strategies. However, at times, both aphasic syndromes appeared to reflect the use of compensatory strategies, indicating that one strategy type reflected processing at different levels. Similarly, at the syntactic level, the employment of reduction strategies appeared to be characteristic of agrammatic patients and the use of compensatory strategies of paragrammatic patients. As different processing mechanisms have been suggested to explain the impairment of these two aphasic syndromes, it would thus seem that the suggested differences in processing are reflected in the employment of two types of strategy. Finally, both reduction strategies and compensatory strategies operated at the lexico-semantic level. However, neither strategy type could be clearly assigned to any particular processing stage. An examination of the strategic behaviour of surface and deep dyslexic patients from the verbal reading errors they produced led to a similar conclusion. Although there was a tendency for code strategies to occur with surface dyslexia and conceptual strategies with deep dyslexia, both types of strategy also co-occurred with deep dyslexic patients.

These observations lead us to conclude that strategic behaviour, although at times suggestive, is not a reliable indicator of a particular processing mechanism. One reason for this is the fact that the processing models proposed are what they are intended to be – merely models, which are continuously discussed, developed and modified, just as the concept of strategy itself is.

Some models are better developed and have more predictive power than others. It is thus not surprising that strategic behaviour cannot always be matched onto processing mechanisms. However, this should not deter us from trying to establish such a match. The psychological plausibility of strategy types can only be elucidated by discussing them within the framework of theories and models of processing relevant for the area of investigation. Ultimately, this may lead us to a better understanding of the relationship between strategic behaviour and its underlying processes.

Taking a somewhat different perspective, we turned to research in which strategies were consciously employed in order to induce particular processing modes, either in order to test hypotheses about processing mechanisms such as in priming studies, or as part of rehabilitation procedures. Such approaches provide yet another way of gaining insight into the relationship between strategies and their underlying processes.

Finally, it should be mentioned that the kinds of strategies used by the population described here share many similarities with the strategic behaviour described in normal speakers struck with the tip-of-the-tongue phenomenon or second language learners struggling to communicate despite a 'deficient' (second) language system. This suggests that strategic behaviour is, to some extent, independent of the nature of the causal factor.

Notes

This study was conducted by the first author under funding from the Medical Research Council of Canada, Grant no. 9004FEN–1037–34749.
1. The situation is different for therapeutic or rehabilitation purposes where teaching particular strategic behaviour is commonly used (see section 6).
2. Problems may also arise due to malfunction of the articulatory apparatus. We will not discuss such problems here.
3. Naturally, these patients' attempts to arrive at the target item are often accompanied by all sorts of mimetic gestures. However, it is beyond the scope of this chapter to include research on non-verbal communication in brain-damaged individuals.
4. Shallice's version of the model is presented here because his adaptations of the model and its nomenclature are more in line with the terminology used in this chapter.

Appendix 5A

Example 1: Speech sample of a Wernicke aphasic (Lecours et al., 1981, p. 17ff.)[1,2,3]

EST-CE QUE VOUS AVEZ DES ENFANTS?

Des enfants où, [1]*Mademoiselle?* ... Oui, j'ai encore une autre [2]*femme* qui est restee depuis le ↓ la [3][bœtʀe] de l'enfant de [4](*ma fils*). [5]*Il* [6]/a/ ↓ Elle avait dix ans quand [7](*mon* lfɛsl) est mort. Et alors, elle est la maintenant. Elle va sur [0]/syz/ ans. Elle va toujours à l'école puisqu'elle se présente les ↓ Je l'avais envoyée à l'école puisque, moi, je travaillais bien dans les [9][syz] ↓ euh à la [10][faʀmid] de ↓ de ↓ de [9][syz]—[11]n'est-ce pas?—de deux [12][ɛtmiʀ]. Et alors, je ↓ Cette [13]/mwazela/, [14]*Ginette* elle s'appelle, elle ↓ elle [15][abil]. Tous les jours, elle venait à Paris pour euh [16][pale] dans les [17][kɔsig], parce qu'elle prenait pour ↓ aussi pour entrer le ↓ euh le [18]*palais*, le [18]*palais* normal bien entendu. euh le [19][namytyʀ], la [20][tɔktœʀ] et l'[21][ãbœtjɛʀ], pour qu'elle sache [22](*tous ces* ↓ *ces choses* ↓) pour qu'elle [23](*sache à*) bien s'[24][ẽskʀyme] ↓ à bien ↓ bien s'[25]/ ẽ/ ↓ s'[26][ẽkyme]. Et c'est là que je suis [27]*morte*, là, cette année. Elle était ↓ Elle allait toujours à l'école. ... Ma fille vient deux fois (par semaine) chez moi ... [28]*Mademoiselle* ↓ ... alors [28]*celle-là* vient le [29]/ʒødim/, puisqu'elle ne va pas en [30]/klis/, et elle vient le [31]/ʒydi/ ↓ le dimanche, puisque nous faisons bonne [32]*filleule* [33]*ici.*

DO YOU HAVE CHILDREN?

Children where, [1]*Miss* [the interviewer was male]? ... Yes, I have still another [2]*woman* who has remained since the-M ↓ the-F [3][bœtʀe] of the child of [4](*my*-F *son*-M). [5]*He* [6]/WAS/ ↓ She was ten years old when [7](*my*-M lBUTTOCKl-F) died. And then, she is there now. She will soon be [8]/SIXTEEN/ years old. She is still going to school since she presents herself since the ↓ I had sent her to school since I myself was indeed working in the [9][syz] ↓ hm at the [10][faʀmid] of ↓ of ↓ of [9][syz]—[11]is it not?—of two [12][ɛtmiʀ]. And then, I ↓ This [13]/YOUNG LADY/, [14]*Ginette* is her name, she ↓ she [15][abil]. Each day, she came to Paris in order to hm [16][pale] in the [17][kɔsig], because she was taking in order to ↓ also in order to enter, the ↓ hm the [18]*palace*, the normal [18]*palace* of course, hm the [19][namytyʀ], the [20][tɔktœʀ] and the [21][ãbœtjɛʀ], in order that she knows [22](*all*-M *these* ↓ *these things* ↓) in order that she [23](*knows at*) [24][ẽskʀyme] herself correctly ↓ *at* ↓ *at* [25]/ẽ/ ↓ [26][ẽkyme] herself correctly. And this is when I [27]*died*, then, this year. She was ↓ She still went to school. ... My daughter comes twice (a week) at my home. ... [28]*Miss* ↓ ... thus [28]*this one*-F comes on [29]/THURSDAYS-SUNDAYS/, since she does not go to [30]/SCHOOL/, and she comes on [31]/THURSDAYS/ ↓ on Sundays, since we make a good [32]*god-daughter* [33]*here.*

Notes

1. This speech sample presents the case of Ms D., whose symptoms were described as follows: 'euarthric logorrheic jargon; severely impaired repetition and reading, with paraphasic and neologistic productions; reduced and paragraphic written expression; and impaired comprehension of spoken and written language' (Lecours et al., 1981, p. 17).

2. Ms D.'s jargon comprised the following deviations:

   - neologisms (3, 9, 10, 12, 15, 16, 17, 19, 20, 21, 24, 26)
   - phonemic paraphasias (8, 13, 30, 31)
   - télescopages (29)
   - semantic verbal paraphasias of the type paradigmatic substitutions (1, 2, 14, 27, 28, 33) or wrong choices that were at least partially determined by a contextual factor (5, 18, 23, 32)
   - compounded deviations (7, 31) (Lecours et al., 1981, p. 19).

3. The conventions for the transcriptions are given on page 124.

Example 2: Speech sample of a conduction aphasic (Lecours et al., 1981, p. 12ff.)[1,2,3]

RACONTEZ-MOI VOTRE VIE AU COURS DE LA GRANDE GUERRE

J'étais encore au[1]|fɔ̃| ↓ sur le [1]|fɔ̃| ↓ J'étais mobilisé encore sur le ↓ sur le [2]|flɔ̃| ↓ le [2]/fa/ ↓ le ↓ la ↓ dans ↓ dans la [3]bataille. ... J'ai été [4]/a/ ↓ [4]/a/ ↓ [4]/ata/ ↓ [4]/a/ ↓ J'ai été ensuite [4]/ata/ ↓ détaché parce que je connaissais très bien l'Allemand. ... J'ai été ensuite chargé, avec juste quelques autres, quand ↓ euh d'[5]/ɛ̃ tɛg/ ↓ de ↓ d'[5]/ɛ̃tɛRɔg/ ↓ euh de l'[5]/ɛ̃tɛga/ ↓ [5]/gɔ/ ↓ [5]/da/ ↓ de ↓ d'[5]/ɛ̃tɛRogosi/ ↓ de ↓ —euh [6]je vais trop vite—d'[5]/ɛ̃tɛRɔ/ ↓ Oui: d'[5]/ɛ̃tɛRɔge/ des [7]/pe/ ↓ des [7]/pe ↓ des prisonniers allemands. ... On recevait euh les papiers et tout ce qu'on avait trouvé sur les Allemands tués ou [8]/plitɔne/ et caetera. C'était même pas ↓ pas drôle quelquefois, parce que j'ai eu à faire ↓ j'[9]/a/ ↓ On recevait ça dans des [10]/sk/ ↓ quelquefois des [10]/saʃk/ ↓ [11]*sous* des grands sacs en jute qui [12]/saRti/ ↓ qui [12]/saR/ ↓ qui [12]/saRt/ ↓ qui sentaient le [13]/tavaR/ ↓ le [13]/tRava/ ↓ les [13]/tɛ/ ↓ les [13]/t/ ↓ le [14]|kavjaR|. Non: l'[15]/epuvɑ̃ɛt/ [13]/tavaR/. Oui: le ↓ le [13]/ka/ ↓ le [13]/kava/ ↓ le [13]/kadRav/ ↓ le cadavre humain, qui a une [16]/ɛskø/ [17]/fal/ ↓ une odeur [17]/fal/ ↓ euh [17]/fals/ ↓ . ... (Je suis souvent nerveux) [18]/da/ ↓ depuis quatorze ↓ de ↓ la guerre de [19]/sa/ ↓ la guerre de [20]|kalis| ↓ de [21]|galis| ↓ de ↓ Oui: C'est la [22]/kɛ/ ↓ C'est la [22]/gɛ/ ↓ Depuis la guerre de [19]/kɔz/ ↓ de mille neuf cent [19]/kasɔz/ ↓ [19]/kœ/ ↓ [19]/ka/ ↓ [23]/katRɔs/. ... C'est une [24]|tɛR| ↓ une ↓ C'est une grande [25]/plɛR/ ↓ une grande place, qui s'appelait la Place des [26]/fizɔ/ ↓ des Philosophes.

TELL ME ABOUT YOUR LIFE DURING THE FIRST WORLD WAR

I was still at the [1]|BOTTOM| ↓ on the [1]|BOTTOM| ↓ I was sent again on the ↓ on the [2]|FRONT| ↓ the ↓ the ↓ in ↓ in the [3]battle. ... I was [4]/DETACHED/ ↓ [4]/DETACHED/ ↓ [4]/DETACHED/ ↓ [4]/DETACHED/ ↓ I was then [4]/DETACHED/ ↓ detached because I spoke German very well. ... I was then charged, with a few others only, when ↓ hm to [5]/QUESTION/ ↓ to ↓ to [5]/QUESTION/ ↓ hm of the [5]/QUESTIONING/ ↓ [5]/QUESTIONING/ to ↓ [5]/QUESTION/ ↓ to ↓ to [5]/QUESTION/ ↓ —hm [6]I am talking too fast—to [5]/QUESTION/ ↓ Yes: to [5]/QUESTION/' [7]/PRISONERS/' ↓ [7]/PRIOONDRO/' ↓ German prisoners ... We received hm the papers and everything that had been found on Germans who had been killed or [8]/CAPTURED/ et cetera. It was not ↓ not even funny sometimes, because I had to do ↓ I [9]/HAD/ ↓ We received this in [10]/BAGS/ ↓ sometimes in [10]/BAGS/ ↓ [11]*under* large gunny bags which [12]/SMELLED/ ↓ which [12]/SMELLED/ ↓ which [12]/SMELLED/ ↓ which smelled of [13]/CADAVER/ ↓ of [13]/CADAVER/ ↓ of [13]/CADAVER/ ↓ of [13]/CADAVER/ ↓ of [14]|CAVIAR|. No: the [15]/DREADFUL/ [13]/CADAVER/. Yes: the ↓ the [13]/CADAVER/ ↓ the [13]/CADAVER/ ↓ the [13]/CADAVER/ ↓ the human cadaver, which has a [16]/FOUL/ [17]/ODOR/ ↓ a [17]/FOUL/ odor ↓ hm [17]/FOUL/ ↓ . ... (I am often nervous) [18]/SINCE/ ↓ since fourteen ↓ of ↓ the war of [19]/FOURTEEN/ ↓ the war of [20]|CHALICE| ↓ of [21]|GALICIA| ↓ of ↓ Yes: It is the [22]/WAR/ ↓ It is the [22]/WAR/ ↓ Since the war of [19]/FOURTEEN/ ↓ of nineteen hundred and [19]/FOURTEEN/ ↓ [19]/FOURTEEN/ ↓ [19]/FOURTEEN/ ↓[19]/FOURTEEN/ ↓ [23]/FOURTEEN-ATROCIOUS/. ... It is a [24]|LAND| ↓ a ↓ It is a large [25]/SQUARE-LAND/ ↓ a large square, which was called the Square of the [26]/PHILOSOPHERS/ ↓ of the Philosophers.

Notes

1. This speech sample presents the case of Mr K., whose speech output was described as follows: 'fluent jargon without arthric distortions; word finding difficulties in spontaneous speech and naming; attempts at repetition and reading aloud led to phonemic paraphasias; attempts at writing showed literal paragraphias; comprehension of oral and written language was nearly normal' (Lecours et al., 1981, p. 12).

2. The following deviations were observed:
   - phonemic approaches (4, 5, 7, 9, 10, 12, 13, 18, 19, 22, 26)
   - phonemic paraphasias (2, 5, 8, 10, 12, 13, 15, 16, 17, 19)
   - phonemic télescopages (23, 25)
   - formal verbal paraphasia (1, 14, 20, 21, 24)

3. The conventions for the transcriptions are given below.

Explanations to examples 1 and 2: Conventions for the transcription of Jargonaphasic samples and their English translations (Lecours et al., 1981, p. 11)

	Transcription in French	English translation
Phonemic deviations		
Phonemic approaches	IPA; within oblique slashes	Target word translated; small capitals; oblique slashes[a]
Phonemic paraphasias	IPA; within oblique slashes	Target word translated; small capitals; oblique slashes
Phonemic télescopages	IPA; within oblique slashes	Target words translated; hyphen; small capitals; oblique slashes
Formal verbal paraphasias	IPA; within vertical slashes	Paraphasic word translated; small capitals; vertical slashes
Morphemic paraphasias	IPA; within square brackets; hyphen between morphemes	IPA; within square brackets; hyphen between morphemes
Neologisms	IPA; within square brackets	IPA; within square brackets
Verbal deviations		
Semantic verbal paraphasias	Bold italics	Paraphasic word translated; bold italics
Predilection words	Italics	Predilection word translated; italics
Filler words	Italics	Filler word translated; italics
Circumlocutions	Italics	Circumlocution translated; italics
Paragrammatic deviations	Italics; within parentheses	Deviation roughly translated; italics; within parentheses
Incomplete production, with or without attempted correction	Arrow pointing down	Arrow pointing down

a Transcribed as in the French original when target word is not obvious.

Example 3: Speech sample of an agrammatic Broca type aphasic (Menn, 1989, p. 166)[1]

Primary transcription

History of illness

(Notes: Loveladies is a New Jersey shore resort not far from Philadelphia, where the patient lives. Hahnemann is a major general hospital; Moss is a rehabilitation hospital. 'Rosa' has been substituted for Mr Eastman's wife's real name.)

Examiner: Would you be willing to tell me something about what it was like when you had your stroke?

Patient: [H] I had a.stroke[4]. Blood [pʷɛ̌šr]—low [pʷɛšr][4]. Low . blood pressure[3]. Period[1]. Ah... pass out[2]. Uh ... Rosa and I, and . friends . of mine[7] ... uh ... uh ... shore[1], uh drink, talk, pass out[4]. (Gesture: slaps table; sighs, laughs softly.)

Ex: And when you woke up—where were you?

Pt: Hahnemann Hospital[2]. ... Uh uh I ... uh uh wife, Rosa[2] ... uh.take.uh. Love.ladies[2] ... uh Ocean uh Hospital an' transfer Hahnemann Hospital amb[ɛ]lance . uh . half 'n hour[10]. ... Uh uh it's[1] ... uh.motion, motion[2] ... uh.bad.patient[2]. I uh.flat on the black[5] (back). Um. It's[1].uh ... shaved, shaved[2]. Nurse . shaved me[3], uh ... shaved me[2], nurse[1]. (Sighs.) Uh. Wheel chair[2] ... uh. Hahnemann Hospital.a week, a week[6]. uh. ... Then uh strength.uh.mood.uh.up.uh.legs and arms, left side uh.weak.and[11].Moss Hospital.two week—. no, two months[7]. (Prosody suggests that missing -s on *week* might be due to breaking off word for lexical self-correction, but it is not possible to be certain.) Yeah[1].

Ex: What sort of hospital?

Pt: Yes[1], uh ... Moss Hospital[2]. Uh. Care.uh.strokes[2] uh ... various of[2] uh ... [dip—dilʌ.—dilʌderi] (rehabilitatory?) ... work[1]. (By intonation, *work* intended as a substitute for the unsuccessfully attempted previous word). (Laughs.) Polish[1]— laughs) uh n:u:c—nuclear physics[2] (laughs) uh ... Harvard[1]. (Mr Eastman uses these terms to comment sardonically on his own unintelligibility.)

(101 words, 35 'syntactic' phrases, 285 seconds, excluding Ex.'s turns)

{Ex: That's not what they told me. (Much laughter from both Ex. and Pt.) You were in business, weren't you? What sort of business?

Pt: Furniture ... business.}

Note

1. The speech sample presents the case of Mr Eastman, who was severely impaired on almost all measures of language performance. 'He omitted 125 of 403 reconstructed word slots (32%, most free grammatical morphemes), and made an additional 5 errors of substituting one category of free grammatical morpheme for another. Forty-six bound grammatical morphemes were correctly supplied, and 12 were omitted (20% of the required total of 58' (Menn, 1989, p. 124). The ability to assemble syntactic structures is limited and he produced nearly no verb embeddings.

PART TWO

Expanding the scope

The chapters in this section examine CS use in a variety of populations (monolingual and bilingual children, L1-using adults, and adult second and foreign language learners), in different modalities of language use (speaking and listening), different native and non-native languages (English, Italian, German, Spanish, Chinese), and most importantly, from different epistemological and theoretical perspectives.

In his chapter, *Lloyd* takes issue with the criticism levelled against the standard referential communication (RC) methodology in education. While acknowledging that RC tasks are 'a prime candidate for an ecological invalidity award', he sees an important role for such tasks in that they resemble the sorts of self-reliant communicative activities young school-age children have to engage in once they have left the 'Cognitive/Communicative Support System' provided by attentive caregivers in the home. A shift from reliance on others to self-reliance is a necessity for meeting the demands of language use in the classroom, requiring the fledgling schoolchild to develop 'autonomous resources'. Consistent with a neo-Vygotskian approach to the 'Zone of Proximal Development', Lloyd discusses how intervention by means of specific clarification requests can help children develop their ability as independent communicators.

It should perhaps be noted here that the emphasis on communicators' autonomy as a key to success in school and society at large may well be an Anglo-European bias. However, as Anderson (1995) demonstrates, even in a cultural context such as Japan, where elementary school education places more weight on children's ability to cooperate in joint tasks, there are still increasing demands on the child's ability to process the input independently of teachers and other students, as well as to deliver sustained autonomous oral discourse in specific speech events.

Moving from RC by monolingual children to bilinguals, *Deutsch, Bruhn, Masche and Behrens* examine grammatical and functional aspects in bilingual (German–Peruvian Spanish) children's object descriptions in comparison with those of monolingual controls. While the bilingual children were just as successful as their monolingual counterparts in functional aspects of referencing, they showed grammatical deviations from native speaker norms in Spanish but not in German. Negative transfer seemed to operate unidirectionally from their stronger language (German) to the weaker (Spanish). An interesting difference was observed between the Peruvian and German monolingual children: the German children did better initially than the Peruvian children on the RC task, the latter providing too little information for identifying the designated referent. The authors venture the hypothesis that this apparent violation of the quantity maxim may reflect a cultural preference, whereby less emphasis is given to cognitive-informative (referential) than socio-emotive dimensions of communication. This suggests that the differences found by Lloyd in his comparison of children's RC in different European countries may likewise be based in variable cultural preferences for communicative style. The issue of cross-cultural variability in RC is in dire need of more exploration since the implementation of the principles underlying RC, such as the Cooperative Principle and its maxims, may vary greatly across speech communities. It would certainly be a fallacy with severe political, social and educational repercussions to impose the communicative style favoured by a particular speech community as a universal norm against which diversity is seen as a deficit.

A concern for bilingual children's 'autonomous resources' also surfaces in *Rodino and Snow*'s chapter on distanced communication skills in working-class minority children. Just like their middle-class counterparts, the Puerto Rican children participating in this study produce longer and more elaborate picture descriptions in decontextualized than in contextualized tasks in both English and Spanish. However, the adjustments they make to the decontextualized condition are smaller, even in their stronger language, Spanish. Examining whether type of instruction has an impact on the children's distanced communication skills in their two languages, Rodino and Snow found no difference between children participating in a bilingual programme and mainstreamed children in the Spanish version of the task, while mainstreamed children performed better on most variables in English. Overall, children performed better in their weaker language, English, regardless of the type of instruction, but this difference was even greater for the mainstreamed children. This study raises important questions about maintenance and attrition of minority languages and the role of bilingual education in both, and about adequate schooling for the educational needs of minority working-class children.

The next two chapters shift the focus from child bilingualism to adult second language use, and from reference to lexis. *Duff* examines the lexical search processes that an adult learner of Mandarin Chinese as a second language engages in while carrying out a conversation. Based on a localist-connectionist model for the analysis of on-line processing and a spreading activation model of lexical access, Duff notes that success in lexical search during discourse production hinges critically on efficient activation of interconnected semantic and lexical features. Such connections may be inhibited through language choice, speaker's intention, discourse constraints and sociolinguistics factors.

Turning from lexical production to comprehension, the chapter by *Ross* investigates the inferencing strategies used by Japanese learners of English in a picture identification task. Immediately consecutive verbal reports reveal that learners attempt to establish links between the aural stimulus and the visual icon at both syllabus and key word level, an approach which can be accounted for in terms of the logogen model of lexical storage and retrieval. More proficient listeners were able to integrate more aural stimuli elements into a referential schema; due to larger short-term memory capacity, they were also able to process more complex input cues when scanning the input for referent candidates. For both the highest and lowest proficiency listeners, the key word processing provided the main input to inferencing strategies, serving as a short-cut for the most proficient listeners and as a processing constraint for the lowest proficiency group.

The last chapter in this section serves as a bridge between psycholinguistic and sociolinguistic perspectives on CS use. *Wilkes-Gibbs* reviews the literature on an approach to referential communication which views listening and speaking in conversational interaction as a collaborative process. Echoing earlier cognitive-sociological approaches (e.g., Cicourel, 1972), the fundamental tenet is that in order to coordinate their actions successfully, conversationalists operate on assumptions about mutual beliefs which they establish initially and subsequently adjust in their contributions to on-line interaction. Following a principle of least collaborative effort, understanding is accomplished when interlocutors display mutual agreement that their current goals are achieved. Importantly, as Wilkes-Gibbs demonstrates, it is not the individual participant's goals but *both* interlocutors' purposes that explain just how much and what kinds of conversational activity are expended.

In theoretical terms, the collaborative principle thus presents an important extension of the principles of cooperation and satisficing discussed by Poulisse in Part I, in that it specifies the procedures adopted by conversationalists when negotiating referential goals. By explaining how knowledge is mutually assumed and interactively constructed, collaborative theory contrasts with the 'single agent' view of RC discussed earlier, which emphasized how individual speakers or listeners bring to bear their autonomous resources on a communication task. At the same time, the approach is cognitive-interactional rather than sociolinguistic because it views conversational participants as collaborators in a joint task rather than as agents in social settings and relationships. Collaborative theory thus 'retains its psychological flavour', as Wilkes-Gibbs comments.

6

Developing the ability to evaluate verbal information: the relevance of referential communication research

PETER LLOYD

Introduction

It is well known that language is used in different ways in different interpersonal and physical contexts. We do not usually speak to the bank manager in the manner and tone that we do to our children. Dialogue in a courtroom is different from that round a dinner table. Aside from these specific examples, there are general claims that can be made about the form and content of communication as a function of context. I wish to examine one of these claims that refers to the sociolinguistic validity of work in the referential communication tradition. The claim, forcefully put by Erickson (1981), is that the results of research into speaker and listener skills are undermined by the artificiality of the paradigm used. Because interpersonal communication is an enterprise in which meaning is socially negotiated, any context which deliberately ignores that fact is of very limited value.

I wish to argue that Erickson is correct in his criticism of the referential communication paradigm but wrong to conclude that the mode is without utility. What is special about referential communication (hereafter, RC) experiments is the onus they put on the *individual* speaker and listener to make the communication situation work. This serves an important purpose in revealing how autonomous resources are organized to solve the encoding and decoding demands of a RC task. In this context, autonomous resources refer to the ability to process verbal information without help from another. It is hypothesized that it is frequently the case in RC tasks that success requires that participants can *detect* inadequacy in what they say or hear, *evaluate* the nature of the inadequacy and try to *resolve* it. They must accomplish this for themselves. The sort of collaborative model described by Clark and Wilkes-Gibbs (1986) is not an option for them.

When placed in a developmental framework, this perspective allows an understanding of the growth of the ability to handle verbal information. A further claim is that the results of RC research are relevant to the educational domain since language in the classroom is not dissimilar to conversation in the RC experiment. Finally, the argument will come full circle by pointing out that there is a place for what might be called 'the rules of normal discourse' to impact on the communication skills approach. That place is in the planning of intervention strategies for helping children who show defects in their speaker and listener behaviour.

The classroom analogy

On the face of it, the RC task would seem to be a prime candidate for an ecological invalidity award. The task uses simple sets of pictorial materials which tap a restricted conceptual and lexical domain such as colour, size, number and form. This, in turn, generates rather simple descriptions on the part of the speaker – adjectival strings such as 'the big, red, square one' – and limited responses on the part of the listener – selecting a referent. As if this was not enough, the whole enterprise is carried on with a screen erected between the participants since only the verbal medium is of interest. I have offered my own criticisms of this approach (Lloyd, 1990; Lloyd et al., 1992) and so will not reiterate them here. What I wish to do, instead, is explain why this apparently barren approach to communication is of value.

The main advantage of the RC approach is that it offers an opportunity to examine the capacity to make sense of oral language in the absence of the supportive framework that characterizes everyday conversation. This is especially important from a developmental perspective since it is still by no means clear how children develop the ability to use language effectively when calling primarily on their own independent resources.

It is generally accepted that the development of communication is greatly assisted by the contribution of the expert interlocutor. Dialogue would not begin unless caregivers were prepared initially to hold up both ends of the conversation. Although the degree of scaffolding begins to be dismantled during the preschool years, the child starting school remains accustomed to communicative support in the home.[1] I have characterized this as a Cognitive/Communicative Support System (CoSS) (Lloyd, 1990) which is best understood in the context of a parent engaging in joint activity with the child. The functions which this system provides include the following:

- *Directing.* Focusing the child's attention on what is relevant rather than merely salient.
- *Organizing.* Introducing information at the appropriate time and at a rate that can be absorbed by the child.
- *Simplifying.* Filtering and interpreting information for the child.
- *Defining.* Defining terms whose meaning is unknown or obscure to the child.
- *Storing.* Holding in working memory and long-term store items beyond the child's capacity.
- *Reminding.* Reminding the child of what is known and what needs to be known, that is, keeping the goal in sight.
- *Sounding out.* Providing a sounding board against which the child can test out hypotheses.
- *Monitoring.* Alerting the child to communicative success and failure.
- *Prompting.* Shifting the child to an alternative procedure when the present procedure is failing.
- *Supporting.* Providing emotional support – praise for success, commiseration for failure, and encouragement to continue.

The presence of such a system in the home, which supplements the child's as yet limited cognitive and communicative resources, is the main reason why the verbal environment in the classroom is a difficult one for the newcomer. A one-to-one, familiar, cooperative context is exchanged for a one-to-many, unfamiliar, relatively unsupportive situation.

A successful user of language in the classroom must be able to appraise the incoming information and construct the appropriate responses to questions asked. As David Wood puts it: 'The use of language to narrate, inform, explain and instruct involves a range of linguistic and intellectual skills in planning and self-monitoring that are *not* a "natural" product of most everyday talk' (Wood, 1988, p. 218). Even though they are skilled communicators with children, teachers cannot monitor the particular linguistic needs and peculiarities – what we might call the verbal micro-environment – of each individual child. It is inevitable, therefore, that children who have problems evaluating the input and formulating utterances are not always going to be noticed. What would appear to be needed in order to address this situation is a clear characterization of the verbal demands of the classroom. And it is in this respect that RC research may have a significant contribution to make. Put bluntly, and to somewhat overstate the case, if we know what a child can achieve in the unsupportive context of the RC task, we have a reasonable idea of what is possible in the classroom.

Speaker and listener skills

It is, of course, an oversimplification to equate the RC experiment with the classroom. There are many more variables contributing to the school dynamic, such as the activity being pursued and the influence of classmates. Nevertheless, in so far as both contexts put the emphasis on autonomous resources, knowing what is typical speaker and listener competence at the beginning of school can inform the applied field.

There are a number of consistent findings which will be briefly summarized. As speakers, young children are relatively successful at discriminating critical features in a referential array and including them in their descriptive message. The larger the array, and the more subtle the differentiating attributes, the more likely it is that information-processing demands will degrade the message provided. If the critical dimension taps a lexical or conceptual area which is cognitively insecure, such as spatial relationships, inadequate descriptions will result. A good speaker is successful at editing messages so that helpful, criterial information is to the fore and unhelpful, redundant material is eliminated or, at least, consigned to a supporting role. Effective speakers are also good at attending to the needs of their listeners. It is here that early school-age children begin to show limitations. If the initial message they provide is insufficient in some way to satisfy the hearer, they should be in a position to remedy the situation by repeating or reformulating the message, as appropriate. The fact that this aspect of speaker competence is incomplete at five years is explained by the level of understanding of the communication process that is present. Thus, if asked why communication failed in a RC trial, that is, the referents of speaker and listener did not match, five-year-old children will attribute blame to the listener (Robinson & Robinson, 1976). This judgement is given whether the child is a speaker or listener at the time, and whether or not the original message is adequate.

Research into listener skills shows that once children understand that in communication tasks their response is contingent on the message they receive, they are usually successful in identifying referents described by adequate messages. Before this idea is grasped, it is not uncommon for the referent to be selected before the speaker has finished (or even started) the message. Listeners' problems become evident, however, as soon as a message is inadequate in some way. Children's understanding of ambiguity has been particularly well researched. Messages that refer to more than one referential item are ambiguous. In the experimental situation the listener is told that:

1. Their goal is to find the item that matches the speaker's selection.
2. They may not know which one to choose since the speaker may sometimes not tell them enough.
3. If they are not sure which one to choose, they are welcome to ask the speaker any questions they wish until they are satisfied that they have the correct object.

Despite the explicitness of these instructions, it is well established that an appreciation of message ambiguity is a concept that eludes five-year-olds. Why this should be is discussed later. First, however, since children in the classroom are mainly consumers, rather than providers, of information, the results of research in this area are of particular interest. Accordingly, some data from a recent study, carried out simultaneously in the UK and Italy, will be presented by way of illustration (Lloyd et al., 1995).

A comparative study

The study used a typical RC task with sets of familiar pictures varying on specific features. For example, a set of four clowns that differed in the colour of their collar and the type of hat worn. One hundred and twenty-eight children were tested, 64 each in Rome and Manchester. These were equally divided for age (six and nine years), sex and socio-economic status (middle and lower SES). Speaker and listener performance were tested but the focus here is on their ability as listeners and since very few errors were made in either age group when messages were unambiguous, attention will be confined to how they dealt with ambiguous messages.

Children were given the instructions outlined above by an adult who also provided the messages. Thus, in the clowns example, if the message was 'The clown with the top hat', the children should want to know the colour of the collar. When children asked appropriate questions the missing information was supplied. Children who thought they already knew the target item were asked if they were sure that they knew. Children who showed uncertainty or gave no response were given a series of feedbeck prompts, including repetition of the message and questions like 'Do you know which one it is?' The aim was to allow the children the opportunity to detect and disambiguate the message through their own efforts if possible. This meant that more information would be provided if the child requested it.

A scoring system was devised to reflect the amount of help that subjects received. For our purposes responses can be divided into three categories.

1. The child was able to detect and resolve message ambiguity by securing the missing information through questioning.
2. The message was disambiguated but only after feedback from the tester, including repetition of the message and various prompts (e.g., Are you sure you know?).
3. No recognition of message ambiguity. Even after feedback, items were selected erroneously based on the original inadequate message.

It can be seen from Table 6.1 that the older children achieved, on average, a better level of ambiguity detection than younger children but it was by no means perfect. Indeed, combining the two national samples, only about one-half of the nine-year-olds were in the first category. This means that 50 per cent of the older children were unable to deal effectively with simple ambiguity without assistance. Furthermore, about 17 per cent of responses were in category 3, showing no recognition of message inadequacy. At six years this behaviour was writ large with the majority of responses being of this type.

Table 6.1 Distribution of listener response categories to ambiguous messages as a function of age and nationality (%)

Response category	Italian		English	
	6 years	9 years	6 years	9 years
1	29.2	35.9	34.4	66.4
2	22.9	40.6	4.2	5.5
3	38.5	15.6	57.3	18.7
Other	9.4	7.9	4.1	9.4

These findings indicate that a majority of children were unable to cope with a simple level of ambiguity in oral messages using their own autonomous resources. When a more stringent criterion was used – the number of children who *consistently* detected ambiguity – only 10 per cent of six-year-olds and about 20 per cent of nine-year-olds could be considered effective processors of oral information. If these findings are replicated, and a larger-scale study is underway, it will signal the need for not only a reliable test of speaker and listener skill but also procedures for remediation.

A further result from this study revealed a learning effect that interacted with nationality. It was found that, in general, children improved their performance across the course of three trials. However, the rate of improvement was much more dramatic for the Italian children. As can be seen from Table 6.1, Italian children showed a much higher incidence of the response category 2. When the effect over trials is added, the picture that emerges – across both ages – is that English children were better at detecting ambiguity unaided at the start of the task but that they did not substantially improve performance over trials. In contrast, the Italians had a low initial detection rate but responded to feedback so that by the end of the task they were performing at about the same level as their English counterparts.[2] The implications of this result for intervention programmes will be discussed shortly.

Factors contributing to communication failure

The argument thus far is that RC research, despite the adoption of an apparently limited, artificial paradigm, has the merit of focusing on how an individual processes language in a largely self-reliant mode. Since the classroom is a location where there is a premium on being able independently to evaluate verbal information – for clarity, ambiguity, level of comprehension, etc. – the analogy between the psychological experiment and the applied setting is worth pursuing. The findings that have been briefly reviewed show that though there is a sense in which speaker and listener capacity is entrenched at the start of formal schooling, important further development continues, certainly up until nine years. Recent evidence, in fact, indicates that there is steady growth from five to 11 years.[3]

In order to assess how children may be aided in their ability to evaluate verbal messages, I will now consider some work that has focused on the factors that account for communication failure. This work arose from dissatisfaction with the standard paradigm for investigating RC to which I have already alluded. The work sought to address what were perceived to be limitations in the *task* used, the *medium* of communication, the *relationship* between participants and the language *measures* employed. These were redressed by using a map task (see Figure 6.1) in which a route across a village community, the actual route being available to only one member of the dyad, had to be described so giving a purposive goal for the participants. Instead of talking through screens, communication was by telephone, a medium intended for purely verbal dialogue. In addition, the participants were pairs of children or adults, completely removing the possibly disturbing influence of the experimenter from the interaction. Finally, in assessing performance, attention went beyond referential outcomes to look at the nature of the discourse to see what it uncovered about communication success and failure.

There are three principal points to be made about this programme of work. First, as soon as a task is complicated slightly, it becomes evident that there is more than one way of solving that task. In the map task some children chose to adopt the standard RC practice of describing attributes of the landmark array (e.g., 'The church with a tower'). Another strategy was to refer to the numerical location ('Go to the second house'). A more sophisticated strategy, especially favoured by adults, was to use typical directions for helping someone to find their way (e.g., 'Turn right, then go straight on until you come to a garage'). Although the above strategies were not guaranteed to work, they all carried the potential of success. This was in contrast to a fourth strategy,

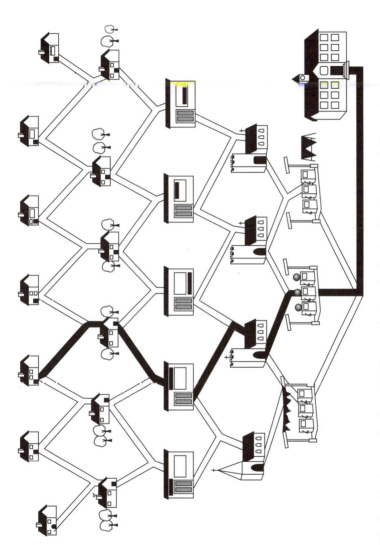

Figure 6.1 'Map' used in the route finding task with example route (available only to the reader) illustrated.
Acknowledgement: This map is adapted from an original that appeared in *Concept Seven-Nine*, published by E. J. Arnold & Son Ltd for The Schools Council.

referred to as Minimal (Lloyd, 1991), which contained no useful route finding information ('Go to the garage, then the church, then the shop, etc.').

A further feature of strategy use was that communicators would combine to produce a conjunction of strategies that would carry more force than the single strategy. This corresponds closely to what Clark and Wilkes-Gibbs (1986) called the collaborative model of communication.

(1) Route instructor: Go up and then left
      Route follower: To the second house?
      Route instructor: Yes, with a tree by it.

In (1) three strategies are in evidence. From a strict RC standpoint, this constitutes redundancy but in the context of a task that could be said to have stronger claims to ecological validity, 'redundancy' represented good practice. Furthermore, successful communication did not terminate either on the passing of an accurate message or on the identification of the referent. In practice, participants continued exchanges *after* what might have been considered the end of the task in RC terms (Lloyd, 1993).

The second point to make is that in more complex situations the role of the listener is vital. Since it is rare for anyone to be at all times lucid and completely unambiguous when conveying information, the listener must be perpetually alert to problems of understanding. These were revealed most obviously in the use of clarification requests. The results showed that the largest degree of communication success was significantly correlated with the use of potential requests for clarification (Garvey, 1979). These are requests that introduce information that was not present in the original message as in the Follower's utterance in (2).

(2) Instructor: Go to the one with the line across
      Follower: In the window or at the top?
      Instructor: The one with the line across at the top, the second one

Results showed that ten-year-old children provided more potential requests for clarification, as against simple requests for repetition or confirmation, than seven-year-olds. Moreover, these requests were very closely correlated (0.86) with the number of inadequate messages received (as judged by independent coders). The correlation coefficient for seven-year-olds was much lower (Lloyd, 1992).

The third finding to be highlighted from the map and telephone task is the dynamics of the interaction process. One of the studies paired mothers with their own children in one condition (related) and with children with whom they had no ties in the other condition (unrelated) (Lloyd, 1993). It was found that although overall task success was not affected by the relatedness variable, the strategies used by related pairs were much more highly correlated than those used by each member of the unrelated pair. Mothers and their children tended to use the same types of strategy when each was in the role of Instructor. In this sense they seemed to be 'tuned-in' to one another. The strategies of unrelated pairs did not match so closely. In addition, there was an effect over time. In the first of the four trials the adults were producing the majority of clarification requests. This difference reduced over time so that by the last trial children and adults were equally contributing in requests made. In so far as this is a measure of task control, it indicates how control can be relinquished by adults and assumed by children in appropriate context-sensitive circumstances.

A tentative approach to intervention

In the final part of this chapter I will show how the results from the more conversational-style communication tasks can inform the conventional, more restricted RC tasks. We have seen that, even in the standard task, there is scope for improvement given that feedback is offered and accepted. In the standard task, however, there is relatively little opportunity for negotiation, circumscribed as it is by a tight procedure and the use of screens. Nevertheless, one national group, the Italians, made more use of the opportunities than the other group. But still, it must be kept in mind that the onus for repairing communication breakdown in classroom contexts falls largely on the child. Therefore, procedures for inculcating that capacity are essential in any training programme that is proposed.

Making requests for clarification is a key part of resolving inadequate communication. Because the classroom environment provides only limited opportunities for posing those questions, it is important that whenever possible, the effective, information-loaded, *potential* clarification requests are used rather than the informationally empty simple requests like What? and How? The way to achieve this has not been fully formulated, but there are some pointers. It is known that children's performance as listeners improves when simply instructed to ask questions (Patterson & Kister, 1981). But, at the risk of labouring the point, some questions are more effective than others. A training procedure that models proper questioning strategies for children who persistently fail to detect ambiguity in messages can help (Pratt & Bates, 1982). Since the model cannot be carried around by children, it must be internalized and be capable of being 'switched on' when required. The type of self-regulating techniques advocated by Meichenbaum (1985) also resonates with neo-Vygotskian procedures that have been tried within a framework like the Zone of Proximal Development (Brown & Ferrara, 1985).[4]

The test of RC skills that is jointly being developed in Manchester and Rome also has as part of its goal a training package. The intervention procedure involves a number of steps:

1. Focus on the procedural knowledge that is necessary to understand that some messages are 'good' – refer to a unique item – and some are 'poor' – refer to more than one item. This means, initially, recognizing how message attributes map on to real-world features. The starting point is simple, familiar pictorial arrays. Once the information-carrying features of the array are determined and, if necessary, the reasons for rejecting redundant features are adumbrated, a modelling process can begin.

2. Unambiguous and ambiguous messages are presented and, having indicated why a good message is acceptable (it achieves its aim), the steps that must follow the articulation of an ambiguous message are explained.

(i) Show how an ambiguous message defines more than one item.
(ii) How can the item pool be reduced?
(iii) By asking appropriate question(s).
(iv) Appropriate questions are those which discover the identity of the missing attributes.
(v) What are the missing attributes?
(vi) What questions should therefore be asked?

3. The procedure set out in (2) must be repeated as often as required for the child to start to produce the required responses spontaneously. This may not be achieved in one remedial session.

The aim is to develop an internal 'programme' that is alert to the possibility of message inadequacy and knows why it is important. Through the process of comprehension monitoring, once an inadequate signal is detected, a plan has to be put into action which will evaluate the message and resolve the communication failure. This will require going through something like the steps given in (2) above.

4. Demonstrations of the success of the intervention procedure will require extending the band-width of competence by using a range of communication materials. It is likely to be beyond the scope of one package to include both the simple situations which model the basic concept and the types of communication problem-solving situations that are encountered in the upper end of primary school. For example, increasingly, the verbal information that the child hears does not have a concrete referent. The tripartite detection–evaluation–resolution process that has to be applied to messages is clearly more demanding at an abstract level. Instead of being at least partially present, the information must be held in whatever amount of working memory is available. It is likely that the acquisition of literacy and the growth of text evaluation skills interact with oral information processing to refine the more maturely functioning system (Bonitatibus, 1988).

Conclusion

The position advocated here is that major discontinuities between, say, communication in the classroom and communication in the playground do not exist; nor do they exist between communication in the psychological experiment and communication in the home. On the contrary, there are important continuities which serve to inform the different contexts. Nevertheless, because support, which is a feature of the asymmetrical communication system between younger and older speakers, does change according to context, one of the developmental lessons that have to be learned is that the responsibility for making sense of verbal communication eventually must become a personal one.

One of the reasons that this is difficult is that two types of communication exist side by side, illustrated by the supportive (CoSS) home context and less supportive classroom context. There is evidence to suggest that some parents are better than others in helping children to manage the transition between the socially supported and the independent modes (Robinson and Whittaker, 1986). The reason that discontinuity is an inappropriate way of looking at this transition is because the support system does not simply drop away. Instead it is internalized. It has to be 'carried around' so that conversations now take place in the head, rather like step 2 in the intervention programme. This means that successful dealers in the commodity of verbal information enact such a procedure whenever communication enters a realm that places demands beyond those of freely negotiated natural dialogue.

Notes

1. While this generalization holds for many societies, it is not universal. Heath (1983), for example, has shown that in some communities children are hardly spoken to by their parents in the early years. More controversially, it has been suggested that socio-economic status (SES) is influential and that lower SES children grow up in an environment that is less supportive linguistically. (See Edwards (1979) for a balanced review and evidence from Wells (1983) that casts doubt on the linguistic deficit position.)

2. It is possible only to speculate about the reasons for this result. Foorman and Kinoshita (1983) compared the performance of Japanese- and English-speaking children on RC tasks. They found the Japanese superior and attributed it to the greater flexibility of adjectival ordering in Japanese. Italian is a predominantly noun–adjective language in contrast to the adjective–noun order of English. If anything, Italian is more flexible than English but, since the results are in the opposite direction, this explanation is not supported. More relevant, possibly, are cultural differences. It has been observed that Italian classrooms are more verbal and more supportive, which may explain both the greater amount of redundancy that was found and the tendency to rely on adult feedback. (Lloyd et al., 1995).

3. An ongoing study is looking at speaker and listener skills from five to 11 years. Six hundred children are being tested and already, with one-third of the data analysed, it has been found that speaker score rises steadily from a success rate of 40 per cent at age five, 70 per cent at age eight, to 90 per cent at age 11. Listener scores on ambiguous messages start at a lower base but show the same line of growth: 20 per cent at five, 50 per cent at eight, and 75 per cent at 11. Significantly, ceiling is not reached by the end of primary school.

4. The Zone of Proximal Development is used by Vygotsky (1978) to refer to the additional intellectual capacity that children can show when given some help. It is not enough to assess children's individual performance as revealed, for example, in mental tests. Given that development is conceived as taking place within a social framework, it is appropriate that children also be evaluated when working alongside a supportive other. All children, therefore, have both an 'actual' and 'potential' cognitive level.

7

Can one be more than two? Mono- and bilinguals' production of German and Spanish object descriptions in a referential communication task

WERNER DEUTSCH, NANCI BRUHN, GOWERT MASCHE
and HEIKE BEHRENS

1. Scope and aims of the study

From the very beginning, research on language acquisition has been dominated by single case studies in which children's approximations to one or more target languages (monolingual or multilingual first language acquisition) or adults' efforts to learn a foreign language (second language acquisition) are documented over a certain span of time. There are good reasons to continue this line of research, since it is difficult, for example, to find homogeneous groups of children or adults for comparative purposes, especially in the realm of bilingualism. Bilingualism itself is so heterogeneous that comparisons across subjects, languages, countries, social classes etc., are difficult to make. Our study may represent an exception since it involves a relatively homogeneous group of 19 children between age five and eight who are growing up with two first languages, German and Hispanoamericano. The children and their families live in or around Braunschweig, Germany. The children's mothers were born and grew up either in South America, Mexico or Spain. Nearly all the families were established outside Germany. The fathers grew up in Germany with German as their first language. They later acquired Spanish as a second language in which most of them became fairly fluent. Many of the children regularly visit their mothers' country of origin during vacations. In Germany the children speak Spanish with their mothers but otherwise German. The families' social background is upper middle class. They support and promote the bilingual development of their children.

In contrast to mainstream research on bilingualism, we are going to focus on a developmental snapshot instead of a longitudinal assessment, and on a particular linguistic fragment instead of a linguistic system. We will be investigating the production of noun phrases modified by colour and size adjectives in German and Spanish. First, we will discuss the theoretical background of our empirical enterprise. Then we will see what inferences can be drawn from a comparative study of the production of German and Spanish noun phrases at a particular point in the children's development.

1.1 Theoretical considerations: structural differences between German and Spanish noun phrases

There is a fundamental structural difference between German and Spanish noun phrases. When noun phrases are modified by one or more adjectives, the noun precedes the adjective(s) in Spanish but follows in German. The prenominal and postnominal word order of adjectival modifications is illustrated in the following examples:

(1) German
Das kleine blaue Auto.
(The small blue car.)

(2) Spanish
El coche pequeño azul.
(The car small blue.)

Examples (1) and (2) are standard forms of modified noun phrases. In Spanish there is another option, in which the colour attribute is expressed by a prepositional phrase, as indicated in (3):

(3) Spanish
El coche pequeño de color azul.
(The car small of colour blue.)

Differences between German and Spanish noun phrases are not exclusively related to word order in adjectival noun phrase modifications. Both languages have gender systems which are dependent on the gender of the noun. Spanish distinguishes between masculine and feminine gender, while German distinguishes between masculine, feminine and neuter. Gender-marking is expressed by determiners; for example the German neuter definite article is 'das' in (1) and the Spanish masculine definite article is 'el' in (2) and (3). Gender-marking is also expressed in the forms of modifying adjectives. These forms depend on the (gender-marked) forms of the determiner system. In German, determiners and adjectives are also used for case-marking, a feature absent in Spanish. There are only certain cases where gender- and case-marking can be distinguished in German. Otherwise they are confounded. Examples (1), (2) and (3) have one characteristic in common: the size attribute precedes the colour attribute. Some studies (e.g., Ertel, 1971; Pechmann, 1989, 1994; Sichelschmidt, 1989; Vendler, 1968) have shown that this ordering is the preferred, if not the only possible word order in German and other languages. Even adult native speakers deviate under certain circumstances from the canonical pattern. The same holds true for Spanish, although we have been unable to find any systematic studies of this issue.[1]

Are our bilingual children able to produce Spanish and German modified noun phrases that meet the respective requirements of each of the two target languages? Do their errors tend to fall into certain categories? Do errors in one language occur more often than in the other? According to E. Clark's (1985) overview of language development for the Romance languages and Mills' (1985) overview for German, monolingual children tend to have mastered the syntax and morphology of complex noun phrases by around the age 5–6. Does the linguistic development of our 19 bilingual children deviate from the normal (monolingual) course of development? If problems occur at all in our bilingual sample, we expect them in one direction. Various authors (e.g., Romaine, 1989) have emphasized that bilingual status is asymmetrical in the vast majority of bilingual speakers, and in particular children, because the linguistic environment is usually biased towards one of the two (or more) languages. Certainly, this is the case in our 19 bilingual children too. In these children, the use of Spanish is limited to interactions with their mothers. The majority of the other interactions occur in German if the children are not visiting their relatives in Spanish-speaking countries. During those visits the dominance relations between the two languages may be reversed.

What is the appropriate standard of comparison in studies of bilingual development? Does the target structure of the language(s) involved provide the only and best criterion? The notion of target structure is usually based either on a prescriptive idea or an idealized version of a native speaker's performance in that language (cf. Deutsch, 1989). In this case, bilinguals' performance is certainly underestimated in relation to other (developing) speakers' linguistic production. A more appropriate standard of comparison can be found in monolingual control groups. In our study, we recruited a group of German-speaking monolingual children who attend the same kindergarten and the same school as the bilingual children. However, the selection of a Spanish-speaking control group constituted a serious problem. It would have been impossible to find a group of the same age and similar social background in the country where the bilingual children live. Furthermore, one has to consider the fact that the bilinguals speak a variant of Spanish, Hispanoamericano, which is not common in Europe. So a control group of European (Spanish) children was out of the question. Our solution was to select a control group of monolingual children from Lima (Peru), who are growing up speaking Hispanoamericano.

No doubt our choice is not an ideal one, since the composition of the control group does not reflect the countries where the mothers of the bilingual children come from. We have to be aware of the fact that the Spanish-speaking control group is more homogeneous than it should be. Practical reasons, however, preclude other choices. Nevertheless, the two control groups do permit the comparison of bi- and monolinguals' production of noun phrases at the same chronological point in development.

1.2 Methodological considerations

In this study, we use a referential communication task to elicit (modified) noun phrases in German and Spanish. Referential communication tasks have been widely used in psychological research in the last 30 years. They were first used in developmental psychology (Glucksberg et al., 1966), and later, mainly inspired by Olson's (1970) theoretical analysis, they came into vogue in adult psycholinguistics (e.g., Clark & Wilkes-Gibbs, 1986; Herrmann & Deutsch, 1976) to study the cognitive and linguistic (sub-) processes underlying the production of communicatively adequate object references. The referential communication task has also been used in studies of second language use and development (e.g., Bongaerts et al., 1987; Poulisse, 1990). Typically, such tasks require a subject to identify a given object from an array of objects, frequently on the basis of a set of instructions provided by a partner who is visually separated by an opaque screen. The version of the referential communication task in this study follows Deutsch and Pechmann (1982).

In contrast to other versions of the referential communication task, in the task reported here the interlocutors could see each other and the relevant set of objects. Moreover, standardized routines of requests for specification will come into play when the subjects' object references do not allow the identification of the intended (target) object on the basis of the initial description alone. The reason why referential communication tasks are especially useful in studying the production of modified noun phrases is that in normal discourse noun phrases are difficult to evaluate in terms of their intended domain of reference and their communicative function. Referential communication tasks introduce standardized conditions in which the extensional and intensional features of a referential domain are explicitly controlled and varied. This allows for an objective assessment of the content, forms and function of object references in a communicative setting. Comparisons among groups are possible, because each member of a group produces his or her object reference under the same structural and functional conditions. Our comparisons concern both structural and functional aspects of object references. The structural aspects have already been outlined earlier.

Is it possible to make any predictions as far as functional differences between bi- and monolingual groups of children are concerned? We might speculate that being brought up in more than one language stimulates children's ability to meet the needs and demands of the interlocutor in a communication task. This one-sided hypothesis about the difference between bi- and monolinguals is based on the fact that children growing up in two languages experience the necessity from early on to select a communicative system that is appropriate for and successful with a certain interlocutor. We will see whether our assumption that bilingual children are sensitive to the addressees' communicative needs can be found in our subjects' object references in both languages or whether this is limited to the dominant language. In our analysis we will distinguish between initial object references which are elicited by the experimenter's question, and specifications of initial object references at the request of the addressee. The latter responses indicate the speaker's ability to deal with feedback, while the initial object references reflect his or her *a priori* sensitivity to the addressee's situation in a referential communication task. Referential communication tasks provide a biased picture of the development of referential abilities, since they are restricted to the introduction of a single object within an array of similar objects. Maintenance and re introduction of reference fall outside this research paradigm.

2. Method

2.1 Subjects

The sample consisted of 60 children, aged 5;0 to 8;0. It was divided into three groups. Each group involved a younger (kindergarten children) and an older (elementary school children) subgroup. The bilingual group consisted of ten children (8 girls and 2 boys) aged between 5 and 6 and nine children (5 girls and 4 boys) aged between 7 and 8. These children live in and around Braunschweig, Germany. The mothers are natives of South American countries, Mexico and Spain, and their first language is Spanish, principally Hispanoamericano. Almost all the families were established outside Germany. The fathers are natives of Germany with German as their first language. Both parents are fluent speakers of both German and Spanish. In communicating with their mothers, the children speak Spanish, while German is used in kindergarten, school and in contact with their fathers. During vacations the children usually visit relatives of their mothers. On such occasions only Spanish is used in interactions. Bilingualism is both highly valued and practised in the predominantly middle-class and upper middle-class families of these 19 children.

The monolingual German-speaking group (n=20) consisted of ten children (6 girls and 4 boys) aged between 5 and 6 and ten children (8 girls and 2 boys) aged between 7 and 8. The younger subgroup attends a kindergarten in Brunswick which is located in an (upper) middle-class area, while the older subgroup attends a Catholic elementary school. It is also located in an (upper) middle-class area of Braunschweig. According to information from the kindergarten and elementary school teachers all 20 children are growing up in German-speaking monolingual families.

The monolingual Spanish-speaking group (n=21) consisted of eight children (2 girls and 6 boys) aged between 5 and 6, and 13 children (9 girls and 4 boys) aged between 7 and 8. They live in Lima (Peru) and were attending a private summer camp situated in an (upper) middle-class area. All 60 children participated as volunteers, after the parents and institutions had been informed about our study. The children received small gifts for having participated.

2.2   *Tasks, materials and procedure*

The subjects' task was to refer to one object out of a set of four objects presented by the experimenter, who elicits the production of an object reference as an answer to the question:

German: Was findest Du am schönsten?
         (What do you like best?)
Spanish ¿Cual prefieres?
         (Which do you prefer?)

If the experimenter could not identify the intended referent, she repeated the given object description in question form. These requests for specification are usually very effective. For example, Deutsch and Pechmann (1982) have shown that children from two years onwards appear to be able to specify ambiguous object references on request. Given a set of four objects only, differing in colour and size, two requests for specification may suffice to reach mutual understanding. After two unsuccessful requests, the experimenter turned to more specific Yes–No questions to finish the particular trial. When the object reference was produced in a piecemeal fashion, the experimenter asked the subject to sum up the pieces of information in one utterance. These utterances were sometimes crucial for evaluating grammatical errors in the production of noun phrases.

The material consisted of ten sets of objects. Each set involved four objects differing in size and colour. Unambiguous descriptions of any one of these objects require a double-modified noun phrase in which the colour and the size of the target object is expressed. Object-class provides redundant information, since each object within a set of four is an exemplar of the same object-dass.

Table 7.1 Composition of the object sets in the referential communication tasks

Object set	Class	Colour	Size
1	(die) Puppe (la) muñeca *(the) doll*	rosa/blau rosado/azul *pink/blue*	groß/klein grande/pequeña *big/small*
2	(die) Maske (la) máscara *(the) mask*	schwarz/gelb negro/amarillo *black/yellow*	groß/klein grande/pequeña *big/small*
3	(das) Auto (el) coche *(the) car*	blau/rot azul/rojo *blue/red*	groß/klein grande/pequeña *big/small*
4	(der) Bär (el) oso *(the) bear*	braun/gelb marron/amarillo *brown/yellow*	groß/klein grande/pequeña *big/small*
5	(die) Schleife (el) lazo *(the) ribbon*	grün/blau verde/azul *green/blue*	groß/klein grande/pequeña *big/small*
6	(die) Blume (la) flor *(the) flower*	gelb/blau amarillo/azul *yellow/blue*	groß/klein grande/pequeña *big/small*
7	(das) Kerze (la) vela *(the) candle*	weiß/blau blanco/azul *white/blue*	groß/klein grande/pequeña *big/small*
8	(die) Vase (el) florero *(the) vase*	grün/Weiß verde/blanco *green/white*	groß/klein grande/pequeña *big/small*
9	(die) Seife (el) jabón *(the) soap*	grün/weiß verde/blanco *green/white*	groß/klein grande/pequeña *big/small*
10	(die) Schachtel (la) caja *(the) box*	rot/schwarz rojo/negro *red/black*	groß/klein grande/pequeña *big/small*

The task was preceded by two training trials with two sets of objects differing in shape, size and colour. Here, the subjects became familiar with the setting and the function of the utterances in a referential communication task. Experimenters were bilingual speakers of German and Spanish who used one language only during the task.

The data were collected at a kindergarten and a private house in Braunschweig, a school in Braunschweig, and a summer camp in Lima during the spring and summer of 1989. Experimenter and subject were seated opposite each other, each with a table in front of them. The distance between the interlocutors was about three metres (ten feet). A microphone was set up on the table in front of the subject, connected to a cassette recorder on the floor close by. The table in front of the experimenter was used to display the sets of the four objects one after the other for the referential communication task. On each side of the table there were two boxes. One box contained the material to be presented; the other one contained the previously presented material. The task itself was embedded into a game in which the subject was asked to help the experimenter to prepare a parcel to be sent to children in Brazil. Each parcel could only contain one object selected from each presented set of four objects. The child's task was to indicate his or her target object within the set. Because of the distance between the children and the presented objects only linguistic descriptions were effective in identifying the subject's target referent. All the monolingual children were tested once in their native language; all the bilingual children participated in the referential communication task twice, with an interval of about 30 minutes during which they had no contact with other subjects in the study. The presentation of the ten sets of objects was randomly determined for each subject. Furthermore, the order of presentation of the German and the Spanish versions of the task was unsystematically varied. It took about 20 minutes to carry out the task with the monolinguals and the first session with the bilingual children. The second session with the bilingual children took about seven minutes less time.

2.3   Data transcription and coding

Transcriptions were made of the discourse recorded during the referential communication task. Children's initial object references after the presentation of an object set were submitted to further functional and grammatical analyses, as were the outcomes of object specifications on request. Utterances summarizing pieces of successively produced descriptions were used to assess grammatical aspects of the subjects' noun phrases. Two independent teams coded the data. There were minor differences in coding between the two teams, but these had no impact on the results of the statistical tests. Here, we will report only on the analysis of the second team. The descriptive analysis of the noun phrases is both functional and grammatical.

As far as function is concerned, children's initial object descriptions were classified into one of three categories, namely *minimally specified* (M), *overspecified* (O) and *underspecified* (U) references. M contains those descriptions in which the colour and the size of the target attribute were mentioned. O applies when the class of the target object appears in the noun phrase in addition to its colour and size. M and O represent communicatively successful initial object references. They allow the identification of the intended target referent without any further requests for specification. This is not the case for U, because here the object description fails to provide the information that is needed for the identification of a unique referent within the presented object set. After the initial object reference further specifications are needed to achieve communicative success. The functional analysis also examines how many requests lead to communicative success.

The grammatical analysis concerns several aspects of the correct or incorrect form of the noun phrases produced in the referential communication task. Our assessment includes the initial object descriptions, supplemented by summarizing utterances when necessary. In particular, the following aspects were looked at:

1. Gender agreement between determiner and noun (DNA): Three dependent categories were distinguished that apply to both languages:
   - DNA+: when the gender-marking of the determiner agrees with the noun gender
   - DNA−: when the gender-marking of the determiner does not agree with the noun gender
   - DNA?: when the correctness of the agreement was unclear due to missing nouns or lexical borrowings from another language

2. Determiner-adjective agreement (DAA): Spanish and German provide different forms of adjectives, depending on the gender-marking form of the determiner. We distinguished between three dependent categories:
   - DAA+: when the adjective form is congruent with the form of the determiner
   - DAA−: when the adjective form is incongruent with the form of the determiner
   - DAA?: when the congruence is unclear, for example due to missing determiners
3. Word order: The basic difference between German and Spanish concerns the position of the modifying adjectives before or after the noun. We distinguished between the following categories:
   - WO+ : when the adjective modification precedes the noun in German standard noun phrases and follows the noun in Spanish standard noun phrases
   - WO− : when the prenominal word order of German and the postnominal word order of Spanish is not observed

As a third category we add the inversion of the conventional positions of size and colour adjectives as a subcategory of WO+:
   - AI: when correct pre- or postnominal noun phrases contain inversions of the size before colour ordering

The acoustic quality of the recorded material is so limited that an analysis of intonation patterns would have been impossible. So we have restricted our analysis to the functional and grammatical aspects of German and Spanish noun phrases which form the dependent variables in our study.

2.4 Statistical analysis

We examine differences between mono- and bilingual groups of children in the functional and grammatical production of noun phrases. To this end, uni- and bivariate analyses of variances (UAV and BAV) were calculated. The independent variables involved the linguistic status of the subject (mono- vs bilingual), the test language (German vs Spanish) and age (younger vs older subgroup).

In the first comparison we looked at differences between bilingual children due to test language. The comparisons concern a dependent sample of subjects, divided into a younger and older subgroup.

In the second comparison, monolingual children were contrasted with their bilingual age mates. Here, the bilingual children were compared with a monolingual Spanish-speaking and a monolingual German-speaking group of children. All groups were divided into younger and older age groups.

The third comparison only involved the two monolingual groups, divided into younger and older subgroups. The three comparisons were carried out for the same list of dependent variables in order to detect main effects of and (unpredicted) interactional effects among the independent variables *linguistic status, test language* and *age*.

A trivariate analysis of variances in which the effects of the three independent variables are tested in one step for each dependent variable is rejected, because of one serious methodological problem. Linguistic status and test language are not independent of each other, since the bilinguals were investigated in each of the two languages. Our step-wise comparisons do have the advantage that the theoretical issues are tested in the most transparent way. It follows that double presentations of data become inevitable. The UAV and BAV required individual test scores for the dependent variables, which were calculated by counting category values over the ten trials of the referential communication task. These values underwent sin-arc transformations before they entered the UAV and BAV. In the presentations of the results we contrast distributions of relative proportions of certain categories between test language and linguistic status. Effects are reported only when they reach the significance level of p=.05 or p=.01. Statistical indices are mentioned only for the significant differences.

3. Results

3.1 The within comparison: bilinguals' object references in German and Spanish

The 19 bilingual children produced 380 initial object references in the referential communication task. In the following tables we compare these references in German and Spanish according to functional and grammatical criteria. In each language relative proportions in percentages are based on 190 initial object references by 19 subjects in ten trials.

Table 7.2   Distribution of functional types of initial descriptions in 19 bilingual children

Type	German (%)	Spanish (%)
U	8	16
M	4	11
O	88	73

Table 7.2 contrasts the relative frequencies of minimally specified (M), underspecified (U) and overspecified (O) initial object references in German and Spanish.

The results of the statistical analyses show the following main effects. In German, bilingual children produced more overspecified and less minimally specified object references than in Spanish (df 1/17; F=5.18; p=.03 for O and df 1/17; F=4.21; p=.05 for M). The older age groups produced more overspecified and less minimally specified object references than the younger age group (df 1/17; F=6.53; p=.02 for O and df 1/17; F= 4.46; p=.05 for M).

The results of the analyses for word order are presented in Table 7.3. The table shows the distribution of correct (WO+) and incorrect (WO−) word order in German and Spanish noun phrases as well as the frequency of size–colour inversions (AI).

Two main effects, both due to the test language, reached statistical significance. Bilingual children's noun phrases contained more word-order errors in Spanish than in German (df 1/17; F=16.42; p=.00). The analogous difference for correct word-order patterns also reached statistical significance (df 1/17; F=15.08; p=.00). No age effects were found. No significant differences between the two languages were found for the following: communicative success of object references; correctness of gender agreement between determiner and noun (DNA); correctness of determiner-adjective agreement marking (DAA).

Table 7.3   Word order in German and Spanish object references of 19 bilingual children

WO	German (%)	Spanish (%)
+	65	33
−	4	42
AI	31	25

The results of our within comparison can be easily summarized. We started with the assumption that one language is often dominant in bilingual children (and adults, too). This dominance is not necessarily stable, since it may switch depending on situational and personal circumstances. As expected, German appears to be the dominant language in the 19 bilingual subjects of our study. However, this dominance does not show up in every comparison of their production of modified noun phrases. Most of these comparisons revealed ceiling effects in both languages, indicating that our children's development has already approximated the ideal standards of the respective target languages.

One difference is striking and can be interpreted as an obvious sign of dominance for German. The bilinguals' Spanish noun phrases often contained prenominal adjective modifications, a word-order pattern that is incorrect in Spanish, but correct in German. We failed to find a substantial amount of the reverse error in German. The relative position of the noun was correct in 96 per cent of the German noun phrases and observed the prenominal pattern of adjective modification (Table 7.3).

The difference between the two languages is not limited to grammatical aspects of the noun phrases. It also concerns functional aspects, since German noun phrases tended to be more explicit than the Spanish ones, at least in the initial object references. This functional difference did not, however, have serious negative consequences for communicative success in referential communication, since the higher degree of explicitness implied a redundant attribute (class membership) of the selected target object. When differences between the younger and the older bilingual subgroups occurred at all, they pointed in the expected direction and were compatible with the findings of Deutsch and Pechmann (1982) for the production of object references in Dutch children.

3.2   The between comparison: German and Spanish object references in mono- and bilingual children

This comparison is based on 200 initial object references (plus necessary specifications) of 20 German-speaking monolinguals and 206 initial object references (plus necessary specifications) of 21 Spanish-speaking monolinguals. Four object references in Spanish are missing due to technical problems. We contrast the

Table 7.4   Distribution of functional types of initial German and Spanish object references in mono- and bilingual children

Type	German Bi (%)	German Mono (%)	Spanish Bi (%)	Spanish Mono (%)
U	8	9	16	26
M	4	12	11	24
O	88	79	73	59

object references of the monolingual children with those of the bilingual children which have already been described in the preceding section. Table 7.4 presents the results for the three functional types of initial object references: minimally specified (M), underspecified (U) and overspecified (O).

The following effects turned out to be statistically significant. Monolingual children produced more minimally specified references than their bilingual age mates in German (df 1/35; F=4.94; p=.03) as well as in Spanish (df 1/36; F=6.47; p=.01). In Spanish, monolingual children produced fewer overspecified object references than their bilingual age mates (df 1/36; F=6.46; p=.01). One age effect was significant in the expected direction. In German, the younger subgroup produced underspecified object references more often than the older one (df 1/35; F=6.30; p=.01).

The next tables contrast the results of the mono- and bilingual children regarding the grammatical aspects of their German and Spanish noun phrases. We begin in Table 7.5 with the gender agreement between determiner and noun (DNA). We distinguish between correct (+), incorrect (−) and unclear (?) agreements.

Table 7.5   Gender agreement between determiner and noun in mono- and bilingual children

DNA	German Bi (%)	German Mono (%)	Spanish Bi (%)	Spanish Mono (%)
+	83	97	81	92
−	10	2	16	8
?	7	1	3	0

Table 7.6 Word order in German and Spanish object references
of mono- and bilingual children

WO	German		Spanish	
	Bi (%)	Mono (%)	Bi (%)	Mono (%)
+	65	67	33	61
−	4	2	42	13
AI	31	31	25	26

Differences between mono- and bilingual children were found
that reached statistical significance in both languages. The direction of the effects was the same in German and Spanish, as the
marking of gender agreement was more often correct in monolinguals' than in bilinguals' noun phrases (df 1/35; F=6.00; p=.01 for
German and df 1/36; F=5.51; p=.02 for Spanish). In German, the
difference for unclear (?) marking was also significant (df 1/35;
F=3.90; p=.05). More unclear gender-marking agreements were
found in the bi- than in the monolingual children. Age effects
(and interactions between linguistic status and age) could not be
observed.

The last comparison between mono- and bilingual children
concerns word order in German and Spanish noun phrases. The
results are presented in Table 7.6, which contains relative proportions of correct (WO+) and incorrect (WO−) word order, as well
as noun phrases with size–colour inversions.

In German, the distribution for the three categories is almost
identical for mono- and bilingual children. Deviations from the
prenominal order of adjective modifications were extremely rare (4
per cent vs 2 per cent), but inversions of the size–adjective ordering
were relatively common, as Pechmann (1989) has already shown
for adult speakers of German. No statistical differences for age and
linguistic status could be found. In Spanish, the distribution of
mono- and bilingual children shows differences that yielded statistical significance for two dependent variables. While the proportion
of adjective inversions is almost identical for the two groups, the
bilingual children's noun phrases were more often incorrect and
less often correct than those of their monolingual age mates (df
1/36; F=7.27; p=.01 for WO− and df 1/36; F=6.69; p=.01 for WO+).
Differences between the younger and the older subgroups were not

detected. No significant differences between monolingual and bilingual children were found for communicative success of object references in either German or Spanish (though the initial level of unambiguous reference is lower in Spanish than in German), or for correctness of determiner-adjective agreement-marking (DAA).

The results of our comparisons do not allow a simple answer to the classic question as to whether monolinguals perform better than bilinguals or vice versa. The answer varies according to whether the comparisons involve the dominant or the subordinate language of bilingual children. In Spanish, the subordinate language of our bilingual children, a substantial number of deviations from the postnominal adjective modifications occurred, whereas in German, their dominant language, no serious word-order deviations could be detected. Bilinguals appear to have certain deficits compared to monolinguals. According to our results, these deficits are highly specific and concern grammatical aspects of modified noun phrases. As far as functional aspects are concerned, bilingual children are at least as good as their monolingual age mates in both their dominant and their subordinate languages.

3.3   The control comparison: monolinguals' object references in German and Spanish

This comparison is based on an analysis of the object references by 20 monolingual German and 21 monolingual Peruvian children. The 200 German and 206 Spanish initial object references are analysed according to functional and grammatical criteria. For the analysis of communicative success, specifications of the initial references are also taken into consideration.

Table 7.7 presents a distributional analysis of three functional types of object reference, namely minimally specified (M), underspecified (U) and overspecified (O) utterances. The distribution

Table 7.7 Distribution of functional types of initial object reference in monolingual German and Peruvian children

Type	German (%)	Spanish (%)
U	9	26
M	12	24
O	79	50

Table 7.8 Communicative success without and with requests for specification in 20 German and 21 Peruvian monolingual children

Requests	German (%)	Spanish (%)
0	91	74
1	5	22
2	2	4
–	2	0

differs in so far as the German object references contained more overspecified utterances, while the Spanish ones consisted of more minimally specified and underspecified utterances. All three differences reached statistical significance (df 1/37; F=12.04; p=.00 for O, df 1/37; F=5.97; p=.01 for M and df 1/37; F=5.24; p=.02 for U). Age effects were not detected.

Table 7.8 refers to communicative success in the two language groups. It shows how often the initial reference was successful (0), how often one (1) or two (2) requests led to success, and how often object references were still ambiguous after two requests for specification (–).

Statistically, the two groups differed significantly at the initial level of communicative success (0). The monolingual German children more often produced unambiguous initial object references, compared to their Peruvian age mates (df 1/37, F=5.24; p=.02). One request for specification usually sufficed to recover lost ground in the initially inferior Peruvian group of children. Age effects were not found.

Table 7.9 presents the distribution of correct (+) incorrect (−) word-order patterns (WO) for modified noun phrases and inversions of the size–adjective order (AI).

Only one difference reached statistical significance. Peruvian children's noun phrases were more often expressed in incorrect

Table 7.9 Word order in German and Spanish object references in monolingual German and Peruvian children

WO	German (%)	Spanish (%)
+	67	61
−	2	13
AI	31	26

word order than those of their German age mates. This puzzling result has a simple explanation. We found out that the majority of the noun phrases with incorrect word order were due to one single child, who, as a later interview revealed, cannot be considered a pure monolingual, since a governess provided some input from Quechua – a language in which adjectival modifications precede nouns as they do in German. Obviously, this child used a Quechua word-order pattern to produce Spanish noun phrases. No significant differences were found between monolingual children for correctness of gender agreement between determiner and noun (DNA), or for determiner-adjective agreement (DAA).

To our great surprise, the two monolingual control groups showed a remarkable difference in the unexpected direction. When the target object is initially described in a referential communication task, Peruvian children tend to say less than necessary or give only just as much information as necessary, whereas German children often say more than necessary. How can this difference at the beginning of a discourse be explained? This issue will lead us to the relationship between language and culture in the final discussion section.

4.   Discussion

According to Grosjean (1982), growing up in more than one language is no longer exceptional. Nowadays, 50 per cent of all children in the world are brought up in bi- or multilingual surroundings. The question is whether it is possible to become a native speaker in more than one natural language. Or does bi- and multilingual development prevent one from becoming native in any language? There are several ways to attack this issue. One could, for example, test subjects who are fully convinced of their native-speaker status in more than one language, and reconstruct their language development. George Steiner's retrospective recollections may illustrate the outcome of this approach.

> I have no recollection whatever of a first language. So far as I am aware, I possess equal currency in English, French and German. What I can speak, write or read of other languages has come later and returns a 'feel' of conscious acquisition. But I experience my first three tongues as perfectly equivalent centres of myself.
>
> (Steiner, 1975, p. 115)

Is Steiner a brilliant exception or only one among many others who possess 'equal currency' in more than one language? The present research on bilingual development does not make extensive use of retrospective data, but instead focuses on prospective studies. The traditional method of longitudinal observation of single cases is still the approach favoured today.

In this chapter, we have chosen a different approach which is not often followed. Our study provides a snapshot only, focusing on the state of development of a particular linguistic structure. This structure – the standard form of a modified noun phrase – was studied in a standardized communication setting, the referential communication task. Our subjects were relatively homogeneous groups of children of the same age and from a similar social background: 19 bilinguals, growing up in Germany with German and Spanish as their two first languages; 20 monolinguals, growing up in Germany with German as their only first language and 21 monolinguals, growing up in Peru with Spanish (Hispanoamericano) as their only first language.

The result of our threefold comparison between bilinguals themselves, between mono- and bilinguals and between the two control groups of monolinguals cannot provide a definite answer to our classic question. However, George Steiner's self-estimation certainly cannot be applied to the performance of our bilingual subjects in referential communication tasks. It is evident that our 19 bilingual subjects do not possess 'equal currency' in the two languages tested. There appears to be a dominant language (German) and a subordinate language (Spanish), as indicated by prenominal adjective modifications in Spanish which, in contrast to German, requires postnominal adjective modifications.

By the age of five, the two languages are separated (see, e.g., Meisel, 1986, on a related issue), but borrowings from the dominant language occurred in the subordinate language. This 'transfer' is highly specific and only concerns the domain of word order in modified noun phrases. Our study leaves open the question of whether this deficit is temporary in nature or may disappear if the bilingual children were to be tested at a later point of development or in a Spanish-speaking environment.

Our results also show that deficits in the correct grammatical form of noun phrases do not have a negative impact upon their communicative function in the setting of a referential communication task. In comparison with their monolingual age mates, bilingual children do not suffer from any communicative impairments. On the contrary, the communicative efficacy of their initial object references was above the level of their monolingual age mates, especially in the subordinate language, Spanish. Our study also included a comparison between two monolingual control groups. The results of this comparison create a new, unexpected problem. According to a processing model developed by Deutsch (1986, 1989), postnominal adjective modifications of noun phrases may facilitate the acquisition of the production of complex noun phrases. The data reverse the predictions, as far as function is concerned. Spanish object references of Peruvian children started at a level that was significantly below the level of monolingual German children. This remarkable difference disappeared after the first request for specification had been asked. How can this unexpected finding be explained?

We can only speculate that the structural differences between languages may be less critical than cultural differences in communication styles. Brent-Palmer (1979) has suggested that highly industrialized ('modern') societies emphasize the cognitive-informative aspect of linguistic communication, whereas traditional societies favour the social-emotional aspects of linguistic exchanges. Is it possible that the development of referential communication is a sensitive indicator of the suggested cultural difference? Is it more important for German children (and adults) to say at least as much as is necessary than for Peruvian children (and adults)? Do Peruvian children (and adults) have a different conception of the goal of the referential communication task? Do they consider communicative success as a joint enterprise in reaching understanding step by step? Do German children, on the other hand, consider the production of unambiguous object references as an individual problem in which social interaction can compensate for production deficits? Where can our bilingual subjects be located in this framework? Do they change their cultural views of the essence of linguistic communication when they speak different languages?

The data, which we should not forget were collected in Germany, point to the fact that the bilingual children are more similar to their German than to their Peruvian age mates. The unexpected and somewhat irritating result of comparing two control groups points to a serious problem. Research on bilingual development should not only focus on structural differences between the languages involved, but also on the cultural context in which the different languages are put to use. So the classic question in bilingualism has to be asked twice. Is it possible to become a native speaker in two (or more) languages, and is it possible to become a native speaker in two (or more) cultures? Referential communication tasks cannot provide definite answers to this two-pronged question, but they do give us a glimmer of the possibilities.

Notes

We would like to thank our 60 mono- and bilingual children in Germany and Peru, the Kindergarten Geschwister Sperling and the elementary school Hinter der Masch in Braunschweig and Thorsten Brants, Gloria Goldberg, Frauke Meibeyer, Hans Przewozny and Markus Wenglorz, who helped us a lot during the various phases of this project. It started as a diploma thesis some years ago (Bruhn, 1990) and was supported by the Max-Planck-Institute for Psycholinguistics in Nijmegen (The Netherlands).

1. A memorandum dated 1990 from Garcia Nieto of 'El Secretario Perpetuo de la Real Academia Española' informs us that both orderings are justified, although the size–colour order appears to be more common.

8

'Y … no puedo decir mas nada': distanced communication skills of Puerto Rican children

ANA MARIA RODINO and CATHERINE E. SNOW

A basic task that children must accomplish in the process of growing up and becoming literate is that of dealing with situations of distanced communication, for example, talking on the telephone, writing a letter to a stranger or giving directions. Effective distanced communication requires analysis of what one's interlocutor already knows, could infer and needs to be told; it requires taking the perspective of a distant, perhaps unknown listener; it requires planning so that one's message is complete and comprehensible, then also monitoring the message on-line to be sure it emerges as planned. Effective distanced communicators must control the linguistic resources of complex sentence syntax and discourse cohesion, as well as considerable analytic and predictive ability. Such abilities can of course be observed (and developed) in oral language contexts, though they are probably demanded most frequently in writing.

Effective distanced communication is often required in everyday life – when conveying information to a group, for example, such that it cannot be individually adapted to each listener. Even quite young school children are held to the standards of distanced communication when delivering sharing time turns, answering teacher questions and writing stories, and those demands increase as children get older. Understanding something about the correlates of skill with distanced communication might well help us understand why some children have an easier time learning about the techniques of distanced communication than others, both for oral and for literate uses.

Skill at distanced communication tasks in oral language has been shown to relate to literacy (Velasco & Snow, 1993); this connection is not surprising if, as Snow (1993) has suggested, the

hardest task in becoming literate is that of acquiring the pragmatics of distanced communication. Thus, we might expect that
children who understand the need for precision, explicitness and
planning in oral language adaptations to the demands of distanced communication would be able to transfer those skills easily
to written texts. This prediction is confirmed, for example, by the
findings of De Temple, Wu and Snow (1991), who looked at children's performance in a picture description task. The children
were asked to describe the picture orally under two conditions –
first, to an adult also looking at the picture, and second 'so that
another child who has never seen the picture would be able to
draw one just like it, from listening to your description'. De
Temple et al. found that performance in the distanced, 'decontextualizing' oral condition correlated strongly with performance
on written picture descriptions – just as one would expect if, in
fact, the major problem in writing is that of considering the
absent, distant audience. Furthermore, they found that children
made a greater distinction between the two sets of instructions in
the oral than the written condition, confirming that the pragmatics of distanced communication are acquired first for use in
oral language.

The De Temple et al. study analysed oral and written picture
descriptions from a group of middle-class children attending a
private school that offered an excellent writing curriculum.
Among the students in the school, almost half were not native
speakers of English; nonetheless the performance of all the children on the various tasks was surprisingly competent and no effect
of status as non-native speaker of English could be found. A
similar analysis of the picture descriptions of 52 of the same children in French (a language they had studied as a foreign language
in school) by Wu, De Temple, Herman and Snow (1993) revealed
the expected deficiencies of performance associated with being a
foreign language speaker (descriptions in French were shorter,
contained more grammatical errors, less complex syntax, and less
detail); nonetheless, the children did adjust their performance in
a way adapted to the needs of a distant listener/reader under the
decontextualizing instructions, even in the foreign language.
Thus, when the instructions were to describe the picture for someone who had never seen it, the children produced descriptions
that were longer and more explicit, that contained more adjectives, more clarifications and more locatives.

The findings by Wu et al. suggest that performance in a second language, even at relatively early stages of acquisition of the second language, can reveal an understanding of the demands of distanced communication, at least for middle-class children such as those they tested. Given the difficulties poor and language-minority children have in achieving as expected in school literacy tests, the question arises whether they control the task-analytic and linguistic skills required to make adjustments like these, in a way similar to more privileged children. In order to pursue this question, we analysed oral picture descriptions from 20 Hispanic fifth graders, to assess their level of performance in Spanish (their home language) and English (their curricular language) as compared to the middle-class children, and most importantly to see whether they also made the expected adjustments under the distanced communication instructions.

Study 1.   Contextualized and decontextualized language use by mainstreamed Puerto Rican children

Research question

The overall research question that guided this study was whether Puerto Rican children who have achieved good proficiency in English, as evidenced by their having been placed in mainstream classrooms, adjust their use of English and Spanish to the demands of distanced communication in a picture description task.

Methods

Subjects and setting

The subjects were 23 children ranging from 10 to 12 years of age enrolled in fifth grade in the New Haven public schools. They came from Puerto Rican working-class families and were native speakers of Spanish. The children attended regular mainstream classes. Intelligibility problems on some tapes forced the removal of two subjects from the original sample. Of the remaining 21 children, 15 had previously attended a bilingual programme, five had never been in bilingual programmes, and no information on previous education was available for one child.

Background data about the community to which the children belonged is provided by an extensive survey of the entire population of Hispanic families with school-aged children in New Haven (Hakuta & Ferdman, 1984).[1] The children in this study came from a community in which adults had commonly left school after ninth grade, and in which unemployment and low-paying jobs were typical. Spanish was still the main language of adult communication at home, though English was also regularly used, with dissimilar levels of proficiency and frequency. Children were brought up speaking Spanish, but by the time of the study they had become active bilinguals at home and were perceived by their parents as having similar proficiency in both languages, or as performing even better in English than in their native tongue.

A previous study that examined the teaching conditions in the New Haven public schools (Lanauze & Snow, 1989) reported that the classrooms were traditional teacher-centred settings. Basal reading series and associated workbooks formed the core of the language curriculum. Instruction in language arts, vocabulary and spelling was based on the typical teacher-led lesson in conjunction with workbook assignments. There were relatively few trade books available in the classrooms, and little writing practice was observed.

The task

The task presented to the subjects was to describe a picture, first under 'contextualizing' instructions and then under 'decontextualizing' instructions. The tasks were carried out in both English and Spanish during individual test sessions held on different days. For each task the child was shown one of four colourful pictures specially designed to include a number of characters engaged in various activities.

The contextualizing instructions simply requested the child to describe the picture to the experimenter, who was seated by the child and looking at the illustration during the process. The directions were: 'Now I am going to show you a picture and I want you to tell me what is happening in this picture.' If the subject gave too brief an answer, the experimenter encouraged further talk: 'Is there anything more you would like to tell me about the picture?'

The decontextualizing instructions also asked the child to describe the picture, with the following additions: 'I would like you to tell about everything that is happening in this picture so that some other child who will listen to this tape recording later on will be able to draw a picture just like this one. Remember, someone else will later on be given a blank sheet of paper and will be asked to draw the picture just like the one you have in your hand from what they hear you say on the tape recorder.' Again, if the description provided was very brief, the child would be prompted: 'Is there anything else you want to say about the picture?' or 'Do you think someone else will be able to draw a picture exactly like this one from what you just said?'

Ricard and Snow (1990), who analysed similar data also from a bilingual setting, stressed that the two instructions differed in three basic ways. The contextualized description was requested for a present listener who could refer to the picture, an adult, and without specification of any particular objective beyond producing a description for its own sake. The decontextualized description was requested for an absent, unknown listener who could not refer to the picture and whose reactions the child could not observe, who was another child, and with the explicit mission of providing a basis for the reproduction of the picture. The contextualizing and decontextualizing instructions were designed to create situations of communication differing in physical context, addressee and purpose of the exchange. Thus, they posed different demands on the speakers who, in order to satisfy them efficiently, had to adjust their linguistic performance.

Transcription and coding

The procedure yielded four picture descriptions for each subject. They are identified here as 'EOC' (English oral contextualized), 'EOD' (English oral decontextualized), 'SOC' (Spanish oral contextualized), and 'SOD' (Spanish decontextualized) (see Appendix 8A on p. 187 for examples). The descriptions were transcribed and coded separately for specific features which reflected the major discourse dimensions that were expected to be sensitive to the change in the instructions in both L1 and L2: quantity, specificity, density, narrativity and fluency. Each dimension under scrutiny was reflected by several variables (see Appendix 8B on p. 188 for more information about coding):

1. *Quantity.* Quantity variables reflect the amount of talk produced by the child. They include total counts of word tokens (TK), work types (TYP), t-units (TU) and noun phrases (NP).
2. *Specificity.* Specificity variables measure the degree of explicitness and precision in the child's description. They include all revisions (RE), clarificatory markers (CM), specific locatives (SL), lexical noun phrases (LX) and adjectives (AJ).
3. *Density.* Density variables are proportional measures constructed to appraise the linguistic complexity and elaboration of the child's language. They present the ratio of several individual features (tokens, verbs, noun phrases and relatives) to the total number of t-units in the text.
4. *Narrativity.* Narrativity variables estimate the inclusion of narrative elements in the description, such as the use of verbs not in present tense (VN), mention of extra-pictorial elements (XP) and reference to the characters' internal states (IS). In addition, a narrativity rating (NA) globally assessed the child's interpretation of the nature of the task on a scale going from 0 (if the account rendered was a straight description) to 4 (if it basically had a story-like quality).
5. *Fluency.* This category combines various variables that measure how eloquent and articulate the child was in using the language. They include conversational features (CF), language switches (LS), direct appeals to an authority – here, the interviewer – (DA) and a global rating of variation on sentence form (VS). The latter ranged from 0 (all t-units showing the same syntactic structure) to 4 (all t-units being as different as their semantics allowed).

Results

The specific research questions addressed in analysing the results were:

1. Were there instruction effects? That is, did instructions which specified a demand for contextualized or decontextualized language affect children's linguistic performance? In English, in Spanish, or in both languages?
2. Were there language effects? That is, did children perform differently as a function of the language used?

3. Was there an interaction between language and instruction? That is, did differences due to instruction vary according to the language used?

A two-way ANOVA was used, with instruction and language as repeated measures factors.

Table 8.1   Means and significant effects for picture description variables under two instructions and in Spanish and English

	English		Spanish		Significant effects		
	EOC	EOD	SOC	SOD	Lang.	Instr.	Interac.
Quantity							
TK	90.38	144.24	50.59	79.95	**	***	–
TYP	44.24	62.48	29.18	38.86	***	***	–
TU	11.33	15.29	6.68	9.64	**	**	–
NP	28.33	43.71	16.77	27.09	**	***	–
Specificity							
RE	1.19	2.48	1.04	2.18	–	**	–
CM	2.52	6.71	1.86	3.73	*	**	*
SL	4.90	8.43	2.59	1.82	***	**	**
LX	21.48	33.48	11.36	18.04	***	***	(*)
AJ	8.05	22.00	2.82	7.23	***	***	***
Density							
TK/TU	8.19	9.48	7.20	8.03	*	–	–
VE/TU	1.29	1.13	1.05	1.22	–	–	–
NP/TU	2.80	3.00	2.45	2.78	–	–	–
RL/TU	0.16	0.06	0.04	0.12	–	–	–
Narrativity							
NA	0.95	0.95	0.59	1.04	–	–	–
VN	1.00	0.48	0.32	0.91	–	–	–
XP	1.33	1.48	0.32	0.73	**	–	–
IS	0.19	0.66	0.04	0.09	**	–	*
Fluency							
CF	0.90	1.00	0.18	0.32	***	–	–
LS	0.00	0.00	1.04	1.45	(*)	–	–
DA	0.05	0.00	0.14	0.27	**	–	–
VS	1.52	1.66	0.91	1.36	*	*	–

(*) p < 0.07   * p < 0.05   ** p < 0.01   *** p < 0.001

Instruction effects

As expected, instructions affected children's linguistic performance noticeably. Decontextualizing instructions produced a significant increase in all measures of quantity and specificity, and in a measure of syntactic variation (see Table 8.1). This means that, under decontextualized conditions, children:

(a) produced more words (TK), more different words (TYP), more utterances (TU) and more referential expressions (NP);
(b) produced a more detailed or explicit language, revising their speech (RE) more, using more lexical references (LX) and introducing more modifiers, including adjectives (AJ), clarifications (CM) and indications of place, direction, source or location (SL);
(c) structured their utterances using more varied syntactic patterns (VS).

The contrast between contextualized and decontextualized use of language appears when we look at both English and Spanish descriptions together (EOC + SOC vs EOD + SOD), as well as when we look at the descriptions in each language separately (EOC vs EOD; SOC vs SOD). The only exception is specific locatives (SL), which only in Spanish were less frequent in the decontextualizing condition.

The strongest effect of the instructions was on length of description. In addition, it is striking that the descriptions were much longer in English than Spanish; accordingly, one must ask whether the increase in specificity in the descriptions may have resulted just from the increase in length by itself. Absolute frequencies of specificity devices might be somehow misleading. In order to control for length, new variables were calculated which expressed specificity indicators as a proportion of utterances.

When using proportional scores (see Table 8.2), some overall differences due to instructional condition disappeared, namely the effects found for revisions, specific locatives and lexical noun phrases. Two variables remained significantly different as a function of instruction: clarifications (CM) and adjectives (AJ).

Density, narrativity and fluency variables were not affected by instruction. There was only a marginally significant effect on one narrativity variable (IS), which in a sense can be interpreted as part of the trend towards increasing specificity: children provided

Table 8.2 Means and significant effects for specificity variables controlling for length

	English		Spanish		Significant effects		
	EOC	EOD	SOC	SOD	Lang.	Instr.	Interac.
RE/TU	0.08	0.12	0.15	0.21	*	–	–
CM/TU	0.23	0.45	0.24	0.40	–	*	–
SL/TU	0.35	0.50	0.36	0.20	**	–	*
LX/NP	0.75	0.78	0.68	0.66	**	–	–
AJ/TU	0.66	1.38	0.45	0.65	***	***	**

$* \ p < 0.05$ $** \ p < 0.01$ $*** \ p < 0.001$

more information about one aspect of the picture (the performers), even though this information was beyond the picture itself, and had to be inferred or imagined by the observer.

In brief, these mainstreamed Puerto Rican children recognized the demand for distanced communication posed by the decontextualizing instructions and adjusted their language accordingly. The most salient adjustments to the decontextualizing condition in both languages were in the amount of talk produced, the degree of attribution incorporated into the text and the degree of syntactic variation.

Language effects

Despite similarities in adjustments observed in Spanish and English, there was an important difference between performance in the two languages. Spanish descriptions were significantly briefer and showed lower scores on several measures of specificity, complexity, narrativity, fluency and syntactic variation.

(a) In Spanish, children talked less – produced fewer words (TK), fewer different words (TYP), fewer utterances (TU) and fewer referential expressions (NP).

(b) Spanish picture descriptions were characterized by less detailed or explicit language – fewer lexical references (LX), fewer adjectives (AJ), clarifications (CM) and indications of place, direction, source or location (SL).

(c) In Spanish, the utterances were syntactically simpler, with a reduced number of words per utterance (TK/TU), and were characterized by less varied syntactic patterns (VS).

(d) When giving Spanish picture descriptions, the children introduced fewer narrative components into the description – they inferred or imagined fewer elements beyond the actual picture, both objects or actions (XP) and actors' emotions (IS).

(e) In Spanish, the children used fewer conversational expressions (CF), made more switches to English language to convey meaning (LS), and appealed more to the interviewer for help in finding the appropriate or intended wording (DA), suggesting reduced fluency.

Even when the specificity measures were adjusted for overall length, the general pattern of less competent performance in Spanish did not change much. Although differences in incidence of clarificatory markers disappeared, locatives, lexical noun phrases and adjectives still occurred less often in Spanish. In addition, revisions per utterance (RE) emerged as more frequent in Spanish, suggesting a more conscious or self-monitored (maybe more insecure?) use of language in Spanish than in English.

Interaction effects

An interaction between instruction and language was found for several specificity variables (CM, SL, LX and AJ) and one narrativity variable (IS). Instruction effects, then, varied according to the language used. In all cases but one (that of SL), the adjustment to the decontextualizing instructions was larger when the children talked in English than in Spanish. The variable SL showed an even more extreme interaction pattern; the decontextualizing instruction produced more locatives in English, while in Spanish it produced fewer. Analysing the specificity variables as proportions rather than raw frequencies eliminated the interactions except for adjectives (AJ) and specific locatives (SL).

Discussion

These Puerto Rican bilinguals showed the richest linguistic performance in English under the decontextualizing instructions: they said more, were more specific, uttered more dense and varied syntactic units, were more imaginative as far as introducing elements not present in the actual picture, and were more secure in their use of the language, not needing to resort to the other language or the interviewer's assistance to express their ideas.

Finding that the subjects adapted their performance to changing communicative conditions was, in itself, not surprising. The result is consistent with prior research evidence from monolingual and bilingual subjects. Several studies on L1 development have confirmed children's early awareness of the pragmatic demands of specific communication situations and have described some of the changes introduced to fulfil those demands (e.g., Sachs & Devin, 1976; Shatz & Gelman, 1973; Wellman & Lempers, 1977). When French–English bilinguals from the United Nations International School in New York were faced with the same picture description tasks (De Temple et al., 1991; Ricard & Snow, 1990; Wu et al., 1993), they exhibited a pattern of adjustment to decontextualizing instructions in both L1 and L2 similar to that of the Spanish–English bilinguals in our sample. What these results add to the picture is confirmation that bilinguals from minority, working-class families with low levels of parental education, those still often regarded as 'high educational risk' and 'restricted code' children, make equally appropriate adjustments. The performance of Puerto Rican fifth-graders from the New Haven public schools proves the ubiquity of the communicative competence needed for effective distanced communication. These children demonstrate their understanding of the need to adjust in both their languages, though their adjustments may be smaller than those of middle-class children even in their stronger language (Snow, 1993), and indeed the children produced shorter and less specific picture descriptions in English than did the middle-class bilinguals.

A disturbing, though perhaps not surprising, aspect of the results from this study is the relatively better performance in English of these native speakers of Spanish. Most of these children had attended bilingual classes, indicating that they had arrived at school speaking 'limited English proficient'. Furthermore, they lived in a vibrantly bilingual community, and in households where many of the adults spoke little or no English. Nonetheless, these children showed evidence of attrition of Spanish skills, at least the skills needed for 'school-like tasks' such as giving picture descriptions. It may be that these children were really losing control over the fluent Spanish needed for complex tasks like this, because of their immersion in an English-language environment at school, or it may be that they were less motivated to work hard at such school-like tasks in Spanish, a language which they might have recognized had little academic value for them. In order to explore

further these possibilities, we compare in Study 2 the performance of these mainstreamed children to 20 fifth-graders from
the same community who were still attending bilingual classes.
The children in the bilingual programme received half their
instruction in Spanish and were still identified at time of testing as
'limited English proficient'; they might thus have been expected
to demonstrate better performance in Spanish than in English,
though previous results suggest that they would demonstrate an
understanding of the need for adjustment in both languages.

Study 2: Comparison of mainstreamed children to children still in the bilingual programme

Subjects

The New Haven Public School from which the fifth-graders tested
in Study 1 were selected also housed a bilingual programme serving
about 150 children. The New Haven bilingual programme follows
the pairing model: a Spanish-speaking teacher and an English-
speaking teacher share two classes, each one working with each
class half a day. The class that had the Spanish-speaking teacher in
the morning had the English-speaking one in the afternoon, and
vice versa. Academic instruction in content areas was conducted in
both Spanish and English, but new and more difficult information
was typically presented in Spanish, and then reviewed in English
(Lanauze & Snow, 1989; Velasco, 1989).

The fifth grade in the bilingual programme included both children born in Puerto Rico and on the mainland. The former were
typically relatively recent arrivals; the latter were likely to have
been retained in the bilingual programme more than the usual
three or four years due to extensive academic problems that suggested they might not be able to handle a full curriculum in
English (Velasco, 1989). In this second case, the reasons for the
placement relate more to the children's weak general academic
performance than to their English proficiency.

The 20 children tested for Study 2 were selected using two criteria: the children had attended the bilingual programme for at
least two years, and they were good readers in Spanish. We selected
only good readers in order to eliminate children with academic
problems and to obtain a more homogeneous group, comparable

to the mainstreamed group (who would have had to score reasonably high on a reading test in order to be mainstreamed).

The community from which this group of children still attending bilingual classes came can also be described using data from the Hakuta and Ferdman (1984) survey of Hispanic families with children in the New Haven Public School. In contrast to the families of the mainstreamed children, the salient feature of the subjects in the bilingual programme is that they came from homes where Spanish remained the primary language of communication for both adults and children. The role of English in family interactions was relatively limited, if present at all.[2]

Procedure

The children in the bilingual group were presented with the decontextualized picture description task described above. Only the decontextualizing instructions were used, since Study 1 had shown that children performed best under these instructions in both languages.

Results

The specific research questions addressed in Study 2 were:

1. How did the two groups of children participating in different school programmes differ in producing picture descriptions in L1 and in L2?
2. Considering the two groups together, did the children perform differently as a function of the language used?
3. Was there an interaction between language and group? In other words, were the differences between performance in English and Spanish the same for both groups?

Bilingual vs mainstreamed children's picture descriptions in English

The two groups differed considerably in linguistic performance in English (see Table 8.3). The mainstreamed group showed stronger performance on almost all variables, with significant differences on most measures of quantity and specificity, on two measures of complexity and on one measure of narrativity. When describing in English, mainstreamed children:

Table 8.3 Means and significant effects for mainstreamed and bilingual programme groups

	English		Spanish		Significant effects		
	Bi-lingual	Main-stream	Bi-lingual	Main-stream	Lang.	Group	Interac.
Quantity							
TK	90.90	144.55*	79.15	84.95	***	–	**
TYP	40.85	62.55**	40.25	40.65	***	–	***
TU	11.65	15.30	10.60	10.60	**	–	–
NP	28.40	43.60*	24.70	28.80	**	–	(*)
Specificity							
RE	1.65	2.50	1.05	2.30(*)	–	–	–
CM	3.80	6.70	4.05	3.85	*	–	**
SL	2.55	8.65***	4.10	1.95**	**	–	***
LX	19.85	33.45**	16.90	19.05	***	–	*
AJ	13.15	22.20	8.50	7.80	***	–	*
Density							
TK/TU	7.38	9.49**	7.18	7.72	*	**	(*)
VE/TU	1.18	1.10	1.12	1.19	–	–	–
NP/TU	2.38	2.99*	2.27	2.67(*)	–	**	–
RL/TU	0.08	0.05	0.11	0.13	*	–	–
Narrativity							
NA	0.60	0.90	0.50	1.05*	–	*	–
VN	0.45	0.45	0.50	1.00	–	–	–
XP	0.80	1.25	0.55	0.75	–	–	–
IS	0.20	0.70*	0.30	0.10	–	–	*
Fluency							
CF	2.00	1.00	0.70	0.35	**	–	–
LS	0.00	0.00	0.05	1.40	–	–	–
DA	0.05	0.00	0.05	0.30(*)	*	–	*
VS	1.40	1.65	1.55	1.40	–	–	–

(*) p < 0.07   * p < 0.05   ** p < 0.01   *** p < 0.001

(a) produced more words (TK), more different words (TYP) and more referential indicators (NP);

(b) produced more detailed and explicit language, using more lexical references (LX), and introducing more adjectives (AJ), clarifications (CM) and indications of place, direction, source or location (SL);

Table 8.4   Means and significant effects for specificity variables controlling for length

	English		Spanish		Significant effects		
	Bi-lingual	Main-stream	Bi-lingual	Main-stream	Lang.	Group	Interac.
RE/TU	0.12	0.12	0.07	0.19**	–	–	(*)
CM/TU	0.31	0.45	0.40	0.34	–	–	**
SL/TU	0.21	0.51**	0.44	0.21**	–	–	***
LX/NP	0.69	0.79*	0.71	0.65	–	*	**
AJ/TU	0.86	1.39**	0.65	0.66	*	***	**

(*) $p < 0.07$ * $p < 0.05$ ** $p < 0.01$ *** $p < 0.001$

(c) constructed utterances containing more words (TK/TU) and more referential indicators (NP/TU);
(d) introduced more inferred or imagined elements relative to the characters' emotions beyond the actual picture (IS).

Even when controlling for length (see Table 8.4), three specificity measures were produced significantly more often by the mainstreamed children: the proportion of lexical noun phrases over the total noun phrases (LX/NP), and the proportion of specific locatives and adjectives per utterance (SL/TU, AJ/TU).

This general pattern is not surprising. Bilingual children are exited to the mainstream programme when they have apparently reached good proficiency in English, at least good enough to allow them to handle all school subjects in that language. The key areas where their linguistic skills in English seem crucial for them to function successfully in the regular classroom are, most probably, quantity and specificity: students have to be able to say as much as necessary, and to say it clearly and accurately. Our data confirm that mainstreamed children demonstrated these skills to a larger extent than children in the bilingual programme.

Bilingual vs mainstreamed children's picture descriptions in Spanish

Though it is not surprising that the mainstreamed children did better in English, one would expect the bilingual programme children to do better in Spanish, a language which they were still using as a curricular language. Unexpectedly, though, there were no relevant differences between the two groups in their linguistic performance in Spanish. Mean scores in most areas that were measured were quite similar (see Tables 8.3 and 8.4). The few statistically significant differences found between the groups showed no consistent pattern. Mainstreamed children had more total revisions (RE), as well as a higher proportion of revisions per utterance (RE/TU); produced more noun phrases per utterance (NP/TU); tended to use a more narrative approach to the descriptive task (NA); and appealed more to the interviewer for help (DA). On the other hand, they used far fewer specific locatives, in total (SL) and per utterance (SL/TU).

In brief, our data did not exhibit a clear, distinct contrast between the groups on their performance in Spanish. A couple of indicators suggest that mainstreamed fifth-graders had a slightly weaker command of their native language than fifth-graders in the bilingual programme – they produced fewer specific references to locations and requested more assistance from the interviewer. But the differences were too few to be generalized as a trend.

Language effects

The main effect of language surfaces forcefully in most of the indicators. Regardless of the programme they attended, Puerto Rican fifth-graders scored higher in English than in Spanish on all the dimensions examined. They consistently talked more (TK, TYP, TU, NP) and more specifically about the picture (CM, SL, LX, AJ) in English. It is interesting to note that increased specificity was basically achieved by expanding the whole text and enriching attribution within utterances. When length was controlled for (see Table 8.4), the only specificity device that showed a significant proportional increment was the use of adjectives (AJ/TU). Furthermore, English picture descriptions contained longer utterances (TK/TU), and included more elements beyond those actually present in the picture (XP). They were articulated with greater fluency, relying more heavily on the use of conversational features (CF), but never on language switches (LS), and almost never on the interviewer's help (DA).

Only one variable, the number of relative clauses per utterance (RL/TU), showed better performance in Spanish than in English. This inconsistent result suggests that children did not have an active command of relativization structures as strong in L2 as in L1. Since relativization is a complex device for integrating information, typically acquired much later than other devices, such as prepositional phrases and coordination (Bloom et al., 1980; Tager-Flusberg, 1989), a plausible explanation is that these Puerto Rican children may not have yet fully mastered it in L2. Furthermore, it must be noted that relativization in English is less clearly marked in discourse surface structure than in Spanish, which may delay its acquisition.

Overall group differences

The influence of group membership on the children's performance was far less marked than that of language. In general, the fifth-graders who were enrolled in the mainstream programme scored higher than those in the bilingual programme, but few differences were significant. The main effect of group surfaced only in two measures of density (TK/TU and NP/TU), the holistic narrative rating (NA), and two proportional indicators of specificity (LX/NP, AJ/TU). Mainstreamed children tended to produce more story-like descriptions, which, though not longer, were structured in longer utterances with more lexical content and adjectives.

Interaction effects

Language and group interacted significantly on a large variety of indicators on all the dimensions examined: quantity (TK, TYP, NP), specificity (in absolute measures of CM, SL, LX, AJ, and all five proportional measures), density (TK/TU), narrativity (IS) and fluency (DA). The basic pattern revealed by the interactions was that the difference between English and Spanish was greater for the mainstreamed than for the bilingual programme group, in general because of the higher quality of their English descriptions rather than the poorer quality of their Spanish.

In summary, all these Puerto Rican children showed more effective distanced communication strategies when speaking in English than in Spanish. While the mainstreamed children performed somewhat better in English, they also showed evidence of some attrition of their Spanish skills, and their performance in Spanish was clearly less good on several dimensions than their performance in English. Surprisingly, continued participation in the bilingual programme had not protected the not-yet-mainstreamed children from similar degrees of Spanish attrition; their Spanish performance was less good than their performance in English, even though they were receiving half their instruction in Spanish and might have been expected to be Spanish dominant if not balanced bilinguals.

General discussion

Two major conclusions can be drawn from the findings reported here. First, children from families with low incomes and little parental education show convincingly that they fully understand the kinds of linguistic adjustment needed to respond to the demands of distanced communication, in both the language they use at home with their families and the language they use at school. Secondly, however, their responses in the language of school and of the dominant society are more elaborated, more precise and more fluent than their responses in the home language, suggesting that the process of first language attrition has begun even before these children exit from bilingual education programmes. These children are clearly operating in a subtractively bilingual situation, one in which acquisition of the second language threatens maintenance of a full array of skills in the first.

It may be that language attrition can be assessed more sensitively in the kind of challenging task used in this study. Providing picture descriptions for a distant audience, and trying to provide the precision, detail and elaboration necessary to fulfil the instructions, may be so difficult that it tests the limits of the children's abilities in both English and Spanish. By testing the limits one may reveal deficiencies that casual conversation never uncovers, for example, in the domain of vocabulary, of complex syntax and of discourse organization. It is striking in listening to the children's descriptions that one often hears explicit statements of incapacity in Spanish (e.g., 'se me olvidó como se llama eso', 'no sé más nada', 'yo no sé el juego ... lo puedo decir en inglés?') as well as many hesitations, false starts and pauses. Explicit requests for help or attempts to code-switch simply did not occur during the English picture descriptions.

The children tested in this study may represent the best hope of American schools to produce good bilinguals with high levels of proficiency in both their languages; yet their schools cannot be absolved of blame for these children's early difficulties in maintaining proficiency in their native language. Even in schools such as they attended, where many children are native Spanish speakers and where Spanish was used as a curricular language by some children, the societal message that English is what counts had clearly had its impact. That impact could be seen most clearly when the children were asked to undertake a challenging task requiring complex and precise language to adjust to the needs of distanced communication.

Notes

The authors would like to express their appreciation to Patricia Velasco for allowing use of data she collected for Study 2, to the Office of Educational Research and Improvement, which funded the data collection through the Center for Language Education and Research, and to the Spencer Foundation, which funded preparation of this chapter.

1. The survey breaks down the information by the grade level of the students and their programme status in the public schools. What follows reviews only the data pertaining to elementary school students in the mainstream classes who had been in bilingual classes in the past, for they constitute 70 per cent of our sample. The adult respondents were the parents (typically the mothers) or guardians of the children. Eighty-six per cent of the adult respondents had been born in Puerto Rico, and two~thirds had lived on the mainland ten years or less. Sixty per cent had received most of their schooling in Puerto Rico, and the mean number of years they had attended school was slightly above nine (9.41 years for the father and 9.29 years for the mother). Forty-three per cent of the heads of household were unemployed. The vast majority (83%) reported knowing English, though self-assessed ability varied greatly: 27 per cent of the respondents said they spoke 'a little'; 32 per cent 'enough to communicate basic ideas'; 12 per cent 'almost as well as a native speaker'; and another 12 per cent 'as well as a native speaker'.

    Half the respondents said they spoke 'only or mostly' Spanish, while 38 per cent said they spoke 'both English and Spanish'. Sixty-six per cent declared their children spoke both Spanish and English at home, having learned the second at school. Children's ability in English compared to Spanish was assessed as being about the same (44% of responses) or even better (another 37%). The majority reported reading regularly both in English and Spanish: 55 per cent said they read one or more English newspapers/periodicals, and 61 per cent said they read one or more Spanish newspapers/periodicals. Seventy-one per cent said they had one or more types of English book at home, while 82 per cent said they had one or more types of Spanish books.

2. Descriptive statistics trace a picture somehow different from that of the families with children in the mainstream programme, not so much in

the socio-economic or educational variables as in the linguistic ones. Eighty-nine per cent of the adult respondents had been born in Puerto Rico, 73 per cent had lived on the mainland ten years or less, 75 per cent had received most of their schooling on the island, and the mean number of school years was less than nine (8.94 for the father and 8.65 for the mother). Fifty-one per cent of the heads of household were unemployed. Sixty-five per cent reported knowing English, but 36 per cent said they could just speak 'a little' and only 29 per cent said they could speak it 'enough to communicate basic ideas' or better. Seventy per cent of respondents said they spoke 'only or mostly' Spanish at home, while 22 per cent said they spoke 'both English and Spanish'. Fifty-two per cent said their children spoke 'only or mostly Spanish' at home, and 40 per cent said 'both Spanish and English' were used. Children had learned English basically at school (69% of responses), though their skills in this language were mostly assessed as being lower than in Spanish (62% of responses). The bulk of respondents reported reading no English newspapers or periodicals regularly (60%), and having no English books at home (46%) or just one type (18%). In contrast, half of the respondents reported reading one Spanish periodical regularly and another quarter, two or more. Thirty-seven per cent had at least one type of Spanish book in the home, and 45 per cent had two types or more.

Appendix 8A: Sample picture descriptions

Clara (pseudonym), 11 years old, attends 5th grade in the mainstream programme. She had previously attended a bilingual programme.

English contextualized:
Ahm ... there's a girl with some flies and plate. And there's a frog by the table. There are two kids with a frog. And there's a fly on the table with the frog. They put the frog close to the fly. They're not too close and one of the girls is looking at something XXX ... and ... the girl's scratching her, her XXX with a XXX and there's flies flying around. And one of the girls has her hand covered, covering her mouth. That's it.

English decontextualized:
There's a board up in front that says 'World history test today', with a punctuation mark after today ... ahm. There's a door almost next to the board. There's a light switch. There's six seat, three in each row. Two rows with three seats in each row. The two first ones are

empty. There's a girls with a book facing the other boy next to her. She has a book on the ... the desk and one in her hand. The boy is looking at her. The boy behind her has a black eye ... and he has his hand over his mouth. He got a blue shirt. And the teacher up in front next to the chalk ... the board ... has three books in her hand ... her hand's pushing her hair. She got a bow, tie ...
EXPERIMENTER: Anything else?
And the door just have like a foot ...

Spanish contextualized:
Están en la ... en la playa. Hay una nena debajo de la arena. Eh ... están jugando con la arena. ... Más na'. Ellos están jugando con la arena y están en la playa.
EXPERIMENTER: ¿Nada más?
Están en la playa, están jugando con la arena. Más na.
EXPERIMENTER: ¿No hay nada más que me quieras decir?
Ellos están debajo de estas ... sombrillas esas grandes. ... Más na'.

Spanish decontextualized:
Hay una bola. La tiraron. Y una nena tiene el bate ready ... pa' batear la bola y los otros están hablando. Uno tiene el pantalón como que ... con dots. El otro tiene pantalón azul ... tenis blancas y negras ... camisa blanca y azul. Pelo amarillo, rubio. La nena tiene pelo rubio, tiene tenis rojas, pantalón rojo, un traje rojo blanco y amarillo. ... Se ve una mano aquí ... de la que draw el picture ... que tira la bola.
EXPERIMENTER: ¿Nada más?
Y hay como una ... como una fence XXX hay una verja ...
EXPERIMENTER: ¿Eso es todo?
El nene tiene un ... un desto un globo ... un ... se me olvidó como se llama eso ... un guante de'sos de cachar la bola ...
EXPERIMENTER: ¿Algo más?

Appendix 8B: Coding of variables

1. *Quantity*

TOK   *Word tokens*
       Total number of words that have meaning, after editing out of the text anything not related to the task of describing the picture (e.g., clarifications of directions, repetitions, false starts). Contractions are counted as one word.

TYP   *Word types*
Total number of different words used.

TU   *T-units*
A t-unit is the smallest unit of syntactically independent speech, that is, a subject–predicate structure with all associated subordinate clauses. Main clauses linked by 'and' are counted as separate utterances, while those linked by 'but' and 'because' are left together.

NP   *Noun phrases*
Total number of noun phrases. Any pronoun, noun or verbal noun is counted as a noun phrase.

2. Specificity

RE   *Revisions*
Any time the subject changes what he or she is saying it is counted as a revision. Repetitions or hesitations are not included. It does not count the number of words but the number of the decisions to alter what is being said.

CM   *Clarificatory markers*
Total number of clauses or phrases which modify a noun, clarifying or expanding on the reference (e.g., 'The boy with the bat', 'The girl in the pink dress', 'The children playing ball'). Adjectives are excluded.

SL   *Specific locatives*
Total number of clauses or phrases that clarify location (e.g., 'Behind the desk', 'In front of the class', 'Under the umbrella', 'To the right').

LX   *Lexical noun phrases*
Lexical noun phrases are all those which are not pronouns or numbers.

AJ   *Adjectives*
Total number of adjectives. Includes possessive but not demonstrative adjectives.

3. Density

TOK/TU   Total number of word tokens divided by t-units.
VE/TU   Total number of verbs divided by t-units.
RL/TU   Total number of relative pronouns divided by t-units.

4. *Narrativity*

VN   *Non-present verbs*
        Total number of non-present indicative verbs. This
        excludes infinitives, but includes present subjunctive.

XP   *Extra-pictorial elements*
        Total number of clauses or events described that go
        beyond the picture. It includes anything that is not obvi-
        ous from the picture (e.g., 'The girls are sisters', 'They
        will soon go home', 'The man entering the classroom is
        the principal').

IS   *References to characters' internal states*
        The number of phrases or lexical items that allude to
        the characters' inner experiences or points of view. It
        includes any references to how the characters feel (e.g.,
        happy, angry, sad) and assumptions such as 'She is hav-
        ing fun', 'He wants to play, too'.

NA   *Narrativity rating*
        0 = there is no narrativity or story-like quality in the
        description; it is purely descriptive.
        1 = there is at least one action or event mentioned as
        being performed by the characters, and the rest is
        descriptive.
        2 = there is a combination of narration and description.
        3 = the text is basically narrative, but inadequate or
        incomplete; there is more narration than description.
        4 = the text is mostly narrative, with any description sub-
        ordinate to the telling of a story.

5. *Fluency*

CF   *Conversational features*
        Total number of I-intrusions (author's voice). It
        includes informal language used to describe the picture
        (e.g., 'He is *like* hiding'), any use of first or second per-
        sons (e.g., you, I, me) and expressions that voice the
        author's doubt (e.g., 'She is three, *maybe* four years
        old') or gratuitous opinion (e.g., 'It is an ugly picture').

LS   *Language switching*
        Total number of switches (not individual words) into a
        language other than the one in which the interview is
        conducted.

DA   *Direct appeal to authority*
Total number of times the child appeals to the interviewer for help (e.g., to find out a word).

VS   *Rating of variation in sentence form*
0 = all t-units have the same structure (e.g., 'there is' or simple Subject–Verb structures).
1 = a combination of two different structures is used with no other sentence patterns.
2 = there is predominantly one structure but at least two other sentence structures are used.
3 = there is no dominant structure but no unusually sophisticated structures are used either; considerable variation.
4 = all t-units are as different as their semantics allows; there is at least one sophisticated structure (e.g., a complex sentence with embedding).

9

The lexical generation gap: a connectionist account of circumlocution in Chinese as a second language

PATRICIA A. DUFF

Introduction

Although interlanguage analysis has typically focused upon the acquisition of second language (L2) syntax, morphology and phonology (see Ellis, 1994; Gass & Selinker, 1994; Larsen-Freeman & Long, 1991, for reviews), a number of papers examining L2 lexicalization processes have appeared in recent years (e.g., in Færch & Kasper, 1983a, 1987a; Schreuder & Weltens, 1993). Much of this work falls under the rubric of research on communication strategies used in second language situations, about which Bialystok writes:

> the familiar ease and fluency with which we sail from one idea to the next in our first language is constantly shattered by some gap in our knowledge of a second language. The gap can take many forms – a word, a structure, a phrase, a tense marker, an idiom. Our attempts to overcome those gaps have been called communication strategies. (Bialystok, 1990, p. 1)

Many of the early lexicalization studies were concerned with identifying learners' strategies in selecting translation equivalents to L1 lexical items. Then, through an analysis of supplied forms and through introspective and retrospective analysis, classifications were derived for the most commonly used strategies. In a few accounts, however, more abstract psycholinguistic models for lexical search and suppliance have been proposed, although until very recently (e.g., Gasser 1988, drawing upon cognitive-computational models; and Schreuder & Weltens, 1993, using psycholinguistic ones), they have tended to be quite general and simplistic in form (e.g., Zimmermann & Schneider, 1987).[1]

As in previous research, one question the present study attempts to address is the following: how does a novice L2 speaker – one with limited linguistic resources in L2 – express intended meanings in that language? Models of lexical search and generation at the discourse (as opposed to sentence) level have been, and remain, underdeveloped and underspecified, as this area has not been widely studied and few computer models have managed to produce appropriately contextualized oral discourse. (McKeown, 1985, is one of the pioneers in this domain.) In studies of natural language processing or artificial intelligence (AI), because of the complexity of modelling, analysis has been mostly restricted to words, phrases and sentences, and parsing or comprehending texts has been a more successful venture than generating them. To illustrate the enormity of the task for the programmer (and the human brain, by analogy), Fantuzzi observes that in Gasser's (1988) research on an ESL speaker's interlanguage, 'a *single sentence* in the model required 292 nodes and 1374 connections!' (Fantuzzi, 1992, p. 323; original emphasis).

While there has been some discussion of the potential contributions of connectionist models to the field of second language acquisition (SLA) theory development and research (e.g., Fantuzzi, 1992; Gasser, 1988, 1990; Klein, 1990; Schmidt, 1988; Shirai, 1992; Sokolik, 1990), precise empirical work is lacking for the most part. In addition, numerous types of connectionist models exist; there are those which incorporate symbolic information in their models, as in localist types and, at the opposite extreme, those which are completely devoid of symbolic information (e.g., represented in nodes) and are, rather, totally distributive with a great amount of inbuilt redundancy (e.g., PDP models; Rumelhart, McClelland & the PDP Research Group, 1986). The somewhat conservative approach taken by Gasser (1988), which falls between the two extremes, is favoured for present purposes because it does not eliminate symbols in the connectionist architecture (Fantuzzi, 1992) and it may provide a helpful account (if only at a metaphorical level) for the complexities of language learning and use found in SLA. Gasser (1988) explains:

> The usual approach in designing connectionist models is to start from the bottom up, that is, to let the networks themselves develop their own representations of a domain given a set of primitive features. The representations that result in such cases are *distributed*; concepts do not appear at particular places in memory. An

alternative, and complementary, approach is to begin with the types of representations that have been found by symbolic models to support basic cognitive processes and attempt to implement these representations in a connectionist network. The resulting representations are *localized*; each concept has a single network node associated with it.   (Gasser, 1988, p. 31)

In addition, the localized approach may be more compatible with existing, empirically tested psycholinguistic and cognitive-linguistic models and furthermore aspires to be 'neurally plausible' (i.e., reflecting true brain activity; although Gasser's model does not exhibit the graceful degradation following activation that neurons do).

I will approach the problem of L2 lexicalization in natural discourse contexts by applying principles from a localist–connectionist model of linguistic knowledge representation and processing. In this chapter, following an overview of the L2 lexicalization literature, I will examine a small corpus of Chinese L2 data with the goal of describing how a learner might activate and then produce functional substitutes for missing or unavailable L2 lexical items.[2] To support my exploration of the phenomenon of circumlocution in L2, I will present some highly simplified schematic representations. Given the preliminary nature of the work, the present account is admittedly both primitive and speculative.

Background to the conceptualization and study of circumlocution

In this section, I will describe lexicalization strategies, semantic competence and circumlocution as they relate to this chapter, first based on general applied linguistics research, and then from an AI perspective. Lexicalization strategies often cited in the applied linguistics literature include two broad divisions and then, within each category, further subdivisions; these are derived from Bialystok (1983b, 1990), Blum-Kulka and Levenston (1983), Tarone (1983), Zimmermann and Schneider (1987). The initial breakdown is (1) use of L1 in borrowings or (conscious) transfer into L2 and (2) use of L2 (or language-neutral semantic features related to the target concept) to generate an L2 item. The latter, in turn, can involve such strategies as: (1) semantic contiguity, substitution, or synonymy; (2) description; (3) word coinage; (4) lexical simplification;

(5) superordinate terms; (6) approximation or overextension; (7) circumlocution; (8) paraphrase; (9) lexical decomposition; and (10) avoidance.

Naturally, overlap exists across these categories, both because they have been operationalized by different researchers, and also because the same utterances may manifest or have embedded within them more than one strategy. However, one point of comparison is the length of supplied forms – although, as Kellerman (1991) notes, this distinction can obscure common, prelinguistic underlying processes across cases of word coinage and circumlocution, for example. A synonym is usually taken to mean a one-word substitute for an individual lexical item; a paraphrase is a phrase or sentence roughly equivalent in length (as well as meaning) to the source item; and circumlocution is a more elaborate description of the features or meanings associated with the source item. Váradi observes that 'while both paraphrasing and circumlocution leave the meaning unaffected, the latter is understood to involve *substantial restructuring of the message, often resulting in awkward verbosity*' (Váradi, 1983, p. 84; emphasis mine). Citing Blum-Kulka and Levenston (1983), Bialystok notes that 'circumlocutions provide all relevant semantic features for an item, while paraphrase is a last resort that points to only a rough equivalent' (Bialystok, 1990, p. 41). And Tarone defines circumlocution thus: 'the learner describes the characteristics or elements of the object or action instead of using the appropriate target language (TL) item or structure ...' (Tarone, 1983, p. 62). For example, in reference to the concept *silk*, a speaker produces: 'It's made by little animals, for their house, and then turned into material' (translation from L2 Spanish; Bialystok, 1990, p. 1). Circumlocution is not restricted to the search for noun replacements, though. In data I collected from Hungarian students, the target concept and English word *splashed* (as in, 'a truck splashed some people when it went through a puddle') elicited numerous extended sequences in oral EFL production, including the following: 'the children got some water in – in their face and clothes; the truck went into water and they became very dirty'.

The extent to which the set of semantic features of the original referent and those of the uttered L2 counterpart match constitutes another difference across the ten categories listed above. When referring to a dog, a superordinate term (e.g., animal) is clearly more general in meaning than *dog*, and therefore the degree of match is different than, say, if a member of the dog category (e.g., *poodle*) were mentioned. Or, in another case, semantic decomposition might yield some but not all of the distinctive features of the referent or hyponym (i.e., where *dog* is realized as *has four legs and barks*, but there is no mention of *has fur*, and soforth), but may still provide a closer match than the superordinate term (*animal*) whose inherited features are of a very general nature.[3]

Blum-Kulka and Levenston (1983) discuss the notion of 'semantic competence' in L1 and L2, which adds a dimension to the broader and more widely used classifications in the L2 literature on communicative competence (Canale & Swain, 1980), highlighting a form of knowledge which might otherwise be considered part of one's grammatical and/or strategic competence. In their account, semantic competence refers to:

(a) The awareness of hyponymy, antonymy, converseness, and possibly other systematic relationships between lexical items, by means of which we can explain why in specific contexts one lexical item can substitute for another.
(b) The ability to avoid the use of specific lexical items by means of circumlocution and paraphrase.
(c) The ability to recognize degrees of paraphrastic equivalence.
(Blum-Kulka & Levenston, 1983, p. 120)

Clearly, the knowledge or awareness described above is central to circumlocution. Identifying relationships among concepts and taking stock of similarities and differences in semantic features for given concepts is critical in that process. The authors even suggest that the more 'semantically competent' individuals are in their L1, the better they will be at circumlocution in their L2 – a hypothesis which is untested and which this chapter will not shed light on, but which is interesting nonetheless.

In her study of L2 oral production data, Bialystok found that 'the best [lexicalization] strategies [used by subjects and judged for communicative effectiveness by native speakers], it seems, are those which are based in the target language and which take account of the specific features of the intended concept' (Bialystok, 1983b, p. 116). For that reason, circumlocution is termed *description* in Bialystok's work (and Færch & Kasper, 1984), of general physical properties, specific features, and interactional/functional characteristics (1983b, p. 106); but this classification does not preclude the use of paraphrase/synonyms together with circumlocution. In her later analysis, Bialystok (1990) presents circumlocution as one

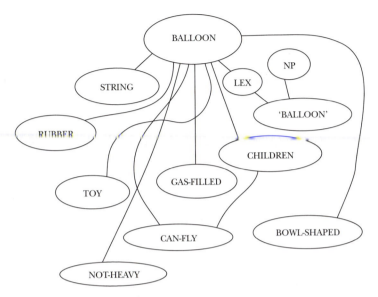

Figure 9.1   Representation of 'BALLOON'

of three categories of paraphrase (after Tarone, 1977), the other two being word coinage and approximation.

Often-cited examples of circumlocution in Váradi's (1983) study illustrate the speaker's analysis and provision of component features associated with the missing lexical element; for the English term *balloon,* Hungarian students produced such phrases as *special toys for children; they are filled by gas;* and *bowls ... they are light and they are flying* (Váradi, 1983, p. 95). The paraphrases/synonyms which Váradi refers to as approximations included *gas ball, air ball,* and *air ring.* (Indeed, these now-classic examples are so commonly cited that Cook observes: '[it is] as if there is no need to get fresh sightings of Bigfoot once one person has glimpsed him' (Cook, 1993, p. 134). Here, some new sightings will be reported.) Therefore, a semantic network for the concept *balloon* contains the following sorts of information for these subjects: special toy, played-with-by-children, gas/air-filled, bowl(ball?)-shaped, light-weight, can-be-flown, etc. (see Figure 9.1). 'LEX' in the following network simply refers to lexical item; in some current psycholinguistic accounts (e.g., Levelt, 1989), this would be broken down into two parts: the *lemma,* which contains semantic and morphosyntactic information, and *lexeme* (form) which contains phonological information. In Gasser (1988) each concept has attached to it grammatical roles (e.g., BOX is an NP, DIR-OBJ), content (this BOX is an instance of the (prototypical) BOX category, perhaps linked to a node for CONTAINER; and with attributes such as SHAPE, COMPOSITION, etc., each of which has attached nodes), and a head ('BOX'); when the latter is fired, it corresponds to the utterance.

Another example of circumlocution presented by Váradi (1983, p. 95) is *line for drying wet clothes* for 'clothesline' (whereas approximations included phrases capturing certain physical features, such as *strong string* and *lace for wet clothes*). The productivity and prevalence of this lexicalization strategy among many L1 and L2 speakers is attested by Bialystok (1990), who reports that in a subset of 78 L2 French utterances (from a total of 324) produced by 18 girls, circumlocution accounted for 80 per cent of the communication strategies they used. Indeed, I believe that many speakers would agree on the basis of personal experience that this is a very natural, common and essential means of communicating.

Here, it is not my intent to scrutinize these taxonomies further, problematic though they may be (see Cook, 1993, Ch. 6, for overview and critique; Kellerman, 1991). I shall focus instead on the processes and semantic features involved in lexical compensatory strategies more generally (see Kellerman, 1991) and the role of spreading activation within the mental lexicon in a broader conceptualization of circumlocution.

Representing circumlocution in a localist–connectionist model

Cognitive models have been developed in an attempt to solve the mystery of how information or knowledge is retained and represented in the mind/brain, how it is accessed in order to carry out particular tasks, and how it is modified and mediated by experience. With regard to language, the questions become more specific:

1. How are word, phrase and sentence structures and meanings stored in memory?
2. How do intentions to comprehend or generate linguistic utterances interact with these stored units of conceptual/linguistic

knowledge to allow humans to understand and produce an infinite number of possible constructions?

3. How is the performance of linguistic tasks related to that of other cognitive skills?

4. How are conceptual schemata represented and what is their relationship to corresponding linguistic elements?

Psycholinguists, computational/cognitive linguists and other scholars have published an array of work that bears on the representation of knowledge structures invoked in the interpretation and/or production of language (see, e.g., Anderson, 1983; Bates & MacWhinney, 1987; Bialystok, 1985; Gasser, 1988, 1990; Grosz & Sidner, 1986; Hatch & Hawkins, 1985; Karmiloff-Smith, 1986; McKeown, 1985; O'Malley et al., 1987; Pienemann, 1984; Poulisse & Bongaerts, 1994; Rumelhart & McClelland, 1986; Schreuder & Weltens, 1993; Slobin, 1985; Waltz & Pollack, 1985). This research increasingly underscores the importance of the mind/brain's massively parallel, distributed representation and processing of language. The common belief now is that language cannot simply be processed in a serial, rule-driven or deductive way. Rather, context, 'real-world knowledge' or schemata, spreading activation, weighted connections, lateral inhibition, graceful degradation, and other claimed properties of the mind/brain (which presumably have both physiological and psychological counterparts) permit the efficient activation of existing knowledge structures that are relevant to cognitive/linguistic tasks (cf. Rumelhart & McClelland, 1986).

The networks stored in the memory of very 'semantically competent' speakers can be viewed as maximally efficient and circumlocution can be one manifestation of differences across L2 proficiency levels in terms of efficiency, automaticity and apparent ease of L2 execution (see McLaughlin, 1987, Ch. 6). For example, the ACTFL Oral Proficiency rating guidelines (Buck et al., 1989) state that for High–Intermediate speakers, 'limited vocabulary still necessitates hesitation and may bring about slightly unexpected circumlocution'; for Advanced speakers, 'circumlocution which arises from vocabulary or syntactic limitations very often is quite successful, though some groping for words may still be evident'; and Advanced–Plus speech, 'often shows a well-developed ability to compensate for an imperfect grasp of some forms with confident use of communicative strategies, such as paraphrasing and circumlocution' (pp. 2–3; cited in Berry-Bravo, 1993, p. 372).

According to Gasser (personal communication, April 1994), this efficiency is related to both representation and processing factors. First, in terms of representation, the networks exhibit maximum connectivity to allow direct and speedy access to relevant semantic components in the mental lexicon and access to possible alternatives where gaps exist. This greater connectivity results from two things: more nodes, that is, more concepts that have been entered into long-term memory, and more connections among the nodes. Secondly, with respect to processing, the two key factors mentioned above are *parallelism* and *constraint satisfaction*: the former refers to the spreading of activation in all directions at once (in contrast to the serial or linear view of processing); and the latter refers to the inbuilt constraints in the system, in the form of variable connection weights. In language production, the network seeks the pattern of activation over all of the units which is most compatible with the inputs, and certain outputs (e.g., paraphrase, circumlocution) are an automatic consequence of this spreading activation, given the system constraints. Because minimally relevant nodes may also be activated during language use, these variable weightings and other constraints on the priming of concepts and lexical items are critical for successful language processing (Waltz & Pollack, 1985).

As mentioned above, in connectionist models as opposed to formal symbolic models, activation spreads quite freely throughout networks once an element in the system is primed. In an analysis of circumlocution, this furnishes some useful effects; for example, multiple semantic features associated with the source concept, paraphrases, synonyms, negated antonyms, and so on, are automatically activated. The lexical items which are connected to these concepts or nodes are activated, and if 'fired' (because of sufficiently high levels of activation from relevant inputs), may be uttered in discourse. (Note that activation is a necessary but not sufficient condition for actual production.) And this is, indeed, what appears to take place in spontaneous, naturally occurring production data, as we shall see below. Of course, what makes matters more complex in depicting the process of lexical generation in SLA is that for each concept potentially one or more lexical entries may exist. Hence, in principle the system must be able to inhibit (through negative weightings) the activation of one language (e.g., Chinese or English, depending on the context) and any unwanted lexical items connected to that language, and yet manage to convey comparable information in the deficient L2. Gasser (1988, 1990) shows in some detail the complexity and significance of this endeavour. For example, his 1988 research examined the ESL knowledge of a native speaker of Japanese (and L1 transfer effects), which was meticulously modelled by means of computer simulations employing a localist–connectionist implementation of memory schemata.[4]

Finally, although not approaching the problem from an AI standpoint, Poulisse and Bongaerts (1994) also adopt a spreading activation approach to the selection of L2 lexical items (lemma), which is shown in a Dutch learner's selection/production of 'boy' for the concept [+HUMAN, +MALE, −ADULT] in L2 English. They explain:

> It should be noted that besides the intended lemma BOY, some lemmas [i.e., MAN, GIRL] are activated which are similar in meaning. In addition, some L1 lemmas which share conceptual information with the intended lemma are activated [e.g., JONGEN]. In this case, the lemma BOY receives most activation and is selected.
>
> (Poulisse & Bongaerts, 1994, p. 41)

Thus, BOY receives inputs from all three relevant semantic features at the conceptual level and from ENGLISH-LANGUAGE, whereas the Dutch equivalent, JONGEN, or the English lemmas MAN and GIRL receive activation from only three sources each.

Circumlocution in L2 Chinese

What might the cognitive (or 'neural') networks associated with circumlocution look like? How might we represent the connections between semantic/conceptual and lexical components? Further, how might both L1 and L2 knowledge be incorporated into the networks, as well as other kinds of knowledge (e.g., world knowledge, semantic composition of referents, pragmatic demands)?[5]

The data for the present study were elicited from a native speaker of English (this author) learning Chinese. The subject (hereafter, P) was engaged in audiotaped face-to-face conversations with native speakers (NSs) of a southern dialect of Mandarin Chinese and with other non-native speakers (NNSs) of Chinese. The tapes were transcribed by trained NSs of Chinese in the months following P's arrival in Hunan Province, P.R. China, in the late 1980s. Upon her arrival, P already had some metalinguistic knowledge of the language from independent study and exposure to small amounts of oral Cantonese and Mandarin elsewhere. During the eight months of data collection, P was unaware that the data would eventually be analysed for properties of lexicalization, as her primary interest at the time was syntactic development. The examples below are presented according to the source concept triggering the circumlocution. A short, uncomplicated paraphrase is presented first and this is followed by more typically expansive cases of circumlocution. However, it is beyond the scope of this analysis to account in a more complete way for the entirety of the discourse produced or to incorporate all the pertinent features in the network. Rather, my primary goal is to examine the resolution of lexical generation gaps for individual concepts/ phrases that emerged in the data. Five short texts will be presented in total, but I will provide sample networks for three examples only. For reasons of simplicity and clarity, I will restrict my formulation of semantic networks and representation systems below by working within a localist–connectionist paradigm (in the spirit – but not nearly the level of detail – of Gasser's Connectionist Lexical Memory model (1988)).

Example 1: Generating the locative complement NEAR
In Example 1, recorded several weeks after P's arrival in China, P tries to explain to a Chinese interlocutor where an acquaintance lives, but without access to the L2 equivalents for the concept NEAR. (Glosses below the L2 utterances are rough translations.)

P: Ta zhu zai nar. Bu yuan **bu yuan**.
She lives there. Not far not far.
I: Zhu zai xuexiao ma?
(She) lives at school?
P: Bu shi xuexiao. Ta-ta de fangjian *bu yuan.*
(It)'s not school. Her- her room is not far. (10/10/86)

Below are listed a number of features in the network associated with the schema for describing relative distance. The numbering is not meant to indicate discrete steps, however.

1.   Simultaneous activation takes place from stimulus inputs to a number of different nodes in the network corresponding to RELATIVE-DISTANCE-ADJECTIVE (REL-DIST-ADJ).
2.   LEX is activated because a lexical item is sought. Both CHINESE-LANG and ENGLISH-LANG are activated through

excitatory inputs from LEX. However, the system has learned to keep English and Chinese linguistic knowledge rather separate through inhibitory connections between the two language nodes. This could be accomplished in one of two ways: either through mutual inhibition between languages (e.g., CHINESE-LANG–ENGLISH-LANG), or in a more complex fashion, between one language, such as CHINESE-LANG, and lexical items in the competing language, such as English 'NEAR' (i.e., CHINESE-LANG–*–'NEAR'). This inhibition, shown with an asterisk, and the inversely excitatory activation of Chinese linguistic knowledge, would also be enhanced by inputs from the discourse context. The previous discussion has all been conducted in Chinese and the topic is related to the Chinese neighbourhood in which P lives. Thus, inputs derived from CHINESE-CONTEXT and CHINESE-INTERLOCUTOR (and language of previous utterance, etc.) over time serve to inhibit ENGLISH-LANG and to activate Chinese knowledge. Even so, English lexical counterparts are also primed to a certain extent, as one might expect in early SLA when some connections are not yet heavily weighted as relatively little learning has taken place; this is a necessary design feature in order to account for occasional code-switching in other excerpts and also contributes to the speaker's understanding that a lexical item for NEAR should exist (as it does in English).

3.   As no item exists in this speaker's memory for the Chinese word directly related to the concept NEAR (e.g., 'JIN'), activation spreads throughout the system; notice that there is no node for the missing lexical item, but that it would be generated through learning at some later point. Furthermore, P has not yet learned Mandarin constructions for verbal complements (e.g., of manner, degree), which are very important in the language. The typical Mandarin construction for 'she lives near here' (N-V-Advl), *ta zhu de hen jin*, requires the complementizing particle *de* after the verb (*zhu*) and then the complement of degree adverbial (for distance), which is actually an adjectival phrase in Chinese grammars, *hen jin* 'very near'.[6]

4.   Activation takes place along the connection linking the pair of coordinates, NEAR–FAR. Although it is the intention of the speaker to communicate the concept NEAR and not the opposite meaning, the two are semantically linked through a relationship of antonymy. Here, the exact nature of the relationship between nodes that is, the significance of the connections is generally not shown.

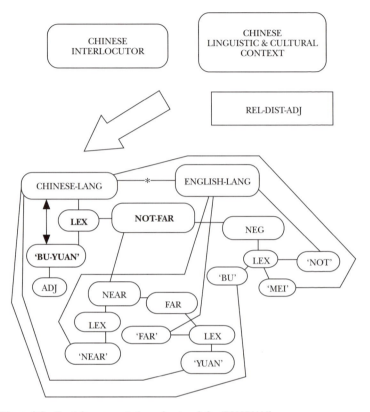

Figure 9.2 Partial representation of network for 'BU-YUAN'

Hence, activation of the antonym FAR in the NEAR–FAR semantic pair automatically occurs with the activation of NEAR, and vice versa. Two factors account for this: (a) P knows the LEX for FAR in Chinese (i.e., 'YUAN'); and (b) perhaps not coincidentally, in the NEAR–FAR pair, FAR is the less marked entry, and thus naturally receives stronger activation than its marked counterpart (cf., Clark & Clark, 1977, pp. 426–7).[7] This kind of default marker passing would be more easily specified in a symbolic model by means of a rule which specifies that when a lexical item is not found for a member of a polar (unmarked–marked) pair of modifiers, the unmarked item should be chosen and negated. However, the same kind of process could also be incorporated into a localist–connectionist model in the following way: circumlocution automatically occurs because

Table 9.1 Dictionary entries for lexical items (Watson, O. (ed.).
(1968). *Longman Modern English Dictionary*. London: Longman.

Chinese target lexical item	English target lexical item	Definition
'JIN'	'NEAR'	at or within a short distance; not far off; not far distance in space (p. 743)
'LINJU'	'NEIGHBOUR'	a person living next door or relatively close to another (p. 745)
'JIERI'	'HOLIDAY'	a day or a part of a day, on which one does not go to work, school, etc. (Br.) away from work, school, etc. for a period of leisure (p. 513)
'HEZI'? (box) 'XIAOCHEZIANG' 'ERTONG GUACHI' or	'CART' (?)	a two-wheeled or four-wheeled horse-drawn or tractor-drawn vehicle, used for carrying loads (p. 169)
'ERTONG TUOCHI' (= carriage for human transportation)	'CARRIAGE' (?)	a wheeled vehicle for transporting people (p. 169)
'DUIHUA'	'DIALOGUE'	a literary work in conversational form; conversation in a novel, play, film, etc.; exchange of opinion between people with opposing interests or points of view, esp. a fruitful exchange (p. 290)
'BAI(XIALAI)'	'MEMORIZE'	to commit to memory; the faculty by which sense impressions and information are retained consciously or unconsciously in the mind and subsequently recalled; a person's capacity to remember; a mental image or impression of a past event, something learned, etc. (p. 697)
'CHONGFU'	'REPEAT'	to say again (p. 942)

NEAR, the somewhat more marked member of the antonym pair, is not lexicalized in P's L2 Chinese. Through repeated experience and spreading activation, this eventually yields NOT–FAR (concept), which in this case is lexicalized as 'BU–YUAN'.[8]

Corresponding to the network outlined above would be a series of roles for the schema of relative distance (REL-DIST-ADJ) (see Gasser, 1988). This schema would specify how the concept selects for (or is associated with) certain kinds of thematic or syntactic roles and relations, information also encoded within the lexicon.

Notice that the information or concept features proposed in this network representation cover many of the concepts captured in a typical published dictionary entry (see Table 9.1); that is, 'NEAR' is defined as 'at or within a short distance; not far off; not far distance in space'.

Example 2: Generating a Chinese noun phrase for NEIGHBOUR

The 'generation gap' observed in Example 1 presents itself again in Example 2 in a rather more elaborate circumlocution. This occurred when P was talking about a book she had read and was trying to describe the heroine's neighbours.

P: Ta yige yue yihou, ta uh bu yuan de zhu, **bu yuan zhu de ren** gaosu ta n – uh

*She one month later, her uh not far live, **not far live person** tells her uh*
ta airen ziji de zuo ta de – tamen de fangzi.
her husband himself made her – their house.

'A month later, a neighbour of hers (Lit: 'a not-far-live-NOM-person')
told her that her husband had constructed their house by himself*
(29/11/86)

To illustrate this, we will build upon the previous network. As in that example, the lexical items corresponding to English 'NEAR' or 'LIVE-NEAR' or 'NEIGHBOUR' (Mandarin 'LINJU') are absent in P's mental lexicon. That being the case, she produces the non-targetlike relative clause 'BU-YUAN-ZHU-DE-REN', (not-far-live-*NOM*-person) to refer to NEIGHBOUR. In Standard Mandarin, the circumlocuted construction would be 'ZHU-DE-BU-YUAN-DE-REN' (live-COMPL-not-far-NOM-person), which also contains a prenominal modifying clause (ZHU DE BU YUAN), in which the verb is followed by the particle (DE) and degree complement of relative distance (BU YUAN) and then a nominalizer (DE) and noun (REN). This construction has not yet been mastered by P; if the knowledge were available, a sequencing mechanism would ensure that the utterance contained appropriately ordered items.

Example 3: Extensive circumlocution related to HOLIDAY

Another problematic concept which yields lengthy circumlocution is HOLIDAY, for which there is no Chinese LEX in P's memory network. In this excerpt, the interlocutor was a young (11-year-old), monolingual Chinese girl from the countryside, who worked as a full-time babysitter/maid in the neighbourhood. She and P often chatted, especially as P passed by on her way to or from work. The following conversation occurred on Christmas Day, a regular workday in the community, but a holiday for expatriate teachers at the university.

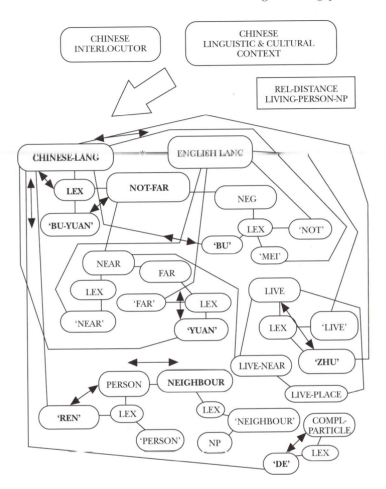

Figure 9.3 Partial representation of network for 'NEIGHBOUR'

I: Ni xianzai hen mang ma?
   Are you very busy now?
P: Ah jintian meiyou ke.   Women meiyou ke.
   Ah today (we do) not have class. We (do) not have class.
   Shi women de – uh waiguo de hen jungyao de – de ri. Meiyou ke.
   (It)'s our uh foreign very important day. (We) don't have class.
   Shi women de wan yi wan de ri. Jintian shi shi'eryue ershiwu hao.
   (It)'s our play-n-play day.   Today is December 25th.
   Shi yige hen jungyao de.
   (It)'s one of the important ones.

*'Today we don't have classes [2 times], it's an important foreign (holi)day
today. It's a day for us to play.* It's December 25th, one of our important
[holidays]' (25/12/86)

The lexical gap in CHINESE-LANG (LEX) created by HOLIDAY,
coupled with differences in Chinese and Western cultural schemata,
obviously causes considerable circumlocution; namely, TODAY (the
topic), the HOLIDAY, CHRISTMAS (the particular instantiation of
HOLIDAY) activates the following attributes for P:

(a) no classes (for the foreign teachers to teach); thus, by implica-
    tion, not busy
(b) foreign, important day (note: probably unfamiliar to inter-
    locutor)
(c) day to play (i.e., enjoy leisure)
(d) December 25th.

The reader might find that P is supplying too much information
in answer to a simple question; that it would suffice to say, 'no it's
December 25th', or simply 'No' – she was not busy, since P didn't
know how to say either 'HOLIDAY' (Mandarin 'JIERI') or
'CHRISTMAS' ('SHENDANJIE'). However, both the cultural holiday schema and the calendar are different for P and her interlocutor, and both individuals have free time at that moment.
Indeed, the question is likely asked to reveal whether P will have
some time to chat while the interlocutor cares for a baby. Hence,
many details are provided to account for why P is not busy.
Furthermore, the young unschooled interlocutor is not familiar
with the holiday which P is observing, and P takes the opportunity
to practise her Chinese and to inform her about the holiday.
    In this example, a complex constellation of features and sche-
mata potentially associated with HOLIDAY comes into play; of
course, it is neither exhaustive, nor sufficiently or uniformly
detailed in this depiction, but simply illustrates certain attributes
or roles and connections that must exist in P's mental lexicon (in
some form) in conjunction with the concept HOLIDAY. Through
spreading activation, given the system constraints, these attributes
are both invoked sufficiently well at the conceptual level and
represented at the lexical level to permit P to render the utterances shown in the text.
    Again, it is interesting to compare this putative knowledge struc-
ture in P's mental lexicon with the dictionary entry for 'HOLIDAY'
in English (see Table 9.1): 'a day or a part of a day, on which one

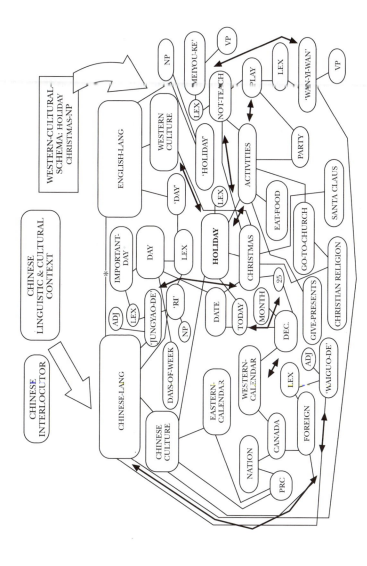

Figure 9.4 Partial representation of 'HOLIDAY' network

does not go to work, school, etc.; (Br.) away from work, school, etc. for a period of leisure' (p. 513). In generating substitutes for the Chinese counterpart to 'HOLIDAY', notice that some but not all of these roles/attributes were uttered – and others, more closely associated with CHRISTMAS[9] were invoked – although all were activated to varying degrees but may not have fired. As McKeown (1985) notes, every attempt to generate a text based on, for example, an attributive schema for HOLIDAY should ideally yield a slightly different set of information, although context and other factors would deem certain facts or attributes of greater relevance than others and these would therefore be primed.

Some of the characteristics of this network follow:

1. ENGLISH-LANG in this communicative context is inhibited, as in previous examples, which creates an environment of relatively higher activation for CHINESE-LANG.
2. Knowledge of differences in HOLIDAY schemata cross-culturally as well as cross-linguistically, is represented in long-term memory and is important in determining what connections are activated most strongly here.
3. Much of the information about the superordinate category HOLIDAY is actually based upon the features for CHRISTMAS; thus the date for this day and not, say, New Year's, is selected; it is naturally also most relevant and thereby satisfies more cooperative conversational principles as well (Grice, 1975). Very culture-specific details related to CHRISTMAS (e.g., Christian religion or culture, Santa Claus, and gift-giving) are avoided because they either do not exist in Chinese or are not sufficiently activated to fire. What is quite remarkable is how in real time, unrehearsed,[10] L2 learners are able to circumvent complete communication breakdown, despite the nature and extent of gaps in the system.

Example 4: Compensating for gaps related to three metacommunicative concepts: (a) DIALOGUE; (b) MEMORIZE; (c) REPEAT

The next excerpt, recorded about a month before the previous one, involves several instances of lexicalization where three complex verb constructions are part of the attendant circumlocution. In this case, both P and her interlocutor are NNSs of Chinese in an informal Chinese practice session together. In the first instance, P's interlocutor struggles to produce the term for DIALOGUE, as she tries to describe the antiquated teaching methods of her Chinese teacher in America and the monotonous language laboratory exercises she had endured there.

1 I: Jizhidai bu – ah meiyou yisi.
  Tape (?) (was) not – ah not interesting.
2 P: Meiyou yisi. Oh.
  Not interesting. Oh.
3 I: Meiyou yisi.
  Not interesting.
4 P: Meiyou yisi.   Ah kewen bu hao – bu tai hao?
  Not interesting. Text not good – not too good?
  Kewen meiyou yisi?
  The text wasn't interesting?
  Kewen.
  Text.
5 I: Kewen meiyou yisi.   Hen chang de ... de ...
  Text (was) not interesting. Very long ...
6 P: Shuo yi shuo?
  Chit-chat? (have a talk)
7 I: Shuo yi shuo! (Laugh) <u>Right</u>!
  Hen uh tai duo de tai duo de uh ke – uh *text?*
  Very uh too much too much uh text
8 P: Kewen.   Uh nimen yinggai – yinggai uh – uh ni ting le nimen
  Text   You had to – had to uh   you heard it you
  yinggai xue le – xue le?   Yinggai <u>remember</u> neige?
  had to learn – learn (it)?   Had to remember it?
  Mei guanxi?
  It didn't matter?
9 I: Um women – women ting le women ting le
  Um we – we heard (it) – we heard (it)
  Women ting le zhei ge women shuo ...
  We heard it that we say ...
  women ting le 'ta shi zhongguoren'
  we heard 'he is a Chinese person'
  women shuo 'ta shi zhongguoren'.
  we said 'he is a Chinese person'.

(24/11/86)

After a long lexical search for the CHINESE-LANG lexical item corresponding to the concept DIALOGUE, in turn #6 P produces the verb phrase 'SHUO-YI-SHUO' (chit-chat, or have a talk) in lieu of the Chinese noun phrase 'DUIHUA'. X-yi-X was a productive reduplicative verb construction the two students had (in P's case only just recently) learned to use in other contexts (e.g., as in Example 3, 'WAN-YI-WAN', or play); its informal, colloquial connotation and application to the problem of the present gap causes both to laugh and it is also ungrammatical because the missing lexical item should be a noun. Their knowledge of this term and its communicative potential, and also their prior experience with this and similar forms, is of course represented in memory and activated on this occasion. English is again suppressed because of the two speakers' resolve to speak only Chinese during these practice sessions. Therefore, in the absence of the target (L2) lexical item for DIALOGUE, the colloquial verb form semantically associated with the schema for SPEAK was activated. Yet the speakers apparently recognized that its usage was marked in this context (i.e., they laughed), although the intended meaning seemed not to be compromised.

In turns #8 and #9, the difficulty for both speakers is that the verbs attached to the concepts they wish to convey, MEMORIZE ('BEI MALAI') and REPEAT ('CHONGFU'), respectively, do not exist in their lexicon. In #8, therefore, P substitutes the CHINESE-LANG LEX equivalents of 'listen and learn' for MEMORIZE; then in #9, her interlocutor first uses the verb 'SHUO' in isolation (the same verb used in connection with DIALOGUE), then decides to demonstrate the meaning of REPEAT by analysing the concept into two sequentially ordered parts: listening to a model ('ta shi zhong-guoren'), then saying the same sentence. This excerpt is too complex to represent schematically; however, it illustrates how spreading activation would need to operate within a system in which better learned items are more heavily weighted and thus more accessible in order for circumlocution to proceed. (For corresponding published dictionary entries for the three items, see Table 9.1.)

Example 4 reveals, then, how verb phrases are circumlocuted – for example, in a procedural fashion (i.e., turn #8 for MEMORIZE, or #9 for REPEAT); with substitution of VP for NP for DIALOGUE; with initially weaker but then stronger priming of the English equivalent ('REMEMBER', in turn #8), to the point that it fires when other linguistic resources were unavailable.

Example 5: Circumlocution related to a new concept – CART/ CARRIAGE

In the final example, some months later, P is attempting to describe to a Chinese colleague an object she observed on a recent trip to Beijing. It is a kind of small, covered, wheeled, wooden cart for which both CHINESE-LANG LEX and ENGL-LANG LEX are unknown to P.

P: haizi qu xuexiao de shihou, zai – tamen you xiaofangzi,
   children go (to) school time,   at – they have small house

fangzili tamen e – houbian, tamen mama haishi baba
house – inside they behind, their mother or father
zixingche houmian zuo, zuo neige fangzili.
bicycle behind go, go this house inside.
I: Hezi. (= candidate expression for missing lexical item; lit. 'box')
    'When children go to school, they have a small house, in the house they
    travel behind their mother or father's bike' (21/2/87)

This instance of lexicalization yielded a decomposition of the concept, entailing an analysis of (a) the physical features of the CART/CARRIAGE, in which it is likened to a small house (i.e., an approximation in some accounts); (b) the function of the covered cart/wagon, in which children travel to school in winter in Beijing; and (c) the manner in which this cart transports its occupants – that is, by being pulled alongside the back wheel of a parent's bicycle. Again, a localist–connectionist network would reveal lexical gaps in P's long-term memory for both the Chinese or English term, although the concept is obviously concrete and stored in memory in such a way that it can be analysed in semantic and functional terms. All of this information is automatically invoked when the speaker plans to mention the object and then struggles to find appropriate L2 structures to convey the information adequately (until in this case a somewhat inadequate target item was supplied by a Chinese NS). Interestingly, there may in fact not be a single target item for that concept even in Mandarin. Some NSs say this object is a Beijing invention, a kind of 'cage on wheels for transporting children' that might be termed *xiao chexiang; xiao tuoche;* or *ertong tuoche* – all referring to a carriage device for children. But these same Chinese nationals were not altogether confident about these candidate lexical items.

Conclusion

In this chapter, I set out to characterize L2 circumlocution by examining a small corpus of data from Chinese as a second language. I highlighted the importance of identifying the semantic features associated with concepts, and how these are interconnected, and suggested (after Blum-Kulka and Levenston, 1983; Gasser, 1988) that it is the efficiency of activating these interconnected semantic and lexical features that determines a person's ability to fill gaps in linguistic knowledge during on-line production. Three examples were depicted in simple semantic networks in which certain connections were activated by receiving various positive inputs, and others, conversely, were inhibited. For example, inhibition was linked to the intended (and expected) language of use (English vs Chinese), speakers' intentions and sociolinguistic factors; whereas greater weightings existed across the most typically or frequently associated features. Discussion of this phenomenon from a connectionist perspective remains necessarily hypothetical without actually testing these proposed representations and procedures using computer programmes, which is an altogether different undertaking. However, even in its present form, this analysis offers a novel representation of lexical generation through circumlocution in a little-researched L2, and perhaps a point of departure for further work along similar lines.

Notes

I wish to thank Mike Gasser, Evelyn Hatch and Anne Hawson for their comments on an earlier version of this chapter, although I take responsibility for the content. I would also like to express my appreciation to the editors of this volume for their patience and encouragement.

1. For example, Zimmermann and Schneider 'suppose that if initial L1 synonym search fails, in at least one strategy of lexical search, learners decompose L1 lexical items into paraphrases and translate them into the L2, or that they form L2 paraphrases right away. Whereas, for some learners, these paraphrases are the final approximations, others go on to condense such paraphrases into shorter lexical phrases and complex words, omitting irrelevant semantic aspects' (Zimmermann & Schneider, 1987, p.180; see also their model on p. 181).

2. In this discussion, *process* and *strategy* will be used interchangeably to refer to a general set of cognitive procedures for searching for, finding and producing L2 forms. Of course, drawing inferences about (mind/brain) architecture and processing from observed behaviours can lead to circular arguments about the way knowledge is structured, as Jacobs and Schumann (1992) point out.

3. One way of testing the degree of match or the retrievability of the referent is to show the alternative (e.g., circumlocuted) forms to native speakers and have them provide the originally intended referent (see, e.g., Bialystok, 1990).

4. In his account, a semantic network or schema is established gradually through experience by the processes of inference, generalization, inheritance, and so on. Those components in the network that are

most often or most closely linked have stronger connections than those which are only distantly or infrequently associated with one another (note that this is not a typical feature of schema-based models, however). The schemata then become 'structured generalizations that are the basis for recognition, inference, and planning' (Gasser, 1988, p. 34).

5. To my knowledge, current connectionist approaches for the most part, although obviously highly sensitive to environmental conditions, contexts and inputs, do not purport to take into account the complexities of pragmatic/social interaction at any level of detail (see Fantuzzi, 1992; Shirai, 1992). Gasser (1988), however, does include speech-act information in his hierarchical model.

6. An alternate way of expressing the same thing would be *ta zhu zai fujin*, 'she lives in the neighbourhood'.

7. Support for the posited connectedness of opposites also comes from Aitchison (1994), who summarizes the results of word association experiments and examples of speech errors (tongue slips). She notes that 'people nearly always pick the partner if the item is one of a pair, as in *husband* and *wife*, or has an obvious opposite, as in *big* and *small*' (p. 83). Further, the links between coordinates such as near/far are said to be 'powerful and long-lasting' (p. 90). Other evidence concerning the unmarked status of the 'positive' element of dichotomous pairs is that it is the form used in questions: e.g., How far/big/heavy is x?, rather than How near/small/light is x?).

8. Evidently, representing negation or non-existence of entities/concepts in this type of network can prove very problematic (M. Gasser, personal communication, 1988). With regard to linguistic properties of Chinese negation, there are two negative particles: 'BU' and 'MEI'. 'MEI' receives less activation because it must be used with a verb (not an adverb or adjective) to provide aspectual information, whereas 'BU' is used with adjectives or in adverbial complements, such as 'YUAN'.

9. The *Longman Modern English Dictionary* (Watson, O. (ed.). (1968)) describes CHRISTMAS as: 'the annual festival observed by Christians on 25 Dec., commemorating the birth of Christ' (p. 197).

10. Certainly, connection strengths are influenced by previous experience, exposure and practice though, and this might be construed as rehearsal at some level.

10

An introspective analysis of listener inferencing on a second language listening test

STEVEN ROSS

Recent interest in second language testing has been focused on revealing the complexities of cognitive processes underlying responses to test task prompts in order to examine construct validity. This interest is motivated by the assumption that our understanding of the validity of test results must go beyond an examination of correlational patterns of item responses with external criteria to include strategic criteria internal to the test-taker (Henning, 1992). Similarly, for applied linguists to understand the nature of comprehension in language processing tasks, other, more subject-centred approaches need to be considered (Cohen, 1987). One approach to exploring comprehension and performance in language processing tasks and tests has been introspection. Through introspective analysis of the processing strategies language learners have used, a new avenue to understanding the validity of item responses and comprehension schemata is potentially opened.

Reference and inferencing in second language comprehension

Current understanding of how inferencing strategies interact with context, schemata and pragmatics during the process of listening comprehension has been summarized in Rost (1990). Inferencing in interactive contexts can be seen as dependent on the availability of a willing interlocutor to provide specific elaborative details matched to the degree of comprehension revealed in the queries and responses of the listener. Rost notes a number of strategies associated with conversational contexts. Common to listening strategies is the initial inferencing hearers make about the possible sense and reference of utterances and then secondarily inferences in schemata induced by the hearing of particular lexical items. The schemata allow for projections on to the subsequent discourse in the form of hypotheses about propositions thought to be thematically related to the understood topic. Subsequent listening serves to confirm or disconfirm the hypotheses about the speaker's intended meaning. When an interlocutor is available, specific schematic hypotheses can be tested and confirmed with the use of clarification questions and checks on the meaning of lexical items unfamiliar to the listener (Rost & Ross, 1991). When no feedback source is available, the hearer must rely on linking the subsequent text to the currently created schematic representation of its meaning. A key question for understanding the process of inferencing in listening is how learners create initial schematic representations and how these are maintained, revised or abandoned in light of discourse accessible after the representations are constructed.

Studies of inferencing in second language learning have suggested that learners use a variety of approaches to associate world knowledge and specific knowledge of the immediate co-text (Bialystok & Fröhlich, 1980). Depending on the response requirements, second language learners may utilize varying hypotheses about the meaning they attempt to decipher (Bialystok, 1983a). Inferencing has been seen as a variably used process that parallels individual differences in achievement and aptitude.

Recent accounts of inferencing in second language comprehension suggest that there are different strategies used by learners at various proficiency levels. Haastrup (1991) concludes that higher-proficiency second language readers utilize world knowledge in their inferencing about the meaning of novel lexical items presented in texts. Lower-proficiency learners, in contrast, tend to focus more narrowly on the available co-text and use it to build meaning from the individual structural components of the words and sentences. Higher-proficiency readers also adopt their inferencing strategies to match variation in the task required by the item type presented in the task. Lower-proficiency readers have a narrower repertoire of strategies and therefore tend to approach different tasks with inferencing strategies that do not lead to successful understanding of the novel lexical items.

In an analysis of comprehension strategies used in interactive listening, Rost and Ross (1991) noted that learners of different proficiency levels tended to rely on inferential strategies in interaction that potentially narrow down possible references in their queries about unknown lexical items encountered in the stream of speech. Specifically, their study suggested that lower-proficiency listeners often opt for a lexically focused query that provides paraphrasing information about the unknown lexical item. Lower-proficiency listeners were found to be less likely to benefit from periphrastic re-runs of information since the rejoinder may not allow a salient synonym to be isolated and matched with the unknown lexical item unless some interactional modification (Long, 1983b) could be provided to make the contents of the rejoinder more accessible. Higher-proficiency listeners, in contrast, started with a clearer identification of where the troublesome lexical element was located in the stream of speech and were more adept at using hypothesis-testing strategies which allowed them to remain engaged in the interaction, while at the same time making relatively better inferences about the meaning of unknown lexical items coming up in the subsequent discourse.

Inferencing studies have used a variety of tasks ranging from isolated sentences with novel lexical items, via cloze gaps, to coherent narratives with exotic lexis included to provoke inferencing or reprisal strategies (Færch & Kasper, 1987a). Relatively few studies have taken responses provided by individual learners and traced their retrospective or introspective accounts back to the source of miscomprehension as evidence of the cognitive strategies used in the unsuccessful identification of possible referents in forced-choice task such as those commonly used in second language testing.

The use of intro- and retrospection

Introspection (think-aloud protocols) and retrospection (*ex post facto* accounts) as methods of test construct validation are still rare in language testing for logistical reasons. MacLean (1984) examined the effect of task difficulty in cloze tests using reader introspection to find varying strategy use for the type of gap encountered. In a study of strategies by both first and second language learners, Cohen (1987) considered the uses of self-report as a method for viewing the process of test-taking, thus providing a perspective on how the task of test-taking is variably undertaken. In a study using delayed introspection, Zimmermann and Schneider

(1987) considered the potential for retrieving the processes involved in lexical searches for learners engaged in the process of translation. Another study that involved the introspection of searches for novel lexical items presented in a written text is that of Haastrup (1987). The impact of retrospection and introspection on our understanding of the cognitive dimensions of tests and tasks has been considerable. Yet relatively few studies to date have considered the use of introspective techniques in the testing of second language listening comprehension, especially modes to examine how listeners with varying likelihoods of comprehending any given test item converge or diverge strategically in the processes of decoding the stream of speech and making inferences about possible referents. Introspection has considerable potential as a tool for investigating the psycholinguistic validity of item response patterns and can offer detailed qualitative data to supplement traditional and probabilistic approaches to test analysis, which have been limited to providing information about who should get items correct, but not why such items were correctly answered.

A study of inferencing strategies in listening

The present study examines introspective accounts provided by second language listeners in a task done immediately after inferencing the meaning and selecting responses to recorded utterances. The utterances were presented on tape and a pictorial reference was selected from a field of alternatives. Immediately after each selection was made the listeners were queried as to the basis on which they chose the particular referent. The analysis of the matching of probability of correct answer and strategy used by the individual listener presents evidence of the range of strategies available in the process of inferencing about a second language.

A picture identification test was originally devised as part of a multi-trait, multi-method construct validation study of listening and reading skills. The picture listening component of the study was designed to assess the effect of aural comprehension without the mediation of the written word. In the multi-trait, multi-method study, picture listening, picture reading, listening cloze, standard cloze, self-assessment of listening and self-assessment of reading tests and surveys were presented to 268 Japanese students. The correlation between the picture identification test and the other direct test of listening, the listening cloze test, was 0.757. As an extension of the study, the picture listening test was later given to a larger sample of Japanese students. The total sample of 582 responses to the 25-item test was subjected to the one-parameter logistic model (Rasch) analysis (Henning, 1987; Wright & Stone, 1979).

The latent trait analysis revealed that although the test showed moderate internal consistency (KR-20 = 0.80), several of the picture identification items showed considerable misfit – listeners whose estimated ability, based on the total number of accurate responses, was closest to, or even surpassed, the difficulty of individual items did not consistently answer those items successfully. Conversely, listeners whose overall performance on the test did not indicate a high likelihood of success on these items could somehow get them correct. Since the test was designed to reduce the guessing factor, the likelihood of improbable correct responses was considered to be revealing of either idiosyncratic test-taking strategies, bias or experiential factors. Our goal in the present study is to explore the interaction of aural processing of the test item input with listeners' introspective accounts for items with unexpected response patterns.

Procedure

Ten of the 25 listening comprehension items from the picture identification test became the focus of the present study. The ten items were chosen to represent a wide range of difficulties as well as a wide item fit range. The fit indicates that listeners whose latent listening ability matches the calibrated difficulty of the item should have a roughly fifty-fifty chance of getting that item correct. When the listeners' estimated ability surpasses the difficulty of the item, the probability of a correct response increases. 'Misfits' are items that are either incorrectly answered by persons with greater latent ability than the items' difficulty, or items that are somehow correctly answered despite the learners' overall pattern of proficiency as indicated by missed items known to be implicationally easier than the 'misfits'. Five of the ten focus items were known to have satisfactory fit to the Rasch model, while the other five showed high misfit for the large sample of Japanese listeners.

A stratified sample of 40 students was selected from two Japanese colleges. Students were selected so as to provide a range

Table 10.1   Descriptive statistics for picture identification test

	Mean	s.d.	Items	N	KR–20
Main sample	11.0	5.1	25	582	0.80
Focus sample	11.8	5.7	25	40	0.87
Introspection	4.2	2.0	10	40	0.60

of scores similar to the range observed in the original item response study involving the larger sample. As in the preliminary study, listeners were provided with a sheet containing 45 picture icons from which they had to choose each of the 25 picture icons that were described on the test tape. In the introspection study, the procedure was modified so that the picture identification test was given to students individually after a short recorded introduction to the procedure of the study, which included an example of introspection presented in the listeners' L1 – Japanese. A researcher was present to stop the tape after each of the ten focus items. At the pause junctures the researcher asked each listener in Japanese to provide an account of what words or phrases were heard in the preceding item, and how these words were related to specific pictures in the selection process. All responses were recorded with lapel microphones for later transcription and analysis.

Each listener's introspection about the word or phrases heard on the tape was categorized according to the apparent processing stage reached, as evidenced by the narrative introspection.

Selection strategies

Analysis of the introspection data for the ten key items revealed a variety of item selection strategies. The selection strategy used for any given item appears to be constrained by the degree of processing of the aural input. At the two basic levels of processing, that of syllables heard in the stream of speech, and at the key word level, listeners seek an association of the word heard to a visual icon. This basis of association supports the notion of the 'logogen' (Morton et al., 1985; Rost, 1990), which suggests how individual lexical items are associated with a web of semantic networks. However, the identification of syllables heard in the stream of speech also indicates that listeners at this level of processing capacity create plausible

semantic networks concurrent with the selection of a visual referent. For picture items to be instantiated (associated to a particular
referent in the field of possible referents), there has to be a minimal pragmatic link between the perceived input and the visual
references. A breakdown of the different processing stages, which
summarizes the accounts provided by the subjects in the present
study, sketches an outline of the ways second language listeners link
what they hear to responses on the picture identification test. The
stages are ordered from simple to more complex.

Noise

Stage		Response	Gloss
N	→	None	No response is made because input was heard as 'noise'

The tape input contains no recognized material that can be related
to the visual referents. From the listener's perspective, the content
of the aural stimulus is too fast, too long, or contains words and
phrases that are completely unfamiliar. In an interactive listening
task (Rost & Ross, 1991), this level of comprehension would most
probably lead to a 'global' reprise – a request for repetition or a
statement indicating non-comprehension.

Distraction

Stage		Response	Gloss
D	→	None	Processing is blocked by a split of attention between the aural input and the previous item

The task of searching the field of pictures for a plausible link is in
competition with the appearance of the next item on the tape. The
listener is faced with a processing overload and cannot continue to
scan the field of 45 pictures and comprehend the contents of the
tape concurrently because attentional resources are focused on the
yet to be completed association task presented by the previous item.

Syllable restructuring

Stage		Response	Gloss
S	→	Restructuring	Listener can hear only a part of a key word and restructures it into a part of a word that was not in the utterance. Association is then based on the misheard key word

This phenomenon involves a syllable being identified and linked onto a neighbouring segment. 'I seem' may, for example, be parsed as 'ice', as the long vowel plus bilabial nasal [m] is projected as 'cream'. The mishearing is then associated with a plausible referent.

Test tape plays:

"I seem to have lost my wallet.'
Listener hears: [ais] +++++++++++++ and instantiates to → ice

Here the listener associates the syllable with any plausible picture in the set. At the lower end of the proficiency continuum, the inferential strategy apparently interacts with a test-taking strategy; visual processing of the pictures often stops after the first plausible association is made.

Syllable identification

Stage		Response	Gloss
S	→	Projection of a syllable to a key word	Listener finds a plausible word or syllable that could be associated with an icon. The syllable or word is projected on to that word

Test tape plays:

'The washing of cars is now done automatically.'
Listener hears: [waʃ] ++++++++++++++ and instantiates to → wash

The listener associates the heard syllable to a plausible word that approximates to the word within the utterance – 'washing' in the utterance. In the picture identification test this strategy is as close to pragmatically motivated 'guessing' as is possible.

Key word association

Stage		Response	Gloss
K	→	Key word	Listener hears a single key word in the input and matches it to a single icon

Test tape plays:

'An artist might use this for painting.'
Listener hears: + artist ++++++++++++ and associates 'artist' with:

The hearing of a key word is the most common processing level for lower-proficiency listeners. It is one that allows the listener to attempt a response by instantiating the key word to a schematically possible referent. The degree of accuracy in the choice crucially depends on the listener's strategic withholding of a selection until all possible associations are scanned and compared. The introspections suggest that the weakest listeners appear to be inclined to go directly to the first association and stop scanning the field of pictures for better choices. This tendency is evidenced by introspections that include only an account of the first possible associated referent. More proficient listeners, in contrast, often include accounts of there having been two possible referents, one of which being less probable as an answer than the one chosen. The single association pattern may be indicative of a less sophisticated test-taking strategy, or perhaps suggests a constraint on the confluence of visual perception and short-term auditory memory for the least proficient listeners.

Linked key words

Stage		Response	Gloss
L	→	More than one key word is heard	Listener establishes a pragmatic link between the two key words and associates them with an icon

Test tape plays:

'Before the development of air travel, this was the only method of transport available for people wishing to make journeys overseas.'
Listener hears: ++++++++++ air +++++++++++++++++++++++ overseas
and associates the two linked words to:

Just as in the case of key word association, linked key words can be mapped pragmatically onto a variety of possible schemata represented in the picture cues. The linking of key words provides a better basis for association so long as the listener exhausts the field of pictures for the most possible selection. In the above sample, the listener does not process the grammatical function words in the first clause, and thus goes for the most likely link between 'air' and 'overseas'. This suggests that listeners' attention is initially focused on the most information-bearing content of the utterance (Schmidt, 1988; VanPatten, 1990).

Phrases

Stage		Response	Gloss
P	→	Whole phrase is processed	As whole phrases are processed, function words can serve to link key words contained in the phrase

Test tape plays:

'This is an automobile which people hire when they want to get from one place to another. People don't often travel very far in one of these.'

Listener hears: This is an automobile which people hire +++++++++
++
+++++++++++++++++++++++++ and associates it with:

When phrases are heard, the number of possible associations represented in the field of pictures is reduced dramatically. The listener can, for instance, eliminate other kinds of automobile or vehicle in the set because they are less likely to be hireable. The listener presumably scans the entire list of vehicles:

until the one that is most 'hireable' is located. Here, as in other picture listening items, the listener's own experience interacts with the process of comprehension to govern the ultimate selection of the 'correct' answer.

Complete Images

Stage		Response	Gloss
C	→	Entire utterance is comprehended	The utterance is chunked into short-term memory and retrieved as the listener scans the field of icons

Test tape plays:

'You might use one of these if you want to talk long distance to one of your friends.'
Listener hears: You might use one of these if you want to talk long distance to one of your friends.
The process of association leads to:

With a complete – or even nearly complete – replay of the heard utterance available in short-term memory, there is greatest likelihood that the field of pictures can be scanned and a number of plausible associations checked and compared before the final selection is made.

An implicational analysis

The matrix of 40 persons by 25 listening items was scored dichotomously as either containing a correct or incorrect response from each person on each item. Classical test analysis was performed on the 40-person by 25-item set and Rasch item analyses were done after adding the 40-person sample to the larger group. The results of the internal consistency analysis performed on the focus sample revealed similar means, variances and item difficulty statistics with those observed in the larger study involving 582 listeners (Table 10.1). A rank order correlation between the difficulty of the ten items in the sample, those for which introspection data had been recorded, and the difficulty of the same ten items in the larger population, revealed a correlation of 0.848. Responses to the ten 'experimental' items were extracted from the larger matrix and were ranked and sorted into an implicational scale. In order to examine better the relationship between the aural processing stage reached and the implicational scaling of the items, each of the dichotomous responses was replaced by the processing stage reached by each individual on each item. Although a Coefficient of Scalability of 0.61 for the ten items suggested only a very rough implicational scale, of main interest for our analysis of listener strategies were introspections about items

ITEMS

Listener	1	13	21	3	16	7	20	15	17	19
Listener1 (9)	C	C	L	C	P	C	C	C	C	C
Listener2 (8)	C	K	P	C	K	C	C	C	C	C
Listener3 (8)	K	P	P	C	P	K	K	C	C	P
Listener4 (8)	K	K	C	K	C	C	C	C	C	C
Listener5 (7)	K	P	P	P	C	K	K	K	P	P
Listener6 (7)	C	K	P	C	P	C	L	C	K	P
Listener7 (7)	K	K	K	C	P	K	K	P	P	N
Listener8 (7)	K	C	L	K	P	C	K	C	C	P
Listener9 (6)	K	P	K	C	L	C	L	P	P	K
Listener10 (6)	K	C	P	P	P	C	L	P	C	P
Listener11 (5)	K	P	K	K	L	S	K	S	K	K
Listener12 (5)	K	C	P	C	C	K	N	P	P	L
Listener13 (5)	K	C	P	C	C	C	C	C	C	C
Listener14 (5)	K	C	K	P	P	K	L	N	K	N
Listener15 (5)	C	C	C	C	N	K	N	P	N	C
Listener16 (4)	K	K	L	K	N	K	K	N	K	N
Listener17 (4)	L	K	P	L	C	K	L	L	C	N
Listener18 (4)	K	K	K	K	P	K	N	N	K	N
Listener19 (4)	K	C	L	K	K	K	K	N	K	N
Listener20 (4)	K	C	L	K	P	K	P	P	C	P
Listener21 (4)	K	P	L	K	P	L	P	S	L	L
Listener22 (4)	K	K	L	K	N	N	K	K	L	K
Listener23 (4)	K	K	K	K	P	K	L	K	K	L
Listener24 (4)	K	K	L	S	N	K	L	N	K	N
Listener25 (3)	K	C	L	S	K	K	N	S	P	N
Listener26 (3)	K	K	K	K	K	N	N	S	P	K
Listener27 (3)	K	K	P	P	P	S	K	N	S	S
Listener28 (3)	K	L	L	K	P	S	K	N	P	N
Listener29 (3)	K	L	L	K	N	K	S	N	K	S
Listener30 (3)	K	P	S	K	K	L	S	N	K	N
Listener31 (3)	K	K	K	K	K	K	K	K	S	K
Listener32 (2)	K	K	L	K	P	K	K	S	K	K
Listener33 (2)	K	L	K	K	N	K	N	N	K	K
Listener34 (2)	K	N	K	K	P	D	N	N	S	N
Listener35 (2)	K	L	L	K	K	N	K	N	K	N
Listener36 (2)	K	D	K	K	N	N	N	N	K	S
Listener37 (2)	K	K	K	D	N	K	K	N	K	K
Listener38 (2)	K	K	K	N	N	S	S	N	L	N
Listener39 (1)	K	K	L	L	L	K	L	K	L	K
Listener40 (0)	K	K	K	K	K	N	N	N	K	K

Figure 10.1   Implication scale of aural processing stages

in which there were instances of improbable mistakes by the most proficient listeners and improbable correct answers by the least proficient listeners. The improbable answers are marked in Figure 10.1 in italics.

The distribution of processing stages suggests a rough hierarchy of processing that forms the basis for the item selection strategy. For the easiest items (e.g., item 1), a simple 'key word' level of processing appears to be sufficient for association to the correct referent. The key word level, however, is ambiguous in that some listeners may have actually comprehended much more of the input than they reveal in their introspective accounts. For more difficult items (15 and 17), Links (L), Phrases (P), and Complete images (C) are the most common stages reached in correct responses.

Of particular interest are the unlikely correct picture selections and the processing stages reached by the low-proficiency listeners compared with the improbable mistakes of the higher-proficiency listeners in relation to their stages of processing of the aural input. Italics indicate the processing stages of the higher-proficiency listeners on unlikely 'misses' in the top left-hand corner of the matrix. Italics in the lower right-hand corner of the matrix likewise indicate processing stages of improbable correct responses by lower-proficiency listeners. The micro-analysis of five cases of unlikely mistakes contrasted with five cases of improbable correct responses suggests that the sources of the response breakdown are inferential errors, experiential biases, mishearing, or a misplaced referent.

In the transcript of Listener 2, whose estimate of listening ability is 1.61 logits[1] greater than the difficulty of Item 7, the introspection revealed that even though he had heard the tape test item in its complete form and could hold the whole utterance in short-term memory long enough to provide a verbatim 'playback', the listener could not associate the content of the heard utterance to the picture it referred to:

(English gloss) 'Number seven is ... um ... I heard "computer programs are often kept on one of these", but I don't know which one it is.'

It is most likely in this case that the listener could not identify the icon of a floppy disk because of lack of first-hand experience with computer paraphernalia. In this case the response task can be thought to indicate an experiential bias, since the listener clearly has the 'latent' listening skill, but cannot demonstrate it on this particular task. Another cause of response breakdown could be related to the fact that the complete set of 45 pictures may create a visual 'maze' to field-dependent listeners that interferes with the task of on-line processing necessary for comprehension (Abraham, 1983; Chapelle & Jamieson, 1986; Hansen & Stansfield, 1981).

In another unexpected incorrect response, Listener 3 on Item 16 (0.28 logits difference) processes the utterance at the phrase level, but evidently mishears a single word, which instigates a set of inferences that make a plausible, but errant, response – given the propositional content of the mishearing. The test item was

'This is an automobile which people hire when they want to get from one place to another. People don't often go very far in one of these.'
According to Listener 3: 'This is something people use when they go out. I heard 'vehicle'. And people don't drive these far, so I chose ...'

If Listener 3 had indeed misheard 'hire' for 'drive', the inference could have been that people might not want to drive their own vehicle too far, so they would rely on some mode of transportation more suitable for long-distance travel.

As the implicational scale of processing stages might suggest, the level of processing determines the likelihood of a correct instantiation of an utterance to a visual referent. Even the most proficient listeners, however, may revert to simpler processing stages, possibly when a salient key word appears near the beginning of the utterance. This phenomenon is suggested by the preponderance of 'key' word introspective accounts for the easiest item. As in the following unlikely error on Item 21 by Listener 1 (1.6 logits difference), an early key word may set off 'selective' listening that leads down a garden path. The test item was:

'Before the development of air travel, this was the only method of transport available for people wishing to make journeys overseas.'
In his account Listener 1 states:
'When people fly, this is what they use. So I chose ...'

In this case the linking of key words may have led to a priming effect and a chain of reasoning that characterizes those frequently used by less proficient listeners. By hearing 'air', 'people' and 'overseas' the most plausible inference is the mode of transport with a common associative link.

Test-taking strategies (see Cohen, 1987) often interfere with the selection of correct responses, especially on forced choice or multiple choice tests. In the following unlikely error (2.09 logits difference), we see that a correctly heard item is edited because it competes with a selection of the same picture near the end of the test.

'If you like music you might have a collection of these – -so I chose the record.'

          is changed to

The listener here assumes that the same response cannot be correct on two different items, so the first (correct) selection is changed to an incorrect one. This response indicates how a test-taking strategy may lead to a response that is independent of the actual comprehension. Since this listener had already used the record icon for a previous (incorrect) response, his assumption was that the same icon cannot be used twice. Even in a test with 45 different selection options, there is still a possibility that certain items will not have complete 'local independence', and thus the reliability and, ultimately, the validity of certain item responses on a forced selection task such as the one used in the present study is threatened.

In a case of different possible schemata being associated with a picture, Listener 4 misses Item 3 (4.68 logits difference);

Tape test plays:

'You might get this on your birthday.'
Listener 4 comments:

'On your birthday, you might go out for a meal.'

What makes this selection unlikely is the fact that the most proficient listeners have the storage capacity to hold an auditory image of the test utterance in short-term memory as they scan the field of potential referents. In contrast, lower-proficiency listeners, perhaps because they also rely on less viable inferential strategies (Haastrup, 1991), tend to instantiate whatever clues they currently have to the first referent that contains enough feature attributes to justify the association. They then stop the scanning process and thus do not find other possible referents. In this study, the use of a visual 'top-down' selection strategy – that is, beginning at the top of the field of pictures and scanning to the bottom until a plausible icon is found – is one that even proficient listeners and strategically competent test-takers sometimes used. A plausible reason for Listener 4's response is not simply a reversion to the top-down, instantiate-and-stop scanning strategy, but is perhaps because the item triggers an 'experiential' bias – a set of experiences that make various schemata potential links to less typical referents.

At the opposite end of the implicational scale were five improbable correct selections of pictures. These misfitting responses were unlikely because they were made by the least proficient listeners on the most difficult items. For example, Listener 31 correctly linked two key words in the test item utterance to associate it with the correct picture on Item 20 even though there were 2.33 logits of difference between the listener's ability and the difficulty of that item. She explains:

'I chose [picture GG]. I heard "luggage" and "pick up" '

The entire item was

'One might expect to find this sign near the place in a terminal where luggage can be picked up.'

We might expect that personal experience in the procedures of air travel would have given this listener an airport baggage claim procedural script necessary to succeed on this relatively difficult item even though she had missed much easier items. It is interesting to note that this listener may have succeeded on Item 20 for the same reason that Listener 2 failed on Item 7 – the birthday present.

For Listener 26's correct response to Item 17 (2.05 logits difference), we find that she managed to process a phrase, as indicated in her introspection:

> 'I thought it was "if people swim there it is dangerous", so I thought the deep water in this picture (DD) is dangerous.'

Interestingly, Listener 26 got the 'right' answer for the wrong reason. The image in the picture represents a shark's fin, and not the deep water that led to the 'correct' selection. It is evident here that listeners often use whatever real-world knowledge they have available to them and extend it in a pragmatically viable way.

For Item 17, the item was:

> 'People might not want to go swimming on a beach where this particular sign is seen.'

Similarly, Listener 30 links across key words in a partial hearing of the same item to find the 'correct' picture (DD) without inferring that the cause of the danger might be the shark-infested waters:

> 'I heard "people play on the beach", but I didn't know which picture it referred to.' *So why did you choose DD?* 'Well, I chose CC for number 4, so I thought it must be BB or DD. I don't know why, but I chose DD.'

Initially, Listener 30 made a pragmatic link between the fact that benches are associated with a set of possible propositions (see

Rost, 1990), some of which can be linked to the visual icons. She thus considers first three water-related referents associated with the heard key word 'beach', and through a process of elimination, which is partially aided by a cognitive strategy, and perhaps some test-taking savvy, ends up with a highly unlikely correct answer.

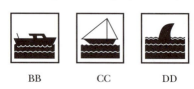

BB   CC   DD

The implicational scale suggests that the assessment of listening skill, as operationalized in the correct identification of the visual referents on the test, is related primarily to the level of aural processing. As the following correct response by Listener 32 to Item 15 (3.59 logits difference) suggests, however, even a 'shoe-string' level of comprehension can lead to a pragmatically viable schema formation, and subsequently to a correct instantiation. The listener appears to process the input at the syllable level – hearing [eyt], which is restructured, possibly with concurrent top-down scanning of the field of icons, to [weyt]. Inferencing takes over and a pragmatic link to a waiting-room script with a wall clock is invoked.

> Item 15:   'One might pay attention to one of these if one is concerned about being late.' Which refers to:

> Listener 32:   'The word "wait" came out so I chose the clock.'

Finally, in a case of syllables being heard, but not identified as referring to even a recognizable word, Listener 25 somehow associates a 'din in the ear' with the correct picture in Item 15.

> 'I heard [graːmey] at the end, but nothing else.'

Interestingly, Listener 25 retained a minimum auditory trace to utilize a 'positional reprise' (Rost & Ross, 1991), or an identification of where in the stream of speech the heard fragment was located. It appears that the only trace available to the listener was an approximation to the diphthong in [leyt]. This listener evidently knows more than she can say about the test utterance, or may have made an extraordinarily lucky wild guess.

Discussion

The analysis of unlikely responses suggests an important role for multiple associations in on-line inferential tasks. In contrast to face-to-face interaction in which queries about references can be made in the form of propositional, lexical or positional reprises (Rost & Ross, 1991), non-interactive comprehension tasks require a more direct reliance on schematic associations to potential referents (Rost, 1990). The introspections provided above suggest that more proficient listeners are capable of integrating more elements from the aural stimuli into a referential schema that leads to a viable instantiation to a visual referent. The more a listener can extract clues from the input and juggle them in short-term memory, the larger the number of candidate referents she can potentially instantiate them to. At this point, the listener may edit the field of candidate referents to a 'shortlist', depending on the pragmatic and schematic memory she possesses about what attributes are potentially associable with each of the candidate references. The interrelation of aural processing stage and item selection strategies is analogous to the processes listeners use in scanning input and attending to form simultaneously (VanPatten, 1990).

The likelihood of schematic association with a visual referent depends primarily on the degree of aural processing of the heard stimulus. As the implicational scale indicates, the degree of processing is distributed from top to bottom to create a roughly ordered hierarchy of processing stages. Of interest to the origins of pragmatic inference is the single processing stage common to both the ten highest- and ten lowest-proficiency listeners in the 40-person sample. As Table 10.2 indicates, the 'key' word processing stage is common to both levels and appears to be the major input to inferencing strategies. For the higher-proficiency listeners, the key word stage appears to trigger a short-cut associative inference path. For the ten most proficient listeners (top row of Table 10.2), the key word processing is used 61 per cent of time on the five

Table 10.2   Frequencies of aural processing stages by proficiency level

Images	Phrases	Links	Key words	Syllable	Distract	Noise
40	25	6	26	0	0	0
0	2	9	56	6	3	22

easiest of the sampled items. Recall that according to the Rasch model, the probability of a correct answer by the ten most proficient listeners is highest when they are matched with the task of comprehending the five most facile items. For the ten least proficient listeners (bottom row of Table 10.2), the key word stage is used with the same five easiest listening tasks 59 per cent of the time. For these listeners, the key word serves not as a short-cut to an inference and association with a correct referent, but is more likely a processing constraint that rarely leads to a pragmatically viable associative chain to the correct referent.

The limits of introspection

As a technique of data collection which aids our understanding of how the processing stages reached in listening are instantiated to visual referents, introspection affords a potentially valuable supplement to item-response theory. It should be considered, however, that introspection only provides data, and that all data are open to some degree of subjective interpretation. In some of the introspection sessions, listeners were only vaguely aware of what they had thought they heard on the test tape – and were thus unsure about how they had arrived at an unlikely correct (or incorrect) response. As the introspections of Listeners 3 and 25 indicate, a listener's account may not provide sufficient evidence about how the processing of aural input is related to understanding without some degree of interpretation.

In addition to a purely probabilistic approach to misfit analysis, such as that used in item-response theory, it may prove beneficial to include supporting introspective data in order for a clearer linking of the psychological dimensionality of item responses with their psychometric properties to be made. Introspective analysis of test performance may well provide such a link.

Notes

Many thanks to Richard Schmidt and Thom Hudson for comments on an earlier draft. All errors remaining on the present version are there in spite of their efforts!

1. The ability logit is a transformation of the total number of correct items on the task for each person. Each item's difficulty is likewise transformed on to the logit scale for direct comparison with the person logit (see Wright & Stone, 1979).

11

Studying language use as collaboration

DEANNA WILKES-GIBBS

In this chapter, I discuss a body of research on first-language communication from the perspective of what I will call the *collaborative theory* (e.g., Clark & Schaefer, 1989; Clark & Wilkes-Gibbs, 1986). This theory treats speaking and listening as fundamentally collaborative processes, and conversing in any language as a strategic, collective activity.

The collaborative theory has guided work on a variety of questions about conversation in recent years. It has been applied to the study of conversations between experts and novices in a domain (Isaacs & Clark, 1987), between people with different conceptual (Wilkes-Gibbs & Kim, 1991) or spatial perspectives on referents (Schober, 1993), or different communicative goals (Wilkes-Gibbs, 1986). It has been used to explore how the number of participants affects a conversation (Thornton, 1990; Wilkes-Gibbs & Thornton, 1993), and to study comprehension by participants and non-participants (Clark & Schaefer, 1987b; Schober & Clark, 1989; Wilkes-Gibbs & Clark, 1992). Further issues that have been examined include the effects of having continuous versus discontinuous evidence of a partner's understanding (Brennan, 1990), and of communicating through an 'intermediary' (Wilkes-Gibbs et al., 1993).

The productivity of the collaborative approach stems, I believe, from one central insight: that any successful communicative act requires its participants to coordinate with one another on many levels (H. Clark, 1985). What we are learning is that the coordination problems they face can be more or less complex, and harder or easier to solve. But recognizing the need for coordinating individual beliefs into mutual ones has moved the study of discourse in a fruitful direction. It helps explain what people are trying to

238

accomplish in different circumstances, and therefore how they use language in the process. To illustrate, I will begin by summarizing some basic elements of the collaborative theory. I will then go on to discuss a sampling of work that has been done since the original description of referring as a collaborative process appeared (Clark & Wilkes-Gibbs, 1986). The studies I will present have consistently affirmed that collaboration is general to many situations of language use. But they also show how the processes and products of collaboration respond to such factors as people's goals, their knowledge, their roles at any point in a discourse, and the evidence they can use to coordinate their beliefs. Each of these influences will be considered in turn.

The collaborative theory

A guiding assumption of the collaborative theory is that, in trying to communicate by using language, people are trying to add to their common ground – their shared knowledge, beliefs and suppositions – in a mutually intelligible way. To contribute to common ground, they may contribute to discourse. But for this, they must do more than utter the 'right' sentences at the 'right' times. The participants must develop mutual beliefs about what they will take such actions to mean to them specifically.

Building a mutual belief out of individual ones is a basic coordination problem (H. Clark, 1985; Lewis, 1969; Schelling, 1960), and the participants share responsibilities for trying to solve it to their collective satisfaction. They act, it has been proposed, according to a *principle of mutual responsibility*: The participants try to establish, roughly by the beginning of the next contribution to their discourse, the mutual belief that they have understood what the contributor meant, to a criterion sufficient for their current purposes (Clark & Wilkes-Gibbs, 1986). To establish evidence for coordinating on a mutual belief, the participants collaborate within a *grounding process*. (The complete name given by Clark and Schaefer (1989) is 'content grounding', but for convenience I will follow them in referring to it as simply 'grounding', or 'the grounding process'.) This process is used both for discovering the boundaries of common ground, and extending them.

In grounding, the basic unit is the *contribution*. A contribution is different from traditional linguistic units. In terms of form, it does not necessarily map on to a standard unit of syntax, such as a grammatical sentence. In terms of function and process, it is not an act that a single agent executes according to a prior plan he or she has formulated. Rather, a contribution is an emergent structure that develops through collective actions. In a conversation, it is built across turns as the participants try to update their common ground in a coordinated fashion. They use a repertoire of procedures for working together as needed, according to their roles in the grounding process at its current point.

Phases in grounding a contribution

In conversation, the process of grounding a contribution divides conceptually into *presentation* and *acceptance phases*. To illustrate, consider the case in which there are two participants. Most contributions begin with an action by A, the contributor. This often consists of A saying something, or 'presenting' an utterance for B to consider, as evidence of what A wants to contribute. Based on the initial presentation, the process enters an acceptance phase in which A and B try to establish that they have a satisfactory mutual interpretation of the action.

Ordinarily, B makes the first move in the acceptance phase, giving evidence that he thinks he does or does not understand what A meant by her initial presentation. In the simplest circumstances, B's continued attention is sufficient to signal that he understands so far. The entire process concludes when A and B think they have a mutual belief that B understood what A meant to add to their common ground, and they can continue their interaction assuming that.

The acceptance phase in grounding a contribution can be virtually invisible or quite involved, and its extent depends on many things. To name a few, it depends in part on the form of the initial presentation itself, which sets up projections about what the next 'move' in the process should be (Clark & Schaefer, 1987a, 1989; Clark & Wilkes-Gibbs, 1986; Wilkes-Gibbs, 1986). Secondly, of course, it depends on whether B does in fact think he understands the presentation. Thirdly, it depends on the medium of communication, and the resources it provides (Clark & Brennan, 1991). Media differ in the constraints they place on speaker change (e.g., face-to-face versus letter writing, telephone, video-conferencing, and so on). Any additional 'costs' of more extensive grounding must be weighed against the potential benefits. But fourthly, those benefits in turn are judged in relation to people's goals, and the level of understanding they think should be sufficient. With a lot at stake, the participants might easily take several turns back and forth to *refashion* an initial presentation until they are satisfied with the accumulated evidence for what they mutually understand (Clark & Schaefer, 1080; Clark & Wilkes-Gibbs, 1986).

As needed, refashioning is accomplished within the acceptance phase of the target contribution. In refashioning, the participants try to diagnose and repair the apparently troublesome part of a presentation, and either expand, revise, or replace it until there is a version on the floor that they can accept (Clark & Wilkes-Gibbs, 1986). Again, this is a coordination problem that A and B collaborate to solve. And again, refashioning involves grounding. Each turn, essentially, is itself a presentation. It initiates a subordinate contribution that must also be mutually understood (see Clark & Schaefer, 1989), and its intended function within the grounding hierarchy must be established as common ground.

So what this means is that the acceptance process is recursive. In negotiating their way through to a conclusion, it has been proposed that A and B are guided in part by a *principle of least collaborative effort* (Clark & Wilkes-Gibbs, 1986). The idea is that they try to minimize the work they both do collectively in grounding any contribution, from initial presentation through acceptance. This, in combination with a *strength of evidence principle* (Clark & Schaefer, 1989), describes how the participants keep the process from going on indefinitely.

Grounding a contribution is thus both an opportunistic and strategic process. It is opportunistic in that participants try to take advantage of precedents in their common ground to help them coordinate their beliefs about a current contribution more efficiently, and those precedents may involve accidental as well as systematic features of their situation (Clark & Brennan, 1991; Schober & Clark, 1989). It is strategic in that participants are trying to balance the effort they expend at any time on a presentation and its refashioning against what they think a misunderstanding might cost them in the future (Clark & Wilkes-Gibbs, 1986; Wilkes-Gibbs, 1986). They also take into account the cost of collaboration itself – the effort of turn-taking and its coordination.

As noted, collaborative costs depend on the communication medium (Clark & Brennan, 1991). As I will describe shortly, other features of the discourse situation may also come into play, such as its formality and the number of participants involved (Wilkes-Gibbs & Estow, 1993; Wilkes-Gibbs & Thornton, 1993).

All else being equal, the more effort that is spent designing and executing the right presentation, the less effort that is likely to be needed for acceptance. However, if a *much* less elaborate initial presentation can get accepted with just a *little* more help from the addressee, then all the better for A and B collectively. In conversation, the efforts of speaking and understanding are distributed. What the participants try to do is distribute them efficiently overall, to satisfy their collective goals.

Grounding a question

To show more concretely how grounding works, Table 11.1 lists just some of many possible scenarios by which the process might be played out in the asking of a question.

Table 11.1   Grounding a question

Present 1:	A: Did you go to the store?
Accept 1/Present 2:	B: Yes. I got the milk.
Present 1:	A: Did you go to the store?
Present 2:	B: Excuse me?
Accept 2/Present 3:	A: Did you go to the grocery store this morning?
Accept 3,1/Present 4:	B: Yes. I got the milk.
Present 1:	A: Did you go to the store?
Present 2:	B: The grocery store?
Accept 2/Present 3:	A: Yes.
Accept 3,1/Present 4:	B: Yes. I got the milk.
Present 1:	A: Did you go to the ... uh ...
Accept 1/Present 2:	B: Store?
Accept 2:	A: Yes.
Accept 1/Present 3:	B: Yes. I got the milk.
Present 1:	A: Did you go to the store?
Present 2:	B: To get milk and eggs?
Present 3/Accept 2:	A: Yes.
Accept 1+2/Present 3:	B: Yes.

The first exchange is an *elementary* one (Clark & Schaefer, 1989; Clark & Wilkes-Gibbs, 1986). A presents an interrogative sentence, and the relevance of B's next utterance lets them establish the belief that the intended question has been asked. It is a collaborative performance, constituted through the actions of both A and B. This is even clearer in the second case, in which B does not immediately accept the initial presentation and initiates refashioning. A does not take the question to have been asked, and presents an *expansion* (Clark & Wilkes-Gibbs, 1986); B then accepts the expanded version by presenting a relevant response, and they can now take it as common ground that the intended question was asked.

The remaining examples in Table 11.1 show some different facets of the hierarchical nature of contributions and grounding. In the third exchange, A and B collaborate to ground the reference in the process of grounding the question, and only then do they take the question to have been asked. In the fourth example, B's presentation is what I have called a spontaneous *completion* (Wilkes-Gibbs, 1986, 1995). Clark and Wilkes-Gibbs (1986) called referential completions *proxy* presentations). Completions present a challenge to traditional, single-agent views of language use (e.g., Searle, 1969). To explain them, one needs a principled means for relating the actions and intentions of multiple agents in the performance of a speech act. The collaborative theory provides the needed tools. In its framework, B is acting as part of his responsibilities in grounding the contribution that A initiated. B's completion is itself a presentation, and here A asserts her acceptance. Finally, the process concludes as B moves on to initiate the next contribution: an answer to the question he helped to get asked.

So in a completion, the integrity of a linguistic unit depends on actions by more than one person. A and B collaborate on form in this way to ground beliefs about the meaning of the underlying contribution. They can use the structural dependencies of their utterances as pointers to the intentional dependencies of their actions within the contribution. The last exchange in Table 11.1 illustrates another case of jointly produced structure, which I have called a *continuation* (Wilkes-Gibbs, 1995). In continuations, A's utterance could have stood alone grammatically, but B elects to build on to its formal structure in the next turn. He collaborates in this way not because A was having trouble getting a superficially complete unit of language on the floor. Rather, by relating his utterance to A's formally, B is again marking its intended relation functionally. Here, he is proposing that the successive presentations be treated, ultimately, as *installments* (Clark & Schaefer, 1987a; Clark & Wilkes-Gibbs, 1986) in a higher-level contribution (Clark & Schaefer, 1989). Whether they will remains for A and B to accept mutually in the grounding process; here, A confirms. So both A and B produced coordinate subunits of an emerging structure, and in this way enlarged the contribution that A initiated. Having helped to build, in this example, a mutually acceptable question, B could then go on to present an answer.

In summary, the collaborative theory assumes that having a discourse is a collective activity. Broadly speaking, many of the things that people must do to coordinate in a conversation are the same as what it takes to coordinate in any collective act, whether it be two people dancing a waltz or an orchestra playing one. Any collective performance is accomplished by means of the individual members doing their parts and adjusting to one another as needed. To succeed at the whole, especially in a dynamic, spontaneous performance, the participants need to coordinate their beliefs and adapt their actions. For this, they rely on mutual beliefs about their past history, about what they are trying to do together now, what they have done so far in the process, and what each may try to do next.

But even though there is a need for mutual beliefs in any collective act, there is no reason to suppose that collaboration should be invariant across different types of discourse activity, different conversations, or even different contributions. Rather, the participants decide how to act at any moment in grounding based on their perceived needs and desires, as well as on the limitations, resources and opportunities their situation affords. The collaborative techniques that can be exploited, and the extent to which they will be, should change with what people think the context demands, allows, or makes worthwhile. This implies that any number of contextual features could change the extent or even the nature of grounding in conversation. However, if the collaborative principles are on the right track, then any such changes should be consistent with them.

In the remainder of this chapter, I will describe some of the work that has been done in recent years to broaden our understanding of collaborative processes in different conversational contexts. By so doing, I hope to illustrate the range of issues to which the collaborative theory has been applied, as well as some of the methods and measures that have proven useful along the way.

Individual goals and collaborative activities

The principle of mutual responsibility explains why people act collaboratively in the performance of a speech act. They need to establish that what the speaker meant to contribute to common ground was understood, and that takes a collective commitment. Not everyone seeks perfect understanding, however, but just understanding 'to a criterion sufficient for current purposes'. Some goals may dictate a generally high criterion, but other purposes could be satisfied by a much lower level of understanding. How do the participants' goals affect the nature and extent of their collaboration? Do conversations among people with lower criteria require the same collaborative assumptions at all?

To examine these and other questions, I did a study several years ago in which the participants in a conversation did not always have to understand one another very well, and did not even always have the same goals (Wilkes-Gibbs, 1986). The basic situation was much like the following. Imagine that you are on the phone with another person, trying to reconstruct a sightseeing tour through San Francisco. You've taken parts of the tour before, and your partner has taken other parts. If you knew that you were going to have to give specific, detailed directions for the whole tour to an influential colleague, you might want to make sure you clearly understand everything your partner can tell you. Your criterion for understanding his or her information should be high. On the other hand, if at this point you just wanted to figure out approximately how long it would take to drive the tour, you might care less about knowing precisely how to navigate from one landmark to another. You should set a lower criterion for your understanding.

In the laboratory analogue I created, two partners who could not see each other were each given different versions of a city map on which a tour route had been drawn. Different portions of the tour were blanked out for each person. Each partner was told that he or she needed to learn about the complete route well enough either to direct another person through it from memory (*High* criterion), or just to estimate travel time (*Low* criterion). So each person knew some things about the route and needed to know others. They needed to coordinate their partial knowledge bases so as to learn where the route would go on a complete map, and they were able to converse as much as they wanted to feel satisfied given their goals.

One basic aim of this study was to compare collaboration between two people who have either High or Low criteria. However, I also paired people who had different objectives (unbeknown to them initially), to compare the notions of individual and collective goals. The collaborative theory assumes that conversation involves collective purposes as well as individual ones. But, of course, people might just *appear* to have joint objectives if their individual goals are all roughly the same. So these *Mixed* conversations were of additional interest for learning more about how individual goals function in collaborative contexts.

Each of 32 pairs did this communication task for maps of three different cities, and their conversations were timed, tape-recorded and later transcribed. As expected, the conversations were structured overall as chains of segments in which the partners traded off giving and getting directions from one location to the next, depending on which one of them had the information about the tour at any given point.

Global effects of criteria

People's goals did indeed affect the extent of their conversations. When both partners had High criteria, they spent an average of 11.5 minutes on each map. When they both had Low criteria, they took only 7.5 minutes to cover the same amount of ground ($t(14)=4.01$, $p <.001$). As this implies, High criterion conversations involved more words, by 1,607 to 1,169 on average ($F(1,28)=4.36$, $p <.05$), and more turns, by 204 to 138 ($F(1,28) = 6.25$, $p <.05$).

So with High criteria, people talked about each tour more extensively. They devoted more effort to grounding for a given unit of *distance* on the map. Surprisingly, however, High versus Low criteria did not much affect the extent of collaboration in a given unit of *time*. When just the first two minutes of conversation about each map were analysed (6 min total per pair), it was the fit between the partners' criteria that made a difference. Matched criterion pairs used about 315 words, but Mixed pairs used about

335 in the same interval (t(30)=2.93, p <.05), and took fewer turns (33 in Mixed, versus 39 in Matched; t(30) = 2.48, p <.05). High- and Low-criterion pairs did not differ reliably from one another when equated for time in this way (ignoring, of course, how much of the tour that was covered in this interval).

Extent of the contributor's participation

Because of the way the maps were designed, it was possible to look at how much effort people devoted to grounding when they had the role of *contributor* (or the person who had the tour informa- tion for a particular segment), versus *addressee* (the person who needed the tour information at that point). Table 11.2 shows the main results for words and turns per tour segment (there were 18 segments in each tour), depending on the participants' criteria.

Table 11.2 Extent of collaboration by contributors and addressees, depending on their criteria

Contributor's criterion:	High		Low	
Addressee's criterion:	High	Low	High	Low
Mean number of words per segment,				
By Contributor:	247	169	205	160
By Addressee:	124	90	82	82
Mean number of turns per segment,				
By Contributor:	22.8	13.1	13.5	13.4
By Addressee:	23.1	14.1	13.5	14.0

Most psychological research on goals and behaviour treats goals as attributes of individuals, and uses them to explain a person's plans and actions in different contexts. But at least in the context of this study, individual goals were rarely sufficient to predict the extent of a person's participation. As contributors, High- and Low- criterion speakers did not differ reliably in how much they said or how often they spoke with Low-criterion addressees. The same pattern held when they had High-criterion addressees. The con- tributor's own goals did not explain her collaborative activities in grounding.

Another possibility was that the addressee's goal might account for how much work a contributor had to do to get her information understood, but that was also not borne out by the data. High-criterion addressees inspired High-criterion contributors to say more, and take more turns. But they did not have such an effect when the contributor had Low criterion. The addressee's goal alone was also not enough to explain the contributor's efforts in these conversations.

Extent of the addressee's participation

Now consider how people with different goals acted as addressees. By most theories it would be the addressee who decides whether or not he has understood to his satisfaction, and so the effects of his criterion might be clearer in this role. But the results for participation by addressees in the different conditions of this study followed much the same patterns as for contributors. As addressees, people with High and Low criteria still used about the same number of words with both High- and Low-criterion partners. High-criterion addressees did take more turns when their partner also had High criterion, but Low-criterion addressees did not.

So whether as contributor or addressee, both participants' goals were needed to explain the extent of one's activities in conversation. Overall, this study confirmed that the extent of grounding does vary flexibly with purpose. But for any contribution, those variations depended on the participants' roles and goals *in combination*. Current purposes are also joint products.

Initial presentations in grounding directions

The types of initial presentation used in grounding are also of interest in relation to people's goals. According to the collaborative theory, they reflect the contributor's judgements of how much collaborative effort she thinks is justified. Clark & Wilkes-Gibbs (1986) identified six different types of initial presentation used in referring, and their relative frequencies agreed with the relative collaborative effort they were suggested to represent.

The same six types accounted for all but three per cent of the initial presentations contributors used in the tour conversations. Examples of how the types would appear as sentence-level presentations (rather than referential ones) are shown in Table 11.3. In

Table 11.3 Illustrating six types of initial presentation in order of frequency

---

Elementary
  A: *Go left on California for three blocks until Taylor Street.*
  B: Ok.
Episodic
  A: *Go left on California. For three blocks. Until Taylor Street.*
  B: Ok.
Installment
  A: *Go left on California for three blocks …*
  B: Mmhmm
  A: *until Taylor Street.*
  B: Ok.
Provisional
  A: *You have to do something weird here. You have to go left on California for three blocks until Taylor Street.*
  B: Ok.
Completion
  A: *Go left on California … uh …*
  B: *for three blocks until Taylor Street?*
  A: Right, for three blocks until Taylor Street.
  B: Ok.
+Dummy
  A: *Go left on whatchamacallit for three blocks until Taylor Street. On California.*
  B: Ok.

---

terms of observed frequencies, only the Dummy category was so rare as to suggest that it does not generalize well beyond referring.

The relative frequencies of these presentation types were again consistent with the idea that they project different amounts of collaborative effort, and that people try to minimize their joint effort when they can. Elementary presentations were significantly more frequent than any other type. Episodic presentations were preferred more than installments; although installments, provisionals and completions were not reliably different. Basically, none of these more elaborate types was used very often in comparison to the less effortful ones.

As expected, the goals people brought to a conversation did affect initial presentation strategies. In High-criterion pairs there was a greater proportion of episodic (28%) and installment presentations (20%) than in Low-criterion pairs (14% episodic and 6%

installment; p < 0.05 all comparisons). By contrast, Low-criterion pairs used more elementary presentations than the High-criterion pairs did (67% versus 36%, p < 0.05). In general, Mixed groups tended to fall in between the High and Low-criterion groups (e.g., 24% episodic, 8% installment, 50% elementary; none of these values is statistically different from either the High- or Low-criterion pairs).

So these findings suggest that the effects of people's criteria in a conversation are consistent with the principle of least collaborative effort. With High criteria, people select more of the higher-effort presentation types. An unexpected finding, however, was that both Low and Mixed pairs used more provisional presentations (11% and 10%, respectively) than the High-criterion pairs did (2%). This would not have been predicted by the original proposals about the relative effort of the types, but it makes sense in retrospect. In a provisional presentation, the contributor goes ahead with an utterance she believes is going to need refashioning, which she intends to provide next. The risk with a High-criterion partner is that he might try to act on the problem before the contributor has a chance, pushing the collaborative process into extra turns. Partners with Lower criteria, on the other hand, may give the impression that they are more likely to tolerate local ambiguities.

Actual understanding with different criteria

A rule of thumb regarding goals and language understanding is that the more motivated a person is, the better one expects comprehension and memory to be. To look at people's actual understanding as a function of the goals they were given, each was asked at the end of the session to draw the three complete tours (from memory) on to new maps. Anytime a drawing missed one of 18 key points in a tour, an error was recorded.

Surprisingly, people with High criteria did not outperform their Low-criterion counterparts, with mean error rates of 24 and 25 per cent, respectively ($F(1,60) = 0.35$, $p > .10$). Instead, the factor that best accounted for recall was one of the group-based predictors: whether both people in a conversation had the *same* criteria. People from the Mixed conversations made significantly more errors on average than people from the Matched pairs ($F(1,60) = 3.71$, $p < .05$). The High-criterion subjects were the key to this, however. They made consistently more errors in Mixed pairs than in Matched ones (p < .01). By contrast, Low-criterion subjects were about equally accurate no matter what their partner's goal was, and their recall was actually *better* than the High members of Mixed pairs (p < 0.05). So again, the bottom line is the same. Knowing whether someone was highly motivated to understand and remember was not enough to explain how well he or she actually did remember the tour information. Rather, the combination of goals brought to these conversations was the better general predictor.

A consistent theme in the results of this study was that people's activities in conversation were seldom explainable with reference to their individual agendas. Sometimes the people with more and less demanding goals acted as differently as one might expect. But just as often, they did not. In a single-agent context, this might be quite surprising. Even for multiple agents in discourse, it makes the best sense when conversation is viewed as involving not just cooperation, but collaboration towards a collective goal. If the partners were merely cooperating to satisfy each other's goals, for example, one would expect that both High- and Low-criterion contributors should say a lot to satisfy High-criterion addressees, and a lot less for Low-criterion ones. Yet this was not what happened. In other words, the technical notions of cooperation and collaboration are not interchangeable. Collaboration presumes cooperation, but takes up where the cooperative principle and its maxims leave off (Grice, 1975, 1978). The cooperative principle does not explain why or how other people get into the act along with a speaker. The collaborative principles do.

Individual and shared knowledge

In the navigation study just described, people had to build a mutual knowledge structure from only partially overlapping parts. Each knew different things about the tours, and they used language to share their expertise with one another. The structure of the task reflects a basic assumption of the collaborative theory: coordinating knowledge and beliefs is a central problem in communication. People in conversation inevitably know different things, or different amounts, about any topic under discussion. Does what they know systematically affect the process and products of collaboration?

Experts and novices in conversation

Isaacs and Clark (1987) studied this question as it pertains to references between experts and novices. In this case, the domain of expertise was New York City. Experts had lived there, novices had never even visited, and their task was to put 16 pictures of New York City scenes into identical arrangements without being able to see one another. Expert *directors* described the postcards to novice *matchers* and vice versa, and references across six trials with the same figures in these two conditions were compared to expert–expert and novice–novice pairs.

All the pairs became more efficient across trials, but more so the more expert each partner was. Overall, pairs with expert directors averaged 2.6 fewer words per postcard than pairs with novice directors. Pairs with expert matchers averaged 1.9 fewer words than pairs with novice matchers. (Both differences were statistically significant. In general, the interested reader should refer to the primary sources for detailed information about statistical tests, significance levels, and so forth. Unless otherwise noted, it is safe to assume that any patterns I refer to as different were statistically reliable.)

Qualitative features of the grounding process also reflected people's judgements about their partner. Consider, for example, a director's initial presentations. Regardless of their own expertise, directors tailored these to fit the expertise of their matchers. Experts talking to novices used proper names for landmarks in the scenes only 50 per cent of the time (e.g., 'Rockefeller Center'), compared to 83 per cent with other experts. Novice directors with novice matchers used only 17 per cent proper names, compared to 47 per cent with expert partners. Likewise, expert directors added descriptions to the proper names they used (e.g., 'Rockefeller Center, with all the flags') more often with novice partners than with experts, by 42 per cent versus 13 per cent. Novice directors adjusted to their partner's expertise in a similar way.

Interestingly, presentations in the mixed and matched groups were most different on the very first trial. For example, descriptions were added to proper names 73 per cent of the time on Trial 1 in expert–novice conversation, versus only 25 per cent in expert–expert pairs. So the partners were *accommodating* to one another's expertise very quickly. But this implies they were also *assessing* that expertise, since they had not been told anything about their partner in advance. As it turned out, they did so in the very process of grounding references to the first few pictures.

Matchers could use the form and content of the director's presentations as evidence of his or her knowledge. One cue, for example, is the choice of a proper name versus a description: 'Citicorp Building' versus 'the building with the diagonal top' Another is whether the director used definite or indefinite articles: 'the fleamarket' versus 'a marketplace'. With a definite reference, the speaker presupposes that the referent should be readily identifiable in common ground. An expert would be more likely to assume this right off the bat than a novice would. Two other sets of cues, more particular to the task studied, involved the perspectives that speakers took: whether they described the target as a place or as a picture of a place, and whether or not their description went beyond information in the picture itself.

So matchers could tell a lot just by how the director initiated the first few presentations. A director, in turn, could judge the matcher's knowledge in the acceptance phase of those same contributions – whether the presentation was accepted right away, whether the matcher added a name or a description, or whether he asked for more information. Each pattern of presentation and response in grounding provides cumulative evidence to the participants about each other's knowledge.

But having assessed their respective knowledge, how did the partners adapt in order to coordinate? Again, the results showed that they did so within the grounding process itself. Experts supplied proper names in their presentations, even as matchers. Novices could then try to adopt them. Over the first two trials, experts corrected a novice's name 8 per cent of the time; they offered names in response to a novice's description another 27 per cent of the time, as here:

Director: Fourteen is the fountain with the arch in the background.
Matcher: Right, Washington Square, good.

So assuming that people can use information only as specific as their knowledge permits, and that they will offer helpful information when they can, Isaacs and Clark (1987) proposed that the experts and novices accommodate to each other in grounding by following a two-part strategy. First, they begin by assuming only as much expertise as they think the partner might share. Secondly, they use the partner's responses in grounding to adjust those assumptions. Having adjusted their assumptions, the participants adjust the language they use in trying to coordinate with one another efficiently. Through the same process by which they make themselves understood, experts and novices build common ground that helps them communicate more efficiently in the future.

Equal but different expertise: collaboration and cognition

According to the collaborative theory, grounding should involve accommodation not only when one participant is highly knowledgeable and the other is a complete novice. To succeed in referring, for example, people must coordinate their perspectives on the referent. Any time those perspectives differ, people may accommodate linguistically to establish that they are focused on the same thing. Contributors try to design noun phrases they think the addressees will understand – that is one sort of accommodation. And if a presentation is not understandable, the participants together refashion it – another sort of accommodation.

In either case, the referring perspective that people establish as common ground may differ from what the speaker might have preferred in another situation. This is true even when there are no major discrepancies in the *amount* of experience each participant has had with a referent, as illustrated in this exchange:

K: So I'm meeting you for the Alpha Delta wine and cheese thing this afternoon?

D: Right. It's in *the big brown building on the corner.*

K: Uh ... you mean *the big brick house,* right?

D: Wait. *On the south corner of the green?*

K: Yeah, that's the one.

D: Ok, so I'll see you at *the brick house on the corner* at 5.

K: Great.

Here, both people were equally familar with the university building in question, but differed in what they thought was salient about it. The grounding process shows evidence of their different perspectives, and they accommodated within it to establish their mutual understanding.

D's purposes in this example are not persuasion but efficient communication, and adopting 'the brick house' might be seen as largely a technical requirement for coordinating with K on the identity of the thing in question. Peter Kim and I wondered if there might be any additional consequences of coordinating in a

A-BIASED RECALL	'A' PERSPECTIVE	ORIGINAL	'B' PERSPECTIVE	B-BIASED RECALL
	CAMEL WITHOUT LEGS		BARN WITH SILO	
	WOMEN SEATED IN CHAIR		SEAL PLAYING WITH TOY	
	VIKING SHIP		PERSON SWIMMING	
	LETTER H		SHACKLED LEGS	
	FACTORY WHISTLE		THICK DAGGER	
	FLYING HUMMINGBIRD		JACKOLANTERN FACE	
	SQUARE ARCH		TWO LEGS	
	SWAN		TOILET	
	TURTLE		FISH	
	FLAGMAN		ANGEL	
	WITCH'S HAT WITH FEATHER		BIRD WITH WING UP	
	BIRD IN FEEDER		BOAT WITH SMOKESTACK	

Figure 11.1   Ambiguous forms from two perspectives

collaborative process (Wilkes-Gibbs & Kim, 1991). To study this, we created the set of ambiguous forms shown in the centre panel of Figure 11.1. We made sure through extensive pretesting that each figure was equally easy to see from either of two perspectives (shown on either side of the original figures). However, the figures had been designed so that switching from one perspective to the other took a distinct shift of focal attention. Loosely speaking, we created a sort of figure/ground problem, such that once one perspective was adopted, the other was harder to appreciate.

Next, we brought people to the laboratory and biased them individually to prefer one or the other of the alternate perspectives on each figure. This was done simply by having them rate how easily they could see a given figure as X (where X was one of the two labels). So what we were doing was providing a verbal label at encoding, and we know from a long tradition of memory studies that this influences people's interpretations (e.g., Carmichael et al., 1932). From here on, I will refer to these encoding biases as a person's *private perspectives* on the figures.

We then asked pairs of people to do a referential communication task. They matched arrangements of the same 12 figures six times (without being able to see one another), and their conversations were timed and tape-recorded. Half of the pairs were in a *Matched* condition, in which both partners had initially rated the same set of perspectives. The other half was in a *Mixed* condition, in which one partner had rated the list shown on the left hand side of Figure 11.1 (*list 'A'*), and the other partner rated the list shown on the right side of the Figure (*list 'B'*). (The two lists were balanced in advance so as to be equally apt overall.) We had people trade off director and matcher roles halfway through each trial, and had designed the target orders so that each person would initiate references to each figure three times over the entire session.

We expected that the collaborative process should be more extensive for the Mixed pairs because they had to coordinate common views out of initially different private ones. If they kept their criterion high (as people in this task tend to do), reaching it should take more collaborative effort. By contrast, grounding a reference should be easier when people bring the same predispositions to their conversation. That was just what we found.

People in the Matched condition needed significantly less time to complete the task overall (with a mean of 47 sec/trial, as opposed to 105 sec/trial in the Mixed pairs; $F(1,30) = 21.56$, $p < 0.001$). As the transcripts showed, this was because initial presentations invariably matched the director's private perspectives, and the matcher quickly accepted them as shared. By contrast, people in the Mixed pairs had to work harder at first to establish jointly effective perspectives. They presented a wider range of expressions in refashioning the initial presentations, trying to find something that would work for both of them. As expected, then, reaching an ultimately acceptable version was a more extensive process with equal but quite different expertise.

By Trial 6, however, both the Mixed and Matched pairs had worked out stable expressions they could use to coordinate efficiently. We used the presentations on Trial 6 as evidence of a pair's *joint perspectives* for referring in this context. For a subject in a Matched pair, an average of 11.7 (of 12) joint perspectives were the same as his or her private ones. For a subject in a Mixed pair, however, only 4.9 of the joint perspectives were the same ($F(1,56)$ = 350.29, p < .001).

So the collaborative process differed depending on the knowledge that was being coordinated within it. As a result, so did the collective products – at least as represented by the expressions that became common ground for future references in a group. The next question we had was whether collaboration had any other consequences for the individuals involved. In particular, we wondered whether coordinating to make an understandable reference might affect one's private conceptions of a referent, beyond the bounds of a specific discourse.

It has been known for some time, of course, that language and memory are intimately related. Being exposed to misleading questions, for example, can influence what an eyewitness reports about an event later on (e.g., Loftus, 1979; Tversky & Tuchin, 1989). Other research has suggested that writing a description of a face from memory may impair one's ability to recognize that face later among 'verbally similar' distractors (Schooler & Engstler-Schooler, 1990; though see Lovett et al., 1992). And our study was itself based on the established finding that verbal labels at encoding can bias recall of visual forms (e.g., Carmichael et al., 1932).

But we expected that in more conversational situations, any consequences to memory might depend on the collaborative process. To explore this, we asked each person who had done the communication task to draw the 12 figures from memory, and examined their drawings as a function of the original 'A' and 'B' lists of perspectives. (We also looked at people's preferences in a recognition task, as well as the labels they gave to their finished drawings. Both of these measures showed the same basic patterns that I will describe for recall.)

We indeed found systematic memory biases, and some drawings made by different people are shown in the outer columns of Figure 11.1. But what we also found was that some people were more likely to produce such clearly biased drawings than others: namely, people from Matched conversations.

For quantitative information about a drawing's accuracy, two 'blind' coders had rated it on a scale of 0–4 for resemblance to the

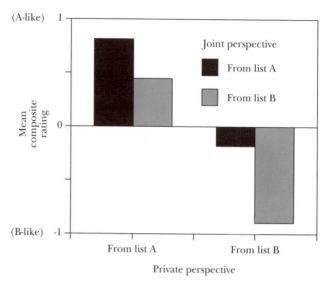

Figure 11.2   Effect of perspective on composite accuracy ratings

original figure (with 0 meaning very little resemblance). Drawings by people from the Mixed pairs got consistently higher accuracy ratings. The means were 2.0 for the Mixed condition, and 1.5 for the Matched condition (F(1,156) = 16.01, p < .001). Still, accuracy alone is not very revealing about specific interactions of private and collaborative experiences with language. We also looked at separate ratings of how much a drawing resembled each of the alternate labels we had initially provided (so, for example, how 'angel-like' a drawing was, and how 'flagman-like' it was as well). Subtracting one rating from the other gave a composite score that reflected the balance of bias in a drawing. The closer to zero a composite score was, the more balanced the drawing was with regard to the A and B perspectives.

The main patterns of results for bias are shown in Figure 11.2. What we found is just what would be expected if memory can be jointly affected by three things. First, a person's drawings in general reflected his or her own private perspective more strongly than the alternate, with an average composite score of about .58 (positive or negative) in its favour (F(1,56) = 169.5, p < .001). Secondly, however, the joint perspective established for referring also had a clear influence. If people had accepted an A-list joint perspective for referring to a figure, their drawing of it was more 'A-like' on average (with a mean composite score of 0.31). Similarly, B-list joint perspectives were associated with more 'B-like' drawings (mean score of -0.23; $F(1,56) - 40.98$, $p < .001$). But the strongest biases in memory came when one's own private perspective on a figure had also been accepted collectively for making references. Drawings were consistently more neutral when people had accepted a different perspective for the purposes of referring ($F(1,56) = 78.84$), $p < .001$).

As expected, however, differences between Matched and Mixed pairs also had a systematic influence. A drawing by someone from a Mixed pair was less likely to favour his or her private perspective more than the alternate. This converges nicely with the finding that it was more accurate overall. The absolute values of bias scores for drawings from the Matched condition were 1.54 on average, versus 0.38 in the Mixed condition ($F(1,62) = 56.16$, $p < .001$).

The explanation for these patterns of interaction lies in the grounding process through which these people solved their different coordination problems. People in the Mixed pairs had to exert more effort to ground their beliefs initially, and to accommodate their different verbal preferences. In accommodating to one another verbally, it appears they were also accommodating conceptually. People in the Matched pairs, by contrast, had the tendencies they brought to the conversation reinforced in grounding.

In terms of more specific mechanisms, there are several ways to think about why collaborative processes could lead to differences in memory. From a social standpoint, one's own views may seem that much more apt if they are easily accepted by the collective, or that much more questionable if they are not. In effect, this would be an example of group polarization (e.g., Myers, 1982) and a demonstration of some cognitive consequences to group members. From a cognitive processing standpoint, when references are easily accomplished, there is less need to consider alternative views, and thus less need to process the figures more deeply within different conceptual frames. And from a specific verbal memory standpoint, when grounding takes less refashioning, there are fewer subsequent encodings of the figures under alternative verbal descriptions. There is a smaller range of verbal labels to compete with one another for reconstructive effects later on.

But no matter which type of explanation one prefers, the basic finding is the same. Collaborative and cognitive processes are intimately connected. The knowledge that people have to coordinate affects the processes by which they use language. Those, in turn, can affect the knowledge with which each began.

Different spatial perspectives

Although it can be more and less difficult to manage, coordinating perspectives is a basic activity in conversation. Putting something into words necessarily imposes a conceptual perspective on it, emphasizing some features and downplaying others. Many references also involve elements of spatial perspective – that is, the physical point of view that a description reflects. Speakers could describe the locations of a referent from their own perspective, for example ('the person on my right'), from their addressee's perspective ('the person on your left'), or from a more neutral one ('the person in between us'). As it turns out, people's choice of spatial perspectives also depends on the grounding techniques available to them (Schober, 1993).

In one study (Schober, 1993), directors had to explain which of two circles on a display in front of them had an X marked on it. They did this so that matchers could mark the right circle on their own version of the display. The matchers were either present on the other side of an opaque screen (*Partner* condition), or were just imaginary (*Solo* condition). Each display explicitly showed the director's vantage point in relation to the circles ('YOU') and also the matcher's ('PARTNER'). When these points of view were offset, the question was what sort of perspective the director would use in her description. Everything that was said during 32 trials was tape-recorded and later transcribed.

Of most relevance here is the finding that speakers with partners used spatial perspectives differently than Solo speakers did. With partners, speakers were more egocentric. In both conditions, people used 'matcher-centred' locatives (true only for the matcher) more often than 'director-centred' ones (by 71 to 7 per cent). But Solo directors favoured the matcher most strongly. On average, they used self-centred locatives (true only for themselves) just 2 per cent of the time, compared to 13 per cent by directors with partners. Overall, people in the Partner condition were much more variable and idiosyncratic in their perspective-setting strategies.

What could explain such a finding? One possibility is that directors with partners felt they could lighten their own perspective-taking load by relying on the partner to initiate refashioning if needed. Trying to distribute the effort, they knew they could risk presenting an expression that might be inadequate. If it was, they could recover in the grounding process and try something different the next time. If it wasn't, then so much the better.

Precedents for this kind of strategy come from such things as 'dummy presentations' (Clark & Wilkes-Gibbs, 1986), in which speakers who are having difficulty elect to go ahead with a word or phrase they expect may need refashioning (e.g., 'the whatchamacallit'). Requests for completion (such as 'He's just, so ... uh ... you know. What's the word?') are another example (Wilkes-Gibbs, 1986). In each case, the speaker proceeds with an imperfect presentation, knowing it can be refashioned – either by herself or her partner.

So the grounding process is a real resource. Solo speakers, following a principle of 'distant responsibility' (Clark & Wilkes-Gibbs, 1986), do not have the safety net of the addressee's direct collaboration. Schober's (1993) results argue that they may therefore feel obliged to take fewer risks. This fits nicely with the well-established finding that directors who are speaking to a tape-recorder do not shorten their references across trials to the same extent as when they can freely converse with real partners (Krauss & Weinheimer, 1966; similar differences in efficiency turned up in Schober's study as well). The collaborative explanation is that the inability to use the usual techniques for grounding in conversation makes the directors less confident in precedents of mutual understanding.

One final thing of note is what happened when directors and matchers in the Partner condition traded roles. If the first person had described a particular object egocentrically ('on my right'), then the new speaker described that object egocentrically, too ('on my left'). Overall, the proportions of self-centred, both-centred, and addressee-centred perspectives taken by each member of a pair were strongly correlated (at .98 on average). It seemed that people were following a norm of reciprocity, matching their partner's perspective-taking strategy with surprising precision. New speakers took their partner's perspectives just as often as the partner had taken theirs.

Overall, this study confirms that the resources of collaboration allow people to distribute their efforts in ways they may not otherwise feel are possible. Using one's own perspective is the easiest option for a speaker, but there is a risk that this might make things too difficult for the addressee. Within the grounding process, speakers can 'test the waters' and get information from the addressee's responses about which coordination strategy is collectively effective (see also Schober, 1993).

Coordinating with more than one person

The referential communication task devised by Krauss and Weinheimer (1966) has proven to be a valuable tool for doing controlled studies of conversation. For largely practical reasons, however, most variants of the task have been designed for just two speaking participants at a time. As a result, we know far less about collaboration in larger group conversations. A basic expectation is that the more variable people's knowledge is likely to be, the more work they may have to do to coordinate on a mutual understanding. And adding more people to a group may increase the chances overall of such knowledge variation.

One line of work that has looked at collaboration in larger groups used a modified version of the map navigation task I described earlier (Thornton, 1990; Wilkes-Gibbs & Thornton, 1993). The basic idea was the same. Each participant had a map showing different information about a tour route, and they conversed to reconstruct the entire tour. In this case, however, people discussed the tours in groups of two, four, or seven participants, and they all expected a memory test.

Briefly, the method was as follows. For a given experimental session, each of seven participants was randomly assigned a letter, from A through G. Subjects A and B would discuss one tour by themselves. Subjects A through D would discuss a different tour (through a different city), and all seven people would discuss yet another tour. Each time, the A subject's version of the map had some information about the tour that no one else had, but was missing other information. All the other subjects had a second partial version of the map, which showed the parts of the tour A's map did not. Although we had to counterbalance for a multitude of order variables, the benefit of this design was that we could watch for changes in the activities of the same two people (A and B) in conversations of three different sizes.

Our main interests were twofold. First, we wanted to see whether group size affected the overall collaborative effort involved in grounding contributions. For this, we compared the extent of collaboration in the different conditions, and also looked at patterns of turn-taking. In addition, we compared the effectiveness of collaboration, as demonstrated by the participants' memory for the tours they discussed. Secondly, we wanted to see whether audience size affected the individual effort of being a contributor or addressee. For this, we examined the extent of each person's participation when they either had information the others needed (contributor role), or needed information that others had (addressee role). As a rough indication of cognitive difficulty, we also compared the frequencies of various speech errors in the different conditions.

In a study of 63 subjects (nine sessions), we found that adding more people to a group did not significantly increase the amount of time they spent discussing a tour. Two people (*Twos*) took 689 seconds on average, compared to 637 seconds for four people (*Fours*), and 754 seconds for seven people (*Sevens*; no comparisons differed statistically). As this implies, there were about the same number of words in all three situations as well, although people's turns were shorter overall in the larger groups (5.7 words per turn in both Fours and Sevens, compared to 7.1 words per turn in the Twos).

So overall, the larger conversations were just about as efficient as the smaller ones – on the surface. But it turned out that people's understanding suffered in the larger groups as a result. The A and B subjects (who both discussed all three tours) made significantly more errors in recalling the tours they had discussed in Fours or Sevens (19.9% and 20.1%, respectively) than the tours they had discussed as Twos (16.8%). What this suggests is that when more people were added to the conversations, A and B could not both maintain the same criteria for their comprehension *and* achieve it with the same amount of grounding overall. So there was a speed/accuracy trade-off. Coordinating with more than two people was more difficult, and in this particular situation, people's response was to accept a lesser degree of understanding.

For our questions about the effects of audience size on contributors, we looked at how much A or B said when they had information that someone else needed. Recall that A always had some unique knowledge of the tour, while B's map was the same as the C–G subjects' (when they were present). This turned out to make a big difference in the effort either person devoted to grounding their information in larger groups. The explanation is a simple one. The demands on a contributor depend on how many other participants know just what one is trying to establish as common ground – that is, on how many other people could potentially share the contributor role. As contributor, A had to do more work in presenting and grounding her information in Sevens than in Twos. She used 279 words in 32 turns when talking to six addressees, but only 188 words in 20 turns when talking to just one addressee (differences significant at p < .01). By contrast, B did substantially *less* work as contributor when there were more participants. B used 287 words in 32 turns in Twos, but just 45 words in 10 turns with Sevens (p < .001, both comparisons). The key is that B was almost always addressing one person (A), no matter what the group size. And in the larger groups, there were more people who could try to do roughly the same thing as B could for a given contribution.

Differential effects on A and B *as* addressees were less pronounced. When collaborating on information she did not herself know, A said more in the Twos than in the Sevens (117 versus 155 words, respectively). There was no significant difference in A's turns (at 12 versus 10 for Twos and Sevens). B expended about the same amount of effort as an addressee in all three group sizes (with regard to both words and turns). So at least in this study, audience size had the biggest effects on people when they were in the role of contributor.

The general conclusion is that people in larger groups may indeed need to do more grounding to achieve the same level of understanding. But as this study also showed, collaborating in a group is not always harder on *everyone* involved. B got by with less effort in larger groups when her contributor role in grounding was shareable, and our analyses of various individual and collaborative 'errors' make much the same point. In terms of problems with *delivery* (such as false starts, hesitations, and so on; see Fromkin, 1980; Levelt, 1989), A and B were about equally dysfluent in the Twos condition. By this rough measure, they were experiencing about the same cognitive load. But in Fours and Sevens, B had a proportionately lower rate of errors than A. This is again presumably because there was less pressure on B when her role in grounding was shareable. A always had some unique knowledge and could not distribute the burden to the same extent.

With regard to problems of *turn-taking*, it should be no surprise that there was more simultaneous speech in the larger conversations. Overall, just 3.6 per cent of the words in Twos were spoken in overlap with someone else's, compared to 10.1 per cent in the Fours, and 13.2 per cent in the Sevens. Coordinating speaker change is indeed harder when there are more people involved. The collaborative process itself 'costs' more in this case. And on *this* measure of difficulty, it was B who had the most problems. B's words overlapped with someone else's 3.3, 13.5 and 19.3 per cent of the time in Twos, Fours and Sevens, respectively. Even though B was in eye contact with everyone but A, it was still trickier to time exits and entrances when more people could potentially act in the same role. So coordinating both speaking turns *and* mutual understanding can be more difficult when there are more people in a conversation. In this particular case, people reacted to increased collaborative costs by shifting their criteria for understanding lower. They managed to keep their collaborative effort about the same, but their actual understanding in larger groups suffered as a result.

Roles in the collaborative process: participants and non-participants

Adding people to a conversation would not affect it in the same way if contributors did not have to worry about whether all the listeners are understanding them. And indeed, they do not always have to. If they are behaving in accordance with the principle of mutual responsibility, then speakers should try to design utterances that the other *participants* in the conversation will understand with a minimum of collaborative effort. But they hold no such responsibilities towards someone who is not recognized as a participant, even though it may be clear that he or she is listening.

This means that a non-participant, such as an overhearer, may face different problems from a participant. Participants can assume that the speaker is designing his or her presentations with their own common ground in mind. Non-participants cannot presuppose this, and may have to guess at the common ground on which the speaker is relying. Similarly, participants can use the grounding process to correct possible misunderstandings as they arise. Non-participants cannot. Together, these observations suggest that non-participants may generally be at a disadvantage compared to participants, and several studies have explored this directly

Comprehension by overhearers

Participants may take one of several attitudes towards anyone else they think is listening to them. Clark and Schaefer (1987b) looked at the case of *concealment*, in which the participants specifically want to prevent an overhearer from understanding. Concealment adds a level of complexity to the usual coordination problems in a conversation. How do speakers get their addressees to understand what they mean, while keeping overhearers from doing the same thing?

In Clark and Schaefer's study, two well-acquainted students conversed to arrange eight pictures of campus landmarks into identical orders, in the presence of an overhearer. In the Concealment condition, the friends were instructed to try to keep as much information about the target orders from the overhearer as possible. They did this for six arrangements of the pictures, and each time, the overhearer played along, trying to get his or her own set of cards into the right order. In the control condition, the overhearer was simply the experimenter, whose understanding was irrelevant to the partners' task.

Not surprisingly, the whole process took more time and effort when the partners were trying to do two things at once with their references: conceal their meaning from the overhearers, but also ground their own understanding sufficiently. They took about 26 seconds to place each picture in the Concealment condition, but only 3 seconds per picture when they were indifferent to the overhearer. And even though it took more time, the process was less successful. The matchers (who were meant to get everything right) were correct 99 per cent of the time in the control groups, but dropped to 92 per cent correct in the Concealment condition. To the partners' credit, the overhearers did do worse than the matchers, at 47 per cent correct. And, unlike the matchers, they did not become more accurate across trials. But, under the conditions of this study, Concealment was both difficult and risky. The matchers' understanding suffered, and the overhearers were still able to understand more than they were supposed to. The transcripts showed that this was largely because the partners accidentally divulged adjunct information that gave their 'private keys' away, or overestimated how opaque their private description was to begin with. Overall, however, an important finding was that the techniques people used to coordinate in Concealment were the same ones they had available to them for more general collaborative purposes: the techniques of grounding.

Would there still be drawbacks to being an overhearer in more favourable conditions? For example, should overhearers be at a disadvantage if the participants were indifferent to them and had no unique past history? The collaborative theory predicts they should be. Even when they share the right background, over-hearers still do not have grounding as a resource. Participants can establish that they have understood one another, and design future presentations assuming that. An overhearer cannot be sure she has understood correctly, and that should be a cumulative handicap in a discourse.

Schober and Clark (1989) tested this prediction. They had unacquainted pairs of people do a referential communication task with 16 tangram figures (using a subset of 12 for any one of six trials), and tape-recorded their conversations. In one condition, overhearers then listened to the recorded conversations and tried to match the target orders on all six trials. As expected, the over-hearers were not as accurate as the matchers, placing the figures with 88 per cent versus 99 per cent accuracy, respectively. This was true even though no one was trying to conceal anything, and the overhearers heard all that was said. Being witness to the build-up of common ground was still not the same as participating in it, and this was true even in a second experiment with overhearers who heard the conversations 'live'. In both situations, the over-hearers were at a disadvantage because they were not part of the grounding process. They could not control the content or the pacing of presentations to reflect their perspectives and state of understanding at any point.

Beliefs about shared information

In a different 'take' on the status of participants and non-partici-pants, Clark and I compared different sorts of information that speakers might use to judge whether common ground established with one participant is likely to be common ground with someone else (Wilkes-Gibbs & Clark, 1992). This study again used a referen-tial communication task in which a director worked for six trials with one partner, but then did another six trials with a different partner (using the same 12 tangram figures). The second partner was either entirely new to the task, or was one of several sorts of overhearers: a *simple bystander* who had heard the conversation but not seen the figures, an *'omniscient' bystander* who had listened to the conversation and seen the director's figures over a video monitor, or a *side participant*, who sat next to the director as a ratified but non-speaking participant in the conversation. So the second matchers differed systematically in their knowledge of the first conversation, as well as their status in it.

We found that the directors assumed more common ground with the side participants than with any of the other second matchers, including the omniscient bystanders who were known to have seen and heard everything. In all four conditions, the pairs worked more slowly when the first matcher was replaced by the second one. But the cost of changing partners was significantly less with the side participants than with any of the others. As reflected either by times, words, or turns, the directors were most efficient with side participants, less so with omniscient bystanders, and least efficient with either simple bystanders or naïve partners.

Choices of definite and indefinite references also reflect the speaker's beliefs about common ground, and they told much the same story as efficiency. On the final trial with the first matcher, directors used an average of 86 per cent definite references (e.g., 'the dog', 'this/that dog'). On the next trial – when the matchers changed – they used 5 per cent *more* definite forms with former side participants, but dropped them for everyone else: by 38 per cent for omniscient bystanders, and by 75 per cent for naïve partners or simple bystanders.

Apparently, then, speakers think people who were silent participants in a conversation have certain advantages over listeners who were not. But those listeners also differed in the objective knowledge they had of the conversation, and this mattered, too. Essentially, the task we created produced different 'levels' of shared information (Wilkes-Gibbs & Clark, 1992). The naïve partners shared no information with the director (other than generic assumptions based on membership in a college community). The simple bystanders shared information about how the director described the figures, but not about the figures themselves. This was apparently no more helpful than having no shared information at all. The omniscient bystanders shared all the information that the director had used in talking to the first matcher, and the director knew this. By most theories of discourse, the director should have treated them as equivalent to the side participants. But by the collaborative theory, directors still had to ground their beliefs with the bystanders. Finally, direct collaborative information should be even better than the indirect collaborative information that directors shared with the side participants, although we did not test this. Had our first matchers continued in the task for a seventh trial, we would have expected that trial to have been the most efficient of all.

The more information two people objectively share, then, the easier it should in general be for them to establish that it actually is shared. But that is the function collaboration serves: to establish reliable evidence for coordinating beliefs about common ground (Wilkes-Gibbs & Clark, 1992). Although many kinds of evidence might be used for building beliefs about common ground (see Clark & Marshall, 1981), the grounding process provides a firmer sense of security about whether or not those beliefs are justified.

Kinds of evidence in grounding

With a few exceptions, much of the experimental work on collaboration has focused on the grounding process as it operates when the verbal channel is either primarily or exclusively all that is available to the participants. In face-to-face conversation, of course, the participants have non-verbal channels as well, which also provide information used for planning and coordinating actions in grounding. As Goodwin (1981) has shown, for example, subtle changes in the addressee's gaze and posture can have anything but subtle effects on a speaker. She will change the course of her presentation mid-stride if her addressee is not continuing to attend in the expected way.

Gestures, too, are a great resource for presenting and grounding contributions. If directors in the referential communication task could be seen pointing to an intended figure, the presentation phase would presumably be much easier. If the matcher could, in addition, just show the director what figure he was selecting, this could serve as evidence of their coordinated understanding. The collaborative theory maintains that communication involves grounding, but not that evidence in the process must be verbal or have propositional content.

So, in face-to-face conversation, non-verbal signs and signals such as gaze, posture and facial expression provide additional evidence in grounding. Visually perceptible evidence may have the additional bonus of not requiring the same sort of turn-taking as spoken evidence. In this way, it can be more continuously available than purely verbal presentations, and also more closely connected in time to a change in the addressee's state. When an addressee's face instantly changes from attentive to puzzled right after the speaker utters a noun phrase, a likely hypothesis is that the reference – as opposed to some other part of the intended contribution – probably needs refashioning.

Presumably, all of this should make the grounding process more efficient, and a recent study examined this expectation in detail. With an innovative measure of 'on-line' collaborative processing, Brennan (1990) showed, among other things, that providing a speaker with continuous, direct evidence of an addressee's state of understanding does indeed simplify – though does not eliminate – the acceptance phase in grounding.

Continuous, direct evidence

In Brennan's task (1990), two people sat at opposite ends of a room, each in front of networked computers that displayed the same map. Each person could control one of two car icons on the computer display by using a mouse input device. When the director clicked her mouse, her car icon would move to a preset target location. The matcher now needed to 'drag' his car to the same location (using his mouse), and the partners could talk to one another as much as they wanted in the process. When satisfied, the matcher clicked to 'park' the car in a final location.

The computer kept a running record of where the matcher's car was at any point in the conversation, and this 'action transcript' was later synchronized within 500 milliseconds or less with a tape-recording of everything the partners said to one another. So what a matcher actually understood could be estimated moment-by-moment according to how close his car was to the target. This could then continue up to the point at which he *committed* to a mutual understanding and parked his car – that is, to the completion point of the acceptance process. It could also be compared to what the participants were doing with their language.

In one condition (*visual*), the director's screen showed both car icons, so she had continuous, visual information about the matcher's progress while they talked (the matcher saw only his own car). In another condition (*spoken only*), both partners saw only their own cars, and thus relied only on spoken evidence to coordinate. The results showed that having both visual and spoken evidence together made the grounding process much more efficient. On visual trials, the director began getting evidence of the matcher's hypotheses as soon as the matcher started to move his car. The evidence was direct, very accurate and continuously available – even while she was in the process of making a presentation. Because of this, she could and did adjust her presentation to reflect their proximity to their goal (and the matcher's apparent needs) more precisely at any moment. Indeed, with visual information directors frequently cut themselves off mid-presentation to initiate acceptance at just about the instant the matcher's car arrived at the target. As all of this would suggest, trials with the visual information were on average half as long as those with spoken evidence only.

The clearest difference in the time course of visual and non-visual trials was in what happened after a matcher reached the target spot. With only spoken evidence, there was a much longer interval between when the matcher's car arrived on target and when he clicked to park it there. And it was exactly in this interval that the partners were doing more lengthy verbal grounding, to confirm that the matcher was indeed in the intended place. So in the visual condition, the director could initiate the final acceptance phase ('Stop right there!'), and the matcher could simply respond by parking with an audible click. In the verbal condition, the matcher had to provide more evidence for his state of understanding.

But, even though more efficient, there were still signs of grounding in the visual condition, and often with even a verbal component. The following exchange from a visual trial exemplifies this clearly (adapted from Brennan, 1990):

1D: ok, I want you to go to the Post Office.
2M: to the Post Office.
3D: right next door to the bookstore.
4M: 'kay. get the icon ok ok?
5D: ok go into the Post Office.
6M: into the Post Office.
7D: click right there.
8M: (AUDIBLE CLICK) gotcha.

In this example, the action transcript showed that when the director (D) began on line 5D, the matcher (M) had already moved his car almost exactly to the target (within 20 pixels). But their interaction didn't stop there. They grounded their mutual understanding that the matcher was there, continuing their interaction for another three turns (which took an additional three seconds, roughly). Still, with only spoken evidence, grounding after the matcher's car was very near the target (again within 20 pixels) was more extensive. The following example with only spoken evidence shows this:

1D: ok now we're at the Post Office, which is in White Plaza?
2M: uhhhh Post Office, yep, found it
3D: ok so you're in the Post Office, you are umm level
4D: with the words Post Office?
5M: ok?
6D: you're completely in the building, and you're a little bit to the
7D: right of centre. So your icon is almost touching the right edge of the building.
8M: ok. (AUDIBLE CLICK)

In this case, the matcher's car was on target by the end of line 2M. Yet it took another 12 seconds or so for them to establish where the matcher's car was *supposed* to be, and to accept that it was there.

As these examples illustrate, the verbal components of grounding were more minimal with strong and continuous evidence of understanding. In the spoken condition, directors and matchers averaged another 35 words from the point at which the matcher's car was actually within 20 pixels of the target to the point at which he clicked to park it. Even when visual evidence was available to the director, however, they still averaged an additional ten words. Verbal grounding was less extensive, but still deemed useful.

Mediated evidence

At the same time that evidence for mutual understanding can be more direct and continuous than the standard communication task provides for, it can also be more indirect and discontinuous. The studies of overhearers illustrate some of the problems that indirect evidence can create. As a final illustration, I will briefly describe some work my collaborators and I have been doing to explore another situation involving indirect, discontinuous evidence: the situation in which conversation takes place through an intermediary (Wilkes-Gibbs et al., 1993).

We wanted to study some of the conditions in effect when conversations are conducted through a translator, but also wanted to keep language constant to avoid additional issues of translatability. In the procedure we devised, an English-speaking director and matcher have the usual task of arranging tangram figures into identical orders without being able to see each other. To do this, they can talk back and forth as much as they want, but not directly. Rather, everything they say is relayed through a third subject, in the role of intermediary. The director sits in one room and the matcher in another. The intermediary is in a third room and can speak by telephone with the matcher, and by intercom with the director. Intermediaries are not given any information about the figures themselves, and their job is simply to be a 'mouthpiece'. Our main interest is whether disrupting the temporal and intentional connections of responses in grounding affects the growth of common ground.

This line of work is ongoing, but several findings are already clear. One is that the mediated directors and matchers *are* able to maintain the same level of accuracy as control groups who speak directly by intercom. But to reach the same criterion for their mutual understanding, the mediated partners work much harder. In one study, they took 432 seconds to complete an average trial, as opposed to 142 for the unmediated groups. This difference is larger than what one would expect if intermediaries simply add redundancy. In other words, if adding a mediator simply causes everything to be said twice (once by the primary participants and one by the intermediary), we would expect mediated groups to take twice as long as unmediated ones. In this study, they took more than three times as long.

Counts of words and turns showed the same patterns. For example, directors in the mediated groups of this study had to use 31.2 words in 3.2 speaking turns to get each figure placed on average. Unmediated directors used just 17.5 words on average, in 1.8 turns, to do the same thing. Note that this direct comparison ignores any words the intermediary said, and so the simple redundancy hypothesis predicts no difference at all in this case. We also find that the mediated groups increase their efficiency more slowly across six trials in the task than the unmediated groups do.

We are looking more closely at the transcribed conversations from this task for more precise information about the problems that mediation causes in this situation, and how the participants solve them. Several related studies are also in progress, including one that asks how well intermediaries actually do understand the conversation in which they play a part, but not as a participant in the usual sense. In another study, we are looking at what happens when mediated directors and matchers are allowed to speak directly on a seventh and eighth trial. Our data suggest that they start out more tentatively on the first few figures than other subjects who had been collaborating directly all along. However, just as Isaacs and Clark (1987) found for experts and novices, our partners firm up their beliefs about their common ground very rapidly, and are quickly indistinguishable from controls.

Conclusion

Overall, each study I have reviewed takes a more interactionist approach to language processing than is common in psycholinguistics. In the collaborative theory, dynamic, social forces in discourse are given more equal footing with cognitive and linguistic ones. At the same time, however, the research I have described retains a psychological flavour that separates it from related work in the sociolinguistic tradition. One difference, for example, is a continued focus on generalizing across individuals – but in collaborative contexts. In this way, the work converges nicely with recent psychological interest in issues of socially shared cognition.

What I have tried to show is how the need for coordinating beliefs and actions within a collective can shape basic processes, and consequences, of language use. In order to build beliefs about common ground, people systematically collaborate for evidence of their mutual understanding. The collaborative process is flexible, and shrinks or expands in response to the coordination problems of a specific discourse, at a specific point. Those problems may differ from one situation to the next, and may be more or less demanding. But a common feature is that their solution is jointly achieved through strategic, collective activities.

PART THREE

Sociolinguistic perspectives

The four approaches to CS in this section are 'sociolinguistic' in the sense that they examine CS as part of socially situated interaction. Yet within this broad category, the approaches take strikingly different perspectives on CS – those of critical sociolinguistics, interactional modification, conversation analysis and cross-cultural pragmatics. Based on analyses of talk involving non-native speakers in different social and institutional settings, the chapters problematize taken-for-granted beliefs extant in the literature on second language acquisition and use about the characteristics associated with the roles of 'learner' and 'non-native speaker', and suggest various ways of expanding the notion of CS.

The initial chapter by *Rampton* sets out with a critical assessment of the psycholinguistic and interactional approaches to CS. Rampton makes the valid point that even if the research focus is on *individuals'* strategic action, sociopolitical contextualization is warranted because macro-social structure is reproduced at the micro-level of intra- and interindividual cognition and communication. Based on previous studies by Aston (1993) and Trosset (1986), Rampton argues against the view of 'non-nativeness' as an interactional if not social handicap and the limitation of CS to emergency solutions when transactional goals are at stake. In his own data on the playground interaction between bilingual Panjabi adolescent boys and their Anglo and Afro-Caribbean friends, Rampton demonstrates how codeswitching to Panjabi functions as a solidarity-creating strategy with no referential importance, serving to construct new ethnic identities that acknowledge diversity and multiple social alignments. While this view of conversational codeswitching has a long history in the literature on functional explanations of codeswitching (see Myers-Scotton, 1993b, for review), it has not received much attention in CS circles until recently. A constructivist view of codeswitching offers an alternative explanation of automatic switches, which had thus far been understood from the perspectives of speech production and conversational principles (see Poulisse, this volume).

Williams, Inscoe and Tasker examine the discourse between international teaching assistants and American undergraduate students in a chemistry laboratory. Adopting the framework of interactional modification proposed by Long (1981), the authors scrutinize how participants collaborate in achieving mutual comprehension. Rather than limiting the scope of analysis to code-based gaps in the non-native speakers' knowledge, information gaps are included as problems that the participants need to solve in order to get on with the laboratory task at hand. In this institutional setting, the commonly assumed distribution of knowledge between native and non-native speakers is reversed because the non-native teaching assistants are in the roles of experts while the native speakers of English are novices in their field of study. CS use is shown to be strongly constrained by the institutional setting, participants' roles, and the overall and local goals that need to be achieved for students to carry out the laboratory task.

Wagner and Firth extend the analysis of CS to yet another type of institutional discourse. Examining lingua franca interaction in a business setting by means of a conversation analytic approach, the authors argue that there are no such things as 'problem' and 'CS' unless conversational activity is overtly marked ('flagged') as problematic by participants. Consequently, many of the stretches of talk that would be traditionally labelled as strategies are excluded in this view. Participants leave lexical and propositional 'problems' unresolved unless they are seen as locally relevant, and only rarely solicit the interlocutor's assistance. In addition to providing a new, strictly interactionally defined view of CS, this chapter also demonstrates that native speaker norms can be inadequate as criteria for communicative success or failure in interaction involving non-native speakers.

Kasper problematizes the dominant research practice in applied linguistics of restricting the investigation of strategic competence to referential and lexical problems and their solutions, and argues for an extension of the research focus to the pragmatics of interpersonal rhetoric. While all communicators have to grapple with communication problems arising from conflicting goals, participants in intercultural encounters are in a potentially more difficult situation because less relevant knowledge is shared and, in case trouble occurs, the strategies employed to solve it are more likely to diverge than among members of the same ethnolinguistic group. The literature in interlanguage pragmatics and related fields is reviewed for reports on pragmatic problems and the strategies adopted by native and non-native speakers to remedy them. Consonant with previous chapters in this section, Kasper argues that an essentialist and deterministic view of 'the non native speaker' overlooks the fact that non-nativeness can be a problem, a resource, or a non-issue in ongoing interaction, and that the local construction of participant identity may be consequential for the pragmatic problems and strategies encountered in intercultural discourse.

12

A sociolinguistic perspective on L2 communication strategies

BEN RAMPTON

The identification and description of communication strategies (CS) has traditionally been the subject of uncertainty and dispute in second language research, but a stage has now been reached where leading scholars question whether there is actually any sense at all in trying to study CS as a distinctive issue in L2 enquiry. In this chapter, I shall argue that communication strategies should indeed be central in L2 investigation, but that their full significance can only be understood if the domain of CS research is expanded beyond the particular kinds of psycholinguistic and interactional approach that currently dominate the field. More specifically, investigation could usefully look beyond grammar and lexis to other kinds of problematic knowledge, beyond referential to social and interpersonal meaning, beyond individuals and dyads to groups, and beyond experiments with undergraduate informants. Widened in this way, the notion of L2 communication strategies can be productively tied into a very large literature outside SLA, and it becomes a rich site for the investigation of interactional, social and educational issues.

The chapter begins by reviewing some of the most radical conclusions of psycholinguistic work on L2 communication strategies. It then refers back to the educational concerns that originally motivated CS research, and it uses these as a starting point from which to elaborate the sociolinguistic perspective that occupies its central sections. With this in place, it then reconsiders the research that it addressed at the outset, and argues that even here, sociolinguistics has much to offer. The chapter finishes with some observations on the way in which the agenda of L2 CS research could be productively expanded.

Scepticism about L2 communication strategies

Scepticism about the viability of communication strategies as a distinctive field of L2 research is most forcefully expressed by Kellerman, Poulisse and Bongaerts (e.g., Bongaerts & Poulisse 1989, 1990; Kellerman et al., 1987). Surveying the field, Kellerman identifies about 50 labels in what he describes as 'a luxuriant jungle of names and strategies' (Kellerman, 1991, p. 146), and he notes that if they are set against criteria of generalizability, parsimony and psychological plausibility most taxonomies fall short. So, for example, it is quite common, claims Kellerman, for CS lists to mix up underlying processing strategies with the properties of the objects that just happen to have been presented to informants in picture tasks (Kellerman, 1991, p. 147; Kellerman et al., 1987, p. 100). Instead, Kellerman, Bongaerts and Poulisse distil a wealth of experimental evidence down into two (or three) basic types of compensatory strategy – the conceptual (subdivided in the analytic and holistic), in which speakers try to communicate by working over their mental representation of the referent that they want to talk about, and the code-focused, in which they try to say what they want by manipulating the communicative medium (through, for instance, neologism, or a switch to L1). This argument leads to several rather radical conclusions. Social interaction is not seen as a relevant concern in compensatory strategy research: 'It matters little whether it is the speaker or the listener who initiates the compensatory behaviour, or whether it is an activity that happens over several conversational turns or a single one' (Kellerman, 1991, p. 153). The distinction between L1 and L2 processes is rejected: '(T)he fundamental difference between a native speaker's and an adult learner's referential behaviour is that the former has a more extensive set of linguistic means available for reaching a particular communicative goal' (p. 154). And there is no place for the view that strategies should be part of the language teaching curriculum: 'Teach the learners more language and let the strategies look after themselves' (p. 158).

There is a good deal of persuasiveness in Kellerman, Bongaerts and Poulisse's lucid critique of the rather *ad hoc* character of quite a few CS taxonomies. But have they really uncovered the fundamental principles organizing the 'luxuriant jungle'? Or have they just tidied the greenhouse?

Problematicity and consciousness in CS research

Kellerman's argument is, then, that social interaction is irrelevant to communication strategies, that CS in the L2 are the same as CS in the L1, and that there is little of any significance for language education. It seems to me that as a verdict on CS research's empirical scope and practical implications, Kellerman's final extrapolations are not really warranted, and to see why not, Færch and Kasper's influential papers (1983a) provide a helpful point of departure.

Færch and Kasper's work during this period rests on a rather uneasy tension. On the one hand, communication strategies are sited within a purely psycholinguistic model of speech processing (drawing heavily on Clark & Clark, 1977), while on the other, quite a lot of emphasis is given to practical usefulness as a criterion for assessing the adequacy of any theoretical formulation. There is no necessary connection between these two strands. Kellerman, Bongaerts and Poulisse's work can be read as a development of the first, but I would like to try to elaborate a little on the second.

In arguing for the importance of practical usefulness as a consideration in the definition of L2 communication strategies, Færch and Kasper emphasize an 'Erkenntnisinteresse ... in foreign language learning and teaching' (1983d, pp. 28–31), and this leads them to analyse CS in terms of problem-orientedness and potential consciousness (see also Corder, 1981; Haastrup & Phillipson, 1983; Paribakht, 1985; Tarone, 1983).[1] They propose that as any attempt to design a syllabus that anticipates the learner's every need is doomed to failure, it is worth trying to identify the most effective ways of coping with occasions when the learner's communicative resources seem insufficient ('problem orientedness'). And in class, the explicit attention to such improvisations is likely to facilitate their performance outside ('potential consciousness'; 1983d, pp. 31–32).

Admittedly, the particular Erkenntnisinteresse emphasized by Færch & Kasper has not won universal recognition for L2 communication strategies. There is some uncertainty as to how and whether problem-oriented, potentially conscious communication strategies can actually be taught in foreign language classrooms (cf. Tarone & Yule, 1989, Ch. 9), and in this context, Kellerman's denial of educational relevance seems fair enough. But this is not the only kind of educational relevance that the CS idea can have: pedagogy inside classrooms where people have come to learn English is only *one* possible context. Language education can be understood more widely than this, and this broader interpretation provides a context – an 'Erkenntnisinteresse' – in which the significance of an L2 speaker's potentially conscious experience of problematicity is much less easily controverted. In the central parts of this chapter, I shall use three case studies to argue this point in some detail. But before doing so, it is worth just remembering how important the notions of problematicity and potential consciousness have been in educational and sociolinguistics in general.

Problematicity and consciousness in educational and sociolinguistics

In one way or another, problematicity and consciousness have figured as major preoccupations in a great deal of educational linguistics, and a concern that language problems might be closely implicated in the widespread underachievement of low income and minority ethnic students has played a central role in sociolinguistics since the 1960s (cf. Hymes, 1972a). Much of this research can itself be seen as an attempt to bring the roots of school failure to (public) awareness, and sociolinguists have consistently seen it as their responsibility to try to use their explanations to influence educational policy.[2] Throughout all of these debates, the identification and explanation of 'language' problems have been surrounded by controversy. It has been hard to distinguish the linguistic from the cognitive from the socio-cultural, and the responsibility for difficulty has been attributed to students, teachers, school systems and indeed to researchers themselves (see, for example, Honey, 1983; Labov, 1969). In addition, at different times and on different issues, particular explanations have been favoured by different political groupings (cf. Rampton, 1988, pp. 515–16).

The first point to draw from this experience is a general one. Controversy about the origin of (purportedly) linguistic problems seems inevitable. Indeed, not only is it impossible for researchers to avoid dispute of this kind, but dispute actually needs to be seen as *part of the data to be analysed*, an active principle in the social fields that researchers try to understand. The second point follows on from this and it is particularly relevant to L2 research: when difficulties arise, it is not necessarily the bilingual, the minority speaker or the second language user who is at fault.[3] Neither of these points are widely accepted in L2 CS research.

In L2 CS research, uncertainty and disagreement about the diagnosis of linguistic problems have been treated much more narrowly. Quite a lot of attention has been given to the difficulties involved in trying to spot and classify problematic moments in L2 production, (e.g., Færch & Kasper, 1983c; Tarone & Yule, 1989, p. 109), but these difficulties have generally been treated as merely technical issues of research methodology. Defining someone's behaviour as a 'problem' often raises political issues, but there has been very little concern with this in work on L2 CS. In addition, where problematic moments can be reliably identified, it is almost invariably the L2 learner who is held responsible (Rampton, 1987, p. 55).

In defence, one might want to argue that sociolinguists and L2 CS researchers are dealing with quite different phenomena: while a lot of the educational and sociolinguistic research that I have alluded to deals with large groups and macro-social processes, CS investigation examines on-line discourse processing among individuals. Unfortunately, the dichotomy at the base of a defence like that is rather artificial. As interpretive sociolinguists have argued at length, it is actually in the details of moment-to-moment interaction that the larger social patterns are produced (e.g., Chick, 1985; Erickson & Shultz, 1982; Gumperz, 1982; Michaels, 1981; Sapir, 1949). Furthermore, *without* losing sight of broader social and political issues, sociolinguistic research on cross-cultural communication overlaps with CS research in some very obvious ways – there are a number of sociolinguistic studies which have included consciousness-raising among participants as part of their design (e.g., Furnborough et al., 1982; Heath, 1983; Roberts et al., 1992). In short, it is not easy for L2 CS research to ignore the kinds of issues that sociolinguistics draws attention to.

In fact, sociolinguistics generates a number of other heterodox implications for L2 CS research, and to see these, one does not need to move any distance from the definition of communication strategies in terms of perceptible problematicity. Communication strategies, it seems to me, constitute the quintessential L2 moment, in which there is an intricate fusion between discourse processing and the recognition of language learner category membership. But as implied in the sketch above, the cultural meaning of learner status is itself very variable, and it is often charged with ambiguities. In consequence, CS investigation needs to approach its subject in a rather more open-ended, ethnographic manner. In Færch's terms, it needs to spend more time 'straying around in the forest' (Færch, 1984, p. 60, also cited in Aston, 1993, p. 230).

Though the need for naturalistic data is quite often emphasized, experimental methodologies have so far been dominant in both psycholinguistic and interactional CS studies, and so from the outset, informant behaviour has been quite tightly constrained by the researcher's own theories and assumptions. In addition, the extra-linguistic factors given focal attention in CS research generally stop at task and setting, and experimental subjects tend to be students who are only differentiated in terms of age, national origin and the length of time they have been doing English lessons (e.g., Bialystok, 1983a, p. 107; Dechert, 1983, p. 177; Haastrup & Phillipson, 1983, p. 141; Váradi, 1983, p. 87; see also Bongaerts & Poulisse, 1990; Færch et al., 1984; Kellerman & Bialystok, 1990; Paribakht, 1985). There is no reference to particular biographies, networks or positions in social structure (though see Fiksdal 1989; Hinnenkamp, 1980; Kleifgen, 1989; Roberts & Simonot, 1987; Schmidt, 1983; Schumann, 1978), and so in general, the CS data base has been rather artificially homogenized. If one steps outside this, however, one can actually see that communication strategies are rather more diverse than they have been hitherto depicted, and three studies can be used to illustrate this.

Aston (1993)

Aston (1993) follows Tarone in being more concerned with the understanding shared between interlocutors than with the speaker's independent competence. But he breaks new ground by highlighting interpersonal rather than transactional negotiation – rapport rather than information transfer, affective more than referential convergence, feelings more than knowledge – and he suggests that it is difficult to set up 'controlled contexts in which the negotiation of rapport is at issue' (p. 230). More concretely, he focuses on conversational actions and sequences through which participants create solidarity and support. The former is defined as shared attitudes to an experience which the partici-pants have in common, and it is typically expressed through routines of agreement (p. 232), while the latter is concerned with shared attitudes to an experience that is specific to only one parti-cipant, and it can be communicated through routines of affilia-tion, compliments, apologies and so forth (pp. 232–3). The extent to which two participants generate solidarity is constrained by the amount of shared experience that they bring along or bring about in an interaction, and support is influenced by the extent to which each participant either shows that they 'know and care' about the other, or can be assumed to do so (pp. 233–5).

Aston suggests that in interaction between first and second language users, the negotiation of solidarity might be impeded by differences in cultural experience, while suspicions about ethnic otherness might hinder the development of support. What he proposes, then, can be seen as an interpersonal counterpart to the transactional problematicity that traditionally concerns CS research, and to point out both the similarities and differences, Aston uses the phrase '*comity* strategies' to describe the ways in which participants overcome these affective obstacles.

In turning to describe L2 comity strategies themselves, Aston then demonstrates the ways in which language learner status itself serves as an interactional resource. The relative lack of a shared background can itself become a joint interest, and by standing outside their respective cultures of origin, participants seem able to establish the solidarity of 'fellow outlaws' (Aston, 1993, p. 238). Beyond that, where one person has only a rudimentary command of their common language 'even routine talk may be problematic, with the result that its successful bringing-off can appear a noteworthy accomplishment, and provide grounds for mutual satisfaction' (p. 239).

And incompetence itself assists the negotiation of support:

> Known incompetence can be a distinctive, individualising feature that, by warranting support in the face of inadequate performance (providing grounds for appeals for assistance to, and displays of benevolent sympathy from, an interlocutor), can constitute an interactional resource. (p. 240)

Aston's research is important in providing detailed empirical leverage on a central dimension of communication that has been hitherto neglected in CS research, even though in reality it is always operating simultaneously with talk's transactional function (Brown & Yule, 1983, pp. 1–4; cf. Roberts & Simonot (1987) for a study that gives explicit treatment to both). It points to some of the pleasures that can be associated with marginal language-learner status, thereby usefully challenging the influential but tacit image of language learners struggling unhappily with their linguistic deficiency. And it produces a list of L2 comity maxims that, in certain circumstances, could be quite sensibly passed on in the classroom ('cite warrants for your attitudes; admit your incompetence; celebrate ordinary success; repair actual incompetence where possible; appreciate benevolence; distance yourself from the stereotypes of your culture' (1993, p. 245)).

In Aston's study, Conversation Analysis is the primary inspiration, and this perhaps partly accounts for a certain lack of wider socio-cultural contextualization. This is given much more fully in Trosset (1986), which, in contrast, aligns itself with the ethnography of communication. So where Aston talks about ethnic and cultural difference in a rather generalized way, Trosset provides an account of how language-learner status is sensitive to interethnic relations in a particular social and historical context.

Trosset (1986)

In contrast to nearly all SLA research, which has been overwhelmingly concerned with the learning of dominant varieties (though see Beebe, 1985), Trosset describes the learning of a minority language – Welsh. Here is some of what she has to say:

> The vast majority of Welsh speakers are first-language Welsh, and their numbers are declining every year. All Welsh speakers by their very existence symbolize the Welsh struggle for linguistic survival. Learners have a special significance because they represent a *reverse* trend in language acquisition. ... The scarcity of Welsh learners, and their obvious expenditure of effort and dedication to the learning of the language, combine with the symbolic implications of their doing so to make successful learners highly visible in the society. Beginning learners are much less significant in this respect, but persons who become at least moderately conversant inevitably draw attention to themselves. ... Largely because of the symbolic implications of the act, Welsh speakers are extremely pleased by any degree of progress on the part of Welsh learners. They are generous with praise and appear to learners to be easily impressed. Any learner who turns up in a group of Welsh speakers will quickly be 'passed around' and introduced, with a strong emphasis on his or her linguistic accomplishment.
>
> (1986, pp. 174–8)

This linguistic celebrity produces communicative problems for the learner:

The aesthetic function is commonly dominant when Welsh speakers listen to Welsh learners. They focus primarily on the medium rather than the content of the learners' speech. Second-language speakers are often frustrated to find how difficult it is for them to engage in normal conversation with native speakers – not because their own Welsh is inadequate, but because the attention of the native speakers seems irrevocably fixed on the linguistic skill being displayed by the learners. Under these conditions the referential function, the content of speech, becomes basically unimportant, or rather inaccessible. Second-language speakers sometimes complain to each other that no one ever listens to *what* they say.

(p. 179)

Trosset reports the following strategic solution:

In their frustration at not being treated as normal speakers, proficient learners may seek to escape from their learners' status ... Since they do not enjoy being second-language speakers, they attempt to 'become' native speakers – that is, they lie about their place and language of origin.   (pp. 187–8)

Several points emerge from this account. First, it is clear once again that L1 speakers can also be a major source of difficulty (see the discussion of *Crosstalk* in note 3). Secondly, language processing plainly involves much more than a movement between linguistic structure and referential propositions. Participants also orient to the social relationships and identities indexed by the linguistic code and this can affect the course of interaction in ways that present learners with difficulty. In fact, 'social meanings' can present learners with difficulties that seem to be the very opposite of the lexical retrieval problems frequently studied in CS research, where learners are generally construed as being concerned with insufficiencies in their own linguistic knowledge. Trosset describes encounters between successful learners and first language users who

speak 'bad Welsh' – that is, Welsh speakers who use a great many borrowed English words ... once when I used the word *ymarfer* ('rehearsal'), my host responded, 'Well you speak better than we do. We say "practice" '. Whether or not such observations have any practical effect on people's speech habits, they do illustrate the consciousness-raising potential of successful learners, who by their acquired command of Welsh can make native speakers more critically aware of their own inadvertent contributions to the decline of the language.   (pp. 176–7)

Here, problems arise from the fact that the second language learner is able to draw on a *larger* L2 lexical store than the native speaker, and more generally, the L2 speaker's capacity to use a more 'correct', more prestigious variety would appear to be far from rare as a source of inhibition.

Corder provides a useful summary of the discussion so far:

> A working definition of communication strategies is that they are a systematic technique employed by a speaker to express his meaning when faced with some difficulty. Difficulty in this definition is taken to refer uniquely to the speaker's inadequate command of the language used in the interaction. This ... is obviously a simplifying assumption, but one which permits a start to be made on investigating a difficult topic.   (Corder, [1978] 1981, pp. 103–4)

This is indeed a simplifying assumption, and Trosset shows why. If these and other idealizations are *abandoned*, the agenda of CS research immediately expands and a range of new strategies present themselves. In Trosset's context, 'pretend to be a native speaker' is clearly a very serious piece of advice. But it doesn't figure in any of the CS taxonomies that I know of.

Indeed, soon after one drops the decision to focus on how individuals and dyads deal with referential communication problems, it becomes clear that 'avoidance' and 'achievement' are themselves inadequate as L2 communication 'archistrategies' (Corder, 1981; Færch & Kasper, 1983d). 'Avoidance' and 'achievement' don't actually cover all of the ways in which people cope with the difficulties that they experience using an L2. There is good evidence, for example, of L2 users actually responding with hostility to the problematic communicative situations that they encounter. Drawing on the contact between Standard and American Vernacular Black English and between Spanish, Quechua and Nahuatl, Hill and Coombs describe the way in which vernacular speakers exploit the dominant language 'as a source of symbolic material for the management of their oppressed status' (Hill & Coombs, 1982, p. 224; see also Reisman, 1974). Standard L2s become the focus of intensive play, their symbolic values are inverted, and they become the objects and instruments of mockery. In this light, it makes sense to propose 'resistance' as a third archistrategy, realized in a range of acts such as accusation, abuse, caricature, symbolic remodelling and maybe also hostile silence (see Rampton, 1991b, extracts 3 & 4).

Trosset concurs with Aston about the interactional significance of a distinctive language learner identity, but she usefully shows the error in any premature generalization about the meaning of this identity. This will always be closely associated with a range of quite particular social and historical influences. My own research takes up a number of the themes mentioned above, and it also underscores the way in which communication strategies can be produced and discussed in quite large social groups. Of course, many CS researchers give this implicit recognition in their concern with the ways in which communication strategies might be taught in class, but there has been very little direct empirical examination of the collective significance that CS might have (though see Hill & Coombs, 1982).

Research on a neighbourhood in the UK

My research draws quite extensively on interactional sociolinguistics and the ethnography of communication, and it focused on a network of adolescents in one neighbourhood in the South Midlands of England. My central concern has been with the use of three learner varieties in a range of different settings (ESL, L2 Panjabi, and Creole as a second dialect; interaction with adults, in the peer group, and around performance art). The emerging portrait is too complex to be described in any detail here (see Rampton, 1991b, pp. 230–7 for a slightly larger fragment, and Rampton (1995) for the full account). But it is worth describing just one of the ways in which L2 status played an important symbolic role, and how it was elaborated in a set of widely celebrated communication strategies.

In playground interaction among boys in early adolescence, it was quite common for Panjabi bilinguals to invite monolingual friends of Anglo and Afro-Caribbean descent to either say things in Panjabi, or to respond to Panjabi questions.[4] These invitations to use another language normally contained elements which lay just beyond the learner's grasp – in Krashen's terms, one might say that proficient Panjabi speakers rough-tuned their utterances at i + 1½ or 2 (Krashen, 1981, Ch. 9). The fact that an important element of what was being said to the L2 learner was *in*comprehensible to them was absolutely crucial, and it was this that produced the fun and games. Learners had to operate just beyond the limits of their linguistic competence, and playfully speaking, their reputations depended on their performance. Here is an example:[5]

Example (1)

Participants: Mohan (male, 13 years, Indian descent wearing a radio-microphone), Sukhbir (M 13 In), Jagdish (M 13 In), David (M 12 Afro-Caribbean), Pritam (M In), others. *Setting:* Breaktime, outside. Mohan, Jagdish and David are best friends.

```
1    Jagdish ((turning to David, speaking in Panjabi)):
2                 [ə tu lɔrə di bʊn mʌregə]
              ((Approximate translation: do you want to bum Laura?))
3    Sukhbir:  ⌈ ha ha ha ha ha
4      Others: ⌊ ((laughter for about three seconds))
5      David: no I don't think so
6    Jagdish: DAVID (.) no I said that – that means that you're –
7              are you going to beat Laura up
8      David: no =
9    Sukhbir: = yeh it does, it does  ⌈ (it does)
10     David: ((smile voice))           ⌊ that – that means [h] are you
11             going to make her pregnant=
12   Sukhbir: =NO::  ⌈ (          )
13    Mohan:        ⌊ no
        ((a few moments later))
21   Jagdish: SAY IT TO HIM (.) say it to him say it to him
22           ⌈ say it to him [meri mãdi _____ ]
            │      ((Trans: my mum's fanny))
23     Others: │ ((laughter))
24      Anon: go on
25     David: I ⌈ don't want to say that
26   Jagdish:   ⌊ NO SAY IT TO HIM GO ON say it to him
27      Anon: ha ⌈ ha ha ha ha
28      Anon:    │ go on
29     David:    ⌊ (it says – your go – )
30             it means that │ MY mum's got a –
31   Jagdish:               │ eh?
32             no say ((... the 'elicitations' continue))
```

Clearly, language learner language was here drawn into traditional playground practice, in variations on the verbal routines which the Opies describe as 'incrimination traps' (Opie & Opie, 1959, Ch. 4).[6] Placed in one of these, a number of communication strategies were available to an L2 Panjabi speaker aware of the insufficiency of their linguistic knowledge, but it is difficult to use existing schemes of classification with any certainty – up to a point, ambiguity was a constitutive element in the activity itself. In the episode above, David's 'avoidance' might be better described as refusal, and it is clear that in this context, Aston's comity maxim 'appreciate benevolence' would leave David with egg on his face, while 'admit your incompetence' would deflate the game as a whole. One common strategy was to ask a friend for help:

'my friend, you know, he swears in Panjabi to English girls, and they go and ask an Indian boy they know, and he tells them and tells them other words and they come and say it to us.'

Consultations of this kind were very commonly construed in pupil–teacher terms, and here cooperative communication strategies slipped over into learning strategies (see Tarone, 1983, p. 67):

A: some people, they revise it for a long time ... Cyril Johns
B: ((laughs)) he doesn't revise it does he?
A: course he does, that's what I heard
B: desperate dudes

It would be premature, however, to classify either of these as achievement strategies, since, as illustrated in the episode above, you would be foolish to trust too much in the instruction provided by friends:

'like Ishfaq tells ... you know Alan Timms, if Alan Timms says "teach me some dirty words", Ishfaq makes him say swear words to himself ((laughs)), so he's saying it to hims ... he goes up to Asif and he says it and Asif starts laughing'

Elsewhere, L2 Panjabi learners appeared to get by by combining rudimentary knowledge of one or two items with inferences drawn from the wider situational and discursive context. It helped, for example, if you could distinguish between 1st and 2nd person pronouns and possessive determiners in Panjabi. David clearly drew on this knowledge in line 30 in example (1), and according to Mohan:

'every time I go to [David] "say [mɛ kʊttʌ]" ((Approximate trans: I'm a dog)), he says "[tu kʊttʌ]" ((You're a dog)). He knows the difference.'

The analysis of communication strategies here is relatively impressionistic, and I haven't tried to match my entire database (comprising about 68 episodes of L2 Panjabi use) against any one or more CS taxonomies. Two points are clear however. First, there is a great deal of relevance in the notion of communication strategy as some kind of improvisational procedure. Adolescents of Anglo and Afro-Caribbean descent didn't have much of a Panjabi interlanguage lexicogrammar on which to draw (cf. Færch & Kasper, 1983d, p. 211) and their production and reception of Panjabi utterances was generally far from automatic – for example, in interview a number of informants had difficulty remembering the words and phrases that they said they typically used (see, e.g., Rampton, 1991b, p. 231, Extract 3). Secondly, in one form or another, communication strategies were widely recognized and reported by adolescents themselves (cf, Færch & Kasper's criterion of potential consciousness). Beyond that, along with L2 Panjabi learner status, they played a significant role in the enunciation of a sense of local interracial youth community. Bilinguals generally regarded the learning of playground L2 Panjabi as an indication of friendship:

> 'if they're our friends, we teach them it'

> 'most of them do really, who hang around with us lot, you see, they all know one word I bet you'

> 'it's mostly the boys ... um I think most ... popular boys ... yeh right, who are not Asian, who get a lot of swearwords because they get them all off their Asian friends'

> '[Billy and Peter who know] quite a lot of words ... these two are one of us'

The Panjabi second language learner was an important (and enjoyable) identity in this adolescent community, and, if suitably expanded, the notion of communication strategy is very apposite in describing the actions and procedures most closely associated with this identity. There was not much sticky sentimentality in the practices which fostered and articulated the loyalties felt between expert and learner users of Panjabi, and the element of challenge and uncertainty implicit in the CS idea fits well with the playfully competitive character of many of these interactions.

But what kind of 'Erkenntnisinteresse' could be served by this kind of analysis? Not one, I think, that focused primarily on foreign language classroom pedagogy. There is little evidence that these communication strategies actually assisted interlanguage development. In most classrooms, it would be difficult to replicate them without rather severe outbreaks of disorder; and when asked, these boys generally said they would not be interested in attending any formal classes in Panjabi – they did not really want to improve their proficiency and were evidently quite happy to remain as permanent pre-elementary language learners. The data also have very little to say about effective referential communication. Referentially, all of these L2 Panjabi communication strategies were highly dysfunctional. If it was the efficient interchange of propositions that the participants were after, then they would be much better off in English, which was spoken much more fluently by everyone.

Instead, the educational relevance of this analysis of communication strategies lies at a more general level. In the part that they played in foregrounding ethnolinguistic difference and turning it into a resource for shared peer group recreation, communication strategies contributed to the emergence of what Hall (1988) calls 'new ethnicities'.

It is not possible here to go into the political dimensions of the sense of multi-racial youth community enunciated through the local use of different ethnic languages (see Rampton, 1995, for a full discussion). However, it is worth pointing out that at present, educational reform in Britain is very heavily oriented to the reassertion of an old ethnicity – an Englishness which suppresses difference and displaces or forgets other ethnicities (e.g., cf. Cameron & Bourne, 1988; Marenbon, 1991). Interpreted for their socio-symbolic import – or in Aston's (1993) terms, as comity rather than communication strategies – the practices described above point to the emergence of a very different sensibility, fundamentally opposed to the spirit of national education policy developments.

This has some very obvious implications for language education. For example, consistent and continuous programmes of bilingual education are discouraged in the UK, and it has sometimes been proposed, in justification, that any classes which turned out to be minority monoethnic would threaten social unity (DES, 1985, pp. 406–7). The description of spontaneous recreational comity/communication strategies shows that as a blanket defence of exclusively monolingual education, this reasoning is spurious. Adolescents do not necessarily require all members of their peer group to speak all its languages with equal proficiency. Linguistic specialization is recognized and youngsters can enjoy the access to different cultural resources provided by their peers' varied linguistic expertise. And in activities demanding a versatile use of communication strategies, marginality can be cultivated as a source of pleasure and an expression of friendship in diversity.[7]

It is worth now summarizing the main points to arise from this review of three (broadly) sociolinguistic studies:

1. CS research needs to give full consideration to interpersonal and social meaning.

2. Doing so shows how a sense of linguistic difficulty is intricately tied to a psychologically and/or interactionally active sense of language learner (LL) identity.

3. The relationship between (i) LL identity and (ii) a sense of communicative difficulty is two-way: communicative difficulty sometimes evokes LL identity (Aston), and LL identity sometimes generates communicative problems (Trosset).

4. Language learner identity is itself closely bound up with other social relations and category memberships, and its evaluation varies accordingly. LL identity can be simultaneously prestigious among target language speakers and stigmatized among L2 users themselves (Trosset); it can be positively rated by both (Rampton), and of course it can also be stigmatized by both. The evaluation of LL identity is highly variable, and the ways in which this impacts on communication strategies have yet to be properly explored.

5. A sense that the L2 user's linguistic knowledge is problematic can be introduced by either party (this is in fact already very well established through L1 and L2 work on conversational repair). Uncertainty about the diagnosis of difficulty can be an active part of the interaction, and both participants can be mistaken.

6. It need not just be the L2 user who is felt to have inadequate linguistic knowledge in L1–L2 interaction (Trosset).

7. Communication strategies are not only significant as on-line improvisations used spontaneously either intramentally or interactionally (or both). They can become celebrated objects of informal commentary, and can be incorporated as a central element in social group rituals.

8. People are not always concerned with improving their L2 interlanguage, LL identity is not necessarily seen as essentially transitional, and communication strategies can be ends in themselves, one of the most important reasons for wanting to use another language (Rampton).

9. Existing taxonomies of L2 communication strategies ought to be considerably expanded, so that, for example, they take something like 'resistance' into account as an architstrategy.

Two questions arise. The first concerns the generality that one can attribute to this list of points. Is it simply based on a few rather rare and exotic studies which are likely to be highly unrepresentative of L2 learning generally? I think not. Support for these points could be adduced from a number of other sociolinguistic studies (Rampton, 1991b, pp. 238, 244), and perhaps more importantly, it is worth asking in reply: which is more likely to produce a representative picture of L2 use – closely controlled experimental elicitations with student subjects, or observations of spontaneous interaction between a wide variety of speakers, in a range of authentic settings and a number of different languages?

This leads, however, into a question that requires a more detailed response. Granted, experimental studies may not be very representative, but are their idealizations necessary, permitting, in Corder's (1981) terms, 'a start to be made on investigating a difficult topic'? Again, I would say that they were not, and that a fair number of issues (1) to (9) could be profitably included in even the most psycholinguistic CS studies. This is an argument that needs to be taken in stages.

Reconnecting with mainstream research on L2 communication strategies

In so far as L2 CS research seeks educational relevance, I do not think it is necessary to elaborate much further on the value of a more sociolinguistic perspective, and reasons for rejecting Kellerman's wider extrapolations, cited at the start of this chapter, are by now fairly obvious. An attempt to reduce the difference between L1 and L2 speakers to a simple question of differing amounts of language structure does not work, because 'language and society [are] parts of a dialectal process in which language both expresses [and] simultaneously constructs social systems and structures' (Roberts & Simonot, 1987, p. 135). In addition, if you ignore conversational sequences and turn initiation, then you lose connection with a very rich body of research on the negotiation of interpersonal meaning (research on face work and on preference organization, e.g., Brown & Levinson, 1987; Heritage, 1984; Levinson, 1983, Ch. 6).

In a sense, though, this is a rather weak statement of the case for (1) to (9), since, after all, Kellerman is saying that conversational negotiation and strategy training are issues in which he *is not* primarily interested. For Kellerman, this is fairly neutral terrain which a different set of concerns has now led him to vacate. The challenge is to show their relevance in the arenas where he stakes his central interest. For example, could a sociolinguistic perspective on L2 use offer anything to research on referential communication strategies? I think it might, both in description and in theory.

For example, Poulisse and Bongaerts (1994) describe Dutch L1 features in the speech of L2 English users. They pay particular attention to the way in which, in the most informal communication tasks – a short chat about everyday topics – learners use Dutch function words, with no hesitation and no morpho-phonological adaptation to English. They call this 'automatic transfer' and analyse it as an error of inattention: Dutch words inadvertently slip in because the speakers are preoccupied with the conceptual content of their utterances and they therefore cannot devote attentional resources to linguistic encoding in the way they do during picture tasks and story re-tellings (see also, Færch & Kasper, 1986). After that, Poulisse and Bongaerts consider the possibility that this inattentive transfer is facilitated by L1 and L2 word forms being linked to a common semantic node.

It is quite possible, though, to begin with a sociolinguistic alternative to this description, and to follow it with rather different psycholinguistic extrapolations. Relaxing in an informal conversation about local cultural topics, the speakers might instead be code-switching in order to explore a mixed Anglo-Dutch identity, which would certainly fit with the Poulisse and Bongaerts' observations about function words and the absence of morpho-phonological adaptation (on the former in a code-switching context, see, e.g., Gumperz, 1982, pp. 77–80, and Romaine, 1989, p. 112; on the latter, Gumperz, 1982, p. 59, and Romaine, 1989, pp. 51, 111). In Poulisse and Bongaerts' general model of speech processing, social identity issues are presumably handled in the prelinguistic processing component – the 'conceptualizer' – which among other things, handles knowledge of the world (see also De Bot, 1992). If this is the case, and if this sociolinguistic description was correct, then processes of linguistic encoding would need to be seen as working in perfect synchrony with the speaker's 'conceptualizer', the switches would not be erroneous and if there was a warrant for considering the relationship between L1 and L2 lexicons, it would be different from the one offered by Poulisse and Bongaerts.

Of course, this is only a suggestion. Its development would involve a much fuller analysis of their corpus, and even then, there is no reason to suppose that an account in terms of purposive code-switching would fit all of their data (see Auer, 1988, pp. 203–5; Auer & di Luzio, 1983). The basic point, though, is that although they may not be very representative of language use more generally, referential communication tasks and laboratory elicitations are still social events, and they do not provide a direct window on intramental activity allowing one to by-pass pragmatic, interactional and sociolinguistic considerations. To be valid, psycholinguistic interpretation requires descriptive input that gives an accurate picture of the systematic organization which speakers themselves produce in their talk. Before trying to model the operation of psycholinguistic processing systems, it is important to be clear whether or not an L2 intrusion is discursively motivated, for example, marking a change of footing, topic shift, sequential contrast, non-first firsts and so forth (Auer, 1988). As conversation analysis amply demonstrates, the same is true with a very wide range of other apparent dysfluencies and deviations from a cannonical standard.

Poulisse and Bongaerts would no doubt accept this point – as always, there are considerable practical difficulties in trying to cover a corpus from every angle, and it is rare to find studies which successfully combine both psycho- and sociolinguistic perspectives. However, a move in this direction is being made in research on L1 referential communication tasks conducted by Clark and Wilkes-Gibbs (referred to in Bongaerts et al., 1987 and Bongaerts & Poulisse, 1989; see also Wilkes-Gibbs, this volume), and it is worth dwelling on this in a little detail, to see the more extensively theoretical contribution of a sociolinguistic perspective on L2 learning and use.

Drawing resourcefully on interaction and conversation analysis in their experimental design and data analyses (e.g., Goffman, 1979; Schegloff et al., 1977), Clark and Wilkes-Gibbs (1986):

> proposed that people collaborate to fulfill the mutual responsibilities they take on when entering a conversation, and that there are particular procedures for doing so. Our goal was to understand how those procedures operate in different contexts, and our initial work took up the case of referring in conversation. ... We suggested that references are accomplished by a cyclic acceptance process, in which the speaker and other participants work together to mutually accept that a reference has been understood before they go on to

the next contribution. That is, when A issues the noun phrase 'the dog next door', he presents this to B as something he has tried to design for her to be able to understand. But B's actions may be needed for them to accept that she has indeed understood what he meant to contribute, and therefore to assume that it is now common ground. The basic point is that B's actions may be an intended part of the performance, making the contribution a joint rather than individual act … collaboration is a natural part of many different acts of speaking in conversation.   (Wilkes-Gibbs, 1990, pp. 1, 6)

Clark and Wilkes-Gibbs' analysis of referential communication tasks is motivated by their interest in a wider theory of collaboration, and one of the assumptions that this builds on is that 'authorized inferences' (comprehension of the meanings which the speaker intended) are a more central issue than those which are 'unauthorized' (inferences that are constructed solely by the hearer, independently of what the speaker meant). Furthermore, the two are seen as entirely separate, and the closely related theory of mutual knowledge is only concerned with the first (Clark, 1982, p. 126; Clark & Carlson, 1982).

Recipient design – the way in which speakers shape their utterances to fit with their perceptions of the listener – is undoubtedly a fundamental feature of language use and it certainly does mean that in crucial respects, utterances are joint rather than individual constructions. But as Hinnenkamp notes in a discussion of foreigner talk (FT)

Recipient design is not socially neutral, even where its conversational role may be that of safeguarding comprehension. In the use of FT we can always recognise overtones as to particular recipients, recipients that are almost always associated with particular membership categories.

(Hinnenkamp, 1987, p. 173; see also, e.g., Bell, 1984;
Volosinov, 1973)

These judgements of social category membership can actually present a considerable obstacle to collaboration and mutuality, and the central thrust of research on cross-cultural miscommunication is that talk between L1 and L2 users often generates a great many *unauthorized*, unintended inferences, which have a significant effect on how the interaction progresses. In consequence, Clark and Wilkes-Gibbs's theory of collaboration may not be adequate for an examination of L1–L2 interactions, and the case for joint rather than individually constructed meanings may be overstated.

There are other ways in which a sense of the social dynamics of L2 use might draw one to question Clark and Wilkes-Gibbs's theoretical model. One might question, for example, whether an account premised on the view that conversation is the fundamental site of language use (Clark & Wilkes-Gibbs, 1986, p. 1) produces a theory that can deal adequately with uses of language which are sometimes bound up, from beginning to end, with contexts of instruction. The more important point, though, is that the case of L2 use is relevant to quite a general debate about comprehension, and that it provides reasons for preferring Sperber and Wilson's (1986) Theory of Relevance, which makes fewer assumptions about communication being governed either by mutual knowledge (pp. 15–21) or by Gricean good faith (p. 162), and which covers both intended and unintended inferences in the same conceptual apparatus (Sperber & Wilson, 1982, p. 78, 1986, Ch. 4; Blakemore, 1992).

There are, then, quite good grounds for supposing that a socio-linguistic perspective on L2 use could make a useful descriptive and theoretical contribution to referential communication strategy research, a key concern among mainstream L2 CS investigators. In fact, the gist of the immediately preceding discussion of Clark and Wilkes-Gibbs was that the case of L2 use can be drawn in as evidence relevant to assessment of the relative value of models of communication that have hitherto only addressed L1 discourse. This leads in the direction of a more important point. The recommendation that there should be a confluence of socio- and psycholinguistic approaches to L2 CS does not simply add up to a one-sided 'you-come-over-here'. There are also problematic areas in sociolinguistic research which could derive a significant benefit from SLA research on L2 communication strategies. Two spring to mind quite rapidly.

In the first instance, sociolinguistic discourse analyses of conversational code-switching have often tended to de-emphasize linguistic non-proficiency as a salient interactional issue (Auer, 1991, p. 339; Gumperz, 1982, p. 65). In addition, studies of code-switching concentrate overwhelmingly on speakers who are regarded as bicultural and as having a full entitlement to both (or all) of their languages. More recently, however, models of code-switching discourse have started to incorporate linguistic non-proficiency as an issue that participants orientate to in the course of interaction (Auer, 1988, 1991), and research is beginning to explore code-switching by people who are not accepted members of the communities associated with the languages they employ, thereby raising all sorts of questions about the social legitimacy of other language use (Hewitt 1986; Hinnenkamp, 1987; Rampton, 1995). On both counts, there is much potential relevance in L2 CS research. Obviously, this is explicitly concerned with a participant sense of problematicity (Færch & Kasper, 1983b, p. xviii), and more generally, though it does not often say so in so many words, SLA has the *crossing* of language group boundaries as its central theme.

Secondly, it has sometimes been argued that sociolinguistic research on cross-cultural communication neglects the creativity with which people overcome their difficulties. McDermott and Gospodinoff (1979) argue, for example, that there has been a tendency to overemphasize the determining influence of linguistic and socio-cultural convention. Sometimes participants in cross-cultural interaction are seen as the prisoners of their communicative inheritances, it is forgotten that people either enjoy or overcome differences in language or cultural style, and adequate attention is not always given to the way in which participants can accentuate or play down differences according to their immediate situational needs and purposes. Particularly if it is expanded in some of the ways suggested in previous sections, L2 CS research provides a very valuable corrective to these misconceptions.

Conclusion

L2 CS research has identified an extremely fertile research site. First, its concern with moment-to-moment discourse processing tunes well with contemporary interests in sociolinguistics, and it also provides an opportunity to connect with analyses of the ways in which social reality is constructed through interaction (e.g., Collins, 1981; Heritage, 1984, Ch. 7; Sapir, 1949). Secondly, problematic moments are a particularly rich research area. Of course, much communication is conducted without any sense of problematicity, and a sense of problematicity can either be hidden or pervasive (see, e.g., Færch & Kasper, 1983c, p. 235; Hinnenkamp, 1987, p. 150ff). Nevertheless, moments of actual or potential trouble provide an invaluable window on participants' social values, their perceptions of social order, and the procedures they use to maintain, restore or disrupt it (Brown & Levinson, 1987; Garfinkel, 1967; Goffman, 1971). And thirdly, L2 learning and use are an ineradicable part of the experiences of migration and globalization, central elements in massive contemporary social change. Unfortunately, however, like much of SLA, CS research has tended to neglect the socio-cultural dimension of L2 use, keeping the lid of Færch and Kasper's 'situational assessment' box quite tightly shut (1983d, p. 27). I have tried to argue that unless it is opened, our understanding of communication strategies is in danger of being stunted, maybe even stifled.

Admittedly, investigation of issues (1) to (9) is likely to lead in a lot of different directions. The following propositions seem to me to be fairly uncontroversial:

(a) CS research already looks beyond the individual to the interactional dyad;
(b) communication strategies can be the concern of social groups as well as pairs and individuals;
(c) people can try to devise problem-solving strategies by looking back on past communicative difficulties;
(d) it is already common to think of education as an extension of the learner-caregiver dyad, as a form of elaborate scaffolding (e.g., Edwards & Mercer, 1987; Wells, 1985a, 1985b).

But with these taken as given, I can see no logical reason for excluding institutional strategies – hiring interpreters, enrolling in classes, campaigning for language rights – from the domain of conscious, goal-oriented attempts to overcome L2 communicative difficulty. Certainly, in this light, CS investigation could no longer be exclusively concerned with on-line discourse processing and the field would require a range of different research skills. Scholars might need to find new ways of articulating the relationship between the particular aspects of the issue that they were interested in, and current efforts to bring order to the field would need to be rethought. But if L2 learning and use is to be situated within wider social scientific debate about the relationship between micro and macro levels of social and cultural organization, these are necessary steps and, in my view, the potential benefits outweigh the costs.

Notes

I am grateful to both the Economic and Social Research Council (Project C00232390) and to the Leverhulme Trust for generous funding for my own research. I would also like to thank Eric Kellerman on a number of accounts. Responsibility for errors remains exclusively my own.

1. Kellerman is quite consistent in giving considerably less emphasis to problematicity and potential consciousness:

    > ... to define compensatory strategies (whether in L1 or L2) in terms of the potential presence of conscious awareness of a problem to be solved ... may artificially distinguish between processes where there is no metacognitive awareness and those where there is ... it would be better to see consciousness and problematicity as epiphenomena, serendipitous by-products of the adult use of compensatory strategies (Kellerman, 1991, p. 155).

2. Hymes's notion of 'sociolinguistic interference' (1972b) was, for example, an attempt to provide a linguistic and cultural explication for difficulties that were typically considered to derive from cognitive deficiency, while conversely, Labov's notion of 'linguistic insecurity' (1970) advocates a reconsideration of folk views about linguistic inadequacy (suggesting that these are a reflection of social difference rather than the linguistic inferiority which they claim). Bilinguals have also been drawn into these debates. Cummins' theory of BICS and CALP operates as a cognitive/linguistic corrective to a tendency to underestimate the educational potential of bilinguals during their early years at school (e.g., Cummins, 1984), while a formal enquiry by the Commission for Racial Equality decided that among education officials, the linguistic categorization of Asian pupils as ESL learners constituted a form of race discrimination (CRE, 1986; see also Rampton, 1983, 1988). In different ways, all of this research has tried to raise general levels of awareness about problematicity in language use.

3. This is well illustrated in the *Crosstalk* video (Gumperz et al., 1979). This adopts a mutual knowledge perspective in the same way as CS researchers who take an interactional approach (e.g., Tarone, 1980; Tarone & Yule, 1989): the speaker's perception of the listener's understanding is seen as having an extensive influence on their speech production and interactional conduct. But in its conclusion, *Crosstalk* doesn't simply lay responsibility for communicative difficulty with the second language user. In the social security interview, for example, the monolingual advisor considerably underestimates the L2 speaker's linguistic and cultural knowledge, he simplifies his lexis unnecessarily, and as a result, he makes a major contribution to their mutual dissatisfaction and to their transaction's abortive character (Gumperz et al., 1979, Ch. 3).

4. Among monolinguals of Anglo and Afro-Caribbean descent, there was a small stock of Panjabi words and phrases in general circulation,

and this comprised a selective if rather predictable cocktail of nouns referring to parts of the body, bodily functions, animals, ethnic groups and kin; adjectives describing personal physical attributes; locative and possessive postpositions; a few numerals; verbs of physical violence and ingestion; and a few other items (cf. Rampton, 1991a, pp. 395–6). It was generally some part or parts of this collective lexicon, which few individuals commanded in its entirety, that featured in the utterances that Panjabi bilinguals tried to get their friends to engage with.

5. The following transcription conventions are used:

[	overlapping turns
=	two utterances closely connected without a noticeable overlap, or different parts of a single speaker's turn
(.)	pause of less than one second
{1.5}	approximate length of pause in seconds
l.	lenis (quiet) enunciation
f.	fortis (loud) enunciation
CAPITALS	fortis (loud enunciation)
(( ))	'stage directions'
( )	speech inaudible
(text)	speech hard to discern, analyst guess
Bold	instance of crossing of central interest in discussion

6. Typical examples in English would be 'Adam and Eve and Pinchmetight went down to the sea to bathe. Adam and Eve were drowned and who do you think was saved?', and

A: Count on. I one a rat
B: I two a rat.
A: I three a rat.
and so on up to eight.

7. See Rampton (1991c) for a full discussion of the educational policy implications of different adolescent interpretations of the significance of second language learning.

13

Communication strategies in an interactional context: the mutual achievement of comprehension

JESSICA WILLIAMS, REBECCA INSCOE and THOMAS TASKER

Introduction

Undergraduate courses at North American universities, particularly in the sciences, are increasingly being taught by international teaching assistants (ITAs). Their communication difficulties in the classroom have been the source of much hand-wringing and complaint, leading to a burgeoning number of studies. Most previous investigations of the discourse and interaction of these ITAs have attempted to pinpoint their difficulties and failures, specifically, how their performance falls short of that of native-speaking teaching assistants. In contrast, the outcome of the interaction in the chemistry laboratory sessions in this study is largely successful; that is, the students manage to complete their experiments and subsequent reports. Their comprehension of the task may be due in large part to their having read the written material provided in the laboratory manual. However, all questions that arise in the course of the experiment must be resolved during the lab session between the NNS (non-native speaker) teaching assistant and the native speaker (NS) undergraduates in order for the experiments to be executed successfully.

It is important to underscore that these NNSs are not highly proficient; they continue to have marked accents and to use non-target-like structures in their speech. In spite of this, the majority of questions and communication difficulties are eventually resolved. The communication does not proceed without difficulty, however. It has been suggested that interlanguage, particularly early interlanguage, is a relatively inefficient vehicle for the kind of referential communication that is required here. Young states, 'When loss of meaning is important to the conversation or task at hand, then there are two options available to the learners and their interlocutors: negotiation of meaning through conversational modifications or by means of communication strategies' (Young, 1993, p. 93).

Both of these options are taken up by the participants in the ITA classroom. The aim of this study is to shed some light on the question of how these NNSs, with rather limited oral proficiency, and NSs can achieve mutual comprehension in this setting. It is primarily a descriptive study that attempts to characterize the contributions of the interlocutors in reaching their goal. We have chosen not to include baseline NS data for comparison because we believe that NS teaching assistants and NNS teaching assistants achieve success in very different ways (Williams, 1992). Our aim is to examine the ITA data on their own terms. The results suggest that this mutual comprehension is related to the communication strategies that the NNSs and NSs employ during this task. Their success may be attributed in part to what we will call their *conservative* questioning strategies and to the apparent awareness of both parties of the potential for miscommunication and the need for gradual and often prolonged negotiation of meaning.

This is not a total success story, however. It has been said that the strategies that facilitate communicative performance are not necessarily ones that lead to successful second language acquisition (Sato, 1986, p. 42). This appears to be the case for the NNSs in this study: while the task is performed successfully, the evidence suggests that the laboratory setting is not one conducive to language learning.

There are three areas of previous research that bear on the current study: (a) communication strategies; (b) analysis of the discourse of ITAs; and (c) interactional modifications, negotiation of meaning and their impact on second language acquisition.

Communication strategy research

Much of the research conducted on communication strategies (CSs) has been rather narrow in that it has focused predominantly on learners' gaps in lexis, and has been conducted almost exclusively using elicitation tasks. These studies have examined the effect of various factors on strategy use: the effects of learner proficiency, problem source, personality and learning situation (Ellis,

1986; though see Poulisse, 1990). In addition, researchers have focused overwhelmingly on individual production (versus achievement of comprehension and the mutual construction of discourse). As such, many studies bear little relevance to our current investigation. However, of potential relevance to the current project are studies such as Wagner's (1983) which take into account the situated nature of real communication by examining the effectiveness of CS use in facilitating communication. This study involved an interactive, instructional task, whereby one member of a pair of adult Danish learners of German instructed the other in a task of either making a clay pot or building a house from Lego blocks. The 'instructor' of the pair was first instructed in the task by the experimenter to ensure understanding of the procedure. Wagner points out that 'the verbal interaction is structured by the goal and contextual conditions of the entire communication' (Wagner, 1983, p. 161), specifically, by the sorts of interactional expectations set up by the nature of the task (one participant has knowledge the other needs in order to complete the task), and by what Wagner calls the 'shared perceptual universe' (p. 166) of the participants. Here CSs function more widely to adjust the communicative plan to the situation, rather than being strictly a response to a 'problem' (i.e., compensatory) or the result of an isolated internal process. That is, 'each individual utterance is to be seen as strategic' (p. 167). So the selection of CSs is determined by the nature of the situation – the interactive goal – as well as the roles of the participants – 'expert' versus needing information. He has broadened the conception of CSs by showing how they have a specifically context-sensitive communicative function for all interactants, rather than as just means for individual L2 users to overcome obstacles to production.

Like Wagner's study, the present investigation differs from earlier work in three important ways. First, it extends the notion of CS to situations involving other kinds of gap in knowledge, for example, gaps which are primarily *information*-based, rather than *code*-based. Specifically, we look at episodes in which either the NS or the NNS fails to comprehend some aspect of the task or another participant's actions and must seek some way of resolving the problem. Ellis refers to the goals of such interaction as 'message-oriented', as opposed to 'medium-oriented' (Ellis, 1984, p. 107). Secondly, such gaps in knowledge tend to show up in *comprehension* problems rather than in production. Thirdly, we will examine the CSs of *both the NNSs and NSs* because we believe that the achievement of comprehension is a joint process. While the NNSs and NSs do appear to have different strategies, they must be viewed together, rather than separately. These strategies share the earlier construal of problematicity in only a limited way: while granting that individuals encounter problems of both production and comprehension, we focus on comprehension problems in particular, both how they are rooted in the interactional context and how they are resolved.

ITA research

There has been an increase in the number of investigations into the difficulties of ITAs in US and Canadian colleges and universities, where they play a crucial role in undergraduate education. Much of this research has examined problems in ITA production – pronunciation, comprehensibility, coherence etc. – rather than ITAs' interaction with their students (Douglas & Myers, 1989; Rounds, 1987; Tyler, 1992; Williams, 1992). Indeed, results of these studies reveal that they have a variety of problems in their language production. Hoekje and Williams (1992) maintain, however, that we will never have a complete understanding of ITAs' problems and those of their undergraduate students until we begin to focus on the interaction between these two groups. Indeed, this is the spirit of more recent ITA research (Madden & Myers, 1994; Shaw & Bailey, 1990). This study is a part of this changing trend in that it examines the contributions of both parties and focuses not on ITA deficits, especially in comparison to NSs, but on the achievement of comprehension.

The role of interaction and interactional modifications in second language acquisition

The role of interaction, interactional modifications and negotiation is thought by many to be crucial in the process of second language acquisition. Although the goal of this study is to explore communication strategies in interaction, it is also important to examine the potential role of these strategies in the acquisition of English by the NNSs, particularly since many of the strategies that are used to facilitate communication have also been singled out as important in second language acquisition, because they (1) provide interactional modification of input to second language learners and (2) they may increase the 'pushing' of modifications in second language learner output (Long, 1981; Pica, 1991; Pica et al., 1987; Pica et al., 1989; Varonis & Gass, 1985a). Ellis (1990) uses the term 'pushed output' to describe learner production that is modified towards the target in response to an interlocutor's signals that the speaker has fallen short of the communicative goal.

We are by no means the first to underscore the need to link the findings of CS research with those of interlanguage negotiation research (see Yule & Tarone, 1991). It is necessary to point out, though, that this setting differs substantially from many that have been used in studying interactional adjustments, and thus is likely to have different consequences for second language acquisition. First, most studies that have involved NS–NNS interaction have not used classroom settings. Secondly, those that have investigated classroom data largely target NNS–NNS interaction. The setting examined in this study is somewhat unusual in that it is an instructional one in which most of the interaction is one-to-one between an NS and an NNS. In addition, the role relationship between participants is radically different from those found in the ESL/EFL classroom. In this case, the NNS is the expert in terms of content knowledge, while the NSs are the experts in terms of language proficiency. Both relative level of content expertise (Woken & Swales, 1989; Zuengler & Bent, 1991) and dominance of interactive role (Yule & MacDonald, 1990) have been found to have a significant effect on the quality and quantity of interaction. Since the most important area of expertise in this setting is chemistry and not English, the natural flow of information is from NNS to NS. Indeed, in this respect, the interaction in this context may resemble a lab led by a NS, rather than any of the contexts that have been the focus of research on second language acquisition and performance.

Finally, the quality of this setting as an environment for second language acquisition takes on greater importance because, by self-report, for the ITAs in this study, these classes are the *only* settings in which they need to communicate in English (Williams & Tasker, 1992). Other researchers have reported similar findings (Ard, 1987), suggesting that the participants in this study are not unique in this regard.

The study

The data consist of three videotaped organic chemistry laboratory sessions, lasting about two hours each. Each session began with a brief non-interactive introduction to the experiment. Only the following interactive portions, which constitute the bulk of the lab session, are included for analysis. The initial portions are examined in an earlier study (Williams & Tasker, 1992). The sessions were transcribed and coded by the three authors. These particular labs were chosen because we wished to avoid the kinds of management and behaviour problems that we had seen in the lab sessions associated with introductory courses for non-majors. The NS students in this study were in the class because they had chosen a chemistry or related major, not because they had to be there to fulfil a requirement. Because the course is an advanced one, it also means that the students were somewhat older than those found in introductory courses. Thus, in general, it can be said that their attitudes were generally positive; the NSs and NNSs seemed to share the common goal of the successful completion of the experiment.

The NNSs are all L1 Mandarin men in their late 20s or early 30s. As mentioned above, their oral proficiency was far from extraordinary. Although their TOEFL scores (some recorded up to a year before the taping) ranged from 597 to 610, their SPEAK[1] scores (recorded approximately three months prior to taping) were rather low, ranging from 160 to 200. Indeed, at many major universities such scores would exclude them altogether from duties that include student contact. All were participating in a university ITA preparation course during the time of the taping.

Method of analysis

The lab sessions are divided into discrete episodes. Each new NS–NNS interaction constitutes a new episode. Most episodes centre around a comprehension problem of one of two types: (1) the NS student seeking an explanation from the NNS of lab procedure or equipment; or (2) the NNS, often sensing there was a problem, attempting to rectify it, or at least to determine the student(s)' activities up to that point. This definition is essentially one of problematicity in interaction used in an earlier study by Varonis and Gass who examined 'those exchanges in which there is some overt indication that understanding between participants has not been complete' (Varonis & Gass, 1985b, p. 73). This indication is usually evident in the initiating utterance of the interaction where the source of the problem becomes clear. A single episode might contain more than one comprehension problem or a series of related ones. There are also just two interactions that fall outside the guidelines; these appear to be interactions with primarily social goals (e.g., a discussion of preferences for coffee or tea). While these may be important for maintaining a positive affective atmosphere, because they account for such a small portion of the data and because they are so different from the bulk of interactions, they will not be examined in the present study. Interactions are almost exclusively between a single student and the ITA, although on several occasions, there are two students involved in the interaction.

The following coding categories were used in analysing the data:

Confirmation checks

This term has been used in previous research on interactional adjustments to describe utterances that seek to confirm that the material in an interlocutor's previous utterance has been heard or understood (Long, 1981; Pica & Doughty, 1985). In this study, because both NNSs' and NSs' questions address issues and material that extend far beyond the previous utterance, we define these checks as utterances seeking confirmation of anything contained in the entire preceding written or spoken discourse. This is considerably broader than the definitions contained in earlier studies (though see Woken & Swales, 1989) in that it hinges on the confirmation or disconfirmation of information in the common domain rather than on our judgement as to the listener's hearing or understanding. We realize that this definition may blur the usefulness of the earlier one, including as it does utterances that might be considered clarification requests by other researchers. However, because of the overwhelming number of utterances of this kind and because the function of these utterances clearly is confirmation-seeking, the term seems necessary and appropriate.

There are three basic kinds of confirmation check. The first is essentially code-based (or medium-based) and easily fits the earlier definition of confirmation checks described above. These are mostly fragmentary echoic responses containing part or all of the previous speaker's utterance, usually with rising intonation. These appear to seek confirmation of the actual language used in the previous utterance, that is, to confirm that an utterance has been heard and understood.

> (1) S: This is my aqueous layer.
> ITA: Aqueous layer?

The second and third types fit our broader definition of confirmation check. They may not relate to the immediately preceding utterance; indeed, there may be no preceding utterance. The speaker may be seeking to confirm an earlier utterance, instructions in the written material, some non-verbal demonstration, etc. Among these confirmation checks, there are differences in orientation and, as a result, in their form. According to Quirk and Greenbaum, a question is positively oriented if it 'is presented in a form which is biased towards a positive ... answer' (Quirk and Greenbaum, 1973, p. 193). In positively oriented confirmation checks, the speaker offers the listener information and implies that he or she expects confirmation of it.

> (2) S: I stick it in the hood, right?

In neutrally oriented confirmation checks, the expectation of the speaker is not made clear, although the information is still presented for confirmation/disconfirmation.

> (3) S: Is this the water layer?

This difference in orientation is evidenced in the form of the utterance. The positively oriented checks are presented in declarative order, sometimes with tags, whereas the neutral ones are presented in interrogative word order. Both positively and neutrally oriented confirmation checks are similar in that they require little work from the respondent in terms of production.

Clarification requests

Once again, we borrow this term from the literature on interactional modifications in second language learner conversations and once again, we extend this definition, which has been limited to the clarification of the interlocutor's previous utterance, to *anything* in the preceding written or oral discourse. There have been other attempts to discuss the function of clarification requests in greater detail (Rost & Ross, 1991). As in this study, they extend the locus of clarification beyond the preceding utterance. At the same time that this is a broader understanding of the term, it is also a narrower category than the clarification requests of earlier studies because it excludes utterances that simply seek confirmation of the information presented. For instance, Pica and Doughty define the response in the following excerpt as a clarification request rather than a confirmation check because it does not reflect a problem with hearing or understanding the preceding utterance:

(4) A: This is very bad ... I think she never estay home.
    B: You're opposed to that?

(Pica & Doughty, 1985, p. 236)

In our study, such a response would be classified as a confirmation check because it presents information for confirmation. Clarification requests, unlike confirmation checks, do not present the listener with information to respond to. Thus, in these cases the respondent has to do more interactional work since the request is an open one, as in the following episode-initiating clarification requests.

(5) ITA: Why you do that?
(6) ITA: How are you doing?

The results of Pica et al. (1989) suggest that in contrast to NS confirmation checks, which provide most of the language to the NNSs, the more open-ended nature of NS clarification requests may force NNSs to modify their output. In addition, as in the case of confirmation checks, some seem to limit the scope of the ongoing interaction more than others by requiring less work from the interlocutor. For instance, (5) and (6) are completely open clarification requests, potentially requiring a substantial response from the (in this case, NS) interlocutor. More limiting clarification requests include:

(7) S: Which one is the water layer?
(8) S: If it's cloudy, what does it mean?

Comprehension checks

These are utterances that attempt to confirm that the listener has understood what the speaker has said. Again, these are not limited to code, but are extended to comprehension of the task. They may be as simple as 'Understand?' or may take more extended form, such as in the following display question.

(9) ITA: How can you decide which layer is which?

Other-/self-repetitions/reformulations

Other-repetitions and self-repetitions are exact duplications of what has been previously uttered, while reformulations offer some modification of the first utterance. These reformulations are of particular importance since most include both modifications of NNS output (self-reformulations) or NS models of NNS production (other-reformulations) (see Pica, 1991). Both repetitions and reformulations are defined by form only and may play a variety of functions in negotiating meaning.

Results

The results show a divergent pattern of NNS and NS strategy use. For both parties, however, there is a clear trend towards keeping the goal of each exchange modest and assisting each other in maintaining mutual comprehension. The following are components of what we call their *conservative* strategy of not demanding too much of one another in terms of interactional work.

Most exchanges are relatively closed, that is, the options presented to the interlocutor are limited in some way, diminishing the potential for miscommunication (see Table 13.1). Specifically, there are more confirmation checks than requests for clarification, more positively oriented confirmation checks than neutral ones, and more limiting clarification requests (73% of all clarification checks) than open ones. For NSs, 82 per cent of their confirmation checks are positively oriented, while for NNSs, they account for 77 per cent of their total confirmation checks. In general then, the dominant questioning strategy is the (positively oriented) confirmation check.

An episode may begin with a clarification request but the problem is most frequently resolved by a series of confirmation checks that gradually isolate and rectify it in an often lengthy negotiation process. The following excerpt is a typical example of such a sequence.

Table 13.1 Interactional modifications

		NS		NNS		Total
		n	%	n	%	
Confirmation checks						
by orientation	positive	244	82	57	77	301
	neutral	52	18	17	23	69
	or choice	1	0	0	0	1
by function	process	285	96	6	8	
	past action	3	1	52	70	
	code	1	0	7	9	
	knowledge	0	0	9	12	
	management	8	3	0	0	
Total		**297**		**74**		**371**
Clarification requests						
Limiting		50	76	12	63	62
Open		16	24	7	37	23
Total		**66**		**19**		**85**
Comprehension checks						
of utterance (code?)		5	100			
of task				51	78	
of knowledge				14	22	
Total		**5**		**65**		**70**
Self-reformulations			25		10	
Self-repetitions		6		15		
Total		**31**		**25**		**56**
	with signal	27	87	9	36	
	without signal	4	13	16	64	
Other-reformulations			4		3	
Other-repetitions		30		15		
Total		**34**		**18**		**52**

(10) S: Which one – which one should we extract with the methyl chloride? This?
ITA: Yea. See?
S: The top layer?
ITA: The bottom layer. The top layer is also this layer.
S: Which is the water layer?
ITA: Here water layer
S: Right.
ITA: So you will – after –

S: Again
ITA: Again
S: 15 ml. methyl chloride?
ITA: Yeah. here 15 ml.
S: And do it again?
ITA: Yea. Just add 3 ml.
S: 15?
ITA: No. See, this? Now here.
S: I did that already.
ITA: Yeah? Twice?
S: Twice.
ITA: OK
S: The methylene chloride will be the bottom layer? The methylene chloride?
ITA: Yeah.
S: And the water layer is up here?
ITA: Yeah.
S: Now it says to combine the aqueous extracts and carry out extraction with two 15 ml. of methylene chloride –
ITA: – to remove – yes. yes.
S: This one, right?
ITA: That means you get the – this is the water layer – the water layer.
S: Right.

Confirmation checks are overwhelmingly the province of NSs; they make 80 per cent of all confirmation checks in the corpus. These are not limited to checks on comprehension of the previous utterance; instead, they are primarily information-based and may refer to a wide range of problems in the lab session. For NSs, the vast majority of these checks (96%) refer to the equipment, material or laboratory procedure. In Table 13.1, these are referred to as 'process' in the function column. In only one case did an NS attempt to confirm a specific lexical item.

The confirmation checks used by the NNSs tend to be part of instructional talk, checking on the past actions of the students to ensure that they are operating within the parameters of the task. This category appears with greater frequency than any other, representing 70 per cent of all NNS confirmation checks. These do not generally arise in direct response to a specific student utterance; rather, they are initiated by the ITA.

(11) ITA: Have you added the sodium hydroxide?
(12) ITA: Are you sure you added the methylene chloride?

These checks also serve an orienting function for the ITA in that they help him to identify and address potential or actual problems. They establish reference points against which both the student and the ITA can measure the progress of the task.

In contrast, comprehension checks are used almost exclusively by the NNSs (93%), while NSs almost never check that their message has been understood. When they do, however, the checks do appear to be on NNS comprehension of their utterances and thus are labelled 'code' on Table 13.1. All five of those included in the corpus are some variation on 'know what I mean?' Most NNS comprehension checks, in contrast, refer to comprehension of the task rather than of specific utterances.

    (13) ITA: You do two times, OK?
             S: Yea. This is the second time.

There are also a few display questions checking on students' knowledge. The commonest type, again, are those that are relatively closed, that is, those which simply require confirmation or disconfirmation of comprehension. These are reflected in Table 13.1 as confirmation checks of knowledge (n=9).

    (14) ITA: You know that dichloromethane is heavier than water, right?

There are also a small number (n=3) of utterances that check students' comprehension more indirectly. These are more open-ended, that is, a more extended response is required.

    (15) ITA: If you don't know the density of the organic solvent, how can you decide which layer is which?

Still less common (n=2) are the completely open checks on NS student knowledge, such as:

    (16) ITA: Why is that?

We see a similar pattern, then, to that described for confirmation checks, that is, the more frequent type of check is relatively closed, leaving the respondent with few options. Less frequent are the open-ended checks that require more interactional work from the respondent.

Reformulation and repetitions are not common in the data. Most NNS self-repetitions and self-reformulations are preventive (64%), that is, there is no intervening NS spoken signal (see Pica et al., 1989) that prompts them to repeat or reformulate. Such preventive moves have sometimes been called strategies (Long, 1981), although reformulations have rarely been included among lists of preventive strategies. Most NS self-repetitions and reformulations, on the other hand, serve a repair function (87%), that is, they are in response to an NNS signal that there has been a problem in comprehension with the first instance of the utterance. These reactive or repairing moves have sometimes been referred to as tactics (Long, 1981).

Most other-repetitions (and the few rare other-reformulations) are uttered by NNSs and are, for the most part, echoic requests for repetition. Secondarily, they are used – and again more by NNSs than NSs – as verifications to their listeners of their own comprehension and to provide confirmation of information offered.

Reformulations are primarily made by NSs, and most of these are self-reformulations, as noted, in response to NNS signals. Most provide some kind of syntactic modification of an earlier utterance: some decompose, simplify and remove embeddings, while others elaborate and embed. The following is an example of a decomposition.

(17) S: You want this to clear up before you put it down, right?
     ITA: Pardon me?
     S: What are we waiting for? For this to clear up?

There are also a number of lexical modifications which appear to be attempts to provide a lexical item of greater specificity than in the earlier utterance.

(18) S: The second one?
     ITA: Second?
     S: The second 3 ml.?

The few instances of NS reformulations of NNS utterances are limited to lexical and phonological modifications.

(19) ITA: Use two beak.
     S: OK. Two beakers.

In other words, the NS students rarely provide the ITAs with reformulated target-like models of their own utterances. NNSs seldom reformulate their own utterances and still more rarely, those offered by the NSs. In sum, the NNSs rarely modify their own output or respond to NS models with renewed attempts of their own at target-like production. In the few instances of reformulations that do occur, they are lexical, generally providing a synonym for an item in the earlier utterance.

(20) ITA: Use a dessicator to dry.
      S: Use what?
      ITA: This is hydrogen sulfate. It is a dessicator. This is used to dry the solvent.

This is clearly not a case of the ITA producing a non-target-like utterance, prompting a need for modification of his output; rather, it is a case of the student's failure to understand a technical term. The ITA provides the student with an example as well as a definition.

There is, in fact, only one clear example in the data of modification of output in response to an NS signal and subsequent model. It is a phonological one.

(21) ITA: Use /s n/ to heat it.
      S: Sun?
      ITA: Sun.
      S_1:   What's sun?
      S_2:   /saend/
      ITA: Sand, yeah, I'm sorry, sand.

NSs are responsible for initiating the bulk of the episodes (NS=71, 68%; NNS=34, 32%). The contributions of the NNSs, both initial and subsequent, can be described as follows, in order of their frequency:

(a) Direct instruction. The vast majority of NNS speech (60% of all NNS turns) provides instructional information, sometimes in response to NS confirmation checks and clarification requests, and sometimes without prompting. This direct instruction contrasts with the checking functions of (b) and (c) below. Example (22) is in reponse to an NS confirmation check, while (23) is spontaneous instructional talk.

(22) S: We add this three times?
      ITA: No, this is your funnel, OK? You transfer the solution to it and add 20 ml.

(23) ITA: Let me show you how to drain it. Drain it very carefully, OK? Little bit higher. See? There, slowly.

Such instructional talk is also the most frequent NNS method of initiating episodes. It is not always absolutely clear, however, that the initiating utterance actually begins the episode. Many appear to be in response to some problem, demonstrated non-verbally, that the NS is having.

(24) (in response to some NS fumbling of the apparatus)
    ITA: Hold the – this separation funnel. Iron ring – do you
        have an iron ring?

(b) Confirmation checks of students' past action. This accounts for the next largest category of utterances by NNSs.
(c) Checks on student knowledge. This last category is relatively infrequent, as noted above.

Discussion

The success of these interactions may be attributed to the efforts of both parties to break down the task into manageable and comprehensible chunks and to limit the scope of interaction with extensive use of conversational adjustments to negotiate meaning. In the laboratory setting, the NSs pose questions that demand relatively little from their NNS interlocutors, that is, they usually require the NNS to respond with yes/no or with a choice that has been provided by the NS questioner. For this reason, we have called this strategy conservative. In addition, the narrow scope of interaction is certainly due, in large part, to the specificity of the lab setting. Therefore, there is little need for the NNSs to create language outside their content expertise or beyond the exigencies of the task. The adjustments which are so frequent in this setting were virtually absent from the interaction of these same ITAs in non-instructional settings (Williams & Tasker, 1992). The non-instructional contexts differ in two important ways. First, topics were wide-ranging and unpredictable. Secondly, accuracy in conveying referential information was considerably less crucial than in the laboratory.

Would these strategies work in any ITA-led laboratory setting? We have said that the ITAs in this study are of limited proficiency, but it is likely that there is a floor below which even the relatively limited demands of these conservative, message-focused strategies will be confounded by an ITA's low proficiency. An earlier study examined the interaction in lab sessions led by ITAs with even lower proficiency than the participants in this study (Williams &

Tasker, 1992). The following excerpt is from a lab led by an ITA with a TOEFL score of 547 and a SPEAK score of 130. It shows a complete failure to achieve mutual comprehension, in part because of the ITA's inability to understand and make herself understood, and in part because of the students' total incomprehension of the task. The ITA opens the episode with a simple 'what?' when she realizes that the students are having difficulty. Compare this with the more situation-appropriate openings seen earlier.

(5)   ITA: Why you do that?
(6)   ITA: How are you doing?

Repeated attempts by the students to ascertain what they had done wrong were met only by the ITA's admonition to repeat the procedure.

(25)   ITA: what?
       S_1:   This second one – our color hasn't changed.
       S_2:   It's all the same.
       ITA: So before do the lab, you must clean it.
       S: Yeah, we did. Everything was –
       ITA: Yeah?
       S: Yeah. We cleaned it, rinsed it.
       ITA: Well, you can see – no gas here. This means no gas. So, finish this and do it again, OK?
       S: Do it all over?
       ITA: Yeah yeah.
       S: So what did we do wrong then?
       ITA: You must do it again.
       S: But what did we do wrong?
       ITA: The color, you mean the color? Must see the color –
       S: – Yeah, but what did we do wrong –
       ITA: – The color have been change
       S: – When we made that one?
       ITA: So you can do next one. Then after finish, you can do this one, OK?
       S: Oh, OK.

This particular interaction also shows that these students are less conservative in their communication strategies in that they do not limit themselves to the negotiation process of the incremental confirmation checks that were characteristic of the interactions in the current study. The combination of the failure to use a conservative step-wise questioning strategy and the use of more open-ended questions, which are evidently not understood by the ITA, makes for a frustrating interaction for all parties.

This kind of miscommunication can also occur in the class-rooms of ITAs with higher proficiency if the interlocutors fail to adhere to the conservative strategies that have been found success-ful here. In the following episode, the NS initiates an episode with little orientation or negotiation, and fails to narrow down the question sufficiently, so that it is up to the ITA to seek the specifics. The impasse is eventually resolved only by non-verbal means.

(26) S: So, OK, when do you stop boiling?
     ITA: Boiling?
     S: When do you stop?
     ITA: Stop?
     S: Yeah, I know when you start. I'm about to start my boil-
            ing, but I want to know when does the process stop.
     ITA: Stop? Take it out?
     S: When do I stop boiling? I don't even know when to stop
            boiling.
     ITA: (looks) Oh! This is methyl chloride?

The division of interactional labour in the laboratory session is influenced by the nature of the task and, more specifically, by the roles of the participants engaged in the task. The ITA is the expert/authority and the expected flow of information is from the NNSs to the NSs. However, since the goal of the laboratory ses-sion is primarily student driven, that is, since it is in the students' interest to secure the correct information needed to complete the task successfully, and since they have more access to their own uncertainties, knowledge gaps and problems in executing the task, they are strongly motivated to take responsibility for seeking out the information they require. It is no surprise, then, that the majority of the interactions reflect the students' need to appeal to the ITA's expertise in order to confirm or clarify their knowledge of the task. The fact that NS confirmation checks and clarification requests predominate indicates that they are actively pursuing that goal. The ITA's contribution to the joint enterprise of achieving mutual comprehension can also be seen as a reflection of their specific role in the laboratory task. The bulk of their talk func-tions to provide, confirm, or clarify information the students need to complete the task. They also take a more active role by check-ing that the students are on track with the experiment, and exhibit a sensitivity to the potential for miscommunication by shouldering the greater burden of checking that they and the task are understood.

We have found that the interactions in these settings are largely successful. It has been suggested that the types of strategy we have examined in this study play an important role in second language acquisition. If such interaction-based accounts of second language acquisition are accepted, however, we must conclude that this particular setting is a relatively poor one for acquisition by the ITAs. In fact, it is ironic that the very characteristics of these interactions which lead to successful communication – what we have called a conservative strategy, limiting the demands on the NNSs in particular – are also those that are unlikely to promote second language acquisition. Specifically, there is little of the risk taking behaviour, or 'pushing' NNS modification of output. The NNSs do not request modification of input from the NSs, as seen in the tiny quantity of code-based interactional modifications. NSs do reformulate their utterances, but almost always in response to information-based, rather than code-based enquiries. They rarely provide models by reformulating the ITAs' utterances, thus denying the ITAs the opportunity to receive target-like versions of their own production. Even when target-like models are provided, NNS modifications in response to them are virtually non-existent.

It is likely that the ESL/EFL classrooms that have been the focus of earlier studies of interactional modification are substantially different in terms of opportunities for language acquisition from the setting examined here. This is not surprising, given that the goal is the execution of a chemistry lab project by students, not language acquisition by the teacher. However, because this setting is one in which the emphasis is on referential communication and not on language, the findings may shed some light on the possibilities for acquisition through negotiation of meaning in other, non-classroom settings.

Note

1. The SPEAK test is an institutional version of the Test of Spoken English, produced by the Educational Testing Service.

14

Communication strategies at work

JOHANNES WAGNER and ALAN FIRTH

Introduction

It is almost two decades since the first studies of communication strategies (CS) appeared in print. Since its inception, the field has moved from broadly addressing foreign language *learners'* attempts to solve a host of encoding and decoding problems in a foreign language towards a more specific focus on learners' speech encoding and management of problematic lexical items.

By analysing data from authentic, naturally occurring[1] business interactions in section 2 below, we will demonstrate that an interactional approach to CS, although infrequently pursued and thus undeveloped within the literature, has the capacity to cast light on to a tenebrous terrain of current CS research: the *social* and *contextually contingent* aspects of language production, including, though not exclusively, aspects that are characterizable as 'problematic'. In outlining what such an approach involves and consists of, one of our main intentions throughout this chapter is to attempt to provide conceptual and analytic impetus for the advancement of CS research that more engagingly adopts an interactional perspective. By so doing, we shall also endeavour to shed light upon hitherto neglected facets of CS research.

1.   Interactional approaches to the study of CS

The need to study CS *in interaction* has been emphasized by Tarone and Yule in several publications (e.g., Tarone, 1980, 1983; Yule & Tarone, 1991). However, it is arguable that the advocated approach has been unable to define its research agenda in an adequate way, or to produce insights comparable to studies undertaken within the psycholinguistic paradigm. One reason may be that CS studies undertaken on learner interactions have been interested in several phenomena at the same time, phenomena which at first glance appear to span the 'cognitive-social' divide. Tarone's 'interactional' studies, for example, attempt to develop *taxonomies* of CS as well as investigate 'negotiated input' as a learner resource. Such studies are interested in conversational 'adjustments' made by speakers in native–non-native speaker communication (Hatch, 1978; Long, 1983a, 1983b; Varonis & Gass 1985a; for an overview, see Larsen-Freeman & Long, 1991). These interests are pursued while retaining an interest in the (psycholinguistic) issues surrounding second language acquisition. It is precisely this dual retention that has given rise to theoretical problems surrounding the issue of compatibility, that is, compatibility with the CS research agenda as laid out by more psycholinguistically oriented studies. In short, it is not clear whether, or to what extent, an interactional/social perspective on language can be reconciled with cognitive/individualistic (CS) perspectives. This issue of compatibility between 'interactional' and 'cognitive' research domains has been raised several times in the literature, both within and without CS studies (see, e.g., Roger & Bull, 1989).[2]

In a recent paper, Yule and Tarone argue for a return 'to the "more humble approach" of describing both input and learner performance in action, and refraining from making claims about acquisition which are based upon untested assumptions' (Yule & Tarone, 1991, p. 170). Without claiming to share the view that such an approach is 'more humble' than any other, we submit that an interactional perspective on CS implies different, and in many ways incompatible, research interests and goals than the psycholinguistic paradigm. As such, we contend that the interactional approach is – temporarily at least – best served by cutting its theoretical ties with the psycholinguistic question of language acquisition.

Clearly, however, this is not an easy task. Yule and Tarone suggest that analysts should make 'use of an analytic framework which encourages the analyst to look at both sides of the conversational exchange' (1991, p. 169). What the two authors call a 'suggestion' is, though, a *conditio sine qua non* for an analysis of communication – if, indeed, communication is perceived as an *interactive* endeavour. That it has to be 'suggested' at all indicates how firmly CS research is rooted in a paradigm of meaning transfer between autonomous individuals.

While the psycholinguistic approach to CS is interested in speech production, the essence of the interactional approach – the approach we are espousing here – investigates how communication is accomplished as a situated, contingent, 'locally managed'[3] achievement.[4] Since code-related problems are a prominent feature of (some) native speaker–non-native speaker discourse-based interactions, its study may shed light on encoding problem-solving techniques in interactions – as far as these problems are related to meaning and, crucially for us, *made public* in the talk. As a consequence, an interactional approach defines CS as *elements of the interaction*, while psycholinguistic approaches define CS as *elements of the speaker's cognitive processes*.

An interactional perspective looks at CS primarily as elements in the ongoing and contingent meaning-creating process of communication. 'Disruption markers' not only show researchers that a speaker appears to experience a problem in expressing what he or she wants to say. They do the same for the interlocutor. They effectively 'flag' an (upcoming) problem in discourse encoding, thereby signalling that a CS is imminent. This procedure is comparable to the 'cueing' of irony in talk: by changing voice quality or intonation contour, by pausing, changing rhythm or by using other elements, speakers routinely mark utterances which are not to be understood in their literal or conventional sense. What we are calling 'flagging', then, approximates to what Gumperz (1982) has called a 'contextualization cue', in the sense that 'flagging' provides the interlocutor with information about how one's actions or utterances are to be interpreted and acted upon. Thus:

> ... constellations of surface features of message form are the means by which speakers signal and listeners interpret what the activity is, how semantic content is to be understood and *how* each sentence relates to what precedes or follows. ... Although such cues carry information, meanings are conveyed as part of the interactive process. ... Their signalling value depends on the participants' tacit awareness of their meaningfulness.   (Gumperz, 1982, p. 131)

Whether flagging of elements leads to any extended negotiation of meaning over several turns is a different point, one that we deal with briefly below.

An interactional approach defines instances of talk as CS if, and only if, the *participants themselves* make public in the talk itself an encoding-related problem and by so doing engage – individually or conjointly – in attempts to resolve the problem. CS, then, are available to the analyst only to the extent that they have been produced and reacted upon by the parties to the talk. The encoding problem may either be a purely linguistic one or a combined linguistic and conceptual problem. The 'flagging' may be done by the above-mentioned 'disruption markers' or by other verbal or non-verbal signals, in general by any kind of 'contextualization cue' in the sense of Gumperz (1982, Ch. 6). Thus, we hope, the main distinctions between a psycholinguistic and an interactive definition of CS becomes clear: while the psycholinguistic definition locates and identifies CS in relation to both 'overt' and 'covert' elements, and upon so doing seeks to investigate and classify the cognitive bases of the CS, the interactional definition sees CS as a publicly displayed ('overt') phenomenon, rendered visible through participants' actions. Once so identified, the interactionally oriented analyst then seeks to explicate *how* the parties – individually or conjointly – endeavour to overcome the encoding difficulty. Here, then, the emphasis is on the *social*, rather than individual or cognitive, processes underpinning talk.

In this chapter, we employ an interactional approach in order to examine talk occurring within a variety of workplace settings. Peculiar to each of the workplaces considered is that foreign language interactions are routine, daily occurrences. In what follows, we analyse transcripts of audio-recordings of naturally occurring telephone interactions extracted from the workplaces. By paying close turn-by-speaking-turn attention to the talk produced, our overriding analytical goal is to explicate how speakers and listeners together make sense in situations where they possess neither fully developed nor stable linguistic/pragmatic competence in the foreign language they are using.

2.　The present study: CS in business communications

2.1　*The data*

The data examined in this chapter have been collected as part of a wider project on international communication between commercial companies (Sonne Jakobsen et al., in preparation; Wagner, 1995a, 1995b). Over an extended period of time, telephone communications between employees of different Danish companies and their foreign partners were audio-recorded. Work-related exigencies deem it necessary for the employees to communicate intermittently in a foreign language. Analyses of data are supplemented by copies of relevant written documents and by ethnographic information gathered at each of the workplace settings.[5]

The foreign languages spoken in the data are predominantly English and German and, to a lesser degree, French, Swedish and Danish. Part of the data are communications in a 'lingua franca', that is, the language of communication is a foreign language for both participants (see Firth, 1990). The larger part of the lingua franca data are in English, the smaller part in German.

2.2 The origin of non-target-like elements – a case example

A preliminary analysis of the data shows a much smaller number of CS than reported by current studies which use elicitation techniques. In the Nijmegen data, for example, 3,203 'clear cases of CS' had been found in 'approximately 110,000 words' (Poulisse, 1993, p. 165). That makes about 3.5 per cent of all words a lexical CS. Although the number of clearly identifiable CS in the data examined in this chapter have not been calculated, a cursory estimate suggests the number here would be significantly smaller.

The surprising aspect of the business data, though, is not the overall smaller number of CS. This could be expected since, in our data, no CS are elicited. The surprising element is the small number of 'flagged' CS in relation to the larger number of instances which resemble non-flagged CS. We refer to these instances as 'non-target-like elements'.[6]

This specific aspect of the business data will now be illustrated by a series of examples from two telephone calls between an employee of a Danish producer of large metal constructions and his German business partners, both of whom are engineers. The German company is in the process of building a power station in Denmark. The Danish company delivers parts for the construction. In the first extract, the leading engineer of the Danish company (D) calls his German colleague (F) to clarify details of the construction. D is unable to see in the drawing whether parts of a grid above which a large valve is positioned may be cut out to provide space for the 'legs' of the construction which carries the valve. This intention becomes clear later in the talk and from a post-event interview with D.

Example (1)

1 D: .h ich=ich habe::(.) ein=ein=ein frage (.) o:b die o – e:
        ehm ob die: ventil (.) e: auf der (.) [I=I have (.) a=a=a
        question (.) if the er if the valve (.) er is placed on the
        (.)]
2 F: ja? [yes?]
3 D: e::m ts auf der e:m auf der bühne s=stEht oder steht es (.)
        auf die e:m .hhhh die e:m die risten(.) [er is it plAced er
        on the on the hoist or does it stand (.) on the er .hhhh the
        er the *risten* (.)]
4 F: ich (.) nehme (.) an daß das ventil e:::m (1.0) nicht auf
        der bühne abgestützt wird (.) [I (.) believe that the valve
        er (1.0) is not supported on the hoist (.)]

In turn 1, D announces that a question is about to follow. While asking the question, D 'flags' an encoding problem by hesitation, lengthening of vowels, filled pauses and false starts. By producing 'yes' with a rising intonation contour in turn 2, F cooperates in the interaction in the sense that he displays understanding of what has been said in the preceding turn (though spoken dysfluently) while acknowledging that his interlocutor's turn is propositionally incomplete. Thus the interlocutors establish the valve as the 'topic' of the question which D is currently attempting to formulate. In turn 3, D completes his question in an 'either–or' format. In the 'or' part, he 'flags' an encoding problem pertaining to a noun by producing two false starts and an extended audible inbreath. The flagged item is *risten* (Danish *rist* = German *Rost* = English *grid*). According to the normal interpretation of hesitation signals, it can be said that D is using a CS, classifiable as *foreignizing*. The Danish stem *rist* is inflected with a German affix *en* marking the plural of nouns. F does not react to this flagged element. Instead, in the next turn, he refers to the 'either' part of the question. D has clearly not been able to ask his question in a way which allows F to supply the information which D seeks. Later in the telephone call, D therefore attempts to ask the question again:

Example (2)

1 D: und das ist ein frage ob die .h ob die riste: e:m
        (1.0)
        [and that is a question if the .h if the *riste* erm
        (1.0)]
2 F: ob das richtig? [if it is right?]

3   D: rUm rUm die d – rUm die e: ventil geht oder Unter dem
          ventil [runs arOUnd arOUND the th – arOUnd the valve
          or Under the valve]
4   F: mm hm

Again, D displays an encoding problem pertaining to the
(German) word *Rost*. In turn 1, he uses the same item *rist* as previously (extract 1), again in the context of a repeated false start
and a pause following the item. A pause of one second is relatively lengthy in this conversation. In turn 2, F reacts by 'offering'
the word *richtig*, presumably because he inferred that D in the
preceding turn was attempting to say *ob das richtig* (rather than
the foreignized form *ob die riste*). But in the next turn (turn 3) D
moves on, without responding to F's preceding attempt to
rephrase the foreignized item. D asks in a rather convoluted way
if he should cut out holes in the grid. This indicates that D
focuses not on the lexical problem (i.e., the *form* of the utterance) but rather on something else, namely the message itself –
the substantive information sought from F.

In examples (1) and (2), D uses *rist* twice in a marked way. In the
first example, F does not react to the flagging. In the second, F
reacts, offering a rephrasing of the perceptually 'marked' utterance
form. But D apparently focuses on a different part of the utterance.
The flaggings mark two different elements in the two examples. In
turn 3 of example (1), *rist* is flagged as a CS which invites a reaction
from the interlocutor. In turn 1 in example (2) the speaker does
not 'flag' *rist* by his hesitation signal but announces upcoming
problems pertaining to the local placement of the valve; however,
in this case, the hesitation phenomena are interpreted by F as flagging the CS *rist* and F reacts accordingly.

This finding illustrates at least one serious problem in the CS
discovery procedures mentioned above. Hesitation signals are not
unambiguously related to a specific lexical item. Quite clearly,
analysts' interpretations of the problematic elements in the discourse can be at best irrelevant as far as the interaction and the
participants are concerned, and at worst simply wrong. In principle, the researcher is in a comparable situation as F in example
(2): D flags production problems, and F tries to relate the flagging
to one problematic lexical element. For the analyst, the hesitation
signals in example (1) seem to mark the onset of a CS – the
foreignizing of *rist* – but on this occasion the interlocutor, F, does
not react to it. Already, from this cursory analysis, we can see that

CS are contingent products of interaction, can be ambiguous in their identifiability, and have differential relevance *vis-à-vis* the participants' communicative concerns.

The second problem worth mentioning here is that D in example (1) marks an element as a CS and, without getting any positive responses, re-uses the same element subsequently without any kind of marking. Does this indicate that D (and F) have added a new item to their lexis? We return to this question presently.

Subsequently in the talk, F abandons the task and refers to another engineer, G, who produced the actual drawing. D then calls G immediately and the following ensues during the call:

Example (3)

1   D: un unda er (.) dafür möchte ich (.) die riste: (..) rUm (.)
         der ventil g gehn [an and (.) therefore I want (.) the grids
         (rist) run arOUnd the valve]

2   G: ja rum nicht (.) rum brauchn wa nìcht (..) herUmgehen
         meinen sìe oder was [yes around not (.) around we don't
         need (..) walk arOUnd you mean or what]

3   D: ja? [yes?]

4   G: ja wir brauchen nicht herumgehen wir brauchen – sie
         kommen von der (..) von der fahrenden bühne (.) da las-
         sen wa ja die das geländer offen [well, we do not need to
         walk around we need – you are coming from the (..) from
         the moving hoist (.) there we leave the gallery open]

5   D: ja? [yes?]

6   G: und treten auf diese bühne drauf und gehen praktisch bis
         so: drei viertel herum aber sie können theoretisch können
         sie noch ganz herum gehen nur nicht ganz herum weil ja
         er zwei rohrleitungen führen ja er vom ventil [and step on
         the hoist and actually walk up to three quarters around.
         But you may theoretically you may walk all the way but not
         all the way because yeah two tubes lead from the valve ...]

D's turn 1 is a close paraphrase of turn 3 of example (2). Again, the marked form *rist* is not flagged. The actual flagging in the utterance is related to *around*. The verb *herumgehen*, which may take an animate or an inanimate subject, is flagged by a filled pause and by emphatic intonation. Now, D is interested in whether he may cut a piece out of the grid, not if the grid may run around the valve, despite his formulation to the contrary. In terms of CS, it could be classified as an 'achievement' strategy (see Færch & Kasper, 1983d, pp. 36–40). This gives two interesting items in turn 1, the unmarked foreignizing *rist* and an achievement strategy.

It appears, though, that G does not understand *rist* and tries to infer the meaning of the element D has been focusing upon: *herumgehen*. D reconstructs an animate subject and talks about somebody walking around the valve. Being unsure about his inference, he checks for understanding in turn 2. In G's rephrasing of the prefix, the same vowel is emphasized as in turn 1, thereby presupposing the second part of the verb, *gehen* (*walking*). As D confirms in turn 3, G then explains the problems of walking around the valve. After having G explain the walking conditions on the hoist, D returns to the grid:

Example (4)

1   D: ja in welchen kot – kote (2.5) in welcher hÖhe (1.0) [yes in which kot – kote (2.5) in which height (1.0)]

2   G: ja momènt ehm w – w – wir sprechn doch jetzt noch von meim entwurf ne? (1.0) oder von welcher bühne sprechn wir [yes just a second er w – w – we are talking about my drawing er? (1.0) or which hoist are we talking about]

3   D: ja? e: enwurf sch – eses heißt er bedienungsbühne (..) ha be [yes er drawing sh it it is called er hoist (..) HB]

4   G: ja? genau. [yes? exactly]

5   D: ja ha? [yes?]

6   G: genau (..) [exactly]

7   D: .hhh und – un – ich ich meine HHH .hh die=dic rist (.) man – darauf man geht ja? [.hhh and – an – I I mean HHH .hh the the grid (rist) (.) one – one walks on er?]

8   G: ja [yes]

9   D: hhh er (.) muß ich e – herausschneiden (.) in diesem rist für die punkte [.hhh er (.) I have – to remove (.) from this grid the spots]

10   G: ja ok – also sie mein e:: die: diese er ngg – das gItterrost müssen {sie [yes o.k. – but you mean er the these er ngg – the grId you have to]

11   D: ja:} [yes]

12   G: (.) ausnehmen [remove]

In his topic shift in turn 1, D flags a new element *kot*. In the next turn, G discloses that he cannot identify the referent in the preceding turn. In turn 3, D rephrases the element with a target language word *hÖhe* (*height*). The mutual point of reference is established in turns 3 to 6.

In turn 7, D returns to the issue raised in example (1), turn 3 – the *rist*. Again he flags *rist* emphatically by heavy breathing and by a paraphrase (*one walks on*). At the end of the turn D invites a reaction, and G in the next turn indicates understanding. But it appears that it is first after the next turn that G is able to discover the sense which D had intended throughout; this is demonstrated in his collaborative provision of the German word *Gitterrost* (turn 10).

In turn 3 of example (1), D uses a CS. In turn 10 of example (4), his interlocutor grasps the point and supplies the adequate lexical item. The question is now, why does D flag *rist* in example (4)? Clearly, it is not an incidental artifact of language production. In fact, D has just used *rist* twice in an unmarked context. A possible explanation might be that D in example (4) wants to focus on *rist* and wants to ensure that his interlocutor is able to make sense of this crucial reference. That is, the CS makes public the problematic lexical item for a specific purpose during *this* particular point in the interaction.

A related question is why *rist* is not flagged in examples (2) and (3), even though it did not work out in example (1). Apparently, *rist* is at that time not judged to be crucial in the meaning-creating process in which the speakers are engaged. And in this case the lexical problem remains unresolved by both speakers until the element is perceived to have a critical role. *The problem is resolved when it becomes interactionally relevant, and the CS plays an important role in this resolution process.* In the remaining part of the chapter we examine a comparable phenomenon.

2.3   Possible explanations for unmarked non-target-like elements

In the data corpus, clear instances of CS are found, that is, cases where speakers flag through hesitation markers that he or she has difficulties finding the right word (comparable to the case of *rist* in examples (1) and (4)). Frequently in this corpus, speakers use non-target-like items without marking them.

In example (5), a Danish employee (O) of a large supermarket chain talks with an employee of his German subcontractor (S). The Danish chain had opened several supermarkets in Germany at the end of the 1980s. O is in charge of the delicatessen sections. His German partner is a high-ranking manager of a large German delicatessen wholesale company. S has only one regular customer: O.

S does not speak Danish. O speaks English, and German to a very limited degree. Both talk frequently to each other on the telephone and meet regularly. All communications between them are in English (here English is a 'lingua franca'), but occasionally some code-switching into German does occur.

Example (5)

O is complaining about several deliveries which have been cancelled:

1   O: there was three lieferschein [bill of delivery] and er
2   S: mm mh
3   O: one of them there was er about er I see ten product four of them was taken out and lieferschein nummer two I've send you a copy there was er seven product four of them was was taken out

In example (5), two items are of interest: *Lieferschein* and *taken out*. Though the two items are not flagged they are both clearly non-target-like elements.

The case of *Lieferschein* could be explained as unmarked *code-switching* in the sense of Myers-Scotton (1993a, 1993b). According to this explanation, a number of unflagged non-target-like elements can be related to studies on code-switching. As Myers-Scotton has shown in her overview of the current literature (Myers-Scotton, 1993b), code-switching is frequent in multi-ethnic encounters. By switching from one code to another, speakers can negotiate meaning and identities. In this sense, code-switching is a contextualization cue for the speakers' intended meanings.

For business encounters such as those examined in the current corpus, the 'sequential unmarked choice' of code-switching would be relevant. Here speakers 'switch from one unmarked code to another when situational features change during an interaction such as the unmarked choice changes' (Myers-Scotton, 1993a, p. 480). When talking about business topics, speakers change between the language of communication and the language of the buyer or seller, depending on the issue they are addressing. This explanation holds true for a number of unmarked non-target-like elements in the data. In a large number of instances, however, code-switching is not a convincing explanation. This is the case when speakers do not have several codes at their disposition, that is, if they are not 'bilingual peers' (Myers-Scotton, 1993b, p. 119). Furthermore, speakers often switch to their first language, which their communicative partners quite openly do not master. This brings us back to the case of *taken out* in example (5).

Taken out in example (5) – in the sense of 'cancelled' or 'not delivered' – could be based on an approximation from a Danish *tage ud* in the same way as *rist* in examples (1)–(4). *Taken out* might have developed out of a flagged CS into a 'provisional lexical entry'. Few examples of a development like this can be documented in the data. But what is found are frequent elements comparable to the case of *rist* in examples (2) and (3), that is, elements which look like a CS without being flagged.

These instances lead to the hypothesis that speakers establish a contextually relevant, and therefore motile, *working argot* to cover their situated, work-related language needs. In this argot, lexical gaps may provisionally be filled by CS. These improvisations may become more or less fixed during the course of the communication, depending on their role in the meaning-creating process. In routine interactions between well-acquainted interlocutors, low numbers of flagged CS would be expected. Working argots may be particularly prominent in lingua franca data, since it cannot unproblematically be assumed that the participants aspire to producing 'native' forms of the language. The code adopted, while being predicated upon a 'native' model, is also motile, and, in circumstances where the parties quite clearly give precedence to the message and the concomitant work-based *task*, rather than the *form* of the message, a wide range of linguistic resources is drawn upon. In this light, CS are important resources that parties use to *contextualize* the import and situated relevance of the topic, task and 'point' being developed in the talk. Talk between O and S contains large numbers of non-flagged, non-target-like elements. Both explanations given until now may be accounted for in the way the two men know each other. S is O's main English-speaking contact. O speaks a little German. Since the talks refer to marketing practices in Germany, unmarked code-switching is a resource at hand.

We submit that the concept of argots, or working codes, has consequences for the study of CS in natural talk. The consequence would be that at least in naturally occurring data, CS can be studied in relation to situated codes and certain speakers' idiolects. The communicative biography of the speakers would necessarily be a part of the analysis of CS. This 'code' hypothesis provides compelling reasons for classifying only those instances of non-target elements as CS where the data in any way indicate that the speaker has a lexical problem.

As a consequence, in talk between familiar interlocutors, more CS should be found when the speakers approach a non-routine topic than in parts with known topics. This seems to be the case. In example (6) an employee of a Flemish company (FC) and his Danish partner (C) are talking about product specifics. They are using German as the lingua franca.

Example (6)

FC is trying to explain a technical detail of the unit in question. The machine is supposed to work in a very wet environment with aggressive fumes and liquids. So the question is whether the unit should be treated in a special way, for example by coating, in order to be able to withstand the forces of the environment.

1   FC: aber ich ich meine is das eh eh die die unten die diese unterteile von von was innen in das gerät da ist sind das ehm edelstahl er ausführung oder is das er galvenisiert einfach oder versch {xxx [but I I mean is the er er the the low the this lower part of of what is inside in the unit is that er stainless steel design or is it er galvanized simply or]

2   C: das} is edelstahl also die kondenswasserwanne is edelstahl [that is stainless steel well the sump for the water of condensation is stainless steel]

3   FC: ja die kondenswasserwanne aber weitere teile wo das feuchte {die [yes the sump but other parts where the damp the]

4   C: ja} [yes]

5   FC: die feuchtige luft mit in beziehung kommt [the damp air is in contact with]

The two interlocutors talk with each other often. Even though FC in general flags more CS than his colleagues do in other talks, CS become increasingly frequent when new technical details are discussed. Following the hypothesis of a situated working code, this can be explained by the fact that FC in these instances is approaching an unfamiliar topic and therefore neither has target-like words nor an established private code at his disposal.

The explanation of a private code or argot covers a number of instances in the present corpus, but it is not sufficient to explain the low number of flaggings in all cases of non-target-like items. As in the case of *rist* in examples (1)–(4), a number of instances can neither be analysed as code-switches nor as private codes. *Rist* is certainly not a code-switch, since G and F do not understand Danish. It is not a private code for both participants either, since, as we have seen in the analysis of examples (1) and (2), the inter-locutor does not understand the item.

Consequently, a third explanation may be forwarded which has already been mentioned in section 2.2: interlocutors use CS in cases where they do not have at their disposition the item which they consider to be the appropriate one. But CS do not do what they traditionally are supposed to – solve the meaning problem or trigger an extended negotiation of meaning. Instead, CS may func-tion as a 'blind spot', so to speak, which is left unattended until these items are rendered critical in the process of meaning crea-tion. We have attempted to demonstrate this in examples (1)–(4).

In examples such as (2) and (3), these improvisations seem to function as 'frozen CS', that is, CS which work as a 'dummy' ele-ment to keep a linguistic problem open. Frozen CS indicate an overall strategy. Often, the interlocutors do not understand each other, but until these blind spots are moved to the centre of the meaning-creating process, the interlocutors effectively live with them. In many cases they may carry out their work without solving the communication problem at all. In general, keeping a lexical or propositional problem unresolved is a prominent feature in the data. In this sense, the 'argot' notion has to be modified. Argots are neither well-defined, nor fixed nor generalizable lists of lexical entries but provisional, situationally motile elements which may serve communicative purposes for a longer or shorter period.

In the next example, we examine a related example of this tech-nique of keeping problems unresolved. In example (7), H, a Dane, talks to a British employee (A) he has not spoken to previously. H orders spare parts for a Danish production company. Since his business partners are often located outside Denmark, he speaks German and English on a daily basis. Not having received language training, his competence in English and German is poor.

Example (7)
H has called A at a spare part-producing company in the UK.

1 A: (.) good afternoon can I help you
2 H: .h good afternoon this is from ei bi: si: mainframes in Denmark .h my name is mister Jens Hansen .hh e:r Samantha Smith (.) has sent me a (.) fax from the twenty June
3 A: yeah
4 H: and we have sent this fax er once more that is our order (.) number ei bi: (.)

```
5   A:  yes
6   H:  er five four six five seven
7   A:  ye::s
8   H:  that is from the twenty one (.) in this month
9   A:  yes
10  H:  I would ask to you ha=have you er got this message from
        us (.)
11  A:  I am sure we have can you hold the line one moment
12  H:  mm mh thank you (20 secs.)
13  A:  hello
14  H:  =hel
15  A:  I can't see that the fax has come in todAY e:r maybe it hasn't
        been sent yet
16  H:  mm w we have sent er this fax er once again at the (.)
        twenty two in this month and that is time (.) ten (.) thirty
        (...) næ (...) ten twenty three that was {the time when we
        sent it
17  A:  xxxxxxxxxxxxxxxxxxxxxxx} I see it was on the twenty first
        you actually sent it
18  H:  yes
```

Even though Hansen's English is weak he nevertheless appears to speak fluently. There are few planning pauses in his talk and there are no overt indications that he is using CS. His speech production does not look as if he is encountering difficulties. We shall consider two issues in this example. First, it transpires that ABC Mainframe sent several telefaxes to Samantha Smith, not a single telefax as A, the native English speaker, appears to understand (see A's *it*, turn 17). Secondly, the English employee gets the date of the sending of Hansen's telefax wrong.

The second issue is ironed out subsequently during the call (not reproduced here), but the first remains unresolved. It does not become clear whether Smith actually has sent a telefax to Hansen. The number of telefaxes sent and the existence of an earlier telefax by Smith simply do not matter for the task at hand. Consequently, these interactional 'blind spots' in the communication remain unattended. A never discovers that H has sent several telefaxes because the issue does not become relevant in this particular encounter.

In this section, three different explanations have been discussed for why non-target elements are often not marked on the surface. Some examples can be explained in that the speakers code-switch between the lingua franca and an at least partly familiar code. A second group could be explained in the way that speakers use a provisional argot. The third explanation is that CS are not marked as long as they are viewed by the participants as playing an insignificant role in the negotiation of meaning. Only if they become a key element for the process of meaning creation are they focused upon and 'flagged'. This last argument is critical in that it designates a different role to the flagging of CS from those that are artifacts of the planning process. They become – through the efforts of the participants – elements of the meaning-creation process. At this point of the analysis, then, the question why CS are not marked has to be turned around. Instead of asking why non-target elements are not flagged, the question is now why they are flagged at all. The answer is to be found in the dynamics of the interaction.

2.4   The inferencing potential of CS

Example (8)
In the second half of a long telephone call, S suggests that certain commodities could be offered from two different placements in O's supermarkets.

1	S:	and er er I ve (.) two other (.) er things Ole
2	O:	yeah
3	S:	the question is .hh is it er possible with Allkauf in the Allkauf shops .hh to have their (.) second placement (0.5)
4	O:	second placement
5	S:	er er er er pallet placement (1.0)
6	O:	please say it again
7	S:	er do – do you have in the Allkauf market .h er pallet (.) placement (.) so for example .hh is it possible to (.) to to do (.) brathering ((fried herrings))
8	O:	ja
9	S:	fümpfhunnert gramm ((five hundred grams))
10	O:	ja
11	S:	that are pasteurized product
12	O:	oh now I understand yeah
13	S:	(.) er (.) can you put it on a on a quarter pallet
14	O:	.hhhh yeah
15	S:	or on a half

S prepares his case carefully. In turn 1 he reveals via a 'pre'-announcement (Schegloff, 1980) that two more points are to be broached. In turn 3 he introduces the first of them, preclassifying it as a question. By using a very short (micro)pause, he sets the last element of the question apart.

We can only speculate on whether or not this is a planning pause. It would seem reasonable to surmise that it is not, even though *second placement* may be an instance of phrasal coinage, that is, S's own creative construction. But the intonation context of the pause sounds different from a 'normal' planning pause. The pause in turn 1 is very short, difficult to measure in length, but clearly an audible interruption of the stream of sounds. While this pause looks like an intended marking of the element to follow, the filled pause in turn 5 indicates S's difficulties in accessing a lexical item.

His interlocutor, O, has marked the string *second placement* as well. His turn 4 is introduced by a longer pause. The pause and rising intonation of the repetition indicates O's difficulties in understanding the expression. In turn 6, pause and indication of non-understanding is repeated. Here O 'triggers' S into repeating the critical element a third time and paraphrasing it (turn 7). Again, S marks *pallet placement* with two short pauses preceding each of the two elements. *Secondary* or *pallet placement*, S explains later in the talk, means to offer a best-selling commodity on a pallet besides its normal placement on the shelf or in the freezer. The idea is to make the commodity more visible and hereby to increase its saleability. This marketing concept is obviously not unknown to O, but he has not previously applied it to the products for which he is responsible. His conceptual problem is to apply it to a new type of product.

S's pauses in turns 1, 3 and 7 are among several elements which increase O's attention to the concept to follow. Pre-announcements and pauses together flag the upcoming element as crucial. In this way the listener's attention is heightened, thus facilitating the effective communication of a complicated message. Accordingly, the flagging of CS is afforded a new, hitherto undescribed function. 'Flags' are not merely deployed to indicate that the speaker has a problem and is currently planning; the resource is also deployed to indicate that the speaker will use an element in a special, perhaps 'marked' way; the interlocutor's inferencing 'work' is thereby facilitated. To put things another way, speakers flag their linguistic problems in order to allow their communicative partners the opportunity to infer as intended. CS, as well as their onset signals, thus bear heavy inferential loads in the discourse.

This observation allows us to promulgate the possibility of analysing CS as objects that are free from psycholinguistic baggage. From a discourse point of view, CS in communication can be targeted towards, and designed specifically for, the interlocutor to give him or her an improved chance of grasping the speaker's intended meaning. By using a CS, the speaker's marking of utterances are keys that unlock inferential doors, thereby calling forth not only his or her own resources but the resources of the co-interactant as well. Simply put, speakers put out 'flags' when they anticipate potential difficulties in the joint creation of meaning.

In example (8), S flags an element to introduce a potentially difficult concept. It could very well be, as argued above, that S does not experience planning difficulties, but simply endeavours to direct O's attention in a particular direction. O reacts by marking the same element himself and thereby establishes it as an element whose comprehension requires that both parties' inferential capacities be keenly marshalled. Example (8) shows clearly that CS do not work just because they are intended as such by the speaker alone, but because they are taken up by the listener as a resource that aids in the creation and negotiation of interpersonal meaning. This reflexive use of a CS by speaker and listener is not always as obvious as in example (8). Normally, the listener accepts the CS by sharpening his inferencing. That is, a CS will commonly entail extra inferential work on the interlocutor's part; but this is not always visible in the discourse.

So, if flagging has an inferential-aiding function, it is not a cry for help, as many CS studies posit. This explains that listeners in our data rarely overtly assist their interlocutor (in the form of, say, utterance completions or candidate completions). Instead, they check whether or not their inferences correlate with the speaker's intended sense, a task that is routinely undertaken through 'formulations' (prototypically formatted as '*so you're saying* ...'; see Heritage & Watson, 1980), by asking control questions or by rephrasing certain topics.

Example (9)
H has ordered a spare part and talks about delivery conditions

1   H: perhaps you could send it by flight and er parcel post
2   A: send it by air parcel post
3   H: yes is that possible

H marks an element in turn 1 by a filled pause. A's rephrasing takes the form of an 'other repair', as has been described by Schegloff et al. (1977). The point is that the 'other repair' not only delivers the right word but that its main function is to indicate that A has understood the concept to which the speaker was referring. Consequently, H confirms the intended word in turn 3 but does not repeat it. Both speakers are oriented towards the conjoint task of sense *making*, and not towards the correction or accurate enunciation of linguistic form (see Firth, in press). In general, this holds for the examples examined above. By putting up flags, speakers raise their listener's attention and effectively put 'scare quotes' around potentially problematic words or expressions. They thereby increase the chances of getting their intended meanings across successfully. If speakers do not flag code switchings, foreignizing and other lexical operations, they heighten the risk of misunderstandings arising and the subsequent requirement for extended procedures to regain the common ground.

In naturally occurring data we suspect that speakers are more oriented towards meaning creation and sense-making than towards linguistic form. The essential condition for communicating successfully is to get the intended meaning across, to get the listener to understand what is meant here and now. The conventionally 'right' lexical item certainly helps in accomplishing this, but it is not the only way. This is the overall communicative condition for the success of CS. Only if speakers can assume that their listeners will be able to do inferential 'work' from what is said, will they be able to exploit successfully the inferential power of CS.

3. Conclusion

The interactional analysis of CS has demonstrated certain methodological problems. As shown in examples (1)–(4), it is not always clear if surface phenomena (e.g., hesitation markers) refer to a certain lexical item or not. The reference and relevance of the hesitation markers is negotiated and established by the speakers themselves in the emerging context of talk. This feature does not go unnoticed in the majority of CS research, though it is alluded to rather than discussed in any detail. This can be seen in the strict design of current psycholinguistically oriented studies, where 'learners' ' language output is very tightly controlled in terms of topic and speaker intention. Such strictures are applied in the hope that the analyst may unproblematically be able to identify CS as they arise.

The main point of this study was to demonstrate that certain phenomena associated with CS have been overlooked in previous research and that interactionally fused studies of CS offer new and challenging perspectives. It has been argued that one central feature in conversation is that participants constantly and conjointly stretch their meaning-creating potential; often, it seems, to the limits. Many studies spanning a wide range of approaches to talk and social interaction have shown that speakers attempt to use all available information in a conversation as a resource to create and continually (re)negotiate interpersonal meaning. Therefore speakers use formats such as pauses and other markers, and listeners deploy mechanisms such as repairs, formulations and control checks to clarify whether they have inferred the meaning in the sense the speaker had in mind.

CS studies adopting the psycholinguistic approach investigate CS to discover more about an individual's language processing. CS is a very prominent element in speech production and therefore an important element of natural discourse. As such it deserves to be studied within a broader remit, one that specifically and centrally includes the interactional facets as well as the cognitive. How and whether the interactional, social perspectives can be reconciled with the acquisitional and cognitive perspectives is presently a moot point, one that we must leave for the future. Of course, interactional studies that focus on CS are not primarily interested in CS *per se* either, but in explicating the ways in which conversationalists make ongoing sense in the myriad social settings within which people interact. Naturally enough, such settings will frequently involve foreign language speakers as well.

Notes

We are grateful to Lene Gyngø Jensen and Grete Anthony for allowing us to use their data. The ideas on the interactional role of CS have been stimulated by unpublished papers by Firth (1988) and by Firth and Kasper (1990). Finally, our thanks to the editors for helpful comments on an earlier version of this chapter. Remaining shortcomings are, of course, our responsibility.

1. The term 'naturally occurring' refers to the nature of the data. It specifies a data-type that would have occurred regardless of the investigator's interventions or research aspirations. In this sense the 'naturally occurring' epithet can be contrasted with 'experimental' or 'simulated' data materials; that is, interactions that have been instigated by the researcher for research-related goals.

2. It may be tempting, though, to question the assumption underpinning such studies, namely that (individual) speakers' actions or utterances can legitimately be focused upon without attending in detailed ways to the interactional domain, which centrally includes the situated and contingent (re)actions of the interlocutor(s). We cannot develop this point further here; suffice to say that we suspect that what individual-oriented studies attribute *a priori* to the individual's cognition may well be accountable and sensitive to the *social* as well as *individual* facets of the interaction. Such a postulation, informed by findings made within ethnomethodological conversation analysis (see, e.g., Atkinson & Heritage, 1984; Ten Have & Psathas, 1994), deserves, and would surely repay, empirical examination.

3. The term 'locally managed' refers to the way interactive talk is ongoingly managed, negotiated and made meaningful *in situ*, in the turn-by-speaking-turn context of situation (see Sacks et al., 1974, p. 729).

4. It is here we acknowledge our intellectual debt to the interactionally oriented research undertaken by scholars who pursue a social (as against a mentalistic or cognitive), situated, 'locally managed', microanalytic perspective on interactive discourse and context. Such scholars include, among many others, Bilmes (1986), Duranti and Goodwin (1992), McDermott and Roth (1978), Moerman (1988), Sacks (1992), Sacks et al., (1974), Streek (1980) and Wootton (1989).

5. The data from each company form a data set. Each set consists of between five and 90 telephone calls and covers between one and a half and ten hours of talk. All spoken data have been transcribed. The following transcription conventions have been used:

(.)	indicates a very short gap in the speech.
{ }	indicates turn overlap.
[ ]	marks translation.
gIve	capitalizations indicate emphatic stress.
(0.5)	indicates pause hand-timed in tenths of seconds.
((…))	indicates omitted text.
hhh	indicates audible inbreath.
gi(h)ve	bracketed h indicates breathiness, typically occurring in laughter.
(xx)	indicates inaudible segments.
?	indicates rising intonation.

gi::ve   colons indicate lengthened sound.

H H H   indicates coughing.

=   indicates repetitions without an audible onset.

gi –   dash indicates cut-off in flow of speech.

6. Our use of the term 'target' should *not* be construed as indicating the participants' desires or intentions to strive towards an idealized level of competence in the foreign language. We do not wish to speculate on interactants' foreign-language related ambitions, motives or desires, were such things to exist.

15

Beyond reference

GABRIELE KASPER

1. Introduction

In applied linguistics, models of communicative competence serve as goal specifications for L2 teaching and testing. A widely cited proposal of this kind was offered by Canale and Swain (1980), which included the components of grammatical, sociolinguistic and strategic competence. Sociolinguistic competence comprises socio-cultural rules and rules of discourse. Strategic competence is seen as an aggregate of communication strategies (CS), serving to 'compensate for breakdowns in communication due to performance variables or insufficient competence', where 'competence' includes both grammatical and sociolinguistic competence (Canale & Swain, 1980, p. 30).

In a model of communicative competence suggested ten years later, Bachman (1990) reorganized and elaborated upon the earlier proposal. In this model, the two main components of linguistic competence are theorized as organizational competence, including grammatical and discourse competence, and pragmatic competence, which subdivides into illocutionary and sociolinguistic competence. Strategic competence operates on all of these components, but in a wider sense than proposed by Canale and Swain. While the ability to solve receptive and productive problems due to lack of knowledge or accessibility remains an aspect of strategic competence, it is now more generally thought of as the ability to use linguistic knowledge efficiently. This conceptual expansion is consistent with the view that as a type of goal-related behaviour, language use is always strategic (see Introduction, this volume). Consonant with the views of Canale and Swain (1980) and Bachman (1990), CS have been regarded as applicable to problems arising from a lack of linguistic or sociolinguistic rules (Tarone, 1983), or to planning or execution problems in attaining referential, illocutionary, or relational goals (Færch & Kasper, 1983d). In actual research practice, however, most studies have limited their scope to CS serving to remedy referential problems, usually focusing on lexical knowledge and retrieval. This gap between proposals of strategic competence at the conceptual level and the small subset of strategic competence that has been examined in database studies is not very satisfactory. If a function of theory is to initiate and guide research, theories of communicative competence have not proven terribly productive precisely in the area in which theories of communicative competence in an L2 differ from those developed for native speakers (NS). Neither Habermas's (1971) nor Hymes's (1971) theories of communicative competence include a strategic component – obviously not because native speakers do not have strategic competence, but because this was not a salient issue from Hymes's sociolinguistic point of view and Habermas's social-philosophical perspective. It is quite ironic that strategic competence, added by Canale and Swain (1980) because of its salience in non-native speakers' (NNS) communicative ability and presumably kept and expanded by Bachman (1990) for the same reason, has only partially been investigated.

2. Pragmatic communication strategies

2.1   *What's the problem?*

If we define pragmatics as 'interpersonal rhetoric' (Leech, 1983) and maintain problematicity as critical to the notion of CS, then problems in pragmatics are communicative events which fall short of participants' actional (illocutionary and perlocutionary) and relational goals. In NS communication, such problems frequently occur because of various types of goal conflict: between interpersonal or intrapersonal, and between actional and relational goals. Interpersonally, participants' goals may conflict at the level of action (e.g., A wants to borrow B's car and B does not want to give it to her) or relationship definition (e.g., A wants a more distanced relationship than B); intrapersonally, types of goal may compete against each other (e.g., B wants to refuse A's request for the car [actional goal] and at the same time maintain a harmonious relationship with B [relational goal]). The best-known theory to account for participants' solutions to multiply conflicting goals is Brown and Levinson's politeness theory (1987), wherein the fundamental conflict is one between efficiency (reaching actional goals at low cost and with maximal benefit) and face wants (need for social acceptance and self-determination). Damage to face can be attenuated through different redressive strategies, for instance indirectness, mitigation of face threatening acts, or aggravation of face-supportive acts. In a different approach, O'Keefe (1991) proposed three basic strategies by which conflicting multiple goals can be reconciled: (a) subsidiary goals may be traded off ('selection'); (b) subsidiary goals may be treated in different parts of the message ('separation'); or (c) the goal may be redefined or avoided ('integration'). It is true that goal conflicts are not always happily resolved, for instance when an indirectly conveyed message is understood differently from what the speaker intended (Blum-Kulka & Weizman, 1988). But while miscommunication among native speakers is a fact of social life (cf. contributions to Coupland et al., 1991, examining miscommunication in different social domains), on balance, NS communicate much more successfully than unsuccessfully, at least when they are members of the same speech community and cultural group. To the extent that NS communication is *intra*cultural communication, its high success rate appears to hinge on two properties. The first is that intracultural communication is based on shared socio-cultural assumptions and conventions of means and form. Interlocutors by and large share their perceptions of each others' rights and obligations, and of the imposition involved in particular acts; they presuppose rather than explicate taken-for-granted assumptions; they *know* (though not necessarily *use*) the same strategies of indirection and repertoire of pragmatic formulae to perform recurrent activities routinely (Nattinger & DeCarrico, 1992). In situations of diverging multiple goals, members of the same speech community will use similar approaches to reconcile conflicting demands (Janney & Arndt, 1992). Because sociopragmatic and pragmalinguistic knowledge is shared intraculturally, members are able to engage in reciprocal perspective-taking and to operate on an 'etcetera' principle (Cicourel, 1972). Linked to shared pragmatic knowledge is a second feature of intracultural communication: members' tendencies to avoid unnecessary costs to their own speech production and their interlocutor's processing resources. Unlike Habermas's and

Hymes's proposals for an *ideal* communicative competence, the notion of communicative competence favoured in communication science is 'the ability to avoid problems, to conduct encounters and relationships in a manner that is adequate or merely "good enough" rather than excellent or perfect' (Coupland et al., 1991, p. 2). This reality-checked concept of communicative competence is compatible with the principle of 'satisficing' (Simon, 1957), denoting problem-solvers' orientation towards a balance between the resources invested in reaching a specific goal and the overall available resources (cf. Poulisse, this volume). Since satisficing is a mutually recognized metastrategy of L1 communication, there is no contradiction between Coupland et al.'s assertion that 'language use and communication are in fact pervasively and even intrinsically flawed, partial, and problematic' (1991, p. 3), and my earlier observation that intracultural communication is more often than not successful, if 'success' is understood as a mutually acceptable outcome rather than the total match of participants' speaker meanings and listener interpretations (were this ever possible) at all times.

In intracultural communication, then, the fundamental problems are to balance conflicting multiple goals, and to use (*available, shared*) resources maximally effectively at minimal cost to self and other. In *inter*cultural communication, the same fundamental problems obtain, but they are exacerbated in two ways.

First, while any communicator will adopt some sort of a satisficing policy, just what satisficing means is a different thing altogether when it comes to intercultural encounters. In intercultural communication, at least some portions of participants' pragmatic knowledge are *not* shared. Again, this situation can be examined from an intrapersonal and an interpersonal perspective. In interlanguage pragmatics, the predominant approach has been intrapersonal, comparing the pragmatic knowledge and actions of NNS to those of NS. While the pragmatic competence of NNS is influenced by linguistic proficiency and input factors such as second versus foreign language context and length of residence in the target community (Kasper & Schmidt, 1996, for review), all but very advanced NNS have been shown to differ from NS in their sociopragmatic assessments of context factors (e.g., Bergman & Kasper, 1993; House, 1989; Olshtain & Weinbach, 1993; Robinson, 1992; Shimamura, 1993; Takahashi, 1995) and their pragmalinguistic knowledge, especially of L2 specific patterns of indirection and L2 routines to convey illocutionary force and politeness (Kasper, 1995, for review). From an interpersonal perspective, *all* parties in an intercultural encounter lack a shared assumptive framework and resources – NNS because they do not have the contextually relevant knowledge, and NS because they cannot use such knowledge without adjustments. Because – especially in initial encounters – pragmatic knowledge is not shared, or not enough of it, there is no basis for an allusive style of interaction (Aston, 1993). Secondly, in cases of intra- or interpersonal goal conflict, participants' approaches to conflict solution are likely to diverge to a greater or lesser- extent, depending on the overlap between their context assessments, available and usable pragmalinguistic knowledge, and assessment of how contextually appropriate the usable resources are. Under such circumstances, 'satisficing' is a more deliberate metastrategy which may be implemented by participants in different ways.

2.2 Some solutions

Several studies have presented evidence for L2 learners' verbosity, at least under certain task conditions. As found in interlanguage pragmatics, verbosity, or (less benevolently) 'waffling' (Edmondson & House, 1991) does not just imply saying the same thing in more words (which, measured against NS norms, would be a violation of the maxim of manner), but giving more information or making information more explicit (a violation of the quantity maxim, if NS norms are a criterion). For example:

- Learners justified their *requests* more than NS (Blum-Kulka & Olshtain, 1986; Edmondson & House, 1991; Færch & Kasper, 1989; Kasper, 1989).
- In *apologizing*, learners provided more explicit statements of responsibility (Bergman & Kasper, 1993; Edmondson & House, 1991; House, 1989), offered more repair and verbal redress, and downgraded their apologies more (Bergman & Kasper, 1993).
- Learners' *complaints* were significantly longer than those of NS (Olshtain & Weinbach, 1993).
- In a variety of speech acts, learners expressed propositions explicitly where implicit formulations were the more idiomatic choices, preferred by NS (Kasper, 1981, 1982).
- Learners tended to provide 'complete responses', repeating parts of their interlocutor's initiating act instead of using ellipsis (Scarcella 1981).

In short, several studies have documented a tendency for learners to use more transparent, complex, explicit and longer utterances than NS in comparable contexts, and to favour literal over non-literal interpretations.

As Edmondson and House (1991) noted, at the same time, learners' speech acts are often noted for their bluntness (lack of mitigation) and directness (Kasper, 1981; Robinson, 1992; Tanaka, 1988). I earlier referred to this feature in interlanguage pragmatics as 'modality reduction' (Kasper, 1979), arguing that since learners have to accommodate their communicative goals to their processing capacity, they may forego marking their speech acts for politeness while maintaining their illocutionary and propositional goals. I suggested that modality reduction was a 'reduction strategy', that is, a CS which deletes some aspect of the speaker's communicative goal.

While waffling and bluntness appear to be contradictory strategies in interlanguage pragmatics, they may well be motivated by the same properties of interlanguage knowledge and intercultural communication. Edmondson and House (1991) offer a psycholinguistic explanation. Both waffling and bluntness, they argue, have to be seen in relation to yet another feature of interlanguage pragmatics – the lack of formulaic routines in learners' interlanguage. The reason that NS can manage multiple goals seemingly effortlessly rests largely on their rich repertoire of formulaic linguistic knowledge, which reduces processing costs in utterance production and frees attentional capacity for newly created utterance components. Learners, especially those with little opportunity for input and sustained activation of their pragmatic knowledge in interaction, may either lack adequate routine formulae altogether, or not have them sufficiently automatized for use in speech act realization. For such learners, then, both waffling and bluntness are compensatory strategies, redressing the absence of routinized pragmalinguistic knowledge.

The psycholinguistic explanation suggested by Edmondson and House (1991) can be complemented by a sociolinguistic account. As outsiders to the target community, NNS might feel that they have to explain themselves and their actions more, take less for granted, and make explicit information that would remain implicit in intra-cultural communication. In fact, this need would still obtain in a situation where NNS have a fair amount of routinized pragmalinguistic knowledge at their disposal. For instance, Weizman (1993) found that NNS did not use non-conventionally indirect request strategies (hints) instead of conventionally indirect ones, that is, as a compensatory strategy. And yet, the same NNS would still use more elaborated hints than NS. Similarly, NNS apologizers used the requisite routine formulae *and* more additional apology strategies (Bergman & Kasper, 1993). What these findings suggest, then, is that even when learners' routinized pragmalinguistic resources are adequate to the purpose at hand, in the absence of a shared assumptive framework, they will need to establish rather than presuppose common ground (Aston, 1993; Janney & Arndt, 1992). While the discourse completion design adopted by most interlanguage pragmatics studies does not inform us about interlocutors' contributions to the discourse, an extension of collaborative theory (Wilkes-Gibbs, this volume) from transactional to interpersonal discourse would predict that participants jointly create a shared context for the ongoing interaction. This is indeed emphasized by Janney and Arndt, who make the point that in intercultural communication, the cultural frames of reference that participants operate on in intracultural encounters have to be replaced by an 'ad-hoc frame of reference, which is roughly prescribed by the partners' immediate interests, activities, or goals. ... For the purpose of sustaining conversation, the partners tacitly agree to become members of a common, transcendent positive-reference group' (Janney & Arndt, 1992, p. 38f). Positive-reference groups serve to make participants' actions more predictable and to 'create a sense of affiliation' (p. 39) between them. Establishing task-oriented co-membership can thus be seen as a major strategy of *tact* in intercultural communication (Janney & Arndt, 1992). Shea's (1993) study of interpersonal encounters between NS of American English and Japanese NNS lends empirical support to Janney and Arndt's proposal, demonstrating how the socio-cultural context in these conversations is constructed on-line and locally through recipient design and task orientation. While participants' L1-based conversational styles shaped the discourse to some extent, intracultural frames of reference were modified by the ongoing interactional process. The constructionist rather than essentialist view of cultural identity in intercultural communication is compatible with the insistence of interlanguage theory on the L2 learner's active, creative role in language acquisition.

The need for participants in intercultural encounters to rely on more explicit forms of communication transcends 'propositional explicitness'; it also includes discourse management. While it has been amply demonstrated in the literature on conversational adjustments, repair, and CS that metalingual and metacommunicative activity increases in interaction involving non-native participants because there is more occasion for *non*-comprehension or *mis*understanding, there is also more need for explicitly signalling *successful* comprehension. This was in fact the case in Kasper (1981), where I found that both participants in NS–NNS dyads backchannelled considerably more than participants in NS dyads did.

Further empirical evidence to support Janney and Arndt's proposal comes from recent studies of intercultural communication in institutional settings and interpersonal encounters. Building on earlier work by Erickson and Shultz (1982), which had demonstrated how establishing co-membership serves as a major collaborative strategy in counselling sessions, Fiksdal (1990) found that in academic advising sessions, participants establish alignment through various strategies of rapport-building (such as seeking agreement and asserting common ground) and rapport-maintaining (such as framing corrections and bad news). In a study of casual encounters between NS and NNS of English, Aston (1993) showed how participants adopted a number of strategies to create interpersonal alignment, or 'comity'. Such strategies[1] did not only compensate for the lack of common ground but in fact exploited 'non-consociacy' and incompetence as resources for negotiating solidarity and support. They included the following: citing warrants for one's attitudes; admitting incompetence; celebrating ordinary success; repairing actual incompetence where possible; appreciating benevolence; and distancing oneself from the stereotypes of one's culture (Aston, 1993, p. 245). Shea (1994) discussed similar alignment strategies from the vantage point of a theoretical model comprising the dimensions of perspectival congruence and discourse production. In successful conversations between Japanese NNS of English and their NS English interlocutors, perspectival congruence was achieved by positive politeness strategies such as soliciting background information, referring to similar experience and shared values, friendly teasing, expressing positive affect, and speaking in the NNS's voice; these were complemented at the level of discourse management by the conversational adjustments known from the interactional modification literature (rephrasing, restatement, completing the NNS's utterances).

Whereas Aston (1993) and Shea (1994) observed the registered alignment strategies in intercultural encounters where talk served predominantly to establish and maintain interpersonal relation- ships, Piirainen-Marsh (1995) explored how face-threatening acts were collaboratively managed in ongoing NS–NNS discourse. Participants in her study thus had to cope with the double prob- lem of conflicting actional and relational goals as well as unequally distributed communicative resources. While the prag- malinguistic and sociopragmatic knowledge of the NNS indeed proved limited, they used the same range of face-saving strategies as their NS interlocutors; this finding is consistent with the inter- language pragmatics literature on speech-act realization (Kasper, in press; Kasper & Blum-Kulka, 1993). Of the strategies operating on the sequential organization of discourse, preparatory strategies were regularly used devices for external speech-act modification. Such pre-sequences not only announced and thereby cushioned the upcoming face-threatening act, but also gave the NS inter- locutor the option to infer the speaker's goals and pre-empt the conflictive act by a cooperative alternative, for instance, pre-empt- ing an anticipated request by an offer or a jointly negotiated pro- posal. Despite the obviously limited L2 proficiency of the NNS, their non-nativeness was not always a salient issue in the interac- tion; at times NS would respond to conversational problems by adopting a letting-it-pass strategy (Wagner & Firth, this volume); at other times, manifest NNS difficulty in understanding or pro- ducing a contribution would invite overt NS assistance and cooperation, while extreme deference of the NNS in some con- texts would elicit stronger displays of solidarity and alignment on the part of the NS.

Re-inventing the status of *learner* or *non-native speaker* as an inter- actional resource rather than as a debilitating condition is also a prime concern in Rampton's analysis of interracial discourse between early adolescents (1995, this volume). In these encoun- ters, the Anglo and Afro-Caribbean participants converge to their Panjabi friends by code-switching to Panjabi, thus reconstructing their cultural identity as members of a joint interethnic group. That an important sociopragmatic function of code-switching is to serve as an 'act of identity' is, of course, well-known (cf. Myers- Scotton, 1993b, for review). However, especially in low-proficiency NNS, code-switching is mostly regarded as a strategy to compensate for insufficient linguistic knowledge. This standard explanation does not cover the switches from L1 to L2 observed in Rampton's L2 Panjabi speakers. In a very different, intracultural context of a classroom activity, Legenhausen (1991) observed how German learners of French code-switched between their L1 and L2, and again, these switches were neither compensatory nor motivated by referential goals, but indexed the students' participation in multiple identities. Similarly, Burt (1990, 1992, 1993) demonstrated how fairly low-proficient learners of each others' native language regularly code-switched to their interlocutor's L1. Again, such patterns of convergence could not be explained as compensation for linguistic deficit, but made sense in light of Brown and Levinson's (1987) politeness theory: in this framework, converging code-switching can be seen as a positive politeness strategy.

What these studies suggest, then, is that non-nativeness and non-consociacy in and of themselves do not constitute interactional problems and can even be turned into a conversational and relational resource when participants' relational goals converge on solidarity, achieved through various perspectival and discoursal alignment strategies. Importantly, however, some of the same studies also point out that the convergence strategies used by NS to achieve mutual comprehension and to facilitate NNS' conversational participation can in fact result in *divergence*, by creating or exacerbating the very problems they were designed to forestall or solve. Frequent foreigner talk adjustments such as completing, rephrasing and restating the NNS' utterances can produce an asymmetrical distribution of 'interactional authority' (Shea, 1994). Explicit other-repair, rather than solving conversational trouble, may reinforce problems by casting the NS as the junior partner in the business of conversation; face-concerns as well as sequencing constraints may thus disfavour explicit other-repair in intercultural encounters just as much as in NS discourse (Færch & Kasper, 1982; Piirainen-Marsh, 1995). The practice of expert–novice-convergence, well-attested in American socialization interaction between children acquiring their first language and their caretakers (e.g., Schieffelin & Ochs, 1986) and adult ESL learners in classroom settings (Poole, 1992), appears more ambiguous in its social messages than is usually assumed: instead of facilitating novice participation, it may accentuate asymmetry and produce psychological divergence (Giles et al., 1991).

Lastly, the assumption that participants in intercultural encounters invariably strive for solidarity through cooperation and mutual convergence of perspectives presupposes fundamentally shared social interests, a presupposition that is naïve at best and potentially harmful in that it ignores conflicting social stances that may pre-exist and become salient in the discourse or emerge as a product of the interaction itself. As Apitzsch and Dittmar (1987) noted in the discourse of adolescent Turkish immigrants in Germany, discoursal 'acts of identity' may in fact emphasize cultural distinctiveness from, and *dis*identification with, the target community (Blum-Kulka, 1991), serving as a strategy of resistance against the discrimination that Turkish immigrants suffer in German society. A related but different type of resistance strategy was observed in multiethnic workplace discourse in Sweden, where a Vietnamese worker resorted to non-participation in protest to ethnification as Chinese by her co-workers (Day, 1994). Adopting a constructivist attribution-theoretical perspective to the discourse of expatriate Chinese scientists in the Netherlands, Shi-Xu (1994) identified a number of strategies operating in the discoursal construction of cultural identity and attribution, such as countering underestimation and negative evaluations by the host community, praising the host community, imputing abnormality to ingroup social forces, (dis-)crediting the identity of cultural groups, and re-orienting cultural actions.

These studies of intercultural discourse in a variety of interpersonal and institutional encounters demonstrate that strategy choice not only varies with the transactional and relational goals that participants pursue during their encounter, but that strategies may be related to such aspects of participant status as cultural identity and attribution. Since an important trait of participant status in intercultural communication is that of the non-native speaker, it will be useful to summarize how this status characteristic has been addressed in the literature.

3. 'The non-native speaker' reconsidered

Non-nativeness as problem. In interlanguage pragmatics (see section 2.1 above for references) and early interactional sociolinguistics (e.g., Gumperz, 1982), non-nativeness was seen as the main source of pragmatic failure or miscommunication. Especially in interlanguage pragmatics, deviances from NS behaviour have regularly been regarded as communicatively disruptive regardless of whether they actually caused trouble or not, and whether or not manifest problems were easily repairable, with no further consequences for the interaction, or caused major disruption at the interpersonal or transactional level (cf. Clyne's, 1977, distinction between 'communication breakdown' and 'communication conflict' and its recent adoption by Meeuwis, 1994).

Since the impetus to interactional sociolinguistics rests on the assumption that conflicts in interethnic relationships are largely due to miscommunication, it is a given that unsuccessful communication is central to the approach. A causal link between 'nonconsociacy' and problematic talk is assumed rather than explored. In NS–NNS encounters, pragmatic failure is usually attributed to the NNS participant's lack of target (pragmatic, discourse, sociolinguistic) knowledge rather than viewed as jointly constructed.

Non-nativeness as resource. As reviewed in the preceding section (2.2), participants can get considerable mileage out of acknowledged non-nativeness and non-consociacy. Most of the research points to alignment and solidarity-creating strategies through which participants construct themselves as members of a positive reference group (e.g., Aston, 1993; Rampton, 1995, this volume). As Meeuwis notes, 'mutual recognition of nonnativeness allows for smooth continuation of the conversation that would be unlikely in any type of conversation involving native speakers' (Meeuwis, 1994, p. 398). If NS participants opt for a metastrategy of 'communicative leniency' (Meeuwis, 1994; cf. the 'letting-it-pass' strategy noted by Wagner & Firth, this volume), they help implement a satisficing principle that is adequate to the communicative ability of the NNS and the purpose of the ongoing encounter.

But as discussed above, non-nativeness and non-consociacy can be exploited to emphasize divergence and disidentification as well. Attributing lack of participation or non-native-like discourse behaviour to deficient communicative competence may fail to recognize the strategic emphasis of otherness for the purpose of dissociation.

Non-nativeness as unattended. While it is true that any participant attribute *can* become salient in ongoing discourse, many attributes do not and non-nativeness is one of them. Whether or not non-nativeness is foregrounded seems largely determined by the overall goal of the encounter at hand. When salient participant features towards that goal are professional competence and a history of previous successful encounters, as in lingua franca discourse in different institutional settings (e.g., Wagner & Firth, this volume), participants tend to disregard non-target-like features in each others' contributions because such features are irrelevant to participants' goals and attending to them would sidetrack attention and discourse development.

From the perspective of discourse participants, the three categories of non-nativeness can be regarded as discourse options, available in any conversation but differentially tapped into depending on the goals and context of the current encounter. As some studies demonstrate, all three versions of NNS status can be present in the same conversation (Piirainen-Marsh, 1995; Shea, 1994), but a particular encounter can also be dominated by any one of them.

Since the treatment of non-nativeness by discourse participants and researchers alike has an impact on both problems and strategies in intercultural communication, it will be useful to briefly review the epistemological positions which have been adopted in the literature. There are basically three of them.

The deterministic, essentialist position views non-nativeness as an independent variable which determines conversational behaviours (usually the dependent variable). A unidirectional causal relationship is presupposed between a participant's pre-existing identity as NNS or specific aspects of it, such as ethnolinguistic background, proficiency level in L2, length of residence in the target community, and sometimes also other demographic traits such as gender and age. There is no room for negotiation and change of participant identity from the demographically pre-given through the conversational interaction. Predicated on an analytical-nomological paradigm of (social) science, this position conceptualizes its 'subjects' and their world as stable objects, regulated by pre-given normative models that exist independently of social interaction. A deterministic-essentialist stance typically underlies quantitative studies in interlanguage pragmatics and sociolinguistics.

The myopic constructionist[2] position holds that participant identity in an encounter is locally produced rather than pre-existent. No participant attribute matters unless it is conversationally manifest, publicly attended to and thus constructed on-line as the discourse unfolds. Non-nativeness becomes a matter of discoursal contingency which does not exist as a category, attribute, or identity trait outside its discoursal construction. Context information, cultural norms, values, beliefs, or conventions may serve the researcher as interpretive resources only to the extent that participants demonstrably attend to them in the course of the analyzed interaction. 'Context' is thus reduced to the microcosm of the ongoing encounter and stops right there. In de-historizing, de-contextualizing, and de-culturalizing discourse practices, myopic constructionism adopts a micro-analytic bottom-up approach to discourse, where the top is defined by the boundaries of the ongoing conversation. This position is represented by the more dogmatic versions of Conversation Analysis.

A *contextualized constructionist position* acknowledges the influences in intercultural communication of historically and biographically constituted pretexts, such as beliefs, values, ideologies, conventions and practices extant in a community. Such pretexts, which may be metaphorized as the frames and schemata that constitute an individual's knowledge structure, inform and predispose, but by no means determine, action in discourse. By allowing for top-down processing, they help establish the link between the immediate context of the interaction and the wider institutional and societal context in which intercultural discourses are embedded. At the same time, participants are seen as constructive agents who reconstitute and restructure identities, attributions, social knowledge and practices through the dynamics of the interaction they are engaged in, thus feeding the discoursally constituted information bottom-up to contexts beyond the immediate conversation. Such analysis connects micro and macro levels of social organization by recognizing the autonomy of agents in intercultural encounters as relative, contextually mediated and itself negotiable. The contextualized constructionist position is best illustrated by ethnographic microanalysis and current work in interactional sociolinguistics and has recently been discussed by Meeuwis (1994) in his rebuttal of different critiques of the interactional sociolinguistic approach.

4. Conclusion

This chapter has reviewed some approaches to and findings about problems and strategies in intercultural communication. Recent studies suggest that both types of discourse event are co-constructed on-line but informed by pretexts and practices that participants can have recourse to during interaction. There is some evidence that a balanced participation structure provides the best opportunities for successful communication (Piirainen-Marsh, 1995; Shea, 1994), but it is unclear whether this is true across discourse domains and speech events. Most studies indicate that verbosity is highly task-dependent, appearing in written responses to discourse completion tasks but not in role-play (Edmondson & House, 1991, Eisenstein & Bodman, 1993; Piirainen-Marsh, 1995). On the other hand, Nyyssönen (1990) did find waffling in conversational discourse. Janney and Arndt (1992) recommend explicitness as a general strategy to counteract conflict in intercultural communication. However, this recommendation may reflect an Anglo-European bias. One may wonder how 'culturally neutral' strategies in intercultural communication can in fact be.

In view of these and many other question marks, a research agenda on communication strategies in intercultural pragmatics and discourse should address such issues as:

- problems and strategies under different context conditions, such as different discourse domains and speech events;
- problems and strategies in different interlocutor constellations (social class, status, ethnicity, social and psychological distance, age, gender, linguistic background);
- functions, forms and use in context of alignment and distancing strategies;
- participation frameworks in relation to problems and strategies;
- the role of culture in creating and solving pragmatic problems;
- the role of transfer in pragmatic problems and strategies;
- the role of L2 proficiency and acculturation;
- strategic options relating to identity maintenance and reconstruction;
- the effect of different strategies, both in the ongoing encounter and over time.

Acknowledging that human beings, among many other things, are limited-capacity information processors, and that non-native speakers and outsiders to a community are even more afflicted by this condition than native speakers and social members, it should be a prime research task to determine what 'satisficing' means in different contexts for the pragmatics of interpersonal communication.

Notes

1. Aston refers to these behaviours as 'maxims'. However, since they describe quite specific goal-related actions and are in part directly observable, it seems more adequate to view these behaviours as strategies.

2. What I refer to as 'myopic' and 'contextualized constructionist' are both versions of social constructionism. A useful recent discussion of (radical) constructivism, (social) constructionism, their epistemologies, methods, and relevance for education is offered in Steffe and Gale (1995).

Bibliography

ABRAHAM, R. (1983). Relationships between use of the strategy of monitoring and the cognitive style. *Studies in Second Language Acquisition, 6,* 17–32.

AITCHISON, J. (1994). *Words in the mind* (2nd edn.). Oxford: Blackwell.

AMMERLAAN, T. (1984). A process-oriented approach to lexical strategies in referential communication. Unpublished master's thesis, Nijmegen University, Nijmegen, The Netherlands.

ANDERSON, F. (1995). Classroom discourse and language socialization in a Japanese elementary-school setting: An ethnographic-linguistic study. Unpublished doctoral dissertation, University of Hawaii at Manoa, HI.

ANDERSON, J. (1983). *The architecture of cognition.* Cambridge, MA: Harvard University Press.

APITZSCH, G., & DITTMAR, N. (1987). Contact between German and Turkish adolescents: A case study. In K. Knapp, W. Enninger & A. Knapp-Potthoff (eds), *Analyzing intercultural communication* (pp. 51–72). Berlin: Mouton de Gruyter.

ARD, J. (1987). The foreign TA problem from an acquisition-theoretic point of view. *English for Specific Purposes, X,* 133–4.

ASTON, G. (1993). Notes on the interlanguage of comity. In G. Kasper & S. Blum-Kulka (eds), *Interlanguage pragmatics* (pp. 224–50). New York: Oxford University Press.

ATKINSON, J., & HERITAGE, J. (eds) (1984). *Structures of social action: Studies in conversation analysis.* Cambridge: Cambridge University Press.

AUER, J. (1988). A conversation analytic approach to code-switching and transfer. In M. Heller (ed.), *Code-switching: Anthropological and sociolinguistic perspectives* (pp. 187–213). Berlin: Mouton de Gruyter.

AUER, J. (1991). *Bilingualism in/as social action: A sequential approach to code-switching.* Paper presented at the ESF Symposium on Code-switching in Bilingual Studies, Strasbourg, France.

AUER, J., & DI LUZIO, A. (1983). Three types of linguistic variation and their interpretation. In L. Dabene, M. Flasaquier & J. Lyons (eds), *Status of migrants' mother tongues.* Strasbourg: ESF.

BACHMAN, L. (1990). *Fundamental considerations in language testing.* Oxford: Oxford University Press.

BARDOVI-HARLIG, K., & HARTFORD, B. (1990). Congruence in native and nonnative conversations: Status balance in the academic advising session. *Language Learning, 40,* 467–501.

BATES, E., FRIEDERICI, A., & WULFECK, B. (1987). Comprehension in aphasia: A cross-linguistic study. *Brain and Language, 32,* 19–67.

BATES, E., FRIEDERICI, A., WULFECK, B., & JUAREZ, L. (1988). On the preservation of word order in aphasia: Cross-linguistic evidence. *Brain and Language, 33,* 323–64.

BATES, E., & MACWHINNEY, B. (1987). Competition, variation, and language learning. In B. MacWhinney (ed.), *Mechanisms of language acquisition* (pp. 157–93). Hillsdale, NJ: Erlbaum.

BATES, E., & WULFECK, B. (1989). Comparative aphasiology: A cross-linguistic approach to language breakdown. *Aphasiology, 2,* 111–42.

BATES, E., WULFECK, B., & MACWHINNEY, B. (1991). Cross-linguistic research in aphasia: An overview. *Brain and Language, 41,* 123–48.

BEEBE, L. (1985). Input: Choosing the right stuff. In S. Gass & C. Madden (eds), *Input in second language acquisition.* Rowley, MA: Newbury House.

BEEBE, L., & TAKAHASHI, T. (1989). Do you have a bag? Social status and patterned variation in second language acquisition. In S. Gass, C. Madden, D. Preston & L. Selinker (eds), *Variation in second language acquisition: Discourse and pragmatics* (pp. 103–25). Clevedon, UK: Multilingual Matters.

BEHRMANN, M., & BUB, D. (1992). Surface dyslexia and dysgraphia: Dual routes, single lexicon. *Cognitive Neuropsychology, 9,* 209–52.

BÉLAND, R., CAPLAN, D., & NESPOULOUS, J.-L. (1990). The role of abstract phonological representations in word production: Evidence from phonemic paraphasias. *Journal of Neurolinguistics, 5,* 125–64.

BELL, A. (1984). Language style as audience design. *Language in Society, 13,* 145–220.

BENSON, D. (1988). Classical syndromes of aphasia. In F. Boller & J. Grafman (eds), *Handbook of neuropsychology* (Vol. 1, pp. 267–80). Amsterdam: Elsevier.

BERGMAN, M., & KASPER, G. (1993). Perception and performance in native and nonnative apologizing. In G. Kasper & S. Blum-Kulka (eds), *Interlanguage pragmatics* (pp. 82–107). New York: Oxford University Press.

BERRY-BRAVO, J. (1993). Teaching the art of circumlocution. *Hispania, 76,* 371–7.

BIALYSTOK, E. (1983a). Inferencing: Testing the hypothesis testing hypothesis. In H. Seliger & M. Long (eds), *Classroom oriented research in second language acquisition* (pp. 104–23). Rowley, MA: Newbury House.

BIALYSTOK, E. (1983b). Some factors in the selection and implementation of communication strategies. In C. Færch & G. Kasper (eds), *Strategies in interlanguage communication* (pp. 100–18). London: Longman.

BIALYSTOK, E. (1984). Strategies in interlanguage learning and performance. In A. Davies, C. Criper & A. Howatt (eds), *Interlanguage* (pp. 37–48). Edinburgh: Edinburgh University Press.

BIALYSTOK, E. (1985). Psycholinguistic dimensions of second language proficiency. In W. Rutherford & M. Sharwood Smith (eds), *Grammar and second language teaching* (pp. 31–50). New York: Newbury House.

BIALYSTOK, E. (1990). *Communication strategies: A psychological analysis of second-language use.* Oxford: Blackwell.

BIALYSTOK, E. (1991). Metalinguistic dimensions of bilingual language proficiency. In E. Bialystok (ed.), *Language processing in bilingual children* (pp. 113–40). Cambridge: Cambridge University Press.

BIALYSTOK, E. (1992). Selective attention in cognitive processing: The bilingual edge. In R. Harris (ed.), *Cognitive processing in bilinguals* (pp. 501–13). Amsterdam: North Holland.

BIALYSTOK, E. (1993). Metalinguistic awareness: Development of children's representations of language. In C. Pratt & A. Garton (eds), *Systems of representation in children: development and use* (pp. 211–33). Chichester: John Wiley & Sons.

BIALYSTOK, E. (1994). Analysis and control in the development of second language proficiency. *Studies in Second Language Acquisition, 16,* 157–68.

BIALYSTOK, E., & FRÖHLICH, M. (1980). Oral communication strategies for lexical difficulties. *Interlanguage Studies Bulletin, 5*(1), 3–29.

BIALYSTOK, E., & KELLERMAN, E. (1987). Language strategies in the classroom. In B. Das (ed.), *Communication and learning in the classroom community* (pp. 160–75). Singapore: SEAMEO RELC.

BIALYSTOK, E., & MITTERER, J. (1987). Metalinguistic differences among three kinds of readers. *Journal of Educational Psychology, 79,* 147–53.

BIALYSTOK, E., & RYAN, E. (1985). A metacognitive framework for the development of first and second language skills. In D. Forrest-Pressley, G. Mackinnon & T. Waller (eds), *Metacognition, cognition, and human performance* (Vol. 1, pp. 207–52). New York: Academic Press.

BILMES, J. (1986). *Discourse and behavior.* New York: Plenum Press.

BLAKEMORE, D. (1992). *Understanding utterances.* Oxford: Blackwell.

BLOOM, L., LAHEY, J., HOOD, L., LIFTER, K., & FIESS, K. (1980). Complex sentences: Acquisition of syntactic connectives and the semantic relations they encode. *Journal of Child Language, 7,* 235–61.

BLUM-KULKA, S. (1991). Interlanguage pragmatics: The case of requests. In R. Phillipson, E. Kellerman, L. Selinker, M. Sharwood Smith & M. Swain (eds), *Foreign/second language pedagogy research* (pp. 255–72). Clevedon: Multilingual Matters.

BLUM-KULKA, S., & LEVENSTON, E. (1983). Universals of lexical simplification. In C. Færch & G. Kasper (eds), *Strategies in interlanguage communication* (pp. 119–39). London: Longman.

BLUM-KULKA, S., & OLSHTAIN, E. (1986). Too many words: Length of utterance and pragmatic failure. *Studies in Second Language Acquisition, 8,* 165–80.

BLUM-KULKA, S., & WEIZMAN, E. (1988). The inevitability of misunderstandings. *Text, 8,* 219–41.

BLUMSTEIN, S., & MILBERG, W. (1983). Automatic and controlled processing in speech-language deficits in aphasia. Symposium on automatic speech, October 1983. *Abstracts of the 21st Annual Meeting of the Academy ofAphasia,* Minneapolis, MN.

BONGAERTS, T., & POULISSE, N. (1989). Communication strategies in L1 and L2: Same or different? *Applied Linguistics, 10,* 253–68.

BONGAERTS, T., & POULISSE, N. (1990, April). *A closer look at the strategy of transfer.* Paper presented at the 9th World Congress of Applied Linguistics, Thessaloniki, Greece.

BONGAERTS, T., KELLERMAN, E., & BENTLAGE, A. (1987). Perspective and proficiency in L2 referential communication. *Studies in Second Language Acquisition, 9,* 171–200.

BONITATIBUS, G. (1988). What is said and what is meant in referential communication. In J. Astington, P. Harris & D. Olson (eds), *Developing theories of mind.* Cambridge: Cambridge University Press.

BRENNAN, S. (1990). Seeking and providing evidence for mutual understanding. Doctoral dissertation, Stanford University, Stanford, CA.

BRENT-PALMER, C. (1979). A sociolinguistic assessment of the notion of 'immigrant semilingualism' from a social conflict perspective. *Working Papers on Bilingualism, 17,* 135–80.

BRODERSEN, D., & GIBSON, K. (1982). Kommunikationsstrategies i folkeskolen, *Sproglæreren, 7,* 26–36.

BROWN, A., & FERRARA, R. (1985). Diagnosing zones of proximal development. In J. Wertsch (ed.), *Culture, communication and cognition: Vygotskian perspectives* (pp. 273–305). New York: Cambridge University Press.

BROWN, G., & YULE, G. (1983). *Discourse analysis.* Cambridge: Cambridge University Press.

BROWN, P., & LEVINSON, S. (1987). *Politeness: Some universals in language usage.* Cambridge: Cambridge University Press.

BROWN, R. (1965). *Social psychology.* New York: The Free Press.

BRUHN, N. (1990). Die Objektreferenz bei monolingualen und bilingualen Kindern [Object reference in monolingual and bilingual children]. Unpublished diploma thesis, Technische Universität Braunschweig, Braunschweig, Germany.

BUB, D., CANCELLIERE, A., & KERTESZ, A. (1985). Whole-word and analytic translation of spelling-to-sound in a non-semantic reader. In K. Patterson, M. Coltheart & J. Marshall (eds), *Surface dyslexia* (pp. 15–34). London: Erlbaum.

BURT, S. (1990). External and internal conflict: Conversational code-switching and the theory of politeness. *Sociolinguistics, 19,* 21–35,

BURT, S. (1992). Code-switching, convergence and compliance: The development of micro-community speech norms. *Journal of Multilingual and Multicultural Development, 13,* 169–95.

BURT, S. (1993, August). *Code choice in intercultural conversation: Speech accommodation theory and pragmatics.* Paper presented at the 10th World Congress of Applied Linguistics, Amsterdam, The Netherlands.

BUTTERWORTH, B. (1982). Speech errors: Old data in search of new theories. In A. Cutler (ed.), *Slips of the tongue in language production* (pp. 73–108). The Hague: Mouton.

BUTTERWORTH, B., & HOWARD, D. (1987). Paragrammatism. *Cognition, 26,* 1–38.

CAMERON, D., & BOURNE, J. (1988). No common ground: Kingman, grammar and the nation. *Language and Education, 2*(3), 147–60.

CANALE, M., & SWAIN, M. (1980). Theoretical bases of communicative approaches to second language teaching and testing. *Applied Linguistics, 1,* 1–47.

CAPLAN, D. (1985). Syntactic and semantic structures in agrammatism. In M.-L. Kean (ed.), *Agrammatism* (pp. 125–52). New York: Academic Press.

CAPLAN, D. (1987). *Neurolinguistic and linguistic aphasiology.* Cambridge: Cambridge University Press.

CAPLAN, D. (1992). *Language: Structure, processing, and disorders.* Cambridge, MA: MIT Press.

CAPLAN, D., VANIER, M., & BAKER, C. (1986). A case study of reproduction conduction aphasia: I. Word production. *Cognitive Neuropsychology, 3,* 99–128.

CARAMAZZA, A., & HILLIS, A. (1990). Where do semantic errors come from? *Cortex, 26,* 95–122.

CARMICHAEL, L., HOGAN, H., & WALTER, A. (1932). An experimental study of the effect of language on the reproduction of visually perceived form. *Journal of Experimental Psychology, 15,* 73–86.

CARROLL, J. (1980). Naming and describing in social communication. *Language and Speech, 23,* 309–22.

CHALLIS, B., & BARTOSZKO, I. (in preparation). *Within- and between-language priming in Polish–English bilinguals.* University of Toronto, Toronto, Canada.

CHAPELLE, C., & JAMIESON, J. (1986). Computer-assisted language learning as a predictor of success in acquiring English as a second language. *TESOL Quarterly, 20,* 27–46.

CHEN, S.-Q. (1990). A study of communication strategies in interlanguage production by Chinese EFL learners. *Language Learning, 40,* 155–87.

CHICK, J. (1985). The interactional accomplishment of discrimination in South Africa. *Language in Society, 14,* 299–326.

CICOUREL, A. (1972). *Cognitive sociology.* New York: Free Press.

CLARK, E. (1985). The acquisition of Romance, with special reference to French. In D. Slobin (ed.), *The crosslinguistic study of language acquisition: Vol. 1. The data* (pp. 702–43). Hillsdale, NJ: Erlbaum.

CLARK, H. (1982). The relevance of common ground: Comments on Sperber and Wilson's Paper. In N. Smith (ed.), *Mutual knowledge* (pp. 124–7). New York: Academic Press.

CLARK, H. (1985). Language use and language users. In G. Lindzey, & E. Aronson (eds), *Handbook of social psychology* (3rd edn., Vol. 2, pp. 179–231). Reading, MA: Addison-Wesley.

CLARK, H., & BRENNAN, S. (1991). Grounding in communication. In L. Resnick, J. Levine & S. Teasley (eds), *Perspectives on socially shared cognition*. Washington, DC: American Psychological Association.

CLARK, H., & CARLSON, T. (1982). Speech acts and hearers' belief. In N. Smith (ed.), *Mutual knowledge* (pp. 1–36). New York: Academic Press.

CLARK, H., & CLARK, E. (1977). *Psychology and language*. New York: Harcourt Brace Jovanovich.

CLARK, H., & MARSHALL, C. (1981). Definite reference and mutual knowledge. In A. Joshi, B. Webber & I. Sag (eds), *Elements of discourse understanding* (pp. 10–63). Cambridge: Cambridge University Press.

CLARK, H., & SCHAEFER, E. (1987a). Collaborating on contributions to conversations. *Language and Cognitive Processes, 2*, 19–41.

CLARK, H., & SCHAEFER, E. (1987b). Concealing one's meaning from overhearers. *Journal of Memory and Language, 26*, 209–25.

CLARK, H., & SCHAEFER, E. (1989). Contributing to discourse. *Cognitive Science, 13*, 259–94.

CLARK, H., & WILKES-GIBBS, D. (1986). Referring as a collaborative process. *Cognition, 22*, 1–39.

CLYNE, M. (1977). Intercultural communication breakdown and communication conflict: Towards a linguistic model and its exemplification. In C. Molony, H. Zobl, & W. Stölting (eds), *Deutsch im Kontakt mit anderen Sprachen* (pp. 129–46). Kronberg, Germany: Scriptor.

COHEN, A. (1987). Using verbal reports in research on language learning. In C. Færch & G. Kasper (eds), *Introspection in second language research* (pp. 82–95). Clevedon, UK: Multilingual Matters.

COLLINS, A., & LOFTUS, E. (1975). A spreading-activation theory of semantic processing. *Psychological Review, 82*, 407–28.

COLLINS, R. (1981). On the microfoundations of macrosociology. *American Journal of Sociology, 86* (5), 984–1014.

COLTHEART, M., PATTERSON, K., & MARSHALL, J. (eds) (1980). *Deep dyslexia*. London: Routledge & Kegan Paul.

COMMISSION FOR RACIAL EQUALITY (CRE) (1986). *Teaching English as a second language: Report of a formal investigation in Calderdale Local Education Authority*. London: CRE.

COOK, V. (1993). LINGUISTICS AND SECOND LANGUAGE ACQUISITION. London: Macmillan.

CORDER, S. (1981). *Error analysis and interlanguage.* Oxford: Oxford University Press.

COUPLAND, N., GILES, H., & WIEMANN, J. (eds) (1991). *'Miscommunication' and problematic talk.* Newbury Park, CA: Sage.

COUPLAND, N., WIEMANN, J., & GILES, H. (1991). Talk as 'problem' and communication as 'miscommunication': An integrative analysis. In Coupland, N., Giles H. & Wiemann, J. (eds), *'Miscommunication' and problematic talk.* Newbury Park, CA: Sage.

CUMMINS, J. (1983). Language proficiency and academic achievement. In J. Oller (ed.), *Issues in language testing research* (pp. 108–26). Rowley, MA: Newbury House.

CUMMINS, J. (1984). *Bilingualism and special education.* Clevedon, UK: Multilingual Matters.

CUTLER, A. (1983). Speakers' conceptions of the functions of prosody. In A. Cuder & D. Ladd (eds), *Prosody: Models and measurements* (pp. 79–156). Heidelberg: Springer.

DAY, D. (1994). Tang's dilemma and other problems: Ethnification processes at some multilingual workplaces. *Pragmatics, 4,* 315–36.

DE BOT, K. (1992). A bilingual production model: Levelt's 'speaking' model adapted. *Applied linguistics, 13* (1), 1–24.

DE GROOT, A. (1992). Determinants of word translation. *Journal of Experimental Psychology: Learning, Memory, and Cognition, 18,* 1000–18.

DE GROOT, A. (1993). Word-type effects in bilingual processing tasks: Support for a mixed representational system. In R. Schreuder & B. Weltens (eds), *The bilingual lexicon* (pp. 27–51). Amsterdam: John Benjamins.

DE PARTZ, M.-P. (1986). Re-education of a deep dyslexic patient: Rationale of the method and results. *Cognitive Neuropsychology, 3,* 149–77.

DE TEMPLE, J., WU, H., & SNOW, C. (1991). Papa Pig just left for Pigtown: Children's oral and written picture descriptions under varying instructions. *Discourse Processes, 14,* 469–95.

DECHERT, H. (1983). How a story is done in a second language. In C. Færch & G. Kasper (eds), *Strategies in interlanguage communication* (pp. 175–95). London: Longman.

DELL, G. (1986). A spreading activation theory of retrieval in sentence production. *Psychological Review, 93,* 283–321.

DEPARTMENT OF EDUCATION AND SCIENCE (DES) (1985). *Education for all: The report of the Committee of Enquiry into the education of children from ethnic minority groups (the Swann Report).* London: HMSO.

DEUTSCH, W. (1986). Sprechen und Verstehen: Zwei Seiten einer Medaille? [Speaking and understanding: Two sides of the same coin?] In H.-G. Bosshardt (ed.), *Perspektiven auf Sprache* (pp. 232–63). Berlin: Mouton de Gruyter.

DEUTSCH, W. (1989). Vom Ende zum Anfang: Ein Prozessmodell für die

Entwicklung referentieller Kommunikation. [From the beginning to the end: A process model for the development of referential communication]. *Zeitschrift Literaturwissenschaft und Linguistik, 73,* 18–32.

DEUTSCH, W., & PECHMANN, T. (1982). Social interaction and the development of definite description. *Cognition, 11,* 159–84.

DICKSON, W., MIYAKE, N., & MUTO, T. (1977). Referential relativity: Culture-boundedness of analytic and metaphoric communication. *Cognition, 5,* 215–33.

DÖRNYEI, Z. (1995). On the teachability of communication strategies. *TESOL Quarterly, 29,* 55–85.

DÖRNYEI, Z., CSOMAY, E. & FISCHER, A. (1992). *On the teachability of communication strategies.* Unpublished manuscript, English Department, Eötvos University, Budapest, Hungary.

DÖRNYEI, Z., & THURRELL, S. (1991). *Conversation and dialogues in action.* Hemel Hempstead: Prentice-Hall.

DOUGLAS, D., & MYERS, C. (1989). TAs on TV: Demonstrating communication strategies for international teaching assistants. *ESP Journal, 2,* 169–79.

DURANTI, A., & GOODWIN, C. (eds) (1992). *Rethinking context.* Cambridge: Cambridge University Press.

EDMONDSON, W., & HOUSE, J. (1991). Do learners talk too much? The waffle phenomenon in interlanguage pragmatics. In R. Phillipson, E. Kellerman, L Selinker, M. Sharwood Smith & M. Swain (eds), *Foreign/second language pedagogy research* (pp. 273–86). Clevedon, UK: Multilingual Matters.

EDWARDS, D., & MERCER, N. (1987). *Common knowledge.* London: Methuen.

EDWARDS, J. (1979). *Language and disadvantage.* London: Edward Arnold.

EISENSTEIN, M., & BODMAN, J. (1993). Expressing gratitude in American English. In G. Kasper & S. Blum-Kulka (eds), *Interlanguage pragmatics* (pp. 64–81). New York: Oxford University Press.

ELLIS, R. (1984). *Classroom language development.* Oxford: Pergamon.

ELLIS, R. (1986). *Understanding second language acquisition.* Oxford: Oxford University Press.

ELLIS, R. (1990). *Instructed second language acquisition.* Oxford: Blackwell.

ELLIS, R. (1994). *The study of second language acquisition.* Oxford: Oxford University Press.

ERICKSON, F. (1981). Timing and context in everyday discourse: Implications for the study of referential and social meaning. In W.P. Dickson (ed.), *Children's oral communication skills* (pp. 241–69). New York: Academic Press.

ERICKSON, F., & SHULTZ, J. (1982). *The counsellor as gatekeeper: Social interaction in interviews.* New York: Academic Press.

ERICSSON, K., & SIMON, H. (1980). Verbal reports as data. *Psychological Review, 87,* 215–51.

ERICSSON, K., & SIMON, H. (1984). *Protocol Analysis.* Cambridge, MA: MIT Press.

ERTEL, S. (1971). Pränominale Adjektivfolgen und semantische Tiefenstruktur. [Prenominal adjective ordering and semantic deep structure). *Studia Psychologica, 13,* 127–35.

FÆRCH, C. (1984). Strategies in production and reception: Some empirical evidence. In A. Davies, C. Criper & A. Howatt (eds), *Interlanguage* (pp. 49–70). Edinburgh: Edinburgh University Press.

FÆRCH, C., HAASTRUP, K., & PHILLIPSON, R. (1984). *Learner language and language learning.* Clevedon, UK: Multilingual Matters.

FÆRCH, C., & KASPER, G. (1980). Processes and strategies in foreign language learning and communication. *Interlanguage Studies Bulletin* Utrecht, *5,* 47–118.

FÆRCH, C., & KASPER, G. (1982). Phatic, metalingual and metacommunicative functions in discourse: Gambits and repair. In N.E. Enkvist (ed.), *Impromptu speech* (pp. 71–103). Åbo, Finland: Åbo Akademi.

FÆRCH, C. & KASPER, G. (eds) (1983a). *Strategies in interlanguage communication.* London: Longman.

FÆRCH, C., & KASPER, G. (1983b). Introduction. In C. Færch & G. Kasper (eds), *Strategies in interlanguage communication* (pp. xv–xxiv). London: Longman.

FÆRCH, C., & KASPER, G. (1983c). On identifying communication strategies in interlanguage production. In C. Færch & G. Kasper (eds), *Strategies in interlanguage communication* (pp. 210–38). London: Longman.

FÆRCH, C., & KASPER, G. (1983d). Plans and strategies in foreign language communication. In C. Færch & G. Kasper (eds), *Strategies in interlanguage communication* (pp. 20–60). London: Longman.

FÆRCH, C., & KASPER, G. (1984). Two ways of defining communication strategies. *Language Learning, 34,* 45–63.

FÆRCH, C., & KASPER, G. (1986). Strategic competence in foreign language teaching. In G. Kasper (ed.), *Learning teaching and communication in the foreign language classroom* (pp. 179–93). Århus, Denmark: Århus University Press.

FÆRCH, C., & KASPER, G. (eds) (1987a). *Introspection in second language research.* Clevedon, UK: Multilingual Matters.

FÆRCH, C., & KASPER, G. (1987b). From product to process: Introspective methods in second language research. In C. Færch & G. Kasper (eds), *Introspection in second language research* (pp. 5–23). Clevedon, UK: Multilingual Matters.

FÆRCH, C., & KASPER, G. (1989). Internal and external modification in interlanguage request realization. In S. Blum-Kulka, J. House & G. Kasper (eds), *Cross-cultural pragmatics* (pp. 221–47). Norwood, NT: Ablex.

FANTUZZI, C. (1992). Connectionism: Explanation or implementation. *Issues in Applied Linguistics, 3,* 319–40.

FATHMAN, A. (1980). Repetition and correction as an indication of speech planning and execution processes among second language learners. In

H. Dechert & M. Raupach (eds), *Towards a cross-linguistic assessment of speech production* (pp. 77–85). New York: Peter Lang.

FIKSDAL, S. (1989). Framing uncomfortable moments in crosscultural gatekeeping interviews. In S. Gass, C. Madden, D. Preston, & L. Selinker (eds), *Variation in second language acquisition: Vol. 1. Discourse and pragmatics* (pp. 190–207). Clevedon, UK: Multilingual Matters.

FIKSDAL, S. (1990). *The right time and pace: A microanalysis of cross-cultural gatekeeping interviews.* Norwood, NJ: Ablex.

FIRTH, A. (1988). *'Interactive fluency' and communication strategies: Bridging the gap.* Department of English Language Research, University of Birmingham, Birmingham, UK.

FIRTH, A. (1990). 'Lingua franca' negotiations: Towards an interactional approach. *World Englishes, 9* (3), 269–80.

FIRTH, A. (in press). Discursive accomplishment of normality: On 'lingua franca' English in conversation analysis. *Journal of Pragmatics 26,* 237–59.

FIRTH, A, & KASPER G. (1990, April). *Problems and solutions in communication strategy.* Paper presented at the 9th World Congress of Applied Linguistics, Thessaloniki, Greece.

FOORMAN, B., & KINOSHITA, Y. (1983). Linguistic effects on children's encoding and decoding performance in Japan, the United States and England. *Child Development, 54,* 148–53.

FROMKIN, V. (ed.). (1973). *Speech errors as linguistic evidence.* The Hague: Mouton.

FROMKIN, V. (1980). *Errors in linguistic performance.* New York: Academic Press.

FURNBOROUGH, P., JUPP, T., MUNNS, R, & ROBERTS, C. (1982). Language, disadvantage and discrimination: Breaking the cycle of majority group perception. *Journal of Multilingual and Multicultural Development, 3* (3), 247–66.

GAGNON, J., GOULET, P., & JOANETTE, Y. (1989). Activation automatique et contrôlée du savoir lexico-sémantique chez les cérébrolésés droits. *Languages, 96,* 95–111.

GALVÁN. J., & CAMPBELL, R. (1979). An examination of the communication strategies of two children in the Culver City Spanish Immersion Program. In R. Andersen (ed.), *The acquisition and use of Spanish and English as first and second languages* (pp. 133–50). Washington, DC: TESOL.

GARFINKEL, H. (1967). *Studies in ethnomethodology.* Oxford: Polity Press.

GARRETT, M. (1980). Levels of processing in sentence production. In B. Butterworth (ed.), *Language production, Vol. 1. Speech and talk* (pp. 177–220). London: Academic Press.

GARRETT, M. (1984). The organization of processing structure for language production: Applications to aphasic speech. In D. Caplan, L. Lecours & A. Smith (eds), *Biological perspectives of language* (pp. 172–93). Cambridge, MA: MIT Press.

GARVEY, C. (1979). Contingent queries and their relations in discourse. In E. Ochs & B. Schieffelin (eds), *Developmental pragmatics* (pp. 363–72). New York: Academic Press.

GASS, S., & SELINKER, L. (1994). *Second language acquisition.* Hillsdale, NJ: Erlbaum.

GASSER, M. (1988). *A connectionist model of sentence generation in a first and second language.* Unpublished doctoral dissertation, University of California, Los Angeles.

GASSER, M. (1990). Connectionism and universals of second language acquisition. *Studies in Second Language Acquisition, 12,* 170–00.

GILES, H., COUPLAND, J., & COUPLAND, N. (eds) (1991) *Contexts of accommodation.* Cambridge: Cambridge University Press.

GLAHN, E. (1980). Introspection as a method of elicitation in interlanguage studies. *Interlanguage Studies Bulletin Utrecht, 5,* 119–28.

GLUCKSBERG, S., KRAUSS, R., & WEISBERG, R. (1966). Referential communication in nursery school children: Method and some preliminary findings. *Journal of Experimental Child Psychology, 3,* 333–42.

GOFFMAN, E. (1971). *Relations in public.* London: Allen Lane.

GOFFMAN, E. (1979). Footing. *Semiotica, 25,* 1–29.

GOLDSTEIN, K. (1948). *Language and language disturbances: Aphasic symptom complexes and their significance for medicine and theory of language.* New York: Grune & Stratton.

GOODGLASS, H. (1990). Inferences from cross-modal comparisons of agrammatism. In L. Menn & L. Obler (eds), *Agrammatic aphasia: A cross-language narrative sourcebook* (Vol. 2, pp. 1365–8). Amsterdam: John Benjamins.

GOODGLASS, H., & KAPLAN, E. (1972). *The assessment of aphasia and related disorders.* Philadelphia: Lea & Febiger.

GOODWIN, C. (1981). *Conversational organization: interaction between speakers and hearers.* New York: Academic Press.

GRICE, H. (1975). Logic and conversation. In P. Cole & J. Morgan (eds), *Syntax and semantics* (Vol. 3, pp. 41–58). New York: Academic Press.

GRICE, H. (1978). Some further notes on logic and conversation. In P. Cole (ed.), *Syntax and semantics* (Vol. 9, p. 113–28). New York: Academic Press.

GROSJEAN, F. (1982). *Life with two languages: An introduction to bilingualism.* Cambridge, MA: Harvard University Press.

GROSZ, B., & SIDNER, C. (1986). Attention, intentions, and the structure of discourse. *Computational Linguistics, 12,* 175–203.

GUMPERZ, J. (1982). *Discourse strategies.* Cambridge: Cambridge University Press.

GUMPERZ, J., JUPP, T., & ROBERTS, C. (1979). *Crosstalk: A study of cross-cultural communication.* London: National Centre for Industrial Language Training.

HAASTRUP, K. (1987). Using thinking aloud and retrospection to uncover learners' lexical inferencing procedures. In C. Færch & G. Kasper (eds), *Introspection in second language research* (pp. 197–212). Clevedon, UK: Multilingual Matters.

HAASTRUP, K. (1991). *Lexical inferencing procedures or talking about words.* Tübingen: Gunter Narr Verlag.

HAASTRUP, K., & PHILLIPSON, R. (1983). Achievement strategies in learner/native speaker interaction. In C. Færch & G. Kasper (eds), *Strategies in interlanguage communication* (pp. 140–58). London: Longman.

HABERMAS, J. (1971). Vorbereitende Bemerkungen zu einer Theorie der kommunikativen Kompetenz. In J. Habermas & N. Luhmann (eds), *Theorie der Gesellschaft oder Sozialtechnologie?* (pp. 101–41). Frankfurt: Suhrkamp.

HABIB, M., JOANETTE, Y., & PUEL, M. (1991). *Démances et syndromes démentiels: Approche neuropsychologique.* Paris: Masson.

HAKUTA, K., & FERDMAN, B. (1984). *Characteristics of Hispanic students in the New Haven public schools: A survey.* Unpublished manuscript, Yale University, New Haven, CT.

HALL, S. (1988). New ethnicities. *ICA Documents, 7,* 27–31.

HANSEN, J., & STANSFIELD, C. (1981). The relationship of field dependent–independent cognitive styles to foreign language achievement. *Language Learning, 31,* 349–67.

HATCH, E. (1978). Discourse analysis and second language acquisition. In E. Hatch, E. (ed.), *Second language acquisition: A book of readings* (pp. 401–35). Rowley, MA: Newbury House.

HATCH, E., & HAWKINS, B. (1985). Second-language acquisition: An experiential approach. In S. Rosenberg (ed.), *Advances in applied psycholinguistics* (Vol. 2, pp. 241–308). New York: Cambridge University Press.

HEATH, S. (1983). *Ways with words: Language, life, and work in communities and classrooms.* Cambridge: Cambridge University Press.

HENNING, G. (1987). *A guide to language testing.* Rowley, MA: Newbury House.

HENNING, G. (1992). Dimensionality and construct validity of language tests. *Language Testing, 14,* 1–10.

HERITAGE, J. (1984). *Garfinkel and ethnomethodology.* Oxford: Polity Press.

HERITAGE, J., & WATSON, D. (1980). Aspects of the properties of formulations in natural conversations: Some instances analysed. *Semiotica, 30,* 245–62.

HERRMANN, T., & DEUTSCH, W. (1976). *Psychologie der Objektbenennung.* [The psychology of object naming]. Bern: Huber.

HEWITT, R. (1986). *White talk, black talk: Inter-racial friendship and communication amongst adolescents.* Cambridge: Cambridge University Press.

HILL, J., & COOMBS, D. (1982). The vernacular remodelling of national and international languages. *Applied Linguistics, 3,* 224–34.

HINNENKAMP, V. (1980). The refusal of second language learning in interethnic contex. In H. Giles, P. Robinson & P. Smith (eds), *Language: Social psychological perspectives* (pp. 179–84). Oxford: Pergamon.

HINNENKAMP, V. (1987). Foreigner talk, code-switching and the concept of trouble. In K. Knapp, W. Enninger & A. Knapp-Potthof (eds), *Analyzing intercultural communication* (pp. 137–80). Amsterdam: Mouton.

HOEKJE, B., & WILLIAMS, J. (1992). Communicative competence and the dilemma of international teaching assistant education. *TESOL Quarterly, 21* (2), 243–69.

HOLLAND, A.-L. (1977). Some practical considerations in aphasia rehabilitation. In M. Sullivan & M. Kommers (eds), *Rationale for adult aphasia therapy* (pp. 167–80). University of Nebraska Medical Center, Omaha, NE.

HONEY, J. (1983). The language trap: Race, class, and 'standard English' in British schools. Kenton, Middx: National Council for Educational Standards. Extracts reprinted in N. Mercer (ed.) (1983). *Language and literacy from an educational perspective: A reader* (Vol. 1, pp.163–89). Milton Keynes: Open University Press.

HOUSE, J. (1989). 'Oh excuse me please...': Apologizing in a foreign language. In B. Ketteman, P. Bierbaumer, A. Fill & A. Karpf (eds), *English als Zweitsprache* [English as a second language] (pp. 303–27). Tübingen: Narr.

HYMES, D. (1971). *On communicative competence.* Philadelphia: University of Pennsylvania Press.

HYMES, D. (1972a). Introduction. In C. Cazden, V. John & D. Hymes (eds), *Functions of language in the classroom* (pp. xi–lvii). New York: New York Teachers College Press.

HYMES, D. (1972b). On communicative competence. In J. Pride & J. Holmes (eds), *Sociolinguistics: Selected readings* (pp. 269–93). Harmondsworth: Penguin.

ISAACS, E., & CLARK, H. (1987). References in conversation between experts and novices. *Journal of Experimental Psychology: General,* 116, 26–37.

JACOBS, B., & SCHUMANN, J. (1992). Language acquisition and the neurosciences: Towards a more integrative perspective. *Applied Linguistics, 13,* 282–301.

JANNEY, R., & ARNDT, H. (1992). Intracultural tact versus interculutral tact. In R. Watts, S. Ide & K. Ehlich (eds), *Politeness in language* (pp. 21–41). Berlin: Mouton de Gruyter.

JAREMA, G., & KADZIELAWA, D. (1990). Agrammatism in Polish: A case study. In L. Menn & L. Obler (eds), *Agrammatic aphasia: A cross-language narrative sourcebook* (Vol. 2, pp. 817–93). Amsterdam: John Benjamins.

JOANETTE, Y., GOULET, P., & HANNEQUIN, D. (1990). *Right hemisphere and verbal communication.* New York: Springer.

JOANETTE, Y., KELLER, E., & LECOURS, A. (1980). Sequences of phonemic approximations in aphasia. *Brain and Language, 11*, 30–44.

KARMILOFF-SMITH, A. (1986). Stage/structure versus phase/process in modelling linguistic and cognitive development. In I. Levin (ed.), *Stage and structure: Reopening the debate* (pp. 164–90). Norwood, NJ: Ablex.

KASHER, A. (1977). Foundations of philosophical pragmatics. In R. Butts & J. Hintikka (eds), *Basic problems in methodology and linguistics.* Dordrecht: Reidel.

KASPER, G. (1979). Communication strategies: Modality reduction. *Interlanguage Studies Bulletin Utrecht, 4*, 266–83.

KASPER, G. (1981). *Pragmatische Aspekte in der Interimsprache.* Tübingen: Narr.

KASPER, G. (1982). Teaching-induced aspects of interlanguage discourse. *Studies in Second Language Acquisition, 4*, 91–113.

KASPER, G. (1989). Variation in interlanguage speech act realization. In S. Gass, C. Madden, D. Preston & L. Selinker (eds), *Variation in second language acquisition: Discourse and pragmatics* (pp. 37–58). Clevedon, UK: Multilingual Matters.

KASPER, G. (1995). Routine and indirection in interlanguage pragmatics. In L. Bouton (ed.), *Pragmatics and language learning* (Vol. 6, pp. 59–78). Urbana, IL: University of Illinois at Urbana-Champaign.

KASPER, G. (in press). Interlanguage pragmatics. In H. Byrnes (ed.), *Perspectives on research and scholarship in second language learning.* Modern Language Association.

KASPER, G. & BLUM-KULKA, S. (eds) (1993). *Interlanguage pragmatics.* New York: Oxford University Press.

KASPER, G., & SCHMIDT, R. (1996). Developmental issues in interlanguage pragmatics. *Studies in Second Language Acquisition, 18*, 149–69.

KELLERMAN, E. (1991). Compensatory strategies in second language research: A critique, a revision, and some (non-)implications for the classroom. In R. Phillipson, E. Kellerman, L. Selinker, M. Sharwood Smith & M. Swain (eds), *Foreign/second language pedagogy research* (pp. 142–61). Clevedon, UK: Multilingual Matters.

KELLERMAN, E., AMMERLAAN, T., BONGAERTS, T., & POULISSE, N. (1990). System and hierarchy in L2 compensatory strategies. In R. Scarcella, E. Andersen & S. Krashen (eds), *Developing communicative competence in a second language* (pp. 163–78). New York: Newbury House.

KELLERMAN, E., & BIALYSTOK, E. (1990, April). *Towards a psycholinguistic model of compensatory strategy use.* Paper presented at the 9th World Congress of Applied Linguistics, Thessaloniki, Greece.

KELLERMAN, E., BONGAERTS, T., & POULISSE, N. (1987). Strategy and system in L2 referential communication. In R. Ellis (ed.), *Second language acquisition in context* (pp. 100–12). Englewood Cliffs, NJ: Prentice-Hall.

KELLERMANN, K. (1991). The conversation MOP: II. Progression through the scenes of discourse. *Human Communication Research, 17*, 385–414.

KLEIFGEN, J. (1989). Communicative inferencing without a common language. In S. Gass, C. Madden, D. Preston & L. Selinker (eds), *Variation in second language acquisition: Discourse and pragmatics* (pp. 84–102). Clevedon, UK: Multilingual Matters.

KLEIN, W. (1990). A theory of language acquisition is not so easy. *Studies in Second Language Acquisition, 12,* 219–31.

KLIMA, E., & BELLUGI, U. (1979). *The signs of language.* Cambridge, MA: Harvard University Press.

KOLK, H., HELING, G., & KEYSER, A. (1990). Agrammatism in Dutch: Two case studies. In L. Menn & L. Obler (eds), *Agrammatic aphasia: A cross-language narrative sourcebook* (Vol. 1, pp. 179–280). Amsterdam: John Benjamins.

KRASHEN, S. (1981). *Second language acquisition and second language learning.* Oxford: Pergamon.

KRASHEN, S. (1985). *The input hypothesis.* London: Longman.

KRAUSS, R., & WEINHEIMER, S. (1964). Changes in reference as a function of frequency of usage in social interaction: A preliminary study. *Psychonomic Science, 1,* 113–14.

KRAUSS, R., & WEINHEIMER, S. (1966). Concurrent feedback, confirmation, and the encoding of referents in verbal communication. *Journal of Personality and Social Psychology, 4,* 343–6.

KRAUSS, R., & WEINHEIMER, S. (1967). Effect of referent similarity and communication mode on verbal encoding. *Journal of Verbal Learning and Verbal Behavior, 6,* 359–63.

LABOV, W. (1969). The logic of non-standard English. *Georgetown Monographs on Language and Linguistics, 22,* Washington DC: Georgetown University Press. Extracts reprinted in N. Mercer (ed.) (1983). *Language and literacy from an educational perspective: A reader* (Vol. 1, pp. 143–62). Milton Keynes: Open University Press.

LABOV, W. (1970). The study of language in its social context. *Studium Generale, 23,* 30–87.

LANAUZE, M., & SNOW, C. (1989). The relation between first- and second-language writing skills: Evidence from Puerto Rican elementary school children in bilingual problems. *Linguistics and Education, 1,* 323–39.

LARSEN-FREEMAN, D., & LONG, M. (1991). *An introduction to second language acquisition research.* London: Longman.

LECOURS, A., & LHERMITTE, F. (1979). *L'aphasie.* Paris: Flammarion.

LECOURS, A., OSBORN, E., TRAVIS, L., ROUILLON, F., & LAVALLÉE-HUYNH, G. (1981). Jargons. In J. Brown (ed.), *Jargonaphasia* (pp. 9–38). New York: Academic Press.

LECOURS, A., TAINTURIER, M.-J., & BOEGLIN, J. (1988). Classification of aphasia. In F. Rose, R. Whurr & M. Wyke (eds), *Aphasia* (pp. 3–22). London: Whurr.

LEDORZE, G., & NESPOULOUS, J.-L. (1989). Anomia in moderate aphasia: Problems in accessing the lexical representations. *Brain and Language, 37,* 381–400.

LEECH, G. (1983). *Principles of pragmatics.* London: Longman.

LEGENHAUSEN, L. (1991). Code-switching in learners' discourse *International Review of Applied Linguistics and Language Teaching (IRAL), 29,* 61–73.

LESSER, R., & MILROY, L. (1993). *Linguistics and aphasia. Psycholinguistic and pragmatic aspects of intervention.* London: Longman.

LEVELT, W. (1983). Monitoring and self-repair in speech. *Cognition, 14,* 41–104.

LEVELT, W. (1989). *Speaking: From intention to articulation.* Cambridge, MA: Bradford Books/MIT Press.

LEVELT, W., SCHRIEFERS, H., VORBERG, D., MEYER, A., PECHMANN, T., & HAVINGA, J. (1991). The time course of lexical access in speech production: A study of picture naming. *Psychological Review, 98,* 122–42.

LEVINSON, S. (1983). *Pragmatics.* Cambridge: Cambridge University Press.

LEVINSON, S. (1987). Minimization and conversational inference. In J. Verschueren & M. Bertuccelli-Papi (eds), *The pragmatic perspective* (pp. 61–129). Amsterdam: John Benjamins.

LEWIS, D. (1969). *Convention.* Cambridge, MA: Harvard University Press.

LINEBARGER, M., SCHWARTZ, M., & SAFFRAN, E. (1983). Sensitivity to grammatical structure in so-called agrammatic aphasics. *Cognition, 13,* 361–92.

LLOYD, P. (1990). Children's communication. In R. Grieve & M. Hughes (eds), *Understanding children: Essays in honor of Margaret Donaldson* (pp. 49–70). Oxford: Blackwell.

LLOYD, P. (1991). Strategies used to communicate route directions by telephone: A comparison of the performance of 7-year-olds, 10-year-olds and adults. *Journal of Child Language, 18,* 175–89.

LLOYD, P. (1992). The role of clarification requests in children's communication of route directions by telephone. *Discourse Processes, 15,* 357–74.

LLOYD, P. (1993). Referential communication as teaching: Adults tutoring their own and other children. *First Language, 13,* 339–57.

LLOYD, P., BOADA, H., & FORNS, M. (1992). New directions in referential communication research. *British Journal of Developmental Psychology, 10,* 385–403.

LLOYD, P., CAMAIONI, L, & ERCOLANI, P. (1995). Assessing referential communication skills in the primary school years: A comparative study. *British Journal of Developmental Psychology, 13,* 13–29.

LOFTUS, E. (1979). *Eyewitness testimony.* Cambridge, MA: Harvard University Press.

LONG, M. (1981). Input, interaction and second language acquisition. In H. Winitz (ed.), *Native language and foreign language acquisition.* Annals of the New York Academy of Sciences (Vol. 379, pp. 259–78). New York: New York Academy of Sciences.

LONG, M. (1983a). Linguistic and conversational adjustments to nonnative speakers. *Studies in Second Language Acquisition, 5,* 177–93.

LONG, M. (1983b). Native speaker/non-native speaker conversation and the negotiation of comprehensible input. *Applied Linguistics, 4,* 126–41.

LOVETT, S., SMALL, M., & ENGSTROM, S. (1992). *The verbal overshadowing effect Now you see it, now you don't.* Paper presented at the annual meeting of the Psychonomic Society, St Louis, MO.

MACLEAN, M. (1984). Using rational cloze for diagnostic testing in L1 and L2 reading. *TESL Canada Journal, 2,* 53–63.

MADDEN, C., & MYERS, C. (eds) (1994). *Discourse and performance of international teaching assistants.* Washington, DC: TESOL.

MARENBON, J. (1991). Extracts from *English our English*: The new orthodoxy examined. In T. Crowley (ed.), *Proper English? Readings in language, history, and cultural identity* (pp. 243–60). London: Routledge. (Originally published 1987.)

MARSHALL, J., & NEWCOMBE, F. (1973). Patterns of paralexia: A psycholinguistic approach. *Journal of Psycholinguistic Research, 3,* 175–99.

MCDERMOTT, R., & GOSPODINOFF, K. (1979). Social contexts for ethnic borders and school failure. In A. Wolfgang (ed.), *Non-verbal behaviour: Application and cultural implications.* New York: Academic Press. Reprinted in H. Trueba, G. Guthrie & K. Au (eds) (1981). *Culture and the bilingual classroom* (pp. 212–30). Rowley, MA: Newbury House.

MCDERMOTT, R., & ROTH, D. (1978). The social organization of behavior: Interactional approaches. *Annual Review of Anthropology, 7,* 321–45.

MCKEOWN, K. (1985). Discourse strategies for generating natural language text. *Artificial Intelligence, 27,* 142.

MCLAUGHLIN, B. (1987). *Theories of second-language learning.* London: Edward Arnold.

MEEUWIS, M. (1994). Leniency and testiness in intercultural communication: Remarks on ideology and context in interactional sociolinguistics. *Pragmatics, 4,* 391–408.

MEICHENBAUM, D. (1985) Teaching thinking: A cognitive-behavioural perspective. In S. Chipman, J. Segal & R. Glaser (eds), *Thinking and learning skills: Current research and open questions* (Vol. 2.). Hillsdale, NJ: Erlbaum.

MEISEL, J. (1986). Word order and case marking in early child language. Evidence from simultaneous acquisition of two first languages: French and German. *Linguistics, 24,* 123–83.

MENN, L. (1989). Comparing approaches to comparative aphasiology. *Aphasiology, 3* (2), 143–50.

MENN, L., & OBLER, L. (1990). Cross-language data and theories of agrammatism. In L. Menn & L. Obler (eds), *Agrammatic aphasia. A cross-language narrative sourcebook* (Vol. 2, pp. 1369–89). Amsterdam: John Benjamins.

MICELI, G., & MAZZUCCHI, A. (1990). Agrammatism in Italian: Two case studies. In L. Menn, & L. Obler (eds), *Agrammatic aphasia: A cross-language narrative sourcebook* (Vol. 1, pp. 717–816). Amsterdam: John Benjamins.

MICHAELS, S. (1981). 'Sharing time': Children's narrative styles and differential access to literacy. *Language in Society, 10,* 423–42.

MILBERG, W., & BLUMSTEIN, S. (1981). Lexical decision and aphasia: Evidence for semantic processing. *Brain and Language, 14,* 371–85.

MILLER, G., & FELLBAUM, C. (1991). Semantic networks of English. *Cognition, 41,* 197–207.

MILLS, A. (1985). The acquisition of German. In D. Slobin (ed.), *The crosslinguistic study of language acquisition, Vol. 1. The Data* (pp. 158–249). Hillsdale, NJ: Erlbaum.

MOERMAN, M. (1988). *Talking culture: Ethnography and conversation analysis.* Philadelphia: University of Pennsylvania Press.

MORTON, J. (1969). The interaction of information in word recognition. *Psychological Review, 76,* 165–78.

MORTON, J., HAMMERSLEY, R., & BEKERIAN, D. (1985). Headed records: A model for memory and its failures. *Cognition, 20,* 1–23.

MOSIORI, K. (1991). The effects of consciousness-raising about communication strategies on the second language strategic performance of adult learners of French as a foreign language. Unpublished doctoral dissertation, University of Toronto, Toronto, Canada.

MOTLEY, M., CAMDEN, C., & BAARS, B. (1982). Covert formulation and editing of anomalies in speech production: Evidence from experimentally elicited slips of the tongue. *Journal of Verbal Learning and Verbal Behavior, 21,* 578–94.

MYERS, D. (1982). Polarizing effects of social interaction. In H. Brandstatter, J. Davis & G. Stocker-Kreichgauer (eds), *Group decision making* (pp. 125–61). New York: Academic Press.

MYERS-SCOTTON, C. (1993a). Common and uncommon ground: Social and structural factors in code-switching. *Language in Society, 22,* 475–503.

MYERS-SCOTTON, C. (1993b). *Social motivations for code-switching. Evidence from Africa.* Oxford: Oxford University Press.

NATION, P. (1990). *Teaching and learning vocabulary.* New York, Newbury House.

NATTINGER, J. (1988). Some current trends in vocabulary teaching. In R. Carter & M. McCarthy (eds), *Vocabulary and language teaching* (pp. 62–82). London: Longman.

NATTINGER, J., & DECARRICO, J. (1992). *Lexical phrases and language teaching.* Oxford: Oxford University Press.

NESPOULOUS, J.-L., DORDAIN, M., PERRON, C., SKA, B., BUB, D., CAPLAN, D., MEHLER, J., & LECOURS, A. (1988). Agrammatism in sentence production without comprehension deficits: Reduced availability of syntactic structures and/or of grammatical morphemes? A case study. *Brain and Language, 33,* 273–95.

NESPOULOUS, J.-L., JOANETTE, Y., BÉLAND, R., CAPLAN, D., & LECOURS, R. (1984). Phonological disturbances in aphasia: Is there a 'markedness' effect in aphasic phonemic errors? In F. Rose (ed.), *Progress in aphasiology: Advances in neurology* (pp. 203–14). New York: Raven Press.

NEWELL, A., & SIMON, H. (1972). *Human problem solving.* Englewood Cliffs, NJ: Prentice Hall.

NYYSSÖNEN, H. (1990). The Oulu project. In H. Nyyssönen, L. Kuure, E. Kaerkaeinen & P. Raudascikoski (eds), *Proceedings from the Second Finnish Seminar on Discourse Analysis* (pp. 7–26). Oulu, Finland: University of Oulu.

O'KEEFE, B. (1991). Message design logic and management of multiple goals. In K. Tracy (ed.), *Understanding face-to-face interaction* (pp. 131–50). Hove, UK: Erlbaum.

O'MALLEY, J., CHAMOT, A., & WALKER, C. (1987). Some applications of cognitive theory to second language acquisition. *Studies in Second Language Acquisition, 9,* 287–306.

OLSHTAIN, E., & WEINBACH, L. (1993). Interlanguage features of the speech act of complaining. In G. Kasper & S. Blum-Kulka (eds), *Interlanguage pragmatics* (pp. 108–22). New York: Oxford University Press.

OLSON, D. (1970). Language and thought: Aspects of a cognitive theory of semantics. *Psychological Review, 77,* 257–73.

OPIE, L, & OPIE, P. (1959). *The lore and language of schoolchildren.* Oxford: Oxford University Press.

OXFORD, R., COHEN, A., & SUTTER, W. (1992). Language learning strategies: Crucial issues of concept and classification. *Applied Language Learning, 3,* 1–35.

PALMBERG, R. (1979). Investigating communication strategies. In R. Palmberg (ed.), *Perception and production of English: Papers on interlanguage* (AFTIL, 6) (pp. 33–75). Åbo, Finland: Åbo Akademi.

PARIBAKHT, T. (1985). Strategic competence and language proficiency. *Applied Linguistics, 6,* 132–46.

PATE, D., SAFFRAN, E., & MARTIN, N. (1987). Specifying the nature of the production impairment in a conduction aphasic: A case study. *Language and Cognitive Processes, 1,* 43–84.

PATTERSON, C., & KISTER, M. (1981). The development of listener skills for referential communication. In W. Dickson (ed.), *Children's oral communication skills* (pp. 143–66). New York: Academic Press.

PATTERSON, K., MARSHALL, J., & COLTHEART, M. (eds) (1985). *Surface Dyslexia: Neuropsychological and cognitive studies of phonological reading.* Hillsdale, NJ: Erlbaum.

PECHMANN, T. (1989). Incremental speech production and referential overspecification. *Linguistics, 27,* 89–110.

PECHMANN, T. (1994). *Sprachproduktion* [Speech production]. Opladen, Germany: Westdeutscher Verlag.

PENN, C. (1984). Compensatory strategies in aphasia: Behavioural and neurological correlates. In K.W. Grieve & R.D. Griesel (eds), *Neuropsychology II.* Pretoria: Monicol.

PICA, T. (1991). Do second language learners need negotiation? *Penn Working Papers in Educational Linguistics*, 7 (2), 1–35.

PICA, T., & DOUGHTY, C. (1985). The role of group work in classroom second language acquisition. *Studies in Second Language Acquisition*, 7, 233–48.

PICA, T., HOLLIDAY, L., LEWIS, N., & MORGENTHALER, L. (1989). Comprehensible output as an outcome of linguistic demands on the learner. *Studies in Second Language Acquisition*, 11, 63–90.

PICA, T., YOUNG, R., & DOUGHTY, C. (1987). The impact of interaction on comprehension. *TESOL Quarterly*, 21 (4), 737–58.

PIENEMANN, M. (1984). Psychological constraints on the teachability of languages. *Studies in Second Language Acquisition*, 6, 186–214.

PIIRAINEN-MARSH, A. (1995). Face in second language conversation. Jyväskylä, Finland: University of Jyväskylä.

POOLE, D. (1992). Language socialization in the second language classroom. *Language Learning*, 42, 593–616.

POULISSE, N. (1987). Problems and solutions in the classification of compensatory strategies. *Second Language Research*, 3, 141–53.

POULISSE, N. (1990). *The use of compensatory strategies by Dutch learners of English*. Dordrecht: Foris.

POULISSE, N. (1993). A theoretical account of lexical communication strategies. In R. Schreuder & B. Weltens (eds), *The bilingual lexicon* (pp. 157–89). Amsterdam: John Benjamins.

POULISSE, N. (in press). Slips of the tongue and their correction in L2 learner speech: Metalinguistic awareness and second language acquisition. In H. Dechert (Ed.), *Proceedings of the symposium 'Metacognition and second language acquisition'*. 10th World Congress of Applied Linguistics, Amsterdam, 1993.

POULISSE, N., & BONGAERTS, T. (1994). First language use in second language production. *Applied Linguistics*, 15, 36–57.

POULISSE, N., BONGAERTS, T., & KELLERMAN, E. (1984). On the use of compensatory strategies in second language performance. *Interlanguage Studies Bulletin*, 8, 70–105.

POULISSE, N., BONGAERTS, T., & KELLERMAN, E. (1987). The use of retrospective verbal reports in the analysis of compensatory strategies. In C. Færch & G. Kasper (eds), *Introspection in second language research* (pp. 213–19). Clevedon, UK: Multilingual Matters.

POULISSE, N., & SCHILS, E. (1989). The influence of task- and proficiency-related factors on the use of compensatory strategies: A quantitative analysis. *Language Learning*, 39, 15–48.

PRATT, M., & BATES, K. (1982). Young editors: Preschoolers' evaluation and production of ambiguous messages. *Developmental Psychology*, 18, 30–42.

QUIRK, R., & GREENBAUM, S. (1973). *A concise grammar of contemporary English*. New York: Harcourt Brace.

RAMPTON, B. (1983). Some flaws in educational discussion of the English of Asian schoolchildren in Britain. *Journal of Multilingual and Multicultural Development, 4,* 15–28.

RAMPTON, B. (1987). Stylistic variability and not speaking 'normal' English: Some post-Labovian approaches and their implications for the study of interlanguage. In R. Ellis (ed.), *Second language acquisition in context* (pp. 47–58). Englewood Cliffs, NJ: Prentice-Hall.

RAMPTON, B. (1988). A non-educational view of ESL in Britain. *Journal of Multilingual and Multicultural Development, 9* (6), 503–29.

RAMPTON, B. (1991a). Interracial Panjabi in a British adolescent peer group. *Language in Society, 20,* 391–422.

RAMPTON, B. (1991b). Second language learners in a stratified multilingual setting. *Applied Linguistics, 12* (3), 229–48.

RAMPTON, B. (1991c). Language education in policy and peer group. *Language and Education, 5* (3), 189–207.

RAMPTON, B. (1995). *Crossing: Language and ethnicity among adolescents.* London: Longman.

RAUPACH, M. (1983). Analysis and evaluation of communication strategies. In C. Færch & G. Kasper (eds), *Strategies in interlanguage communication* (pp. 199–209). London: Longman.

REHBEIN, J. (1977). *Komplexes Handeln.* Stuttgart: Metzler.

REISMAN, K. (1974). Contrapuntal conversations in an Antiguan village. In R. Bauman & J. Sherzer (eds), *Explorations in the ethnography of speaking* (pp. 110–24). Cambridge: Cambridge University Press.

RICARD, R., & SNOW, C. (1990). Language use in and out of context: Evidence from children's picture descriptions. *Journal of Applied Developmental Psychology, 11,* 251–66.

RICCIARDELLI, L. (1993). Two components of metalinguistic awareness: Control of processing and analysis of linguistic knowledge. *Applied Psycholinguistics, 14,* 349 67.

RINGBOM, H. (1991). Crosslinguistic lexical influence and foreign language learning. In R. Phillipson, E. Kellerman, L. Selinker, M. Sharwood Smith & M. Swain (eds), *Foreign/second language pedagogy research* (pp. 172–81). Clevedon, UK: Multilingual Matters.

ROBERTS, C., JUPP, T., & DAVIES, E. (1992). *Language and discrimination.* London: Longman.

ROBERTS, C., & SIMONOT, M. (1987). This is my life: How language acquisition is interactionally accomplished. In R. Ellis (ed.), *Second language acquisition in context* (pp. 133–48). Englewood Cliffs, NJ: Prentice-Hall.

ROBINSON, E., & ROBINSON, W. (1976). The young child's understanding of communication. *Developmental Psychology, 12,* 328–33.

ROBINSON, E., & WHITTAKER, S. (1986). Learning about verbal referential communication in the early school years. In K. Durkin (ed.), *Language development in the school years* (pp. 95–116). Beckenham, UK: Croom Helm

ROBINSON, M. (1992). Introspective methodology in interlanguage pragmatics research. In G. Kasper (ed.), *Pragmatics of Japanese as native and target language. Technical Report # 3* (pp. 27–82). Second Language Teaching and Curriculum Center, University of Hawaii at Manoa, HI.

ROGER, D., & BULL, P. (eds) (1989). *Conversation: An interdisciplinary perspective*. Clevedon, UK: Multilingual Matters.

ROMAINE, S. (1989). *Bilingualism*. Oxford: Blackwell.

ROST, M. (1990). *Listening in language learning*. London: Longman.

ROST, M., & ROSS, S. (1991). Learner use of strategies in interaction: Typology and teachability. *Language Learning, 41* (2), 235–73.

ROUNDS, P. (1987). Characterizing successful classroom discourse for NNS teaching assistant training. *TESOL Quarterly, 21*(4), 643–72.

RUMELHART, D., & MCCLELLAND, J. (eds) (1986). *Parallel distributed processing: Explorations in the microstructure of cognition. Vol. 1. Foundations*. Cambridge, MA: MIT Press.

RUMELHART, D., MCCLELLAND, J., & the PDP Research Group (1986). Learning the past tenses of English verbs: Implicit rules or parallel distributed processing. In B. Macwhinney (ed.), *Mechanisms of language acquisition* (pp. 195–248). Hillsdale, NJ: Erlbaum.

RYALLS, J., VALDOIS, S., & LECOURS, A. (1988). Paraphasia and jargon. In F. Boller & J. Grafman (eds), *Handbook of neuropsychology* (Vol. 1, pp. 367–76). Amsterdam: Elsevier.

SACHS, J., & DEVIN, J. (1976). Young children's use of age appropriate speech styles in social interaction and role playing. *Journal of Child Language, 3,* 81–98.

SACKS, H. (1992). *Lectures on conversation*. Oxford: Blackwell.

SACKS, H., & SCHEGLOFF, E. (1979). Two preferences in the organization of reference to persons in conversation and their interaction. In G. Psathas (ed.), *Everyday language studies in ethnomethodology* (p. 15–21). New York: Irvington.

SACKS, H., SCHEGLOFF, E., & JEFFERSON, G. (1974). A simplest systematics for the organization of turn-taking for conversation. *Language, 50,* 696–735.

SAPIR, E. (1949). Communication. In D. Mandelbaum (ed.), *Selected writings in language, culture and personality* (pp. 104–9). Berkeley, CA: University of California Press. (Originally published 1931.)

SATO, C. (1986). Conversation and interlanguage development: Rethinking the connection. In R. Day (ed.), *Talking to learn: Conversation in second language acquisition* (pp. 23–45). Rowley, MA: Newbury House.

SCARCELLA, R. (1979). On speaking politely in a second language. In C. Yorio, K. Perkins, & J. Schachter (eds), *On TESOL '79* (pp. 275–87). Washington, DC: TESOL.

SCHEGLOFF, E. (1980). Preliminaries to preliminaries 'Can I ask you a question?' *Sociological Inquiry, 50,* 104–52.

SCHEGLOFF, E., JEFFERSON, G., & SACKS, H. (1977). The preference for self-correction in the organisation of repair in conversation. *Language, 53,* 361–82.

SCHELLING, T. (1960). *The strategy of conflict.* Cambridge, MA: Harvard University Press.

SCHIEFFELIN, D., & OCHS, K. (1986). Language socialization. *Annual Review of Anthropology, 15,* 163–91.

SCHMIDT, R. (1983). Interaction, acculturation, and the acquisition of communicative competence: A case study of an adult. In N. Wolfson & E. Judd (eds), *Sociolinguistics and language acquisition* (pp. 137–74). Rowley, MA: Newbury House.

SCHMIDT, R. (1988). The potential of parallel distributed processing for SLA theory and research. *University of Hawaii Working Papers in ESL, 7,* (1) 55–66.

SCHOBER, M. (1993). Spatial perspective-taking in conversation. *Cognition, 47* (1), 1–24.

SCHOBER, M., & CLARK, H. (1989). Understanding by addresses and over-hearers. *Cognitive Psychology, 21,* 211–32.

SCHOOLER, J., & ENGSTLER-SCHOOLER, T. (1990). Verbal overshadowing of visual memories: Some things are better left unsaid. *Cognitive Psychology, 22,* 36–71.

SCHREUDER, R., & WELTENS, B. (eds) (1993). *The bilingual lexicon.* Amsterdam: John Benjamins.

SCHUMANN, J. (1978). *The pidginisation hypothesis.* Rowley, MA: Newbury House.

SEARLE, J. (1969). *Speech acts.* Cambridge: Cambridge University Press.

SELINKER, L. (1972). Interlanguage. *International Review of Applied Linguistics and Language Teaching (IRAL) 10,* 209–30.

SHALLICE, T. (1988). *From neuropsychology to mental structure.* Cambridge: Cambridge University Press.

SHATZ, M., & GELMAN, R. (1973). The development of communication skills: Modifications in the speech of young children as a function of the listener. *Monographs of the Society for Research in Child Development, 38,* 5.

SHAW, P., & BAILEY, K. (1990). Cultural differences in academic settings. In R. Scarcella, E. Andersen & S. Krashen (eds), *Developing communicative competence in a second language* (pp. 317–28). New York: Newbury House.

SHEA, D.P. (1993). Situated discourse: The sociocultural context of conversation in a second language. In L. Bouton & Y. Kachru (eds), *Pragmatics and language learning* (Vol. 4, pp. 28–49). Urbana, IL: University of Illinois at Urbana-Champaign.

SHEA, D.P. (1994). Perspective and production: Structuring conversational participation across cultural borders. *Pragmatics, 4,* 357–90.

SHIFFRIN, R., & DUMAIS, S. (1981). The development of automatism. In

J. Anderson (ed.), *Cognitive skills and their acquisition* (pp. 111–40). Hillsdale, NJ: Erlbaum.

SHIMAMURA, K. (1993). Judgement of request strategies and contextual factors by Americans and Japanese EFL learners. *Occasional Papers No. 25*, Department of English as a Second Language, University of Hawaii at Manoa, HI.

SHIRAI, Y. (1992). Conditions on transfer: A connectionist approach. *Issues in Applied Linguistics, 3,* 91–120.

SHI-XU (1994). Discursive attributions and cross-cultural communication. *Pragmatics, 4,* 337–57.

SICHELSCHMIDT, L. (1989). *Adjektivfolgen: Eme Untersuchung zum Verstehen komplexer Nominalphrasen* [Adjective ordering: An investigation into the understanding of complex nominal phrases]. Opladen, Germany: Westdeutscher Verlag.

SIMON, H. (1957). *Models of man.* New York: Wiley.

SLOBIN, D. (ed.). (1985). *The crosslinguistic study of language acquisition* (Vols 1–2). Hillsdale, NJ: Erlbaum.

SNOW, C. (1993). Learning from input in L1 and L2. In J. Alatis (ed.), *Georgetown University Roundtable on Languages and Linguistics 1993* (pp. 23–35). Washington DC: Georgetown University Press.

SOKOLIK, M. (1990). Learning without rules: PDP and a resolution of the adult language learning paradox. *TESOL Quarterly, 24,* 685–96.

SONNE JAKOBSEN, K., SVENDSEN PEDERSEN, M., & WAGNER, J. (in preparation). *Business foreign language communication. A data overview.*

SPERBER, D., & WILSON, D. (1982). Mutual knowledge and relevance in theories of comprehension. In N. Smith (ed.), *Mutual knowledge* (pp. 61–85). New York: Academic Press.

SPERBER, D., & WILSON, D. (1986). *Relevance: Communication and cognition.* Oxford: Blackwell.

STEFFE, L. & GALE, J. (eds) (1995) *Constructivism in Education.* Hillsdale, NJ: Erlbaum.

STEINER, G. (1975). *After Babel.* Oxford: Oxford University Press.

STEMMER, B. (1981). Kohäsion im gesprochenen Diskurs deutscher Lerner des Englischen. *Manuskripte zur Sprachlehrforschung, 18.* Bochum, Germany: Ruhr Universität.

STERNBERG, R., & POWELL, J. (1983). Comprehending verbal comprehension. *American Psychologist, 38,* 878–93.

STILES, J., TADA, W., & WHIPPLE, T. (1990). Facilitative effects of labelling in preschool children's copying of simple geometric forms. *Perceptual and Motor Skills, 70,* 663–72.

STREEK, J. (1980). Speech acts in interaction: A critique of Searle. *Discourse Processes, 3,* 133–54.

SWAIN, M. (1984). Large-scale communicative language testing: A case study. In S. Savignon & M. Berns (eds), *Initiatives in communicative teaching* (pp. 185–201). Reading, MA: Addison Wesley.

SWAIN, M. (1985). Communicative competence: Some roles of comprehensible input and comprehensible output in its development. In S. Gass & C. Madden (eds), *Input in second language acquisition* (pp. 235–53). Rowley, MA: Newbury House.

TAGER-FLUSBERG, H. (1989). Putting words together: Morphology and syntax in the preschool years. In J. Gleason (ed.), *The development of language* (3rd edn, pp. 151–94). New York: Macmillan.

TAKAHASHI, S. (1995). Pragmatic transferability of L1 indirect request strategies perceived by Japanese learners of English. Unpublished doctoral dissertation, University of Hawaii at Manoa, HI.

TAKAHASHI, S., & DUFON, M. (1989). *Crosslinguistic influence in indirectness: The case of English directives performed by native Japanese speakers.* (ERIC Document Reproduction Service No. ED370439).

TANAKA, N. (1988). Politeness: Some problems for Japanese speakers of English. *JALT Journal, 9*, 81–102.

TARONE, E. (1977). Conscious communication strategies in interlanguage. In H. Brown, C. Yorio, & R. Crymes (eds), *On TESOL '77* (pp. 194–203). Washington, DC: TESOL.

TARONE, E. (1980). Communication strategies, foreigner talk and repair in interlanguage. *Language Learning, 30*, 417–31.

TARONE, E. (1983). Some thoughts on the notion of 'communication strategy'. In C. Færch & G. Kasper, (eds), *Strategies in interlanguage communication* (pp. 61–74). London: Longman.

TARONE, E. (1984). Teaching strategic competence in the foreign language classroom. In S. Savignon & M. Berns (eds), *Initiatives in communicative language teaching* (pp. 127–36). Reading, MA: Addison Wesley.

TARONE, E., & YULE, G. (1987). Communication strategies in East–West interactions. In L. Smith, (ed.), *Discourse across cultures* (pp. 49–65). Hemel Hempstead: Prentice-Hall

TARONE, E., & YULE, G. (1989). *Focus on the learner.* Oxford: Oxford University Press.

TEN HAVE, P., & PSATHAS, G. (eds) (1994). *Situated order: Studies in the organization of talk and other embodied activities.* Washington, DC: University of America Press.

THORNTON, D. (1990). Collaborative processes of language use in group conversations. Unpublished master's thesis, Wesleyan University, Middletown, CT.

TROSSET, C. (1986). The social identity of Welsh learners. *Language in Society, 15*, 165–91.

TULVING, E. (1972). Episodic and semantic memory. In E. Tulving & W. Donaldson (eds), *Organization of memory* (pp. 382–403). New York: Academic Press.

TVERSKY, B., & TUCHIN, M. (1989). A reconciliation of evidence on eyewitness testimony: Comments on McCloskey and Zarragoza. *Journal of Experimental Psychology; General, 118*, 86–91.

386   *Communication Strategies*

TYLER, A. (1992). Discourse structure and the perception of incoherence in international teaching assistants' spoken discourse. *TESOL Quarterly*, *21* (4), 713–29.

VALDOIS, S., JOANETTE, Y., & NESPOULOUS, J.-L. (1989). Intrinsic organization of sequences of phonemic approximations: A preliminary study. *Aphasiology*, *3*, 55–73.

VAN DIJK, T., & KINTSCH, W. (1983). *Strategies of discourse comprehension.* New York: Academic Press.

VANPATTEN, B. (1990). Attending to form and content in the input: An experiment in consciousness. *Studies in Second Language Acquisition, 12*, 287–301.

VÁRADI, T. (1983). Strategies of target language learner communication: Message adjustment. In C. Færch & G. Kasper (eds), *Strategies in interlanguage communication* (pp. 79–99). London: Longman.

VARONIS, E., & GASS, S. (1985a). Miscommunication in native/nonnative conversation. *Language in Society, 14*, 327–43.

VARONIS, E., & GASS, S. (1985b). Non-native/non-native conversations: A model for negotiation of meaning. *Applied Linguistics, 6* (1), 71–90.

VELASCO, P. (1989). The relationship of oral decontextualized language and reading comprehension in bilingual children. Unpublished doctoral dissertation, Harvard Graduate School of Education.

VELASCO, P., & SNOW, C. (1993). Cross-language relationships in oral language skills of bilingual children. Unpublished manuscript, Harvard Graduate School of Education.

VENDLER, Z. (1968). *Adjectives and nominalizations.* The Hague: Mouton.

VOLOSINOV, V. (1973). *Marxism and the philosophy of language.* London: Seminar Press.

VYGOTSKY, L. (1978). *Mind and society: The development of higher mental processes.* Cambridge, MA: Harvard University Press.

WAGNER, J. (1983). Dann du tagen eineeeee – weisse Platte – An analysis of interlanguage communication in instructions. In C. Færch & G. Kasper (eds), *Strategies in interlanguage communication* (pp. 159–74). London: Longman.

WAGNER, J. (1995a). 'Negotiating activity' in technical problem solving. In A. Firth (ed.), *The discourse of negotiation* (pp. 223–46). Oxford, UK: Pergamon.

WAGNER, J. (1995b). What makes a discourse a negotiation? In K. Ehlich & J. Wagner (eds), *The Discourse of business communication* (pp. 9–36). Berlin: Mouton de Gruyter.

WALTZ, D., & POLLACK, J. (1985). Massively parallel parsing: A strongly interactive model of natural language interpretation. *Cognitive Science, 9*, 51–74.

WEIZMAN, E. (1993). Interlanguage requestive hints. In G. Kasper & S. Blum-Kulka (eds), *Interlanguage pragmatics* (pp. 123–37). New York: Oxford University Press.

WELLMAN, H., & LEMPERS, J. (1977). The naturalistic communication abilities of two-year-olds. *Child Development, 48*, 1052–7.

WELLS, C. (1983). Talking with children: The complementary roles of parents and teachers. In M. Donaldson, C. Pratt & R. Grieve (eds), *Early childhood development and education* (pp. 127–50). Oxford, UK: Blackwell.

WELLS, G. (1985a). Language and learning. In G. Wells & J. Nichols (eds), *Language and learning: An interactional perspective* (pp. 21–39). Lewes, UK: Falmer Press.

WELLS, G. (1985b). The language experience of five-year-old children at home and at school. In J. Cook-Gumperz (ed.), *The social construction of literacy* (pp. 69–93). Cambridge: Cambridge University Press.

WIEMANN, J., & DALY, J. (1994). Introduction: Getting your own way. In J. Daly & J. Wiemann (eds), *Strategic interpersonal communication* (pp. vii–xiv). Hillsdale, NJ: Erlbaum.

WILDNER-BASSETT, M. (1984). *Improving pragmatic aspects of learners' interlanguage*. Tübingen: Narr.

WILKES-GIBBS, D. (1986). *Collaborative processes of language use in conversation*. Unpublished doctoral dissertation, Stanford University, Stanford, CA.

WILKES-GIBBS, D. (1990, April). *Collaborative processes of language use in native speaker conversation*. Paper presented at the 9th World Congress of Applied Linguistics, Thessaloniki, Greece.

WILKES-GIBBS, D. (1995). Coherence in collaboration: Some examples from conversation. In M. Gernsbacher & T. Givon (eds), *The coherence in spontaneous texts* (pp. 239–67). Amsterdam: John Benjamins.

WILKES-GIBBS, D., & CLARK, H. (1992). Coordinating beliefs in conversation. *Journal of Memory and Language, 31*, 183–94.

WILKES-GIBBS, D., & ESTOW, S. (1993). *Effects of gender and floor on discourse processes in a group decision making task*. Unpublished manuscript.

WILKES-GIBBS, D., & KIM, P. (1991, November). *Discourse effects on memory for visual forms*. Paper presented at the Annual Meeting of the Psychonomic Society, San Francisco, CA.

WILKES-GIBBS, D., MANGELS, R., O'DONOGHUE, J., & LABAY, L. (1993). *Collaborating at a distance: Efficiency, accuracy, and confidence in mediated communication*. Unpublished manuscript.

WILKES–GIBBS, D., & THORNTON, D. (1993). *Collaborative processes in dyadic conversation*. Unpublished manuscript.

WILLEMS, G. (1987). Communication strategies and their significance in foreign language teaching. *System, 15*, 351–64.

WILLIAMS, J. (1992). Planning, discourse marking and the comprehensibility of international teaching assistants. *TESOL Quarterly, 26* (4), 693–711.

WILLIAMS, J., & TASKER, T. (1992, October). *Interlanguage across domains and activity types*. Paper presented at the Second Language Acquisition Forum, East Lansing, MI.

WOKEN, M., & SWALES, J. (1989). Expertise and authority in native-nonnative conversations: The need for a variable account. In S. Gass, C. Madden, D. Preston & L. Selinker (eds), *Variation in second language acquisition: Discourse and pragmatics* (pp. 211–27). Clevedon, UK: Multilingual Matters.

WOOD, D. (1988). *How children think and learn.* Oxford: Blackwell.

WOOTTON, A. (1989). Remarks on the methodology of conversation analysis. In D. Roger & P Bull (eds), *Conversation: An interdisciplinary perspective* (pp. 238–58). Clevedon, UK: Multilingual Matters.

WRIGHT, B., & STONE, M. (1979). *Best test design.* Chicago: MESA Press.

WU, H., De TEMPLE, J., HERMAN, J., & SNOW, C. (1994). L'animal qui fait oink! oink!: Bilingual children's oral and written picture descriptions in English and French under varying circumstances. *Discourse Processes, 18,* 141–64.

YOUNG, R. (1993). Functional constraints on variation in interlanguage morphology. *Applied Linguistics, 14* (1), 76–97.

YULE, G., & MACDONALD, D. (1990). Resolving referential conflicts in L2 interaction: The effect of proficiency and interactive role. *Language Learning, 40* (4), 539–56.

YULE, G., & TARONE, E. (1990). Eliciting the performance of strategic competence. In R. Scarcella, E. Andersen & S. Krashen (eds) *Developing communicative competence in a second language* (pp. 179–94). New York: Newbury House.

YULE, G., & TARONE, E. (1991). The other side of the page: Integrating the communication strategies and negotiated input in SLA. In R. Phillipson, E. Kellerman, L. Selinker, M. Sharwood Smith & M. Swain (eds), *Foreign/second language pedagogy research* (pp. 162–71). Clevedon, UK: Multilingual Matters.

ZIMMERMANN, R., & SCHNEIDER, K. (1987). The collective learner tested: Retrospective evidence for a model of lexical search. In C. Færch & G. Kasper (eds), *Introspection in second language research* (pp. 177–96). Clevedon, UK: Multilingual Matters.

ZUENGLER, J., & BENT, B. (1991). Relative knowledge of content domain: An influence on native–non-native conversations. *Applied Linguistics, 12* (4), 397–415.

Subject Index

389

Name Index